# Conscience and Conflict

# Conscience and Conflict

## Methodism, Peace and War in the Twentieth Century

Michael Hughes

✠ EPWORTH

British Library Cataloguing in Publication data

A catalogue record for this book is available
from the British Library

978 0 7162 0617 0

First published in 2008
by Epworth
4 John Wesley Road
Werrington
Peterborough PE4 6ZP

Typeset by Regent Typesetting, London
Printed and bound in Great Britain by
MPG Books Ltd, Bodmin, Cornwall

# Contents

# Preface

This book is not a work of 'Methodist history' in the narrow sense of the term. It is instead a book by an international historian interested in examining reactions within British Methodism to some of the defining events of the twentieth century: the Boer War; the First World War; the Second World War; and so on. There were three main reasons prompting my decision to embark on a project of this kind. The first was a sense that historians who have written about reactions in Britain to the great events of the twentieth century have been too inclined to generalize about that amorphous phenomenon of 'public opinion', with the result that there is a place in the literature for new studies that tell us in more detail how particular sections of the population have reacted to some of the defining moments of the past hundred years. The second stimulus for writing this book was an equally strong sense that international historians have, with some honourable exceptions, forgotten that 'religion' has for much of the twentieth century played a role in shaping the reactions of millions of Britons to developments taking place in the world around them. The scale of this influence has, nevertheless, been open to question in a century that witnessed an extensive decline in formal religious commitment. It is for this reason that the following pages also seek to determine the extent to which debates within Methodism about issues ranging from conscientious objection through to nuclear deterrence have offered a distinctive 'Christian' perspective on the wider secular debate. I hope that I have in the process also brought to light material of interest for those concerned with the history of the Methodist Church *per se*.

The third stimulus for writing this book has been more personal. It is the work of an historian who comes from a high Anglican trad-ition, and has a life-long interest in the philosophy and culture of the Eastern Orthodox churches. It is also the creation of an author who is by instinct sympathetic to what might be termed a tragic-apophatic reading of the Christian story, sceptical about the extent to which we can ever know or speak about the will of God, and uncertain about the right relationship between St Augustine's heav-enly and earthly cities. It is nevertheless incumbent on anyone who comes from such a tradition to think seriously about the clear ethical import of the Gospels, and the manifest fact that the teaching of the Sermon on the Mount was intended by Jesus to provide his listeners with a direct set of injunctions relevant to everyday life. There is a real wisdom in Kierkegaard's warning that 'The Bible is very easy to understand. But we Christians are a bunch of scheming swindlers. We pretend to be unable to understand it because we know very well that the minute we understand we are obliged to act accordingly.' British Methodism has throughout its history been more inclined than most other Christian traditions to engage seriously with the problems of the world. There has in the last hundred years or so been extensive debate within the Methodist Church of Great Britain and its predecessors about how to respond to the challenge of sup-porting peace in a war-torn world. The study of some of the issues at stake has provided me with a fascinating insight into the differ-ent ways in which countless men and women have down the years tried to think through their faith in the light of real problems posing complex moral dilemmas. The alert reader will I suspect note that I have a deep admiration for those whose faith has led them to follow the path of unconditional pacifism – even if I cannot ultimately agree with their position.

It should by now be clear that this is a work of history and not theology. It is not, as I make clear in the first chapter, concerned with such issues as the 'just war' debate (although the subject does inevitably occur from time to time). Nor, as I note above, is it a work of 'Methodist history'. I do not by this simply mean that it is written by a non-Methodist. I mean instead that it seeks quite consciously to look at Methodism 'from the outside', so to speak, seeking answers to questions of the kind that come naturally to an international historian rather than a church historian. This inevitably raises certain problems. It means that the focus and themes of the book will at times seem unfamiliar to those most concerned with the historiography of Methodism. It may also appear to some readers that the author has at times 'missed the point', or failed to grasp the way that Methodists (and the Methodist Church) debate problems and engage with the world. This will doubtless on occasions be true. I would nevertheless ask readers who come to this book with a strong 'Methodist perspective' (if such a thing still exists) to be patient. There can often be a value in seeing the familiar world through unfamiliar eyes. The things that seem intuitively important or self-evident to those within the Methodist tradition may seem less so to one with a different background and set of interests.

I have incurred debts too many to mention in researching this book, from those who have pointed me towards valuable material, or who have been kind enough to share their thoughts with me on some of the issues discussed in the pages that follow. I would like in particular to thank: Dr Peter Forsaith; the Revd Dr Kenneth Greet; the Revd Dr Leslie Griffiths (Lord Griffiths); Mr Bill Hetherington; Mr Steve Hucklesby; Dr Gareth Lloyd; Dr Peter Nockles; and Dr Peter Richardson. I also owe a huge debt to the staff in the various libraries and archives where I have trawled through what has at times seemed a daunting mountain of archival and printed material: the Bodleian Library (Oxford University); Bradford University Library; the British Library; the British Library of Economics and Political Science (London School of Economics); Cambridge University Library; the Methodist Archives and Records Centre (John Rylands Library, University of Manchester); the Methodist Studies Unit (Oxford Brookes University); and the Sydney Jones Library (University of Liverpool). I would like to thank all those who have given me permission to quote from material to which they hold the copyright. I would also like to thank the *Bulletin of the John*

*Rylands Library* for allowing me to make use of some material from an article I published with them in 2003.

It is as ever true to note that the greatest debts incurred by any author are personal ones. I once again dedicate this book with love to my wife Katie, who must as a life-long Methodist be happy that I have for once written a book in which she has at least some interest. The last few years have been exceptionally busy ones for me, given the demands of life facing the university scholar in the modern age, and I could not have gone through them without her.

# Abbreviations

| | |
|---|---|
| BCC | British Council of Churches |
| CCAD | Council on Christian Approaches to Disarmament |
| CCBI | Council of Churches in Britain and Ireland |
| CO | conscientious objector |
| *Conference Agenda* | *Agenda of the Annual Conference of the Methodist Church* |
| *Conference Minutes* | *Minutes of the Annual Conference of the Methodist Church* |
| COPEC | Conference on Christian Politics, Economics and Citizenship |
| DCC | Department of Christian Citizenship |
| DSR | Department of Social Responsibility |
| MARC | Methodist Archives and Records Centre, John Rylands Library, University of Manchester |
| MPF | Methodist Peace Fellowship |
| PPU | Peace Pledge Union |

# 1

# Introduction

> You have heard that it was said, 'An eye for an eye and a tooth for a tooth.' But I say to you, Do not resist one who is evil. But if any one strikes you on the right cheek, turn to him the other also; and if any one would sue you and take your coat, let him have your cloak as well; and if any one forces you to go one mile, go with him two miles. Give to him who begs from you, and do not refuse him who would borrow from you. You have heard that it was said, 'You shall love your neighbour and hate your enemy.' But I say to you, Love your enemies and pray for those who persecute you, so that you may be sons of your Father who is in heaven; for he makes his sun rise on the evil and on the good, and sends rain on the just and on the unjust. (Matthew 5.38–45 RSV)

War has posed a challenge for the followers of Christ ever since the days of the early Church. The seemingly unambiguous command not to 'resist one who is evil' has for two thousand years created dilemmas for Christians who have been forced to struggle with the practical implications of such a doctrine. If the words are taken at face value, then they immediately raise the problem that such 'non-resistance' might actually allow the triumph of evil and injustice in the world. If they are seen as a more general ethical injunction, which cannot be applied in a straightforward fashion to the complexities of human affairs, the vexed question arises as to how they should be interpreted in any particular situation. Many members of the early Christian Church stubbornly refused to serve in the Roman armies on the grounds that service as a soldier could never be compatible with their faith,[1] a position that often resulted in martyrdom, while Church fathers such as Tertullian (c.160–225 AD) argued passionately that 'Christ in disarming Peter ungirt every soldier'.[2] The conversion of the Roman empire to Christianity during the reign of the Emperor Constantine (306–37 AD) made the situation more complex, raising the question of how Christians should react when commanded to fight by a ruler who professed to share their faith. St Augustine argued in the fifth century that war could be accept- able for the Christian when 'we go to war that we may have peace', thereby laying the foundation for the concept of the just war,[3] a position developed in a more sophisticated form many hundreds of years later by St Thomas Aquinas. Numerous theologians and other religious writers have subsequently sought to identify the condi- tions under which it might be possible to reconcile war with the ethical teaching of the Sermon on the Mount. The works on the subject have indeed become voluminous enough to fill the shelves of a small library.

The possibility of a 'just war' has, however, never commanded universal assent among Christians. During the Middle Ages a vari- ety of sects such as the Bohemian Brethren and the Waldensians preached the virtues of non-resistance to armed force (and were duly treated as heretics and persecuted by the Church). In later centuries, reforming sects like the Anabaptists and the Mennonites also committed themselves to the idea that pacifism was a central tenet of their Christian faith, a position subsequently taken by the Quakers in the seventeenth century, although modified somewhat in the period that followed. Even the briefest glance at the schol- arly literature shows, though, that Christian 'pacifism' has never been a uniform phenomenon with a clear doctrinal foundation.[4] Some Christian pacifists have rejected the idea that the state had the right to employ force even to ensure order within its borders; others have been happy for the legitimate authority to use police powers to prevent challenges to good government. Some Christian opponents of war have chosen to base their argument on scriptural author- ity; others have placed more emphasis on individual conscience as a guide to how to behave in the world. Whatever the form their pacifism took, though, serious consequences have often followed for those whose religious principles led them to refuse to take up arms or to proselytize against those who did. Governments from medieval times down to the twenty-first century have seldom looked kindly on individuals and groups that pose a challenge to their ability to wage war as they see fit. From the perspective of the state, pacifists of whatever kind all too easily appear as members of the 'awkward squad', whose refusal to compromise their ethical principles threatens to undermine the existing social and political order by refusing to live according to its values.[5]

No single book could hope to include in its compass the huge range of responses within the Christian Church to the challenge of war. The aim of this book is far more modest. It seeks to examine some of the reactions within British Methodism to the major international conflicts of the twentieth century, ranging from the Boer War through to the Cold War and beyond, as well as focusing on attempts within Methodism to think creatively about the contribution that the Church should make to the promotion of world peace. The scientific and industrial developments that took place in the last decades of the nineteenth century created the material and technological foundations for an era of 'total war' that destroyed millions of lives during the two world wars. The subsequent Cold War, resting as it did on the threat of mutual annihilation, dominated both international politics and the human imagination for forty years following the capitulation of Nazi Germany in 1945. Numerous other conflicts ranging from Korea to Iraq added their own toll of misery and destruction. And yet, despite this grizzly record, the twentieth century also witnessed some of the most far-reaching attempts in human history to manage and resolve international conflict. The League of Nations and the United Nations were both established to help limit the baneful effects of 'international anarchy' by promoting dialogue between governments. Novel patterns of diplomacy, ranging from the rise of 'summitry' through to the use of special envoys, emerged in response to the changing character of the international system. And, perhaps paradoxically in a century that witnessed some of the most brutal conflicts in human history, international relations were increasingly discussed by politicians and diplomats after 1945 in a way that assumed that the wholesale destruction of human life and property were great evils to be avoided at all costs. The tragic gulf between the rhetoric

3

of peace and the reality of war was perhaps the defining feature of international relations throughout much of the twentieth century.

## Early Methodism and the Question of War: the Eighteenth and Nineteenth Centuries

The correct Christian attitude to war has been a source of some controversy for Methodists from the time of John Wesley.[6] Although Wesley himself was generally reluctant to become too embroiled in controversial political questions, he was much exercised by the rights and wrongs of the struggle for American Independence that erupted into war in the 1770s. In 1775 he wrote to the Prime Minister, Lord North, expressing tentative sympathy for the position advanced by the American colonists on the question of taxation and representation:

> I do not intend to enter up the question of whether the Americans are in the right or in the wrong. Here all my prejudices are against the Americans: for I am an High Churchman, the son of an High Churchman, bred up from my childhood on the highest notions of passive obedience and non-resistance. And yet, in spite of all my long-rooted prejudices, I cannot avoid thinking, if I think at all, these, an oppressed people, asked for nothing more than their legal rights, and that in the most modest and inoffensive manner that the nature of the thing would allow.[7]

The sympathy expressed by Wesley for the colonists in his letter to Lord North proved to be short-lived. Just a few months later, he published *A Calm Address to Our American Colonies*, in which he questioned the legitimacy of resistance to the British crown and warned against a conflict that might lead fellow Christians to 'bite and devour one another'.[8] Wesley's emotions were much exercised by the savagery of the war that finally broke out between the British and the Americans in 1776. In *A Seasonable Address to the More Serious Part of the Inhabitants of Great Britain*, he argued passionately that the rights and wrongs of the dispute were of little relevance compared with the awful reality of 'the blood and the wounds of thousands'.[9] He warned that all warfare had its own deadly momentum, leading inexorably to slaughter and 'lawless plunder', and painted a vivid picture of the 'weeping and disconsolate' widows and fatherless children whose lives had been ripped apart by the conflict in North America. He concluded with a passionate appeal to Christians to refrain from war for fear that they should find themselves 'consumed' by the passions of the world. The *Seasonable Address* was effectively a meditation on the horrors taking place on the far side of the Atlantic, rather than a sustained attempt to unravel the rights and wrongs of the conflict, but it is clear that the founder of Methodism was himself no pacifist. He subscribed to the thirty-seventh of the Thirty Nine Articles of the Church of England, which roundly declared that 'It is lawful for Christian men at the commandment of their Magistrate to wear weapons and serve in the wars', while at the first Methodist Conference in 1745 he responded positively to the question 'Is it lawful to bear arms?'[10] The founder of Methodism nevertheless remained sensitive throughout his long life to the human and financial costs of war.

While it has recently been suggested that Wesley made a concerted effort to define the circumstances under which it was acceptable to wage war, it is hard to deduce anything like a coherent 'just war' theory from his fragmented writings on the subject.[11] In his essay on 'The Doctrine of Original Sin', written in response to a tract by Bishop John Taylor of Norwich, Wesley came close to treating war as a natural phenomenon in a fallen world, the existence of which provided stark evidence of the 'plainest degeneracy' of humanity:

> Who can reconcile war, I will not say with religion, but to any degree of reason or common sense? ... When nation rises up against nation, and kingdom against kingdom, does it not necessarily imply pride, ambition, coveting what is another's; or envy, or malice, or revenge, on one side if not on both.[12]

And yet, true to his belief in the possibility of Christian perfection,[13] Wesley's essay also implied that individual repentance and faith in God's power to redeem humanity could reduce the incidence of war and allow men to become 'reasonable creatures'. Although Wesley believed that war was a part of the human condition, he remained hopeful that a day might come when it would be unthinkable, at least between the Christian nations of the world.

Some early Methodists did in fact espouse a complete and unconditional pacifism, perhaps most notably John Nelson from Birchfield in Yorkshire, the uneducated son of a stonemason who devoted his life to evangelism after hearing Wesley preach. Nelson's zeal in attempting to preach to the masses, when combined with his attacks on the established church, won him a number of enemies in his home county, and in 1744 he fell victim to a plot designed to forcibly dragoon him into the army. When imprisoned in York for refusing to take the King's shilling, Nelson repeatedly told his inquisitors that:

> I shall not fight; for I cannot bow my knee before the Lord to pray for a man, and get up and kill him when I have done. I know God both hears me speak and sees me act; and I should expect the lot of hypocrite if my actions contradict my prayers.

He refused to carry a rifle on the grounds that 'I am a man averse to war, and shall not fight but under the Prince of Peace', and roundly declared that 'I cannot see anything in this world worth fighting for. I want neither its riches nor its honours, but the honour that cometh from God only. I regard neither its smiles nor its frowns, and have no business in it, but to get well out of it.' Nelson did not attempt to provide any sophisticated theological foundation for his pacifism, but instead based his views on a pervasive sense that a personal commitment to live according to the ethics of the Sermon on the Mount was incompatible with the profession of a solider. His stance was an essentially quietist one. While Nelson observed from time to time that 'If all men lived by faith in the Son of God, wars would be at an end,' he was in practice no great crusader in the cause of peace.[14]

The fragmentation of Methodism into a number of different branches following the death of John Wesley makes it particularly hard to generalize about its distinguishing features and outlook. Elie Halévy argued in his celebrated work on the *History of the English People in the Nineteenth Century* that Methodism helped to prevent revolution in Britain during the Industrial Revolution by channelling social discontent into religious fervour, preventing the 'unsettling [of] a social order founded upon inequality of rank and wealth'.[15] Eric Hobsbawm has more recently provided some qualified support for this view, suggesting that the individualist ethos of the various Methodist connexions helped to undermine the rise of a proletarian consciousness among workers in the new industrial cities.[16] Other writers have agreed that Methodism displayed 'distressing signs of a complacent, almost unchristian Conservatism' in the first half of the nineteenth century.[17] The situation did, however, change sharply in the following decades. The death of the influential Wesleyan Methodist minister Jabez Bunting in 1858 paved the way for the start of a gradual change in emphasis during the second half of the century, as ministers like the Revd Hugh Price Hughes began to promulgate a more socially aware Methodism focused on the need to address problems ranging from venereal disease to alcoholism.[18] Hughes also played a central role in mobilizing the so-called Nonconformist Conscience in an effort to influence the activities and policies of government, a development that was in turn bound up with the growing support for the Liberal Party in Wesleyan circles. The radical social and political turn was even more pronounced among other connexions such as the Primitive Methodists and the Free Methodists.[19] Nevertheless, while all the main branches of Methodism began to engage in a more sustained manner with social and political problems as the nineteenth century progressed, they devoted comparatively little formal attention to questions of war and peace. Neither of the two best-known theological works by nineteenth-century Methodists, both Wesleyans, dealt with the subject in any great depth. Richard Watson's *Theological Institutes* (1829) gave little space to social and political questions of any kind, beyond a few profoundly conservative remarks to the effect that 'it is God's appointment that [men] should be subject to those powers whom he, in his government of the world, has placed over them'. William Burt Pope's *A Compendium of Christian Theology* (1880) devoted rather more consideration to the ethical foundations of government, doubtless reflecting the wider changes that were taking place in the culture of British Methodism, but he too had little to say on the morality of war. Even so, while both Methodist theologians and the connexional hierarchies were generally slow to engage directly with the ethical challenges of war and peace, a considerable number of individual Methodists did become personally involved in efforts to promote international peace throughout the nineteenth century.

The Peace Society that was created in London in 1816 was formally non-denominational in character, although Quaker influence was predictably strong among both the leadership and rank and file.[20] Over the following years, branches of the society were set up in all the major English cities such as Liverpool and Birmingham. The Society was formally committed to an unconditional pacifism that rejected even defensive war, although it always remained open to the possibility of close collaboration with 'all friends of peace', who took a less purist view of the subject. The Peace Society at first attempted to operate by moulding public opinion through the publication of books and pamphlets but, as the century progressed, it made more serious attempts to lobby MPs in an effort to get them to look sympathetically at proposals such as binding international agreements to prevent conflicts. There was certainly a good deal of sympathy among some Methodists for the aims of the Peace Society. Forty-one Methodist ministers were happy to sign a declaration circulating in the 1830s that 'all war, whether offensive or defensive, is anti-Christian', while Methodists played a particularly large role in the activities of the Peace Society in Wales.[21] The involvement of leading Methodists in the Peace Society became most pronounced during the closing years of the nineteenth century. Hugh Price Hughes frequently spoke at its meetings in the 1880s and 1890s, while the prominent Wesleyan layman Percy Bunting served as its chairman for a number of years. By the time that Bunting and Hughes were actively involved in the Peace Society, though, it had relaxed its earlier 'absolute' opposition to war in favour of a more sober campaign to promote new forms of international arbitration.

The attitude of most leading figures in the Methodist churches towards international politics was governed in the second half of the nineteenth century by an uneasy combination of *laissez-faire* principles and Gladstonian moralism, rather than by any commitment to a thorough-going and unconditional pacifism. It has often been pointed out that the Wesleyan Church, in particular, attracted a large number of its more prosperous members from the ranks of the mercantile middle classes.[22] The vigorous support for free trade in these circles was predictable, given the benefits that had accrued to such people from the growth of international commerce over the previous few decades. Some of the most eloquent proponents of free trade in Victorian Britain, most notably Richard Cobden and John Bright, repeatedly argued that a *laissez-faire* policy would reduce international conflict by cementing closer relations between nations and eliminating conflict over tariffs. Bright – himself a Quaker – was no pacifist, but he was convinced that war brutalized whole populations and damaged popular welfare, and roundly declared his belief that Britain's foreign policy should be guided by the principle of 'Non-intervention in every case where her interests were not directly and obviously assailed'.[23] These sentiments were echoed by Cobden, who lamented how the passions raised by war clouded clear thinking and destroyed 'all reason and argument; you might as well reason with mad dogs as with men when they have begun to spill each other's blood in mortal combat'.[24] Cobden and Bright were both widely revered in Nonconformist circles in the second half of the nineteenth century, and newspapers such as the *Methodist Recorder* frequently published laudatory comments about their attitudes on a whole series of international and domestic questions. The two men's vocal support of free trade, when combined with their insistence that British foreign policy should be predicated on the principles of peace and non-intervention, struck a chord with many leading Methodists.

There were nevertheless times when this instinctive commitment to a non-interventionist foreign policy came into conflict with an equally pervasive sense that British foreign policy should be guided by ethical considerations. The dilemma was revealed starkly in the 1870s, at a time when the Eastern Question threatened to explode into a European war. The *Methodist Recorder* consistently campaigned against attempts by Disraeli's administration to preserve intact the Ottoman Empire and its Islamic government. The paper shared the general fury that was aroused in the summer of 1876 by tales of the slaughter of Christians in the Turkish province of Bulgaria, noting that the events there 'sent the mind travelling back to the darkest times of human savagery'.[25] It also condemned as 'evil' Disraeli's pointed refusal to respond to the mood of public horror, which the Prime Minister feared would create pressure to end Britain's traditional policy of defending the Ottoman Empire as a bulwark against Russian expansion. Two years later, in 1878, the paper furiously attacked those who called on Britain to go to the defence of Turkey against Russian aggression: 'War for a just cause, to free the enslaved, to lift up the down-trodden? If it must be, yes. But war in league with the slave-holder, the oppressor [ie the Turkish government]? Never.'[26] The *Recorder* instead continued to call for the emancipation of the Christian peoples who lived in the European provinces of the Ottoman Empire, and made it clear that it was willing – albeit reluctantly – to support the expansion of Orthodox Russia in order to liberate Christians from Turkish rule.

While the *Recorder* expressed fervent opposition to any military action designed to defend the Ottoman Empire, it never committed itself to an unconditional pacifism. The paper's defence of wars 'for a just cause' has already been noted above. An editorial published in March 1878 discussed the whole issue at some length, asking rhetorically whether Christians should not 'trust to prayer and Providence' to preserve international peace and justice, which would in turn allow countries like Britain to disband 'at once our armies and our fleets'. After raising such a beguiling prospect, though, the author of the editorial went on to argue that the Old Testament in fact provided countless examples of righteous wars ordained by God, while the New Testament placed an injunction on all Christians to be 'good soldiers of Jesus Christ'. He continued by observing that:

> A righteous peace is indeed a grand and noble thing – a climax the whole earth will reach when the millennium comes, but the time of that climax is not yet, and, it may be, many a purging and purifying war must first be permitted before the righteousness is reached on which alone peace can securely rest. The bloodshed and carnage that destroyed the old Roman empire were a necessity.[27]

In other words, the author suggested, war was an inescapable part of the human condition. While a Christian country should only fight wars that were defensive in character, or designed to promote a just cause such as the abolition of slavery, it was an illusion to believe that conflict could be abolished once and for all in a post-lapsarian world. Even the pursuit of a Cobdenite policy of non-intervention could not guarantee that Britain would not be dragged into war from time to time.

## The Twentieth-Century Context

All the main Methodist connexions became increasingly preoccupied with social and political questions during the final decades of the nineteenth century, as men like Hugh Price Hughes played a critical role in promoting efforts to ensure that the main political parties were 'leavened with Christian influence'. The attention of the Methodist connexions only really began to focus on international affairs in a sustained fashion during the late 1890s, though, when the outbreak of the Boer War created sharp divisions across British society about the rights and wrongs of the Salisbury government's policy in southern Africa. In the century that followed, questions of war and peace were seldom 'off the agenda', a sad comment perhaps on the turmoil that has characterized human history over the past one hundred years or so. The subject was discussed endlessly in the Methodist press, as well as at Conference and district synods, as the Church faced the familiar problem of bearing witness to the Christian faith in a broken world characterized by violence and conflict.

It is no easy matter to gain any insight into the mind of the whole 'Methodist People', to use Wesley's familiar phrase, on the great international questions of the twentieth century. The phrase the 'Methodist People' was, even in Wesley's time, an abstraction that failed to capture the social and intellectual diversity of the religious movement that he mobilized so effectively. Wesley himself may have assumed that the shared bonds of Methodist experience and commitment were more powerful than the fractures of class and geography, but such assumption can hardly be defended in the context of the twentieth century, when huge social pressures ranging from the rise of the electronic media through to greater social mobility have combined to create enormous diversity in the social and political character of British Methodism. At the start of the twentieth century, the chapel still dominated the daily life of its members in many areas.[28] By the middle of the century, following the creation of the unified Methodist Church of Great Britain in 1932, the pressures of modernity and secularism had greatly undermined the traditional character of Methodist congregations, as religious commitment increasingly became a matter of personal choice and conviction.[29] Although it might be expected that such a development would lead to greater unity on a whole range of issues, as individuals actively chose to join a denomination that reflected their own views rather than passively accept the religious affiliations of their family or community, this does not in practice seem to have been the case. The sociological and psychological factors determining choice of religious affiliation are notoriously complex, and seldom owe much to sustained reflection about the theological position or the social teachings of a particular church. Attitudes on such questions as the rights and wrongs of war are instead the product of an immensely complex set of factors, ranging from education and gender through to religious outlook and personal experience.

The debates that have raged within Methodism over international questions have in any case usually only really exercised a small minority of the total membership. The anguished discussion that took place in the Methodist press during the 1930s about the rights and wrongs of pacifism in the face of the rise of fascism was probably not of great concern to the overwhelming majority of Methodists, at least before the critical days of the Munich crisis in September 1938, when it became clear that a second world war was likely to erupt in the near future. The same was true of the debates on nuclear weapons that have so exercised the Methodist Church in the years since 1945. It is therefore inevitable that the following pages give a disproportionate weight to the ideas and activities of an 'elite' within Methodism, who had both the time and the interest to engage actively with important international questions.[30] A great deal of space is given to tracing the formal position taken by the Methodist Church of Great Britain and its predecessors on issues like conscription and the League of Nations, as revealed by such formal documents as resolutions passed by the annual Conference and district synods. A good deal of attention is also given to the debates on international affairs that took place in the Methodist press, since the discussion in newspapers and journals was often less guarded than in the more formal setting of Conference, while the correspondence pages provided 'ordinary' Methodists with a voice that was not necessarily always heard in other settings. The following chapters also examine the views of leading Methodists who have been closely involved in discussions about questions of war and peace – ranging from Samuel Keeble and Leslie Weatherhead through to Charles Coulson and Donald Soper – in order to show how some of the most influential figures in twentieth-century British Methodism have engaged with the challenges posed by the Christian imperative to work for peace. None of these partial perspectives can be accumulated in a simple fashion to present a coherent portrait of reactions within the Methodist Church to the practical and moral challenges involved in combating war and fighting for peace during the bloodiest century in human history. They can however be combined to make some tentative judgements about the tensions and cross-currents that have helped to define the response of British Methodism to the whole question during the past one hundred years or so.

A number of other points should also be made here. This book does not pretend to offer a detailed study of the theological and ethical questions raised by the persistence of war and conflict in human society. Readers will search its pages in vain for any detailed exposition of the theory of the just war or the ideas of writers like Reinhold Niebuhr. Nor is there much sustained discussion of the anguished debates that have taken place among Christian pacifists about how to distinguish between the use of force as a permissible 'police action' to deter violence in a domestic setting and the use of force by the state to defend or promote its national interest abroad. Some effort has been made to explore how formal theological and ethical frameworks both structured – and were structured by – the responses of individual Methodists to conflicts ranging from the Boer War through to the events that took place in New York on 11 September 2001. This book is, though, above all a work of history, concerned with gauging responses within British Methodism to the international turmoil of the twentieth century. Its focus is primarily on the immediate and spontaneous reactions within British Methodism to particular instances of international conflict, along with the way these sentiments and attitudes helped to mould the policies and resolutions adopted at Conference. Such a study is hopefully of value in its own right, helping to illuminate a neglected aspect of the history of twentieth-century Methodism, and fostering wider recognition that the 'history' of British Methodism did not end in 1900 but continues up to the present day. It can also help to provide an insight into broader responses within British society to the international challenges of the past one hundred years or so.

While there is room for debate about the influence of the British churches on government policy throughout the twentieth century, there is little doubt that what might loosely be termed the Christian inheritance has played a role in moulding both individual and collective responses to the challenge of creating peace in a world of violence.

There is perhaps another reason to justify the lack of focus on 'theological' responses within British Methodism to issues of peace and war. The defining motif of Methodism has always rested on its ability to respond in practical terms to immediate challenges. The rise of Methodism in the late eighteenth and nineteenth centuries was indelibly bound up with its ability to adopt a fluid organizational form that responded effectively to the challenges of industrialization and urbanization. The emphasis on 'preaching' to the people, wherever they were, represented a sharp break with the practice of the Church of England with its parochial structure and its emphasis on more formal types of worship. Some recent writing has suggested that Methodist theology is in essence a theology of practice, that needs to be seen less as a coherent doctrine and more as an eclectic set of practices and values, inherently dynamic in character, that can best be understood by focusing on the changing practice of the Church.[31] This claim is almost certainly too simple, and fails to do justice to the work of generations of Methodist theologians and Bible scholars, but there is nevertheless some truth in the argument that the best way to understand British Methodism both now and in the past is to focus on Methodism in action. Nor is it unfair to suggest – the work of writers like John Vincent notwithstanding – that some of the most creative work by Methodist scholars and theologians on war and peace during the past fifty years or so has been carried out across the Atlantic by members of the United Methodist Church. It is certainly difficult to think of a Methodist scholar whose writings on the subject have commanded the respect of a figure like the late Paul Ramsey. It might indeed be suggested that one of the most obvious and arbitrary limitations of this book is that it constrains its discussion to the Methodist Church of Great Britain rather than treating it as one part of a broader worldwide Methodist community. Such a narrow focus is in practice unavoidable given the lack of space. It is also sensible given the focus of this book on actual responses within British Methodism to international conflict in the twentieth-century rather than the more abstract theological and doctrinal issues that such responses both reflected and raised.

It is perhaps worth ending with a few words about the particular perspective of the author, himself a practising Christian, although not a member of the Methodist Church. The framework governing the presentation of the material presented in the following chapters is very much one that comes naturally to an historian who has spent his professional life studying international history in the twentieth century. As a result, the structure and content of the book are determined by the rhythms of the international political system, rather than developments within Methodism itself, an approach which may at times result in a focus that appears unusual to readers who are well-versed in the historiography of British Methodism. Such a perspective can, though, offer fresh insights and understandings into a subject that has not received much discussion in the scholarly literature, as well as providing historians of international politics with a salutary reminder that they should not ignore the impact that 'religion' has had on debates about international politics during the twentieth century. The alert reader will also note that the following discussion is characterized by a quizzically sympathetic approach to its subject-matter, informed by an admiration for all those who have tried to engage creatively with the challenge posed to the Christian conscience by the traumatic events of the twentieth century, while at the same time tending towards a somewhat bleak view that war and violence form an endemic part of the human condition. Such pessimism cannot, though, ever be a justification for inaction. It is surely to be hoped that a book written on this subject at the start of the twenty-second century will make happier reading than one written at the start of the twenty-first, and that the ideals espoused by the Christian Church in all its various guises will have played a part in reducing the bloodshed and misery caused by international conflict.

# 2

# From the Boer War to the First World War

## Introduction

The previous chapter briefly discussed the development of the 'Nonconformist Conscience' during the late nineteenth century, symbolized by a growing readiness of leading figures in the non-established churches to argue that public policy should seek to promote the moral fabric of British society. Although the attention of men like the Wesleyan Hugh Price Hughes and the Baptist John Clifford was usually focused on domestic issues such as education policy, resisting attempts to give the Church of England a privileged place in the running of schools, the conduct of international affairs was not immune from the process of moral scrutiny. The early years of the twentieth century were a turbulent period in Britain's relations with the rest of the world.[1] The sheer size and diversity of the British Empire made it vulnerable to the depredations of rivals such as France and Russia, while closer to home the ambitions of Germany threatened to create a damaging instability across Europe. The lofty imperialism of the Edwardians, manifested in elaborate ceremonies and rituals, in reality concealed widespread and profound unease about the economic and strategic vulnerability of empire.[2] In the first few years of the twentieth century, British public opinion was sharply divided over such important questions as policy towards South Africa and the wisdom of a diplomatic *rapprochement* with the autocratic government of Tsarist Russia. The diffuse commitment to a policy of peace and non-intervention, which had been the hallmark of most Nonconformist thinking on international affairs during the nineteenth century, seemed increasingly outmoded in a world of imperial rivalry and European alliances. The following pages explore some of the debates and arguments that took place within British Methodism on international affairs during the years before 1914, concentrating in particular on the Boer War of 1899–1902, along with the changing pattern of Britain's diplomatic relationships with the other great powers that took place during the decade that followed.

Nobody articulated the traditional Methodist dislike of war during the final years of the nineteenth century more forcefully than the Revd Hugh Price Hughes, who made numerous impassioned attacks on the 'crowning insanity' of war in many of his speeches and sermons.[3] In an editorial published in the *Methodist Times*, in 1887, he vigorously condemned the notion that war was 'the natural and glorious occupation of a gentleman'.[4] Two years later, he preached a powerful sermon at St James's Hall in London attacking 'the deadly militarism' of Lord Wolseley, who had recently called for the introduction of conscription.[5] Hughes was enough of the liberal optimist to hope that humanity would one day be so transformed that 'justice, law and peace' would 'reign with unchallenged supremacy in every land'.[6] There was, though, always a latent tension between the dictates of the Nonconformist Conscience and the traditional commitment of many nineteenth-century Methodists to a foreign policy based on the principles of *laissez-faire* and the supreme importance of peace. A foreign policy conducted according to strictly non-interventionist principles was not on the face of it well-suited to dealing with situations in which the use of force alone could offer the prospect of preventing or ameliorating gross injustice.

The response of the main Methodist connexions to the brutal slaughter of Armenian Christians living in the Ottoman Empire, in the mid-1890s, showed that many of their members were happy to support the use of force when it was designed to achieve a clear moral objective. The massacre mobilized anti-Turkish sentiment among all the Nonconformist churches, since it appeared to confirm a widespread belief that the Muslim Turks were unconstrained by the values adhered to by all the supposedly 'civilized' nations of the West.[7] Numerous denunciations of the Turkish government appeared in the Methodist press when reports of the killings began to circulate in London during 1894 and 1895, while a number of editorials condemned the British government for its passive response to the atrocities.[8] Attitudes began to harden still further the following year, as more and more voices began to clamour for the great powers to use force in order to protect the Armenians. In September 1896, Hughes himself grandly argued in the *Methodist Times* that 'We are quite as much bound to defend Armenia as to defend Kent', a sentiment that was on the face of it at odds with his earlier pronouncements against the use of force to resolve international disputes. He also accused Lord Salisbury's Unionist government of cowardice for refusing to take decisive action against the Turkish government, attacking ministers for pursuing a foreign policy that was governed solely by a calculation of diplomatic consequences.[9] The *Methodist Recorder* was more cautious about the wisdom of British intervention, preferring a diplomatic solution that would allow Russia to destroy the Turkish government's control over territory inhabited by Christians,[10] but both papers were agreed that British policy should be guided by moral considerations rather than arid calculations about the balance of power. Members of the Wesleyan Church seemed happy to endorse the forceful editorial line taken by the *Recorder* and the *Times*. The Revd S.F. Collier called for 'the prompt and energetic intervention of the Christian powers of Europe' when addressing a public meeting in Manchester,[11] while the Revd E.J. Brailsford demanded that Britain should 'draw the sword' in order to protect the Armenians. The district synods that met in September 1896 all called on the British government to take 'the most vigorous measures' against the Turks. The feeling within the Wesleyan Church was so powerful that a special meeting was held in London in late September to discuss the situation in Armenia, concluding with a series of resolutions demanding action to 'end the reign of terror which has so long disgraced the civilised world'.[12] Many members of the Wesleyan hierarchy, including Hughes, also attended a large inter-denominational meeting held at the City Temple on 5 October to protest about the great powers' refusal to act. One correspondent to the *Methodist Times* even urged his fellow Methodists to contribute money for a volunteer force to depose the Sultan should the British government fail to respond to the clamour for a more forceful policy.[13]

Feelings about the situation in Turkey ran equally high in the other Methodist connexions. Senior figures in the United Methodist Free Church called for 'immediate action' to counter the 'misrule and cruelties' of the Turkish authorities, while the author of the Notes column in the *Free Methodist* newspaper argued that Russia should unite with Britain to take resolute action to clip the wings of the Sultan.[14] The General Committee of the Primitive Methodist Church passed a resolution expressing its 'horror and detestation of the wholesale cruelties perpetrated upon the Armenian churches throughout the Turkish Empire'.[15] Numerous chapels used their services and quarterly meetings to protest against the massacres, while at least one Primitive Methodist minister called publicly for a declaration of war.[16] The *Primitive Methodist Magazine* criticized all the great powers for looking 'coldly on' while calculating how they could turn the crisis to their own diplomatic advantage.[17] Opinion in the various Methodist churches was equally aroused in 1897 by the Salisbury government's dilatory response to an attempt by the Christian population of Crete to throw off Turkish rule, a policy that was once again widely condemned for allowing diplomatic considerations to triumph over the dictates of morality. The *Primitive Methodist Magazine* attacked British policy as an 'atrocity',[18] while Hugh Price Hughes thundered hyperbolically in the *Methodist Times* that the reaction of the great powers towards the Cretan rebels and their Greek patrons was 'one of the most disgraceful facts in human history'.[19]

The crises that broke out in the Near East at various times during the 1890s did not create any real divisions within the Nonconformist churches, since their leading figures were virtually unanimous in believing that the western powers were morally obliged to use force to protect Christians in the Ottoman Empire against further attacks. The situation was very different when the Boer War broke out in the autumn of 1899. The conflict in South Africa created deep tensions in British society.[20] Although a majority of the population accepted the Government's argument that the war was a justified defence of the Empire against a dangerous enemy, a vocal minority of 'pro-Boers' repeatedly claimed that Britain's involvement only came about because of the pressure of a small group of financiers and speculators who wanted to gain access to the goldmines located in territory controlled by the Boers.[21] The differences between the two sides frequently erupted in noisy protests and even violence. The division was echoed in all the main Methodist connexions, leading to a split between those who believed that British policy in South Africa represented an attempt to promote progress and civilized values, and others who were convinced that it was driven by much baser commercial instincts. Although the argument between the two sides was seldom about the rights and wrongs of the use of force *per se*, it helped to sow the seeds of a tension that was to become much more marked during the First World War, when a minority of Methodists began to move towards an unconditional pacifism that rejected the use of organized violence under all circumstances.

## Methodist Responses to the Boer War

The Empire played a pivotal role in forging British national identity in the decades before 1914. One young colonial administrator recalled that when he was sent to the Gilbert Islands on the eve of the First World War:

> The cult of the great god Jingo was as yet far from dead. Most English households of the day took it for granted that nobody could always be right, or ever quite right, except an Englishman.

The Almighty was beyond doubt Anglo-Saxon, and the popular conception of Empire resultantly simple. Dominion over palm and pine (or whatever else happened to be noticeably far-flung) was the heaven-conferred privilege of the Bulldog Breed. Kipling had said so.[22]

Many of the rituals of empire reached their height in the late Victorian and Edwardian era,[23] when generations of children were brought up to take pride in a map of the world in which a quarter of the land was coloured pink. Nor was the Empire simply a matter of rituals and high politics. The business interests of many members of the commercial middle classes who flocked to the Nonconformist churches were bound up with imperial trade, while millions of Britons had relatives in such far-flung places as Canada and Australia, the result of decades of outward migration by those driven away by poverty or the search for a new life away from the motherland. The Empire did of course have its critics. Free-trade radicals such as Richard Cobden and John Bright had always been sceptical about the value of the Empire, arguing that it was costly to maintain, and that its mere existence tended to expand the role of the state by assigning it a critical role in the defence of imperial interests.[24] The residual influence of the two men on Nonconformist attitudes towards international affairs was beginning to wane by the closing years of the nineteenth century, though, as their intellectual and emotional legacy was increasingly eclipsed by a growing sense that the British Empire represented a potential force for good in the world. The moral imperative of the Nonconformist Conscience was able to accommodate itself, at least in part, to the realities of empire during the final years of the Victorian era.

There had been a marked 'imperialist' tradition within the Wesleyan Church since at least the middle decades of the nineteenth century. In 1859 the secretary of the Wesleyan Missionary Society, William Arthur, wrote a pamphlet demanding that Britain should annex Fiji in order to prevent the French from colonizing the country and hindering the work of the Protestant missions there.[25]

Although the pamphlet received little attention at the time, the Wesleyan MP (and subsequently Lord Mayor of London) William McArthur returned to the subject in the 1870s. McArthur argued in a speech in the House of Commons in 1872 that the establishment of a Protectorate over Fiji made economic and strategic sense for Britain, and would also benefit the local inhabitants, by offering them the benefits of a 'civil government [that was] urgently required to complete the blessings we had conferred on [the country]'.[26] The establishment of vibrant Wesleyan churches in countries such as Australia during the nineteenth century also helped to forge a powerful sense of the worldwide 'imperial' character of Methodism, while the activities of the Wesleyan Missionary Society fostered a sense that the church had a critical role to play in civilizing the indigenous populations of territories controlled by the British. This commitment to the cause of empire became even stronger in the final years of Queen Victoria's reign, when Hugh Price Hughes became the standard-bearer for Methodists (and indeed many other Nonconformists) who combined in more or less equal measure a passionate commitment to the cause of social reform and a belief in the civilizing virtues of empire.[27]

It has sometimes been suggested that Hughes became more conservative in his final years, as his long-standing social radicalism gave way to an unabashed imperialism that reached a crescendo during the Boer War. The reality was more complex. In a series of sermons preached in London in February 1889, more than ten years before the outbreak of the Boer War, Hughes had already been critical of the 'pacific' wing of the Liberal Party whose adherents believed that colonies should be given full independence as soon as they were sufficiently developed. He argued that the British Empire was not the product of force and conquest, but had instead been created by 'the enterprise of our merchants, the daring of our explorers, the industry of our workmen [and] the unselfishness of our missionaries'.[28] Hughes ascribed a particularly important role to Methodism in cementing the bonds of empire, repeatedly claiming that it was the only true imperial religion, since Anglicanism lacked a popular following in most of the colonies. While he was often sharply critical of the Wesleyan Missionary Society,[29] he was nevertheless greatly influenced by his numerous contacts with missionaries 'in the field', many of whom held it as an article of faith that the British Empire provided a just and civilized form of government that had the added benefit of facilitating their own evangelical work. As a result, Hughes was confident that Methodism could play a vital role in ensuring that the elevated mission of the British Empire was not debased by a cruder jingoism that was concerned only with issues of force and power.

Hughes's ideas owed much to the belief, commonplace in the nineteenth century, that nations had their own distinctive missions to perform in the world. The Wesleyan Minister the Revd John Bond reflected a widely held sentiment when he observed in 1887 that 'the empire of the world had been handed to England because God meant the world to be Christian and Protestant'.[30] Such ideas were expressed in a range of Wesleyan Methodist publications around the turn of the century. The *London Quarterly Review*, a journal with a wide readership among Methodist ministers and educated lay people, published numerous articles emphasizing the importance of Britain's imperial mission. An anonymous piece that appeared in January 1896 on 'The Command of the Sea' argued that sea-power was a 'primordial necessity' to Britain, since 'supremacy at sea' was vital in order to protect the imports of food and raw materials on which the country was dependent. The author also argued that command of the seas was necessary for Britain to promote:

> social progress, our international influence, our power to 'help the right and heal the world's wrong', our mission as the leaders and organisers of the backward and chaotic races that have come beneath our rule, and, what is dearest to the heart of Christian Englishmen, the opportunity to give to all the world the gospel that made us free.

The article concluded with a paean of praise to the diligence of the

English colonist 'in whom the power to open up new countries amounts to genius and has been the wonder and envy of the world'.[31] Another article in the same edition of the *London Quarterly Review* similarly praised the record of British colonialism, particularly in southern Africa, where the history was 'one of which Englishmen may well be proud'.[32] An article on Nigeria, published three years later, argued that the establishment of British rule there would help to advance 'the country and the welfare of the native inhabitants'.[33] Another piece on British rule in India, published on the eve of the Boer War, praised 'the thoroughness and comprehensiveness of the system of paternal government which we have established there'.[34] There was a strong consensus among contributors that the British Empire provided enlightened and effective rule to millions of people previously denied the blessings of such government.

It is not surprising in the light of such attitudes that most senior figures in the Wesleyan Church were confident that Britain was justified in waging war against the two Boer republics. Hugh Price Hughes's rapture for all things imperial grew to a veritable crescendo under the impetus of the conflict. On a trip to the Eastern Mediterranean, in 1900, he gave voice to sentiments that could have flowed from the pen of Rudyard Kipling:

> I have seen many fair and wonderful sights, but the fairest and most wonderful of all was a grinning Tommy Atkins at Alexandria. I sighted him as our vessel was approaching the shore – grinning for all he was worth, and my heart leapt up at him. Oh, my God, the wretched Egyptians have at last obtained something approaching happiness in the world! Everywhere justice and the Pax Britannica.[35]

Hughes ruthlessly excluded critics of the Boer War from the pages of the *Methodist Times* which he had established in 1885. At the outset of the war, he used his 'Current Events' column in the paper to reject pacifism on the quasi-theological grounds that it was an unrealistic strategy in an imperfect world:

We cannot . . . reject the evidence both of Scripture and of human history, that the great principles of the Gospel triumph gradually, and that many things inconsistent with the genius of Christianity were tolerated even by our Lord and his Apostles, because at that time the human race was not ready to receive . . . the ethics of the New Testament.[36]

Hughes was convinced that the Boers had been planning to wage war against the British Empire for many years, building up their military forces in readiness for the battle, and he used this fact to explain away the defeats suffered by imperial forces in the first few months of the conflict. In his articles and editorials he drew his readers' attention to the Boers' atrocious treatment of the indigenous people – a subject that had occupied the Wesleyan Church since the early 1880s – citing such conduct as a moral justification for the war. The *Methodist Times* ran articles describing the joy of the native population in Ladysmith following the defeat of the Boer armies there, and repeatedly condemned the Boer authorities for refusing to allow the native population to own land or to marry without paying an exorbitant licence fee. Perhaps most controversially, the *Methodist Times* also expressed scepticism about reports that hundreds of Boer women and children were dying in 'concentration camps' set up by the British authorities to house the civilian population in the later stages of the war, suggesting instead that the excessive death rates were largely due to 'the exceedingly insanitary habits of the Boer women'.[37] Such language provoked a furious response in some quarters, culminating in a savage attack by the Liberal politician and critic of the war, Henry Campbell-Bannerman, who condemned the *Methodist Times* and its editor for taking a position contrary to 'Christian morality'.[38]

The two most prominent Wesleyan laymen in British politics during this time – Robert Perks and Henry Fowler (later Lord Wolverhampton) – were both wholehearted supporters of the Boer War. Fowler had become the first Wesleyan to obtain a seat in the British Cabinet when he was appointed Secretary of State for India

in 1894, while Perks was active in mobilizing Nonconformist sentiment on the back-benches, helping to establish the Nonconformist
Parliamentary Council in 1898. The two men were closely associated with the 'Liberal Imperialists' who clustered around the former
Prime Minister Lord Rosebery, a movement that eventually found
institutional expression in the Liberal League, but whose members
never really articulated a coherent philosophy or programme.[39] The
Liberal Imperialists were committed to a somewhat ill-defined belief
in a progressive social policy at home, combined with a staunch
defence of empire abroad, a position that was of course markedly
similar to the one promulgated by Hugh Price Hughes on the pages
of the *Methodist Times*. Perks and Fowler both made great efforts
to use their influence to mobilize public opinion behind the war
in South Africa. Fowler set out his position clearly in a speech in
Wolverhampton in November 1899, telling his audience that 'the
war in which we are engaged is a necessary war, and I therefore feel
it to be my duty to support all measures for carrying on that war as
vigorously as possible'. He also argued that 'The Cape Colony and
the Colony of Natal are as much parts of the British territory as
the counties of Cornwall or Kent', and that the British government
was therefore duty-bound to defend their 'honour and integrity'.[40]
Robert Perks took a similar line, although like Fowler he was careful
to condemn a 'jingoism' that placed too much emphasis on military force and failed to understand the elevated mission of empire.[41]
In a speech to his constituents at Louth, in September 1900, he
accused the Boers of making an 'organised attempt' to challenge
the 'British authority and dominion' that represented the best hope
for all the inhabitants of southern Africa.[42] It is no easy matter to
account for the strident character of such Wesleyan 'imperialism'.
Many lay members of the Church were drawn from the commercial
middle classes whose business depended directly or indirectly on
close economic ties with the Empire. The fortune of Perks himself,
for example, was derived from his global interests in projects ranging from harbour construction to railway building. Some Wesleyan
missionaries were certainly convinced that the development of the

British Empire made it easier for them to proselytize among the native peoples and sought to influence attitudes in Britain accordingly. It seems most likely, though, that Wesleyan imperialism was for the most part simply a reflection of broader social attitudes in an age when the rhetoric of empire loomed large in the popular consciousness.

There was in fact rather more opposition to the Boer War among Wesleyan ministers and lay people than was apparent from the pages of the *Methodist Times* – a situation that was echoed across Nonconformism generally. The *British Weekly*, which commanded a wide readership from across the Nonconformist churches, was at one stage forced to close its columns to debate on the subject given the ferocity of the opposing views. Serious attempts were also made to prevent discussion in the National Council of Evangelical Free Churches for fear of the bitterness that might result.[43] Hugh Price Hughes's strident support for the South African war undoubtedly grated on a significant number of those who had previously collaborated with him in his efforts to promote social reform,[44] including such notable figures as the Baptist John Clifford, who had joined with Hughes in the early 1890s in establishing the Free Church Council.[45] Hughes also received many letters attacking his articles and editorials in the *Methodist Times*, while around 500 Wesleyan ministers eventually signed a manifesto condemning conditions in the concentration camps set up by the British.[46] The opposition to the war in Wesleyan circles began to crystallize in February 1900 following an invitation to the Colonial Secretary Joseph Chamberlain to address a lunchtime meeting at the Wesley Chapel in City Road. Hughes, who was a long-standing admirer of Chamberlain, greeted the invitation with jubilation.[47] The same was not true of one of his erstwhile collaborators in the task of social reform. The Revd Samuel Keeble had already established a reputation as one of the most radical and original social thinkers in the Wesleyan Church with his book *Industrial Day-Dreams*, published in 1896, which showed the author's familiarity with the ideas of a number of leading European thinkers including Karl Marx. He reacted with horror when he heard of the invitation to Chamberlain, writing in a letter to the press that:

> To thousands of Wesleyans who are nothing if not patriotic, Chamberlain has not only made the greatest political and diplomatic blunders, but he is guilty of the gravest moral offences and of the lack of true patriotism ... That one of the leading Churches of the land should give such a man the opportunity of making capital out of the position is a startling scandal.[48]

Keeble was not alone in his views. The President of Conference received some three hundred letters of protest about the invitation to Chamberlain. A significant minority within the Wesleyan Church refused to accept the interpretation of the war provided by the British government and promulgated in their own leading publications.

The opponents of the Boer War within the Wesleyan Church were not well-placed to make their concerns known. The Wesleyan Conference of July 1900 showed no inclination to discuss the Boer War in any great detail, while both the *Methodist Times* and the *Methodist Recorder* were effectively closed to critics of British policy in South Africa. It was partly for this reason that Keeble began preparations to publish a new newspaper, the *Methodist Weekly*, which finally appeared in November 1900. Keeble himself served as editor. The paper was designed, in the words of its first editorial, to 'encourage new ideas for adapting Methodism to the ever changing needs of the time'.[49] In practice, Keeble had two main objectives. The first was to develop a newspaper that would be 'alive to the growing importance of the working classes in Methodism'. The *Methodist Weekly* repeatedly echoed the demands of the *Methodist Times* for better housing and educational reforms, but took a far more radical line during its three-year existence by attacking the 'trusts and syndicates' which its editor believed were the hallmark of modern capitalist society.[50] The second main theme that dominated Keeble's editorship of the paper was the war in South Africa. Keeble's opening editorials show that he was not at this stage committed to an unconditional pacifism – as later became the case during the Great War – but was instead critical of the 'spirit of militarism' that he believed was the hallmark of British policy towards the Boers. Many correspondents echoed these sentiments. Dr S. Lunn condemned 'the bloodthirsty spirit which is animating so many millions of our countrymen'.[51] The Revd Michael Elliot, from the Liverpool Peace Society, praised the *Methodist Weekly* for providing 'a newspaper free from the Satanic Spirit of War'.[52] The Revd John Birtwhistle noted that he was 'distressed and perplexed' that so many of his fellow ministers were willing to offer their support for the war. A number of editorials and articles criticized the brutal measures taken by British forces which resulted in women and children being 'turned out on the veldt to starve and, perhaps, to die'.[53]

Contributors to the *Methodist Weekly* were particularly exercised by the impact of the Boer War on the character of British Methodism. In June 1901 the paper responded fiercely to a claim by the Revd E.J. Brailsford, one of the most prominent supporters of the war among Wesleyan ministers, that it had helped to create an 'elevated tone' in national life. Such extravagant praise of the martial spirit was anathema to Keeble and his colleagues, who attacked such words as a 'disgrace to our church'.[54] The paper also attacked the promotion of military instruction in schools, and was particularly distressed by proposals to form a cadet corps at the Leys School in Cambridge, which it feared might 'imbue young lads . . . with the military spirit of the times'.[55] Although Keeble worked hard to avoid direct confrontation with his critics, his paper could not resist pointing out some of their inconsistencies, suggesting that it made little sense for the *Methodist Times* to oppose conscription while so fervently supporting the war.[56] There was in fact always some ambiguity towards the British Empire in the pages of the *Methodist Weekly*. In an editorial published in May 1902, the author (almost certainly Keeble) proclaimed that 'We are not little Englanders' but supporters of a federation of 'free peoples of which England is the mighty mother'.[57] At other times, though, the paper carried enthusiastic accounts of John Bright's sceptical views about the value of the Empire for the mother country. Contributors were, however, agreed that British imperial policy should always be 'exalted by righteousness' rather than crude considerations of economics and politics. Although only a small minority of contributors to the *Methodist Weekly* were committed to an unconditional pacifism that rejected war under all conditions, there was a general consensus that British policy towards South Africa displayed all the worst features of modern imperialism, and that the war against the Boer republics was an unjust conflict being fought for material rather than moral objectives.

The Boer War created even sharper disagreement within the other main Methodist connexions. The potential for division within the Primitive Methodist Church was starkly revealed at a meeting of ministers in the West Midlands District that took place just a few days before the conflict in South Africa finally erupted. One of those present made it clear that he did not support 'peace at any price', while another said he would take an intense delight in 'slapping the Boers in the face'.[58] Other ministers were by contrast appalled at the prospect of the conflict. The two weekly Primitive Methodist newspapers both reacted cautiously to the start of hostilities in South Africa. The *Primitive Methodist* avoided the subject whenever possible, seeking to limit its coverage to brief factual reports, a position that was not appreciated by all its readers. In January 1900, one contributor to its letters page complained that the paper had not published any appeal by a senior member of the Primitive Methodist Church demanding 'peace between the two nations now in deadly conflict with one another', adding that:

> I used to think that by being a member of the Primitive Methodist Church I belonged to a Church that was founded upon the principles taught us by our Lord Jesus Christ. It seems that I entirely misunderstood the constitution, and that instead of being a peace-loving Church, we are sanctioning by our continual silence, if not by actual promulgation, the 'War of Assassination' now raging.

The paper itself responded with a somewhat mealy-mouthed piece on 'The War and Christian Philanthropy', expressing a 'wish that peace may soon be established', and regretting that war had broken out at a time when 'we have been cherishing the hope that we would in the future be spared from witnessing such dreadful conflicts among civilised nations'.[59] The *Primitive Methodist World* took a more critical line towards the Boer War, and in the days leading up to the start of the conflict it roundly condemned a 'poor patriotism that sends out regiments to slaughter and be slaughtered while the patriots sing at home "Britons never shall be slaves"'.[60] A few days after the fighting began, the author of its 'Topics of the Week' column argued that 'the war might have been avoided', and lamented that the conflict would involve 'a great waste of money' and 'precious lives'.[61] The paper printed several appeals from the liberal journalist W.T. Stead's 'Stop the War Movement',[62] an organization that included among its leadership Silas Hocking, a former Free Methodist minister who had subsequently made a successful career for himself as an author.[63] It also resoundingly defended the right of opponents of the war to 'freedom of speech', criticizing magistrates in Andover who dismissed the case of two men charged with smashing the windows of a shop owned by a man who had criticized British policy in South Africa.[64] The paper was not, though, directly critical of the war in the manner of Keeble's *Methodist Weekly*. While it occasionally printed letters from soldiers at the Front giving a brutally accurate picture of the situation there, it was willing to support censorship designed to stop sensitive information from falling into the hands of the Boers,[65] and frequently gave coverage to the activities of those who supported British policy.

Anxiety about the war came to the fore during the Primitive Methodist Conference at Bristol in the summer of 1900, when the subject was discussed at a public meeting attended by many senior figures in the church. The Revd Arthur Guttery's powerful attack on 'the militarism of the age' was well-received and, according to one sympathetic account, 'carried that great meeting of over 2,000 persons completely with him'. On the floor of the Conference itself, there were repeated if rather vague attacks on the 'war-spirit', as well as widespread condemnation of a report from one of the church's committees calling on God to smash Boer rule in order to promote the work of evangelizing the native population. Six months before the Bristol Conference, a former President of the Primitive Methodist Conference had already preached a sermon questioning the morality of the war in South Africa, concluding with a passionate cry that 'God forbid that I should say my country is in the wrong. But I am just as strongly convinced that we are not entirely in the right.'[66] The Revd John Smith, another former President of the Primitive Methodist Conference, was even more critical of British policy towards South Africa. Smith was incensed by the arguments put forward by the Revd George Butt, head of one of the Primitive Methodist missions in South Africa, who had defended British policy in the region during a public meeting held at Aliwal North in July 1899.[67] When the speech was reported in the *Primitive Methodist World*, Smith at once wrote a letter arguing that many of the problems in South Africa had stemmed from the activities of a small group of Britons who wanted to seize control of the gold reserves in the Transvaal,[68] a view he repeated on a number of occasions in the years that followed. Butt himself was forced to flee his mission following the outbreak of hostilities in the autumn of 1899, and spent most of 1900 back in Britain, where he continued to argue that there is 'no alternative for good Government but to bring South Africa under one [British] flag'.[69] His views were supported by another member of the Primitive Methodist mission at Aliwal North, the Revd Edwin Smith, who argued that native South Africans 'were glad to be under the British flag'.[70] Primitive Methodist missionaries, like their Wesleyan counterparts, were frequently among the most zealous supporters of British imperial rule.

Attitudes towards the Boer War within the remaining Methodist connexions echoed the divisions within Primitive Methodism. The *Free Methodist* newspaper – widely read by members of the Free Methodist Church, the Methodist New Connexion and the Bible Christians – carried numerous letters attacking 'the mad and murderous slaughter' in South Africa.[71] Voices were also raised at the Free Methodist Conference in the summer of 1900 expressing anxiety that the current 'military fever' posed a 'grave peril to the young',[72] although others argued equally vehemently that the war against the Boers was a just one. The war in South Africa posed a significant challenge for all the main Methodist churches, forcing them to confront the ambiguities of an imperialism that could be interpreted either as liberating and progressive or as coercive and reactionary. The fact that most Methodists who criticized the war in South Africa continued to pay lip-service to the *potential* value of imperialism is perhaps indicative of the central place occupied by empire in the late Victorian and Edwardian imagination. Even the contributors to the *Methodist Weekly* focused much of their fire on the British government's failure to avoid war in South Africa rather than on the iniquities of imperialism itself. Hugh Price Hughes and his sympathizers were convinced that the Boer War was a justified defence of Britain's lofty imperial mission, while his critics were equally certain that it represented a betrayal. A shared set of moral principles failed to create a consensus among British Methodists over the most important international crisis facing Britain at the start of the twentieth century.

## Methodism and the Build-Up to the First World War

The memory of the bitter debates over the rights and wrongs of the Boer War faded in the years of peace that followed, although discussion about the future of South Africa continued to be a source of disagreement in Methodist circles. The *Methodist Weekly* repeatedly argued that the native population was no better treated under British rule than they had been under the Boers, and demanded recognition that 'the Kaffir is a man and a brother, redeemed by Jesus Christ as much as the white man'.[73] The *Methodist Times* also became increasingly critical of British policy towards South Africa, particularly on the question of the treatment of imported Chinese labour, and was sharply critical of Milner and Chamberlain in the years following the death of Hugh Price Hughes in 1902.[74] One of the most distinguished students of the period has suggested that the 'Nonconformist Conscience' slowly faded away in the early years of the twentieth century, especially (and paradoxically) after the 1906 General Election returned a House of Commons with a huge Liberal majority.[75] The Methodist press nevertheless continued to print many articles and letters demanding that British foreign policy should be guided by moral criteria, providing strong support for the campaign led by the journalist E.D. Morel demanding international action to deal with the situation in the Congo, where ruthless exploitation by the Belgian colonial authorities was costing countless lives among the native population.[76] The issue was also widely discussed at the annual conferences of the various connexions, resulting in numerous resolutions calling on the British government to take measures to prevent the abuses.

Morel's long campaign over the Congo led him to view the British diplomatic establishment with increasing disdain, a position that was articulated most forcefully in his book *Morocco in Diplomacy*, in which he bitterly attacked the Foreign Office and the Diplomatic Service.[77] The chorus of attacks on 'the old diplomacy' that erupted in the years before 1914 found considerable sympathy in the more radical non-Wesleyan press.[78] The *Primitive Methodist Leader* (formed from a merger of the *Primitive Methodist* and the *Primitive Methodist World*) printed numerous articles by Arthur Guttery attacking the British diplomatic establishment.[79] In September 1908 Guttery wrote an article claiming that the Liberal Foreign Secretary Sir Edward Grey had lost control of his officials at the Foreign Office to the point where 'the democracy is slacking in its grip of foreign affairs, and therefore is practically deprived of a decisive voice on questions of naval armaments and military policy'. He went on to suggest that 'The Foreign Office needs a thorough cleansing', and condemned the Diplomatic Service as a 'class preserve ... staffed for the most part by the aristocratic classes'.[80] Four years later, in August 1912, Guttery argued that 'modern diplomacy, with its artificiality and pretence, is breaking down', and needed to be replaced by a system that allowed ordinary people to exert greater influence on international affairs.[81] His views were echoed by the Revd Robert Hind and the Revd Joseph Ritson, who were responsible for writing the 'Current Events' column in the *Primitive Methodist Leader* during these years.[82] Such views reflected widespread concern among those on the radical wing of the Liberal Party, where there was general disquiet about Grey's supposed reluctance to allow frank public discussion of international questions.[83]

There had since the late nineteenth century been calls from a number of British Methodists for new patterns of international negotiation designed to ensure the maintenance of peace. Hugh Price Hughes had proclaimed the virtues of arbitration in a sermon preached to a congregation at St James's Hall in London in 1889, expressing a hope that there would come a time when all states would be willing to accept the authority of a High Court of Nations, charged with resolving 'the international difficulties which keep Europe in a state of continual terror and misery'.[84] When Tsar Nicholas II of Russia unexpectedly called in 1898 for the governments of Europe to discuss new ways of reducing expenditure on armaments,[85] he urged the British government to seize this 'supreme opportunity' to reduce international tension once and for all.[86] Hughes's belief that war was irrational reflected a liberal optimism that was echoed by many contributors to the Methodist press in the ten years or so after his death. All the main Methodist newspapers responded warmly to developments such as the second Hague Conference of 1907, which was widely welcomed by the churches both in Britain and abroad,[87] along with such proposals as one to establish an International Court of the Sea. The decision by the American President William Taft to seek some form of arbitration treaty with Great Britain in January 1911, under which both countries would pledge not to use force to settle any disagreements between them, received a huge amount of positive coverage in the Methodist press. Joseph Ritson used his column in the *Primitive Methodist Leader* to commend the proposal,[88] while the Revd Samuel Henshaw argued optimistically in an article appearing in the same publication that 'A peace built upon agreements of arbitration will be an assured and lasting peace.'[89]

Hugh Price Hughes's old paper, the *Methodist Times*, was also delighted by Taft's initiative,[90] and called on the Wesleyan Quarterly Meetings to forward resolutions expressing their support to Grey at the Foreign Office.[91] The *Recorder* suggested that Methodists had a particular role to play in improving relations between the USA and Great Britain given their large membership in both countries.[92] There was a wide consensus among contributors to the Methodist press that new forms of international agreement could lead to a fundamental change in the fabric of world politics, placing international politics on a more peaceful footing, and reducing the danger of conflict between states.

High military expenditure was a frequent target of criticism in the Methodist press during the years before 1914. The criticism was strongest in the non-Wesleyan papers. The *Free Methodist* fretted in 1907 about the 'millions upon millions' that were spent across Europe maintaining armed forces, and attacked a military culture which it believed was characterized by 'anti-social codes and customs' and the 'immorality of the men and officers alike'.[93] The most persistent attacks appeared in the *Primitive Methodist Leader*. Both Hind and Ritson were deeply concerned about the cost of the naval race that developed between Britain and Germany, particularly given the expense of building the new Dreadnought class of battleships.[94] Hind was at first hopeful that the Liberal victory in the 1906 General Election would lead to reductions in military expenditure, a position taken by many on the radical wing of the Liberal Party, who expected the new government headed by Sir Henry Campbell-Bannermann to adopt a foreign policy designed to prevent Britain from becoming involved in international conflict.[95] Hind was soon disillusioned, however, using his Current Events column to criticize the first set of naval estimates advanced by the new government in March 1906. He went on to argue that the government should refuse to build any more Dreadnoughts, given their enormous cost,[96] and subsequently told his readers that 'Old age pensions would do infinitely more good' than increased naval expenditure. Ritson echoed Hind's complaints when he took over the 'Current Events' column in the *Leader*, repeatedly condemning the 'scaremongers' who exaggerated the extent of Germany's naval power in order to justify higher naval estimates.[97]

The growing disappointment of Hind and Ritson with the Liberal government headed by Campbell-Bannermann and (from 1908) Asquith reflected broader unease among many Nonconformists – particularly those of a more radical disposition – that the election of 1906 had proved less of a triumph for 'the Nonconformist Conscience' than they had originally expected. While many Nonconformists 'liked to claim the Liberal Party as their own', ministers in the Liberal government proved adept at ignoring demands that came into conflict with their own objectives and policies.[98] There was in any case considerable disagreement among Nonconformists in general, and Methodists in particular, even on such an apparently clearcut 'moral' issue as defence spending. While the Wesleyan *Methodist Times* contained regular appeals for a reduction in arms expenditure during the early years of the twentieth century, its contributors were more inclined than their counterparts on the *Primitive Methodist Leader* to believe that big cuts should only be made once a greater measure of international stability had been achieved. The paper was also far less critical of the Liberal government's ship-building programme than the *Leader*, reflecting a long-standing belief in the importance of a strong navy that went back to Hugh Price Hughes's time as editor. The 'Notes on Current Events' that appeared in the paper on 16 January 1908 accepted the need 'to maintain the unchallengeable strength of the navy' given its central role in ensuring imperial security,[99] while a few weeks later the author of the same column argued that 'the Navy should be maintained in the fullest efficiency'.[100] Contributors to the *Methodist Times* did, however, share the distrust of the army that was repeatedly expressed on the pages of the *Leader*, roundly condemning proposals to develop an expeditionary force that could be deployed on the continent, on the grounds that such a move would divert money away from the navy and raise the spectre of compulsory military service.[101] It was only under the pressure of war on the Western Front, in 1916, that a significant section of British Methodism reluctantly began to accept the need for conscription.

Articles and letters that appeared in the Methodist press also reflected considerable differences among contributors over the revolution that took place in Britain's diplomatic alignments during the first decade of the twentieth century. The negotiation of a treaty with Japan in 1902, along with the establishment of ententes with France and Russia in 1904 and 1907, signalled the end of an era of 'Splendid Isolation' that had traditionally been supported by nineteenth-century Nonconformists on the grounds that it reduced the risk of war and promoted trade. Sir Edward Grey, who was appointed Foreign Secretary in the Liberal government that came to office at the end of 1905, was convinced that the agreements with France and Russia could help to counter the threat of Germany. His critics feared that Britain was simply becoming entangled in European power politics.[102] Contributors to the *Methodist Times* and *Methodist Recorder* generally expressed firm support for the foreign policy of the Liberal government throughout the years before 1914. Non-Wesleyan papers such as the *Primitive Methodist Leader* and the *Free Methodist* more often gave their support to Grey's critics.

The establishment of the *entente cordiale* with France in 1904 attracted comparatively little interest in the Methodist press,[103] although the *Methodist Times* welcomed initial rumours of an agreement that began to circulate in the first few weeks of 1904, hoping that such a move would lead to the 'removal of long-standing dangers to friendly feelings between the two Western Powers of Europe'.[104] The rapprochement with Russia proved to be a good deal more controversial. The *Methodist Times* had for years demanded better relations with Russia. Hugh Price Hughes had always been willing to accept the advance of Russian power towards Constantinople as an acceptable price for liberating the Christian subjects of the Sultan, when he edited the paper in the closing years of the nineteenth century. It was therefore hardly surprising that the paper (now under the editorship of the Revd J. Scott Lidgett) greeted the announcement of the agreement with Russia in 1907 as 'welcome news', recalling that 'This journal has consistently advocated a better understanding with Russia at times when that policy was extremely unpopular.' It rejected the claim that an agreement with the autocratic regime in St Petersburg represented a betrayal of liberal principles, arguing that such a position was 'as illogical as the action of those people who will not have intercourse with anyone who is not as pious as they themselves are'.[105] Lidgett and his fellow contributors even remained loyal to the rapprochement with Russia when it came under pressure during the crisis over Persia at the end of 1911.[106] Such an unashamedly 'realist' position, based on the assumption that diplomacy had to take into account broad political realities as well as general moral principles, was not shared by most of those who wrote for the non-Wesleyan press. Robert Hind repeatedly used his column in the *Primitive Methodist Leader* to criticize the tsarist government, reflecting widespread dislike in progressive Liberal circles for an autocratic regime that adopted unashamedly repressive policies to ensure domestic order.[107] He attacked the massacre that took place in St Petersburg on 'Bloody Sunday' in January 1905, writing caustically that the Tsar was 'incapable of devising any method for restoring order save by shooting down the people',[108] and subsequently accused the authorities of using torture on those who were accused of revolutionary activities.[109] It is therefore hardly surprising that Hind reacted with caution to the prospect of an understanding with Russia.[110] When details of the Anglo-Russian agreement were made public in the autumn of 1907, he grudgingly supported the clauses relating to Tibet and Afghanistan, on the somewhat surprising grounds that they might restrain the 'fire-eaters' and jingoes in Britain who had advocated a 'forward' policy in the region over the previous few years.[111] He was, though, deeply sceptical about the clauses dealing with Persia, since he believed that the Russian government would never be content with its limited sphere of influence in the north of the country.[112] His concerns were echoed by the editor of the *Free Methodist* newspaper, who announced that the paper could not support the agreement given the Russian government's brutal treatment of its own people.[113]

Contributors to the *Primitive Methodist Leader* took an even more jaundiced view of the Anglo-Russian agreement in the years following the establishment of the Anglo-Russian rapprochement. Joseph Ritson repeatedly attacked the brutality of the Russian government. Although he condemned the assassination of the Prime Minister Peter Stolypin, in September 1911, he suggested that Stolypin's repressive policies had helped to create the culture of violence that had eventually claimed his life.[114] Ritson also shared the anger felt by many British radicals at the events that took place in Persia at the end of 1911,[115] when the Russian government made a systematic attempt to destabilize the fragile Persian government in order to extend its influence across the heart of the country. While contributors to the *Methodist Times* and the *Methodist Recorder* largely glossed over the crisis in Persia, Ritson launched a furious attack on the Foreign Secretary's handling of foreign affairs. He had already expressed concern on a number of occasions that 'our ententes and semi-alliances may plunge us some day into European war',[116] but Grey's reluctance to respond forcefully to Russian aggression convinced him that 'secret diplomacy' had compromised Britain's freedom of diplomatic manoeuvre, and forced the country into a position where it was bound to support policies of dubious morality.[117] He therefore called on his fellow countrymen to free themselves from 'the hypnotism of Sir Edward Grey's ascendancy', and demanded the adoption of a foreign policy that was guided by ethical considerations rather than *Realpolitik*.[118] He also attacked the entente with Russia as a policy that 'degrades us in the eyes of the world', and lamented that the 'oppressed' could no longer look to Britain for protection.[119] Ritson was even convinced that 'The whole future of Liberalism and social reform is imperilled by the policy of the Foreign Office', and made no secret of his desire to see Grey depart from office, in the hope that his replacement would pursue a foreign policy based on clear ethical principles.[120] Ritson's views on Russia were shared by Arthur Guttery, who condemned Grey's pursuit of a 'Diplomacy that is both callous and cowardly'.[121] It was a lament shared by many radicals in the Liberal Party, whether from a Nonconformist background or not, who believed that ethical considerations should rule out any policy based on accommodation with the autocratic and anti-Semitic regime in St Petersburg.

The Methodist press was also frequently preoccupied with the question of Anglo-German relations, a subject that created sharp divisions in British society in the years before 1914.[122] While some British newspapers and periodicals mounted a strident campaign demanding tougher action against supposed German provocations, there were also calls for improved relations between London and Berlin, a prospect that was widely believed to be an anathema to Grey and other senior officials at the Foreign Office. Many members of the Nonconformist churches instinctively looked to Germany as the spiritual home of Protestantism,[123] and were inclined to feel more warmth for the country and its people than for the Catholic French.[124] The desire for better relations with Germany was strongest in the non-Wesleyan papers. Although Robert Hind used his 'Current Events' column in the *Leader* to attack the 'jingo policy' pursued by the Kaiser, he was optimistic that a better relationship could be established between London and Berlin, expressing a hope that the meeting between the Kaiser and Edward VII that took place in August 1908 could 'smooth the difficulties which at present threaten the peace and progress of the nations of Europe'.[125] His successor as author of the 'Current Events' column was an even more determined supporter of a possible Anglo-German entente. Ritson was inclined to blame France rather than Germany for the genesis of the Agadir crisis that threatened to lead to war in the summer of 1911,[126] suggesting that Berlin's decision to dispatch a warship to the Moroccan port was 'the natural and inevitable' consequence of aggressive French policy in the region.[127] He repeatedly told his readers that 'We have really no question of interests about which we need to quarrel with Germany', and lamented that the naval race had 'swallowed millions which might have gone to help the cost of social reform'.[128] Ritson welcomed the semi-official visit of the Lord Chancellor Richard Haldane to Berlin in February 1912, which was designed to improve Anglo-German relations,[129] and regretted that it had so few tangible results.[130] The *Free Methodist* was a particularly zealous advocate of better Anglo-German relations during the final weeks before it ceased publication at the end of 1907. In November of that year the author if its 'Notes' column described the Kaiser as 'a man of great ability and of good character',[131] and praised him for not responding aggressively to the 'perfect frenzy of jingoism and a high war fever' that often erupted in Britain.[132] The *Methodist Times* also hoped for the establishment of improved relations with Berlin, although its contributors were more sceptical than those in the non-Wesleyan papers about the character of the German regime, conscious perhaps of the potential threat posed to British interests by Germany's naval policy and the rhetoric of *weltpolitik*. The Kaiser himself was periodically rebuked for his 'rash and impulsive nature',[133] while the columnist 'Historicus' unflatteringly described the German monarch as 'the earthquake centre' of Europe.[134] The paper was, though, very supportive of unofficial initiatives to improve relations between Britain and Germany, praising the visit of a group of German municipal leaders to London in the spring of 1906.[135] It also called for greater contact between representatives of the British churches and their German counterparts.[136] The author of the *Methodist Times*'s 'Notes' column called for a new Anglo-German entente in the wake of the Agadir crisis of 1911,[137] and expressed a hope that Haldane's subsequent visit to Berlin would signal a real rapprochement between the two countries. The *Recorder* made fewer pronouncements on the subject, but its contributors too consistently welcomed signs of any easing of the tension between London and Berlin.

Although the 'Nonconformist Conscience' was always an uncertain and elusive phenomenon, there was undoubtedly a real desire among many leading members of the Nonconformist churches to influence social and political developments in Britain during the late nineteenth and early twentieth centuries. The focus was for the most part on domestic issues, ranging from the morality of individual politicians through to the iniquities of the liquor trade, but questions of international politics did not escape scrutiny altogether. The previous pages have shown, though, that there was always scope for disagreement even between those who were in accord about the need to ensure that Britain's relations with the rest of the world were based upon the highest moral principles. Hugh Price Hughes passionately believed that the Boer War was a defence of the British Empire's mission as a force for good in the world, while Samuel Keeble argued equally fervently that the conflict was profoundly immoral. The Wesleyan contributors to the *Methodist Times* supported Britain's naval build-up as a justified response to German aggression, while writers in the non-Wesleyan papers argued that the expenditure on new warships was inspired by a crude jingoism that disfigured the national psyche and diverted money from more important social expenditure. The *Methodist Times* and the *Methodist Recorder* broadly supported Sir Edward Grey's attempt to develop new diplomatic alliances to constrain possible German aggression in Europe and beyond, while the non-Wesleyan press more often than not railed against the immorality of the rapprochement with autocratic Russia that was a natural component of such a policy. A common moral passion did not, in short, lead to agreement on complex questions of practical policy. It was a harsh truth that always tended to marginalize the political significance of the 'Nonconformist Conscience'.

The moral passion of the debates on international affairs within British Methodism was seldom matched by practical discussion about how best to influence government policy. While there was a lively debate in the Methodist press on important questions of defence and foreign policy, none of the main Methodist newspapers ever had the prestige or the circulation to exercise a major influence beyond their comparatively narrow readership. Nor did the election in 1906 of a Liberal government supported by some two hundred MPs from a Nonconformist background really make it much easier to exercise direct pressure on the political process, not least because divisions in the Liberal Party were remarkably similar to those within Methodism, while Sir Edward Grey and the Foreign Office worked hard to insulate themselves from any outside pressure.[138] Although the resolutions passed by the annual conferences of the various Methodist connexions on such matters as the Congo were carefully filed in the government departments to which they were forwarded, ministers in the Campbell-Bannermann and Asquith governments felt little compunction in ignoring the furore that bubbled up from time to time in Nonconformist circles. The election of 1906 at first seemed to reflect the triumph of the Nonconformist conscience, but it quickly became clear that there was no easy compromise between the vicissitudes of practical politics and the politics of moral passion. The next chapter examines how some of these tensions and dilemmas developed during the First World War, a conflict that drove a considerable number of Methodists towards an unconditional pacifism based on a belief that participation in war was always incompatible with the dictates of Christianity. Such a response was, though, only ever characteristic of a minority within each of the main connexions. The First World War played a pivotal role in crystallizing divisions within Methodism about how best to interpret and implement the ethical teaching of Christ in a world racked by hatred and conflict.

# 3

# Methodism and the First World War

## Introduction

The carnage caused by the First World War that erupted in 1914 forced all the main religious denominations in Britain to respond to a conflict that turned out to be far more bloody than any that had occurred before.[1] Around three-quarters of a million Britons died on battlefields stretching from France and Belgium through to Turkey and Palestine. Nor did the horrors of trench warfare and poison gas only scar those who were forced to endure them at first hand. They also entered the consciousness of a civilian population in a way that was quite unlike any previous conflict. Many Anglican churchmen enthusiastically endorsed the war, making excoriating attacks on the enemy powers, and encouraging young Britons to enlist in the armed forces. Although the Archbishop of Canterbury Randall Davidson adopted a more measured tone in his sermons,[2] the impression remained among many contemporaries that the Church of England had effectively become little more than a recruiting arm of the state.[3] The challenge posed by the First World War was perhaps greater for the Nonconformist churches, whose members had traditionally taken the lead in arguing that Britain should avoid being dragged into the folly of war, with all its attendant human and financial miseries.[4] In the event, however, most Nonconformists came to support Britain's struggle against the central powers of Germany and Austro-Hungary. The prevailing attitude of Methodist congregations towards the war did not vary a great deal from the population at large, combining a general sense of patriotism with a determination to see the conflict through to victory, but there were always those who took a different view of the situation. The First World War played a pivotal role in fomenting a division within Methodism between those who were ready to accept that war was on occasion necessary as the price of preventing still greater evils, and a minority who questioned whether such a position could ever be reconciled with the demands of the Christian faith. Although the seeds of the division had been visible for many decades, stretching back to the time of Wesley himself, it was only with the advent of total war that the tension between the two conflicting views became so starkly apparent.

While the Methodist press gave extensive coverage to the perennial crises that bedevilled international politics in the years immediately before the First World War, its contributors initially failed to understand the seriousness of the events that took place in the summer of 1914. They were not alone. Following the upheavals of the two Balkan wars that took place in 1912–13, there was a pervasive sense across much of Europe that the international situation was less dangerous than for some years. In the first half of 1914, the *Methodist Times* (still edited by Lidgett) continued to devote most of its attention to domestic questions. An editorial published in February attributed recent labour unrest to a 'revolt against unbearable conditions of life and labour', and went on to argue that the church had a duty to contribute to 'the social righteousness of the nation',[5] a thinly veiled attack on those Wesleyans who still believed that their Church should avoid becoming embroiled in partisan political controversy. The *Recorder* also focused on domestic and imperial matters during the first few months of 1914. Although the paper published a letter by the Revd J.E. Harlow at the start of the year lamenting that 'We are in the throes of a gigantic conspiracy of international suspicion', neither its editorials nor its 'Notes' column had much to say about European politics in the weeks that followed. The non-Wesleyan press by contrast continued to express a good deal of concern about the 'wretched and ruinous and unproductive expenditure on the munitions of war'.[6] The Revd R.W. Keightley lamented in the *Primitive Methodist Leader* that Europe had become 'an armed camp', and demanded 'the conversion of swords into ploughshares' in order to avoid catastrophe.[7] The paper reacted with hostility to a proposal by Lord Roberts for the introduction of conscription, noting scathingly that 'it is a pitiful thing that super-annuated military men should spend their old age seeking to foster the fighting temper instead of frowning on all that leads to international antagonisms'.[8] The complaint was echoed in the *United Methodist* newspaper, launched in 1908 following the establishment of the United Methodist Church,[9] one of whose authors noted caustically that 'You do not reduce the risk of cutting by sharpening your razor.'[10] Few contributors suspected, though, that the armaments they so deplored would be used quite so soon.[11]

The Methodist press was, like much of the mainstream press, slow to grasp the significance of the assassination of Archduke Ferdinand by Serbian nationalists in Sarajevo at the end of June. It was only in the edition printed on 30 July that the *Methodist Times* finally acknowledged that the tension between Austria and Serbia meant that 'Europe stands in peril of a conflagration more terrible than anything in the memory of living man.' The *Leader* was a little more prescient in its coverage of the assassination in Sarajevo, although it too did not really grasp the possible implications of the outrage. The editors and contributors to the Methodist press were largely drawn from the ranks of the ministry, and it would be quite unfair to condemn them for failing to grasp the significance of international developments that escaped far more seasoned observers. The lack of a sense of impending catastrophe did, however, blind the Methodist press to the harsh reality that their readers would soon be forced to confront in the starkest terms how their faith should shape their attitudes towards the challenge of war.

The Wesleyan Conference that met on the eve of the war discussed the armaments question at some length. The Revd E.A. French moved a resolution suggesting that 'panics concerning international relationships are engineered by armaments contractors', with the result that 'our people would do well to regard with suspicion

statements that the nation is in danger through inadequate armaments', but the somewhat acerbic tone of his words attracted a good
deal of criticism.[12] After a great deal of debate, the resolution was
carried in an amended form that deleted the attack on the munitions industry, and instead urged Methodists to do all they could
'to promote international amity and substantial reduction in armaments'.[13] Britain's declaration of war on 4 August, ostensibly over the
principle of Belgian neutrality, but in reality because of anxiety over
the prospect of Channel ports falling into German hands, forced all
the main Methodist churches to determine their attitude towards
the war against the central powers. The Methodist press once again
provides an important insight into the process. The author of the
*Methodist Times*'s 'Notes and Comments' column – almost certainly
Lidgett – declared his horror at the outbreak of 'an almost universal
war' that appeared as 'the horrible nightmare of a restless sleeper'.[14]
He condemned the German government's 'spirit of aggression'
and its refusal to pay 'the slightest heed to the rights and guaranteed integrity of the smaller nations'.[15] The following week's 'Notes'
column likened 'gallant little Belgium' to the biblical David, confronting the Goliath of the German army. The tone of the *Methodist
Recorder* was a little more restrained, and the language rather more
sober, but it too insisted that '*we* [the British] have not brought to
pass the immediate cause of the catastrophe'.[16]

The *Leader* and the *United Methodist* reacted more hesitantly
to the British government's declaration of war, reflecting the traditional suspicion displayed by the smaller Methodist connexions
towards the use of armed force. The former published an article in
its first edition that appeared after Britain entered the war summarizing a speech that had been made by Arthur Guttery a few days
earlier, in which he condemned the countries of Europe for plunging 'into a fury that is insane'. While Guttery was shortly to become
an enthusiastic proponent of the war against Germany, in the first
days of the conflict he vigorously attacked a 'struggle that may
drown civilisation in blood'.[17] The *Leader's* 'Notes of the Week' column grudgingly accepted the inevitability of the war, but demanded

that the government avoid demonizing the entire German nation. The second edition of the paper to be published after the outbreak of war revealed, though, much firmer support for the British government's decision to enter the conflict. The Revd William Younger argued that the recent publication of the 'blue book' reproducing key diplomatic exchanges between London and the other major capitals in the period leading up to the war showed that the Asquith government had behaved in a 'creditable' fashion.[18] The editor of the *United Methodist* similarly acknowledged that Sir Edward Grey had done all he could to avoid bloodshed, although he was anxious to point out to his readers that the United Methodist Conference alone had the authority to commit the church to any definite position on the war.[19]

## Methodism and the Nation at Arms

The outbreak of war in the summer of 1914 crystallized the latent divisions within British Methodism on the ethics of war. There is little doubt that the population as a whole reacted with a wave of enthusiastic patriotism to the start of hostilities, although recent studies have shown that there was some unease in working-class communities at the prospect of war.[20] Alan Wilkinson has suggested that the social and political attitudes characteristic of most Nonconformist congregations were converging with those of the rest of the population during the first few decades of the twentieth century, and most Methodists certainly shared in the prevailing mood that right was on Britain's side in the conflict.[21] It nevertheless soon became clear that there was a significant minority within each of the Methodist connexions that was unable to endorse such a view. The Wesleyan Minister J. Parton Milum wrote to the *Methodist Times* in August arguing that Christianity was the one true international movement directed against war. He blamed the alliance system that had emerged over the previous thirty years for plunging Europe into war, and concluded with a call for his fellow Methodists to support a 'movement of war against war', particularly as the established Anglican Church was 'hopelessly compromised' in seeking international harmony given the bellicose statements of many of its leaders.[22] The Revd W.F. Lofthouse, Secretary of the radically minded Methodist Union for Social Service, wrote to the same paper expressing his conviction that 'force is no remedy. As followers of the Prince of Peace we know that war, of itself, can settle nothing.'[23] The Revd H. Baird Turner argued that Christ's 'Kingdom had its birth in non-resistance and can only have its continuation in the same'.[24] While such voices were countered by those of men like the Revd F. Warburton Lewis, who argued in somewhat apocalyptic terms that the war against Germany was a 'war not against flesh and blood but against principalities and powers',[25] the correspondence columns of the *Methodist Times* and the *Recorder* showed that a significant minority of Wesleyan ministers and lay members were alienated by the wider public mood of optimism and excitement that followed the outbreak of war.

A similar uncertainty about the war was even more visible in Primitive Methodist circles. Guttery quickly abandoned his early doubts about the conflict and began to contribute numerous articles to the *Leader*, in which he argued that Germany had been responsible for the collapse of attempts to preserve peace.[26] His attacks became increasingly vitriolic over the following weeks, culminating in a piece published on Christmas Eve 1914, in which he suggested that the Kaiser should be hanged after the war unless he was certified mad.[27] However, while most articles published in the *Leader* supported the war effort, there was no shortage of letters condemning the 'utterly unchristian' spirit displayed by some of their authors. One contributor argued passionately that 'Force will never destroy force.'[28] A second who simply signed himself 'Pax' attacked ministers who treated their churches 'as auxiliaries to the recruiting stations' by using their sermons to promote enlistment.[29] A third wrote that war was utterly incompatible 'with the spirit and teaching of our Lord. You cannot love your enemy and *kill* him at the same time.'[30] A fourth complained bitterly about the change of heart that had come over many Primitive Methodists since the outbreak of war in August.

'It is astonishing how the attitude of the Church has changed in rela-
tion to war. At one time the feeling was all against war, but now the
war spirit is with us in both pulpit, school and classroom, and we are
condemned if we dare stand against war.'[31]

While the minority of Methodists who opposed the war was
extremely vocal in the Methodist press, they had little impact on the
way in which the main connexions adapted to the reality of the situation. The Wesleyan Church moved quickly to express its formal support for the British government. Although the Wesleyan Conference
was not scheduled to meet until the following July, the Extraordinary
Committee on Privileges – which constituted the highest decision-
making body in between conferences – met in London in September
to discuss the conflict. The members of the Committee passed a
unanimous resolution noting that while they viewed the war with
'horror', they were 'absolutely convinced that the British government
acted the part of peacemakers . . . and that our country only drew
its sword when plighted faith and national safety left no alternative
course'.[32] A few weeks earlier, the President of Conference, the Revd
Dinsdale Young, praised Wesleyans in the armed forces and wished
them good fortune in the 'righteous course you defend'.[33] By the
time the Wesleyan Conference met in Birmingham in the summer
of 1915, the Conference was happy to pass a 'Loyal Address' assuring
the monarch that 'The Methodist People are convinced that Great
Britain and her allies are fighting the battle of freedom and justice,
and that they cannot retire until victory crowns their efforts.'[34] The
hierarchies of the Primitive Methodist and the United Methodist
Churches also endorsed the war against the central powers, despite
their traditional opposition to 'militarism', and the presence in their
ranks of significant minorities with moral qualms about the legitimacy of war. The Primitive Methodist 'Conference Address to the
Churches' for 1915 did nevertheless tacitly acknowledge that its
members had found it hard to come to terms with the reality of war
during the previous few months:

For the first time in our history the Church has heard the call of
the Nation, and though, as a Church, all our beliefs and training have made us averse to war, the Church has responded to the
Nation's need. Her sons have given themselves to what they and
we believe is the call of God and duty. Nothing but the deepest
conviction that the Nation was fighting for the right would have
led our Church, of all churches, to have responded to the call so
valorously as it has done.[35]

The war against Germany and Austro-Hungary was usually justified in Methodist circles in the same terms that were used by the
British government itself: the defence of Belgium and the need to
uphold international law in the face of aggression.[36] There were,
however, occasional attempts to discuss the whole subject from a
more systematic theological perspective. Prof. J.H. Moulton, from
Didsbury College in Manchester, contributed an article to the *London
Quarterly Review* early in 1915 in which he sought to explain why he
had moved away from his earlier pacifist convictions.[37] He suggested
that the words of Christ in the Sermon on the Mount should not
be read literally but as 'oriental paradoxes ... It is deeply significant
that when Jesus Himself was smitten on the one cheek He did not
turn the other, but offered very dignified remonstrance.' He went on
to offer a staunchly 'realist' interpretation of the human condition,
based on a recognition that 'The State may have to acknowledge
[divine law] as an unattainable ideal, and frame its own legislation
as much as possible in its spirit, with a view to minimizing to the
utmost the evils that it cannot rule out ... if one party determines
to use violence, the other party may have to choose between resistance and extermination'. Moulton concluded by suggesting that it
was incumbent on all Christians to work out for themselves how
to apply the principles of the gospel to everyday life, a position he
followed himself with tragic consequences, enlisting in the forces
before dying at sea when a German submarine torpedoed his boat
in the Mediterranean in 1917.[38] Nor was Moulton alone in trying to
think through systematically the ethical and theological problems

facing those who supported the war. The Revd H.S. Seekings published an article on 'The Morality of the Sermon on the Mount' in the *Holborn Review*, in which he cited Ruskin in defence of his argument that non-intervention in armed conflict could be 'selfish and cruel', and that if it was wrong to kill then it was morally justified to resist the killer.[39] Arthur Wood contributed a piece on the 'Moral Problems Raised by the Great War' to the same publication, echoing (though in less eloquent form) the kind of sentiments expressed by Moulton in the *London Quarterly Review*. Wood suggested that 'Christian ideals are not achieved easily', and went on to argue that 'the dream of a sudden or immediate permanent peace is one of the most foolish fancies man has ever been the victim of'. He concluded that 'Just as our forefathers established a method of punishing those who would not keep laws, so it is necessary for the civilized world to make punishments and laws for nations.'[40]

The various Methodist connexions devoted a great deal of energy following the outbreak of war to practical work designed to respond to the huge changes brought about by the conflict, including the massive movement of people into the armed forces and the munitions industries. There was a good deal of concern among many Methodists about the possible increase in alcohol abuse, both among industrial workers and among women whose husbands had gone to war, reflecting the strong temperance tradition that had been a hallmark of Methodism since the early years of the movement. In many cities up and down Britain, Methodist churches and chapels demanded that local authorities should restrict the opening hours of public houses, and petitioned the government to take action to reduce drinking among munitions workers.[41] The various 'missions' located in the major industrial cities also worked hard to combat 'the horrible excess of drunkenness' that erupted during the war. While some ministers noted that their congregations had increased since the outbreak of the conflict, and were more inclined to think seriously about the nature of their faith, there was widespread concern that the war would undermine public morality and make it harder for Methodism to perform its evangelical mission. Particular attention was paid to the needs of the large number of soldiers who enlisted during the first year of the war (work that was often carried out in co-operation with the other Nonconformist churches).[42] Local Methodist churches and chapels made great efforts to set up recreation centres where soldiers could spend their leisure time in a suitably restrained and sober atmosphere. The Army and Navy Board of the Wesleyan Church developed special Soldiers Homes designed to ensure that troops billeted in Britain would have access to premises suitable for Sunday services and other church activities.[43] Within a few weeks of the start of the war, the Wesleyan Church designated more than three hundred ministers as 'officiating Wesleyan Clergymen', charged with ministering to troops billeted in their area,[44] while other ministers made huge efforts to deal with the growing number of wounded troops convalescing in local hospitals. The figures produced by the district synods provide a graphic insight into the impact of the war on British Methodism, as well as a melancholy reminder of the human cost of the conflict. By May 1916 around 8,000 Wesleyans from the Liverpool District had enlisted or been conscripted into the armed forces, of whom some 260 had died, while a further 400 wounded troops were recuperating in the area.[45] The Nottingham and Derby Wesleyan Synod that met at the same time reported a broadly similar pattern, noting that 35 men from one circuit alone had died in enemy action, while almost 3,000 sick and wounded men were in hospitals and convalescent homes in the region.[46]

One of the most important tasks faced by the Methodist connexions was the provision of chaplains to the armed forces.[47] Wesleyan chaplains had been appointed to the army for many years,[48] but the Primitive Methodist and United Methodist Churches had not previously appointed their own personnel, a situation which changed towards the end of 1914 when a new United Board was set up to provide chaplains charged with ministering to troops drawn from a number of Nonconformist churches.[49] Hundreds of Methodist chaplains were eventually sent into the field, where they helped with practical work in dressing stations and hospitals, as well as conducting services under conditions that were frequently appalling.[50] A number of chaplains were awarded the Military Cross, while four Wesleyan chaplains were killed by enemy fire when carrying out their duties, as were a number of chaplains from the other connexions.[51] In all, more than thirty Methodist ministers died during the war, the vast majority men who had decided that their conscience required them to fight, even though they were formally exempt from military service. The Secretary of the Wesleyan Army and Navy Board, the Revd J.H. Bateson, contributed numerous articles to the *Methodist Recorder* and the *Methodist Times* reporting on the work of the chaplains attached to British forces abroad. So too did the Revd Owen Watkins, who gave graphic accounts of the problems he faced in helping men under fire, as well as describing in stark terms the plight of refugees who told 'heart-rending stories of homes in flames, and ... outrages which make the blood run cold'.[52] The outbreak of the war posed a particular problem for the young men who were preparing for the ministry at the various Methodist theological colleges.[53] A considerable number from Wesleyan theological colleges such as Didsbury and Handsworth followed J.H. Bateson's call in September 1914 for 'all Christian men who can possibly leave their homes to join the Army, not only to help the nation in a great crisis ... [but also so] that the tone and morale of the army may be raised'.[54] One young student from Didsbury, who had recently enlisted in the forces, wrote to the *Methodist Times* at the end of 1914 that he believed he could 'do more good in the Army at this time than in the Ministry'.[55] His views faced criticism from those who could not understand how a young man who had 'dedicated his life to the service of the Prince of Peace can now take the sword to slay his brothers'.[56] Many of the young students who initially enrolled in combatant units were in fact eventually appointed as chaplains themselves, after serving in the trenches for a couple of years, often struggling to meet the demands of their new role. The enormous calls on their time meant, though, that they had little opportunity to reflect on the profound moral questions raised by the war, until the end of hostilities gave them the leisure and perspective to think in more depth about the significance of the experience they had gone through.

## Methodism, Conscription and Conscientious Objectors

The divisions within the main Methodist connexions over the rights and wrongs of the war were magnified enormously when the Military Service Act of January 1916 introduced conscription. Although the Asquith government had previously tried to avoid introducing a measure that was anathema to the liberal principles espoused by many of its members, most ministers reluctantly accepted by the end of 1915 that all able-bodied men who were willing to enlist had already been recruited into the armed forces.[57] During the previous few months, the Northcliffe press had waged a strident campaign for the introduction of conscription, egged on by many conservative figures in the British political establishment, with the result that public opinion was by the start of 1916 ready to accept such a dramatic move. While the Home Secretary Sir John Simon (himself a son of a Congregationalist minister) resigned from the Cabinet over the issue,[58] his colleagues grudgingly accepted the end of voluntary enlistment as a regrettable but inevitable culmination of the pressures posed by total war. Walter Runciman, the most prominent (Wesleyan) Methodist in Parliament, decided to stay in the Cabinet in order to fight for what was left of the *laissez-faire* Liberal tradition.[59]

The Military Service Act paved the way for the conscription of all unmarried men between the ages of 18 and 41, although it permitted exemptions for men who could convince local tribunals that their enlistment would create particular hardship for their families or businesses, or that their health was too poor to allow them to fight. There was not initially any intention to allow exemption from military service on grounds of conscience, but in the wake of Simon's resignation a new draft of the Military Service Bill was printed, allowing exemption from military service 'on the ground of a conscientious objection to bearing arms'. The inclusion of this clause attracted a good deal of derision both in the press and Parliament, but it was still included in the final version of the Bill, and justified by Asquith on the grounds that such a measure had been in place more than a century before when the Quakers were exempted from forced enlistment during the Napoleonic Wars.[60] While the conscience clause appeared unambiguous on paper, its implementation gave rise to endless difficulties throughout the following years. It was assumed when the act was passed that conscientious objectors would be content to undertake non-combatant duties, whereas it quickly became clear that a considerable number would not undertake any kind of work that might be construed as assisting the war effort. Since most of the members appointed to the local tribunals established to deal with these cases were not at all sympathetic to the claims of the conscientious objectors, nor able to grasp the complexity of their position, thousands of the 'absolutists' who refused to undertake alternative service were condemned to prison where they often faced brutal treatment.[61] As a result, the whole issue of conscription became a sensitive political issue in Britain during the second half of the war.

The *Recorder* was at first alone among the main Methodist newspapers in supporting the introduction of conscription. The 'Notes of the Week' column published in the second edition of the paper for 1916 praised the government for taking measures to recruit young unmarried men 'who have not seen fit to accept the duties that belong to them', and the following week contained a stern warning that membership of a Nonconformist church should not be used as a justification for opposing compulsory military service, since 'the Nonconformist does not refuse to obey the state, save as the state interferes with his standing before God'. The author also observed, with more than a hint of sarcasm, that 'There is nothing in Nonconformity, as we understand it . . . alien to the attempt by any Government to preserve freedom on the earth.'[62] The *Methodist Times* edited by Lidgett at first took a different editorial line, blaming the Northcliffe press for pressurizing ministers to abandon the voluntary principle,[63] although it too subsequently came to accept

58

the logic of the move.[64] The *Primitive Methodist Leader* argued that the Asquith government had been 'dragooned' by 'the sinister but terrible power of a certain type of journalist in our midst'.[65] The author of its 'Notes' column wrote that although the opponents of conscription 'may be overborne for the time . . . our opposition will remain, and we believe this is true of the great mass of Free Churchmen'.[66] The *United Methodist* agreed that conscription was 'not a step upwards but a step backwards', and warned that 'trusted Liberal leaders' had 'betrayed one of the most cherished tenets of Liberalism'.[67] All the main Methodist newspapers recognized that conscription was a *fait accompli*, but debate about the rights and wrongs of the whole subject continued to loom large in their pages in the months that followed. It was a pattern broadly echoed in the other main Nonconformist churches.

The *Methodist Times* published numerous letters from readers opposed to conscription. One correspondent pointed out that the New Testament provided no authority to wage war, making it impossible for the Christian to take up arms,[68] while another argued that 'Conscription is altogether unnecessary and can never be of advantage in the present war.'[69] The Revd H.W. Horwill, a United Methodist minister who was himself exempt from military service as a minister of religion, observed that he could never agree to serve because he would not be ready to surrender his conscience to a senior officer.[70] One young intending Wesleyan conscientious objector from Bedminster argued that 'War cannot be justified by Christ's gospel; therefore, as a follower of Christ, I cannot allow even the State to come between God and myself.'[71] There were also many complaints about the treatment of conscientious objectors at the hands of the tribunals, which were widely condemned for 'holding up to ridicule men's claims and opinions which are in most cases based on their religious faith'.[72] The plight of the conscientious objectors (COs) was, however, looked at a good deal less sympathetically by many other contributors. One Scottish Wesleyan argued that 'the State has an absolute call on all its citizens to defend the interests of their country'.[73] Another correspondent attacked the

COs for hiding behind God when seeking exemption from military service, while a third condemned the opponents of conscription as 'quaint old self-righteous pharisees'.[74] The *Recorder* also printed letters criticizing the stand taken by conscientious objectors, including one from the Revd Joseph Dawson attacking them for refusing 'to stand up for their country when it is imperilled'.[75] The divisions over conscription were equally sharp in the other main Methodist connexions. The United Methodist minister the Revd J.E. Black urged his church to oppose conscription on the grounds that it dealt a grave threat to 'the democratic freedoms of our land',[76] while the Primitive Methodist minister Arthur Barham demanded action to protect young COs who faced the 'sneers' of the whole community in defending their conscience before the tribunals.[77] One member of the Primitive Methodist Church even argued that 'Conscription is as much a danger to our religious freedom as our political freedom.'[78] Once again, however, such views faced considerable criticism. John Whittaker contributed a letter to the *Primitive Methodist Leader* arguing that the 'cowardice' of the COs was 'transparent', adding that 'I have little respect for a person's conscience who will allow himself to sit whining at home while murder and rapine and atrocity and devastation are rampant in Belgium and France, Serbia and Poland.' He ended by suggesting that 'If communal conditions are not congenial to them, let them betake themselves to the jungles where reptiles crawl and wild beasts roam, and where every creature is a law unto itself.'[79]

The introduction of conscription gave a renewed impetus within Methodism to the debate about the rights and wrongs of pacifism. While many Methodists who opposed the introduction of the Military Service Act were not themselves pacifists, the advent of conscription clearly posed a particular challenge for all those who questioned whether it was *ever* possible for the Christian to participate in war with a clear conscience. In the first few months of 1916, a considerable number of Methodists began to argue not only that those who refused to fight in battle were entitled to have their views respected by their fellow citizens, but that their renunciation of organized violence represented the only appropriate Christian response to war. Samuel Keeble played a critical role in bringing together committed pacifists in the Wesleyan Church in the wake of the introduction of the Military Service Act in January 1916. Keeble had opposed the Boer War because he rejected the justice of the British government's policy, not because he was opposed to the use of force under all circumstances, a position that he had reaffirmed in a lecture on 'Christianity and War' he gave in Manchester in 1904 when he suggested that war could on occasion be a 'necessary evil'.[80] He even seemed to endorse this position during the opening months of the First World War itself, when his letters to the press fought shy of a commitment to outright pacifism, concentrating instead on demands for the nationalization of the arms industry and an increase of taxation on the rich to pay for the war.[81] By the time the Military Service Act was passed, however, Keeble's position had advanced to the point where he had become opposed to war as a matter of absolute principle. He attacked the Military Service Act on the grounds that it would turn 'the England I love and honour' into a 'servile state', and called on all Methodists to oppose the bill on the grounds that 'Conscription is not in harmony with either freedom, democracy or Christianity'.[82] During the following weeks, he made a vigorous attempt to bring together ministers and lay people who shared his belief that war could never be justified. In the early spring of 1916, Keeble joined with a number of other Methodists in drafting an 'Address to the Methodist People' that denounced war in the most vigorous terms, arguing that 'We believe, if need be, we must be wronged rather than wrong others, and, in the last resort, be killed rather than kill.' The manifesto concluded with a ringing declaration that 'Satan does not cast out Satan', and that war could only be 'overcome by the spirit of love'.

The circulation of Keeble's 'Address to the Methodist People' infuriated many Wesleyan ministers. The Revd J.T. Waddy observed acidly that all Methodists were opposed to war, but that there were times at which 'The only way to peace … lies through war.' The Revd B.C. Spencer believed that Keeble and the other signatories had impugned 'the honour of the nation and of our Church'. The Revd. E. Omar Pearson argued that 'war in certain circumstances is essentially Christian', while the Revd E.H. Jackson said that the expression of such views could weaken the war effort and lead to 'a prolongation of war'. Other correspondents accused the signatories of the address as 'naïve' and argued that it was hypocritical of them to eat the imported food escorted through the blockade by the Royal Navy.[83] A few weeks later, the Revd James Lewis contributed an article to the *Recorder* on 'Quakerism in Wesleyan Methodism', in which he accused Keeble and his collaborators of failing to accept the discipline of the Church, and demanded that the forthcoming Conference should act to impose some kind of order.[84] Keeble was, however, unperturbed by this barrage of criticism. Although he was not successful in securing a debate at the Wesleyan Conference on the whole issue of peace and war, in the summer of 1916 he co-founded the Peace Fellowship of the Wesleyan Church, which survived until 1926. The Fellowship subsequently played an important role in bringing together pacifists in the Wesleyan Church, both in a series of national meetings and via the establishment of local branches, as well as offering practical help to Wesleyan conscientious objectors who fell foul of the law.[85]

The main Methodist newspapers did frequently use their editorial columns to demand that men seeking exemption from military service on grounds of conscience should receive the protection accorded to them by the Military Service Act. All of them were appalled by the sentiments expressed from time to time in newspapers such as the *Sunday Herald*, which ran an item in April 1916 suggesting that although 'conscientious objectors were "not worth the powder and shot" . . . in view of the extreme circumstances perhaps a few rounds might be spared'.[86] Even the bellicose Arthur Guttery, who at one point came close to condemning COs as shirkers hiding behind the 'valour of our sons',[87] eventually complained on the pages of the *Primitive Methodist Leader* that 'Youths who have claimed to obey the dictates of conscience have been deprived of the protection of a law that promised to guard them.'[88] The *Recorder* urged the government to rein in the more headstrong members of the tribunals, while the *Methodist Times* observed that 'certain rights have been conceded to COs and they are entitled to the full exercise of them'.[89] Most of the newspapers were, however, markedly unsympathetic to the 'absolutists' who rejected any form of alternative service (on average around one in four of the conscientious objectors). One columnist on the *Methodist Times* (probably Lidgett) noted in March 1916 that 'We cannot conceive what is the mental attitude of a man who refuses to take non-combatant service . . . so long as he is content to enjoy, and even take part in paying for, the protection afforded by the British Fleet.'[90]

The connexional hierarchies varied in the way they responded to the plight of the conscientious objectors. Although Lidgett joined senior figures from other Nonconformist churches in sending a letter to Asquith in May 1916 expressing concern about the treatment of COs,[91] the Wesleyan Conference that met in London a few weeks later gave little attention to the subject. The loyal address to the crown noted as usual that 'the Methodist people . . . will continue unfailingly to support your Majesty in the prosecution of the war', while the new President's speech once again emphasized that Britain had joined the war to help its allies 'in resisting unscrupulous violations of international covenants'. Brigadier Sir John Barnsley, addressing the Memorial Service for the 5,000 or so Wesleyans who had died during the previous year, told the congregation that 'We glory in the part Methodism has played in this World War.' The district synods that met in 1916 also generally refrained from comment on the whole issue of COs, although a number passed resolutions pointedly expressing their admiration for members of the Wesleyan Church who had 'joined His Majesty's forces and cheerfully taken up this burden of service on behalf of their country'.[92]

The 1916 Conferences of the other main Methodist connexions gave far more attention than their Wesleyan counterpart to the plight of the conscientious objectors. Concern about the treatment of COs by the tribunals had already led many Primitive Methodist district synods to pass resolutions on the subject a few weeks before the

Conference met in June. The Norwich Synod expressed its 'serious alarm and deep indignation' about the plight of the conscientious objectors,[93] while the synods in Darlington and Bristol demanded that the tribunals be instructed to go about their business in a more open-minded and generous spirit.[94] The Primitive Methodist Conference as usual offered a loyal address to the crown, and praised the 'heroic manner' in which tens of thousands of young Primitive Methodists had rallied to their country's call. It also, however, distinguished itself from the Wesleyan Conference by giving students at its Hartley Training College 'entire freedom of choice over whether to enlist' (the Wesleyan Church had by now closed its training colleges for the duration). The Primitive Methodist Conference passed a resolution roundly expressing its 'unqualified abhorrence of the deliberate and savage brutality' with which many conscientious objectors had been treated when condemned to prison for refusing to accept non-combatant service, which was then forwarded to the Prime Minister and a number of other Cabinet ministers, in order to put pressure on the government to end the abuses.[95] The United Methodist Conference also discussed the problems facing conscientious objectors, following a resolution proposed by the Revd R.J. Pollard expressing 'sympathy with all those who suffer because of fidelity to a religious and enlightened conscience'. The resolution provoked heated discussion on the floor of the Conference. The Revd George Graves acknowledged that many of the tribunals had been insensitive in their dealings with the men who came before them, but argued that some of the objectors had also taken up 'unreasonable positions'. It quickly became apparent that 'strong feelings' would be aroused 'on both sides if the discussion continued', which might 'cleave the Church to its very base', and it was therefore agreed to end the debate without forcing the issue to a vote. Although the United Methodist Conference was agreed on the need to offer support to Church members who were fighting in the trenches, many delegates remained incensed that the tribunals were able to ride rough-shod over the consciences of those who refused to fight.[96]

The drift towards pacifism among some Methodists was part of a wider development visible throughout British society during the Great War. Before the First World War, 'the pacifist minority within the Churches had been small and unorganised . . . [while] the Christian basis for its pacifism remained largely undefined'.[97] This changed markedly after 1914 with the emergence of denominational pacifist organizations such as the Anglican Pacifist Fellowship and the Wesleyan Peace Fellowship. The most important interdenominational pacifist organization during the First World War was without doubt the Fellowship of Reconciliation, whose founding manifesto (or 'Basis') declared that 'love as revealed in the life and death of Jesus Christ . . . is the only power by which evil can be overcome and the only sufficient basis of human society'.[98] It concluded firmly that 'as Christians [we] are forbidden to wage war'. The philosophy enshrined in the 'Basis' was echoed by most other Christian pacifist groups, which similarly claimed that a commitment to peace could mobilize spiritual forces capable of undermining the dynamic of hatred that fuelled war. Opposition to the war was not, however, only found among those who believed that organized violence was incompatible with Christian teaching. Criticism of the war against Germany and Austro-Hungary was at times extremely vocal on the left of the political spectrum. Since the Military Service Act did not limit requests for exemption from military service to practising Christians, a considerable number of conscientious objectors sought to establish their claim on the basis of their opposition to the supposedly imperialist nature of the conflict. Conscientious objectors who staked out such a position often attracted the support of such radical politicians as Ramsay MacDonald and Philip Snowden, as well as organizations like the No Conscription Fellowship.[99] Snowden, who was himself raised as a Wesleyan Methodist, became a particularly zealous advocate of the CO cause, using his parliamentary platform to publicize the harsh treatment meted out to conscientious objectors sentenced to imprisonment.[100] While many members of the tribunals sought to operate within both the letter and the spirit of the Military Service Act, listening with care to the claims put forward by those who appeared before them,[101] the attacks of Snowden and MacDonald helped to create in the public mind some unease about their *modus operandi*. The cause of the conscientious objectors was never a popular one in Britain,[102] but even the *Times* felt moved to attack the 'unedifying' approach taken by a small number of tribunal members, such as the chairman of one north-west tribunal who condemned those who sought exemption on grounds of their faith for 'exploiting God to save your own skin'.

The boundary between 'religious' and 'political' dissent was blurred in the minds of some Methodists who opposed the war and demanded fairer treatment for the conscientious objectors. Many of those who committed themselves to an unambiguous pacifism also held radical views on social and political questions. The war in fact created a split among Wesleyan ministers who belonged to such progressive organizations as the Methodist Union of Social Service. While some MUSS members like Samuel Keeble committed themselves to pacifism, others such as Lidgett did not. The complex boundary between the religious and political critiques of war can be seen in the careers of a number of individual laymen with close links to the various branches of Methodism. Wilfred Wellock was a member of the Independent Methodist Church in Lancashire, who came to espouse a radical pacifism that was intimately bound up with his wider Christian faith. He was convinced that the Great War represented 'the apotheosis of [a] corrupting industrialism' which he had come to despise during his years working in a Lancashire mill, and in the wake of the Military Service Act of January 1916 he began publishing the *New Crusader* journal, devoted to articulating its founder's belief that 'Pacifism is simply applied Christianity.'[103] Although Wellock was eventually imprisoned as a conscientious objector, he continued to write numerous letters attacking the 'political and commercial corruption' of modern society, and subsequently became a Labour MP in the 1920s. Jim Simmons, a Primitive Methodist local preacher from East Anglia, also came to prominence through his struggle against the war. Simmons first joined the army as a volunteer in 1911. By the time the war began three years later he was increasingly inclined to explore the political aspects of his faith – he was already a member of the Independent Labour Party – and his sermons often stressed the 'warm, human, inspiring' aspects of Christianity. Simmons was sent to the Front in 1914, where he lost a foot, before returning home to Britain to convalesce. During this time he met a number of the leading radical critics of the war, including Ramsay MacDonald and Noel Buxton, and began speaking at peace rallies under the billing 'Private Jim Simmons with a message from the trenches'. While Simmons later wrote in his memoirs of carrying the 'fiery cross of peace' across the country, most of his speeches actually focused on such essentially secular issues as the need to control the 'war profiteers' and the 'armaments sharks'. His subsequent arrest for sedition, which became something of a *cause célèbre* in Parliament, seems to have radicalized him still further. In later life Simmons like Wellock became a Labour MP, although he was by this time increasingly distancing himself from his Methodist background, coming to believe that he could 'preach the "politics of Christ" and proclaim the "Kingdom of God" more effectively from the soap-box than the pulpit'. He remained convinced, though, that 'socialism [was] ... synonymous with Christianity'.[104]

Most Methodist conscientious objectors were less articulate and determined than Wellock and Simmons in spelling out their position. Since the records of the tribunals that heard their cases have in most cases been destroyed, it is difficult to recreate in much detail their reasons for refusing to fight, although there is enough information to allow some broad generalizations. A majority of Methodists who resisted conscription into the armed forces were happy to accept alternative non-combatant service, although a small number refused to undertake any kind of war-work, and were in consequence often sent to prison. Many of these 'absolutists' seem to have been erstwhile members of the Bible Christians who were absorbed into the United Methodist Church when it was formed in 1907. A few of the Methodist conscientious objectors were drawn from the more educated and literate section of the population, typically schoolteachers, and possessed the confidence and skill to plead their case with some eloquence before the tribunals.[105] Most, however, lacked the ability to make their case effectively. Only a small number of those who sought exemption under the conscience clause of the Military Service Act on religious grounds – whether Methodist or not – seem to have constructed elaborate theological arguments to justify their position. Although the more sophisticated Christian pacifist groups such as the Fellowship of Reconciliation grounded their pacifism on the broad texture of Christ's ethical teaching, most individuals who came before the tribunals simply made reference to *ad hoc* passages in the Bible, most often those which stressed the need to love one's neighbour and forgive one's enemies. When tribunal members responded by citing other biblical passages that expressed a contrary sentiment, the less confident appellants became confused, struggling to justify their position.[106] The available evidence makes it hard to decide whether Methodists were more inclined to seek exemption from conscription than members of other religious denominations. Most conscientious objectors who sought exemption on religious grounds were drawn from minor sects such as the Quakers and the Christadelphians, for whom pacifism was a central and recognized part of their creed.[107] The records of the Pelham Committee, which was charged with finding suitable alternative work for conscientious objectors, suggests that Methodists were far more inclined to be represented among the ranks of conscientious objectors than Anglicans or Catholics, but only marginally more so than other Nonconformists such as Baptists and Congregationalists.[108] At least a hundred Primitive Methodists were eventually imprisoned for refusing to fight or to undertake alternative service, including three men who were later ordained into the ministry.

Methodist conscientious objectors who refused to undertake any form of alternative service, on the grounds that they might simply be 'freeing up' other men for the armed forces, often paid a high price for their principles. They began by facing the usual hostile cross-questioning at their tribunal hearings. One young CO who appeared before the Westminster tribunal was abruptly told that he had no case because it was 'not a part of the creed of the Wesleyans that fighting is a wicked thing',[109] a view articulated in Parliament by some MPs.[110] Individuals who appealed against a tribunal decision often found themselves bogged down in a complex and bewildering bureaucracy, although some were successful in having the initial judgement overturned.[111] Those who failed to gain exemption and still refused to undertake any form of non-combatant service often faced the perils of a prison sentence, normally with hard labour, as well as the hostility of the prison guards charged with supervising them. The experience was harsh enough to break many of them. One young Wesleyan conscientious objector who spent two and a half years in prison was sent home on a stretcher, doomed to spend the rest of his life as an invalid.[112] Another young Primitive Methodist conscientious objector died in Dartmoor, his body stoned by local thugs as it was removed from the prison by his friends.[113] Methodist COs who did manage to gain some form of exemption often faced considerable hostility in their local community, including their local church or chapel, like the young man in a Durham mining village who had the windows of his house shattered by stones.[114] While all the main Methodist connexions urged that conscientious objectors should be treated with dignity and respect, many of their own members shared the scorn for those who refused to fight that was common in Britain throughout the Great War.

A brief biography of one Methodist conscientious objector who suffered for his convictions can help to illustrate some of these issues more clearly. J.H. Brocklesby was a 25-year-old Wesleyan local preacher when the war broke out in 1914. He decided not to volunteer on the grounds that 'God has not put me on the earth to go destroying his children', a position that was partly inspired by the chance circumstances of his youth, when he had known two children who were accidentally shot and killed by a family member.[115] By 1915 he was already coming into conflict with the local Methodist circuits he preached in for arguing that support for the war could not be reconciled with Christian teachings, a position rejected by some of his hearers for not being a 'Methodist doctrine'. When he appeared before the tribunal in February 1916 he was refused permission even for non-combatant service – something he would have accepted – and he was drafted into the army and in due course sent to France. Other conscientious objectors drafted to France were treated with great brutality, tied with arms outstretched to a barbed wire fence, although Brocklesby himself was spared such treatment. He was court martialled in June for refusing to follow orders, and duly sentenced to death, although this was commuted to ten years in prison. On his way back to England he was taunted by soldiers angry that he had been spared the firing squad. Over the next few years he was held in a number of jails, including Wormwood Scrubs and Maidstone, where his pacifist convictions hardened. He praised the Methodist ministers who offered him pastoral care, one of whom was Keeble, but shortly after his release following the end of the war he decided to join the Quakers. Brocklesby's own religious position seems to have evolved during the war towards a more 'personal' faith that was based less on a traditional interpretation of Christian doctrine, and more on the sense of needing to be true to his own inner convictions. His journey towards Quakerism was not an unusual one among Methodists who refused to fight. Their experiences encouraged them to reflect about both their faith and their denominational commitment, leading many of them to seek affiliation with a religious community that appeared to be more sympathetic to their convictions.

## The Methodist Churches and War, 1917–1918

The Methodist connexions continued to do their best to adjust to the demands of war throughout the years of bitter fighting in 1917–18. By the summer of 1917 there were more than 200,000 Wesleyans serving in the various branches of the armed forces, ministered to by some two hundred chaplains, and almost one thousand officiating clergymen. Some 16,000 men had died. Casualty figures in the smaller Methodist connexions were proportionately just as severe. The chairman of the Wesleyan Army and Navy Board, J.H. Bateson, wrote to every single bereaved family to offer the church's condolences. At the annual Wesleyan Conference, delegates attended a solemn memorial service for the dead, a practice followed in the other Methodist connexions. Local churches and chapels also mourned the young members of their congregations slaughtered in the trenches, offering what support they could to the bereaved families. Most Methodists continued to accept the justice of the war against the central powers, instinctively agreeing with Arthur Guttery's argument that the British people should continue to fight for 'the sacred ideals that drove us into this terrible conflict'.[116] The dissenting voices, however, never faded completely in the final two years of war. The debate over the Loyal Address at the 1917 Wesleyan Conference revealed the lingering divisions within the largest Methodist connexion. The draft version called for a continuation of the struggle with the central powers until 'those who willed [it] ... have been utterly and entirely vanquished'. Such strong words evoked a powerful response in some quarters. The Superintendent of the Wesleyan Mission in Birmingham stood up, 'pale and obviously feeling the strain of his position' according to one report, in order to object to the draft resolution on the grounds of 'pacifist principles'. His short speech of protest was continually heckled, a very unusual event at Conference, and the delegates had to be called to order four times by the President. In the end, the Loyal Address was passed in its original form with just fifteen dissenting votes, and the debate ended with 'the fervent singing of the national anthem'.[117] Despite the patriotic mood of Conference, though, there was still some disquiet in Wesleyan circles over the treatment of conscientious objectors. The *Methodist Times* complained in September 1917 about the imprisonment of the prominent Quaker conscientious objector Henry Hobhouse,[118] while the 1918 Wesleyan Conference passed a resolution demanding that all conscientious objectors should be treated in accordance with the Military Service Act. There were, however, still strict limits to the sympathy for those who refused to take up arms. Proposals put forward by the government at the end of November 1917 to disenfranchise conscientious objectors attracted considerable support in Wesleyan circles, and even the normally liberal *Methodist Times* supported the measure on the grounds that it was dangerous to 'place the community at the mercy of an obstinate minority pleading the dictates of conscience as its only guide'.[119]

The issue of conscientious objectors also remained a sensitive issue in the other main Methodist connexions. Arthur Guttery's strictures on the subject led to numerous complaints from some of his fellow Primitive Methodists, who accused him of being 'war-mad' and preaching 'a Christ in khaki'.[120] In the summer of 1917 a meeting at Sheffield condemned the failure of the Primitive Methodist Church to take effective action to protect COs from persecution, and established the quasi-pacifist Primitive Methodist Fellowship for Freedom and Peace, with the active support of at least 120 ministers.[121] The Secretary of the Church's General Committee, the Revd M.P. Davison, rejected suggestions that his church should play an active role in helping Primitive Methodist conscientious objectors to establish their *bona fides*, but he did lead a delegation to the War Office to complain about the activities of the tribunals. The distinguished Manchester University Primitive Methodist Bible scholar A.S. Peake contributed a thoughtful series of articles to the *Leader*, condemning all those who sought to force men 'to act in violation of [their] own conscience'.[122] In 1918 the Primitive Methodist Conference once again passed a resolution calling on the government to ensure fair treatment for the men whose principles prevented them from fighting or carrying out any kind of work that could help the war effort. Many members of the United Methodist Church also continued to protest about the plight of the COs. The editor of the *United Methodist* newspaper, the Revd Henry Smith, condemned their treatment as 'utterly unworthy of our British traditions',[123] while other contributors expressed familiar concerns that the war had fostered a military mentality across British society. Although the number of outright pacifists within the United Methodist Church remained quite small, organizations such as the United Methodist Peace Fellowship were vocal in condemning all the main British churches for blessing a war that was contrary to the spirit of Christ's teaching.[124]

The moral questions raised by the war were simplified for many non-pacifist Methodists in the spring of 1917 by the collapse of the tsarist regime in Russia, which was followed just a few weeks later by America's entry into the war. The alliance with the authoritarian Russian government had always made it hard to present the conflict as a simple struggle in favour of liberalism and democracy, while the refusal of the USA to come to the aid of the 'imperialist' powers before 1917 undermined attempts to present the struggle in terms of a simple conflict between good and evil. It was for this reason that the Methodist press reacted in such rapturous terms to the February Revolution in Petrograd (a reaction that was largely echoed in the British secular press as well), which was described in the *Methodist Times* as 'a supreme triumph of the ideals for which we are at war'.[125] Arthur Guttery similarly rejoiced in the *Primitive Methodist Leader* that Russia had joined 'the family of democratic nations'.[126] The entry of the USA into the war was greeted with equal rapture. An overly effusive editorial on the subject published in the *Methodist Times* in April 1917 proclaimed that 'God Himself has intervened, as the Sovereign Spirit who inspires the onward march of men towards freedom, righteousness and brotherhood.'[127] The dramatic international changes that took place in the spring of 1917 quickly placed the whole question of allied war aims and peace terms still more firmly on the international agenda. Contributors to the Methodist press had penned numerous letters and articles from the start of the war warning against the danger of demonizing the Germans, as well as issuing a number of prescient warnings about the dangers of imposing harsh peace terms that would simply perpetuate international suspicion and tension. The *Methodist Times*'s radically minded correspondent Historicus welcomed the entry of the United States into the war in April 1917 precisely because he believed it would prevent the conflict from being degraded still further into a war 'against the whole German people'.[128]

The *Methodist Times* paid particular attention in 1917 to the proposals for a Stockholm Conference, suggested by representatives of the Second International in Russia and Scandinavia as a means of bringing together socialists from across Europe to discuss ways of ending the war. The strongest advocate of the Conference in the British War Cabinet was Arthur Henderson, General Secretary of the Labour Party, and a long-standing Wesleyan local preacher and regular Conference delegate. Henderson eventually resigned from the War Cabinet when he was unable to convince his ministerial colleagues to support British participation in the Stockholm Conference, winning strong support from the *Methodist Times* in the process.[129] The flurry of discussions about further peace proposals that took place at the end of 1917 and the start of 1918 were followed closely in the Methodist press. A great deal of space was devoted to the celebrated letter by Lord Lansdowne that appeared in the *Daily Telegraph* at the end of November 1917, arguing that 'prolongation' of the war 'will spell ruin for the civilised world', and questioning 'the value of the blessings of peace to nations so exhausted that they can scarcely stretch out a hand with which to grasp them'.[130] The Lansdowne letter's support for a negotiated peace evoked a range of responses from senior members of the Wesleyan Church. Some, such as the Revd Grainger Hargreaves (Chairman of the Oxford District), condemned it as 'most inopportune'. Others, like the Revd Enoch Salt (Secretary of the Committee of Privileges), took a far more positive line.[131] Lansdowne's letter for some reason attracted less attention in the non-Wesleyan press, although the *Primitive Methodist Leader* did publish a number of letters praising its proposals, and attacking those in the British government who continued to believe in the 'knock-out blow'.[132]

The speeches by the British Prime Minister David Lloyd George and the American President Woodrow Wilson setting down their respective countries' war aims at the start of 1918 were widely reported in the Methodist press. In a speech to a trade union audience on 5 January, Lloyd George stated that Britain would be willing to accept a peace based on the sanctity of treaties, the principle of self-determination, and the establishment of 'some international organisation to limit the burden of armaments and diminish the probability of war'.[133] A few days later, President Wilson made his celebrated speech before Congress setting down the 'Fourteen Points' that should inform any peace. Lloyd George, who had become Prime Minister at the end of 1916, generally remained a popular figure in Methodist circles despite rumours of his colourful private life, not least because he was always shrewd enough to make much of his Nonconformist credentials. Woodrow Wilson was also feted in the Methodist press, particularly by those who expected the American President to use his country's power to end the war, and encourage the rebuilding of the international system on an entirely new basis. The columnist Historicus eulogized Wilson in the *Methodist Times* as a man who towered above 'all the leaders and rulers of the world . . . Every time he speaks, he speaks bigger and looms larger by contrast with the smaller men who are filling the stage in Europe'.[134] The speeches of Wilson and Lloyd George were widely praised by prominent Methodists for securing the moral high ground for the allies, while offering the prospect of a post-war settlement that would mark a break with the old cycle of vengeance and suspicion that had dogged the international system before 1914. The General Committee of the Primitive Methodist Church even went so far as to pass a formal resolution welcoming the proposals. There were, though, still some notes of scepticism. Arthur Guttery in particular remained wary of any move that might weaken national resolve and encourage a willingness to contemplate peace on the basis of anything short of total victory.[135]

Both Lloyd George and Wilson made a good deal in their January speeches of the need to establish a 'general association of nations' that would in future provide 'mutual guarantees of political independence and territorial integrity'. Such an idea received enthusiastic support in all the main Methodist connexions, which was hardly surprising given their long-standing commitment to new forms of international arbitration designed to reduce the incidence of global conflict. The 1917 Wesleyan Conference in London had already passed a resolution declaring that a new League of Nations should be set up after the war in order 'to place the international relations of the world upon a basis in accordance with the teachings of Christ'.[136]

The following year, the Conference expressed 'deep satisfaction' over the proposals of Wilson and Lloyd George for a new collective security organization, and called on 'our ministers and people ... to assist in every possible way in the formation and strengthening of public opinion in favour of such a League of Nations'.[137] In the same year, the Primitive Methodist Conference in Northampton passed a resolution proclaiming that the proposed League was 'the only method by which international differences can be justly and equitably settled and the peace of the world preserved'.[138] Although the previous few years of conflict had created sharp divisions within Methodism about how best to respond to the challenge of war, there was widespread agreement that governments should in future seek to establish a just and sustainable peace based on the principles of internationalism and collective security.

## Conclusion

The Methodist churches were very successful in mounting a practical response to many of the challenges facing Britain between 1914 and 1918. British Methodism had developed rapidly during the Industrial Revolution in large part because it was more effective than the Church of England at dealing with the needs of the growing urban population, and the fluid organizational heritage of the various connexions allowed them to react quickly to the outbreak of hostilities in 1914. Chaplains were sent to minister to troops at the Front, while officiating clergy were appointed to deal with the large concentration of soldiers and sailors in towns such as Aldershot and Portsmouth. Camp homes were constructed to offer new places of worship and sober entertainment. Local churches and chapels made great efforts to keep in contact with members serving in the armed forces, and extended comfort and help to the numerous bereaved families in their midst. City missions in large cities like London and Liverpool continued to reach out to broad sections of the population at times of social upheaval and uncertainty. The sheer scale and horror of the conflict did not, however, only raise practical problems of organization and ministry. It also posed more profound questions about the problems inherent in any effort to reconcile the Christian ethic of love with the brutal reality of war.

It was seen in earlier chapters that the cluster of principles grouped together under the heading of the 'Nonconformist Conscience' seldom yielded straightforward conclusions about how best to confront complex social and political problems. Although all the main Methodist connexions formally committed themselves to the view that Britain was fighting in a just cause, a significant minority of their members remained convinced that it was impossible to reconcile support for the war with the ethics of the Sermon on the Mount. The language that was used by each side to defend their position was seldom distinguished by great theological depth or subtlety. The sophisticated reflections of men like J.H. Moulton and A.S. Peake on the ethical problems posed by war were the exception rather than the rule. Most of those who supported the war against the central powers used a language that was strikingly similar to the one used by senior figures in the government, arguing that Britain was fighting in defence of international law and against unprincipled aggression. Most of those who opposed the war contented themselves with the simple claim that the use of organized force by the state to defeat its enemies could not be reconciled with the general texture of Christ's ethical teachings. The differences between the two sides inevitably created a degree of tension. Although the traditional commitment to freedom of conscience within Methodism meant that the right of pacifists to speak their mind was seldom questioned, there was often a strong undercurrent of bitterness in the debates that took place in the Methodist press and at annual conferences and district synods.

The historian Martin Ceadel has made a useful distinction between 'pacifism' and 'pacificism' in his classic work on the development of the peace movement in Britain between 1914 and 1945.[139] He suggests that the first term should be used to describe individuals and groups who were absolutely opposed to the use of violence to resolve international crises, while the second is best applied to those who accepted that a resort to force could on occasion be a necessary if regrettable measure to prevent aggression or defeat gross injustice. As Ceadel himself recognizes, each position was capable of an almost infinite number of permutations, but the basic distinction remains of value when discussing attitudes towards peace and war among British Methodists during the First World War. Both those who opposed the war and those who supported it were united in believing that there was nothing glorious or heroic about military conflict; rather they disagreed about whether a resort to force was sometimes unavoidable, either to defend other important principles, or to promote the long-term prospects for a more peaceful world. The end of the conflict in 1918 did not resolve these differences. While there was widespread support within all the connexions for the League of Nations, created at the Paris Peace Conference in 1919, the divisions between 'pacifists' and 'pacificists' continued to create considerable tension throughout the inter-war years. The following chapter explores the response of British Methodism to the challenges posed by such developments as the rise of fascism in Italy and Germany in the 1920s and 1930s, and examines how the divisions were at times serious enough to pose a real threat to the unity of the new Methodist Church of Great Britain that was formed in 1932. The search for the principles to inform what a later generation would call an 'ethical foreign policy' proved as elusive and contested in the inter-war years as it had ever been.

# 4

# British Methodism and the Inter-War Crisis

## Introduction

The widespread hope that the First World War might prove to be the 'war to end all wars' quickly proved illusory in the twenty years or so after 1918. Some historians have even argued that the years between 1918 and 1939 are best understood as a time of perennial crisis, sandwiched between two periods of bitter conflict, which together marked the beginning and the end of a thirty-year-long European civil war.[1] International politics during the 1920s was dominated by attempts to deal with the aftermath of the cataclysm of 1914–18, ranging from questions of war debts and reparations through to discussions about how best to establish and maintain a new security architecture capable of maintaining peace in Europe. The economic depression precipitated by the Wall Street Crash of 1929 made the problems still worse, fuelling the growth of an economic and political nationalism that fostered the rise of Nazism in Germany, and destabilized political life by encouraging the development of political extremism across much of the continent. The League of Nations that was established with such fanfare in 1919 failed to cope with attempts to undermine the international *status quo*, responding feebly to Japan's invasion of Manchuria in 1931, and doing little to oppose the attack by Mussolini's Italy on Abyssinia four years later. The spectre of war haunted the imagination of the British public throughout the 1930s, fuelling support for a growing pacifist movement manifested in the creation of such organizations as the Peace Pledge Union. The British government's failure to respond more robustly in the face of the Nazi challenge had many causes, but it was at least partly due to the Cabinet's recognition that public opinion was reluctant to contemplate the prospect of another war so soon after the carnage of the Somme and Passchendaele.

The Protestant churches in Britain engaged with problems of peace and war during the inter-war period in a far more sustained manner than before 1914. The inter-denominational Conference on Christian Politics, Economics and Citizenship (COPEC), held at Birmingham in 1924, produced two lengthy reports on 'International Relations' and 'Christianity and War'. The report on 'Christianity and War' freely acknowledged that its members had 'divergent views' on the subject. Some believed that the application of 'permanent and universal principles' had to be 'relevant to time and place', with the result that injunctions to 'turn the other cheek' and 'to love thy neighbour as thyself' could not be taken as proof that war should be considered wrong under all possible conditions. Others firmly rejected the idea 'that war under any circumstances can be right', arguing that Christians should not 'willingly use evil means [even] to achieve good ends', not least because history showed that war invariably led to 'a progressive deadening of the moral sense of the nations engaged'.[2] The members of the Commission that compiled the report did, however, work hard to devise a common platform building on the 'very large measure of unity' among Christians about the need to work for peace. They demanded greater support for international organizations like the World Alliance for the Promotion of Friendship through the Churches, in the hope that closer co-operation between their members could play a role in promoting better relations between nations.[3] The main British churches welcomed the development of the global ecumenical movement as evidence that Christians around the world were determined to resolve the differences that divided them.

Support for the international ecumenical movement was particularly strong within British Methodism, engaging the sustained attention of such prominent figures as the Revd R. Newton Flew and the Revd William Lofthouse, who were both active in the main conferences and meetings that took place during these years. The inter-war years also witnessed fresh ecumenical initiatives in the domestic arena, manifested among other things in the creation in 1932 of the new Methodist Church of Great Britain, a development that followed many years of anguished debates within the various connexions. While Methodist union was in large part a practical response to the decline in membership that had set in following the rapid expansion of the Victorian period,[4] the general enthusiasm for the *international* ecumenical movement was prompted above all by the desire to contribute to world peace. The new Methodist Church was nevertheless divided from its creation about how best to respond to the challenge of supporting peace in a fractious world. There was during the 1920s broad agreement among its members that the promotion of collective security through the League of Nations represented the best way of preventing war, but the League's failure to maintain world peace in the more turbulent climate of the 1930s undermined this consensus. The deteriorating international situation led to the re-emergence of a sharp debate within British Methodism between those who were committed to an unconditional pacifism and their critics who believed that such a stance was both morally and practically flawed in a world of violence and turmoil.

## British Methodism and Support for Internationalism in the 1920s

While there had been a general consensus within British Methodism during the war over the need to avoid imposing a punitive peace settlement on the defeated countries, there was in the event some support in the Methodist press for the Treaty of Versailles that was signed in the summer of 1919, despite its harsh clauses on such questions as the payment of reparations by Germany.[5] Arthur Guttery contributed a decidedly acerbic article to the *Primitive Methodist Leader* hinting that Germany had no real regrets about its actions during the previous five years.[6] Most contributors to the Methodist press nevertheless remained opposed to any peace that smelt of vengeance rather than justice. 'Historicus' condemned the Lloyd George government in the *Methodist Times* for pursuing a policy towards Germany that was 'blinded by . . . national hate',[7] while Samuel Keeble contributed a number of letters to the same paper calling for 'a different kind of peace' based on the principles of equality between nations.[8]

The creation of the League of Nations was welcomed by all the Methodist connexions as a valuable attempt to 'end the rule of force and set reason upon the throne'.[9] The League was established at a time of great international confusion, and none of the victor powers represented at the Paris Peace Conference had a clear vision about how best to translate into practice the lofty principles articulated in its charter.[10] There was always something naive about the high hopes placed on the League by many people around the world in the years after 1918. The author of the Editorial Notes in the *Methodist Times* spoke for many of his readers when he observed hopefully that all the member states of the League would have to understand that 'A partnership of nations, like any partnership . . . restricts the activities of its individual members.'[11] Few governments were ready to accept such a radical challenge to the principle of state sovereignty. The refusal of the United States Senate to ratify the Versailles Treaty, which in effect meant that the country remained outside the League, gravely weakened the organization's moral authority throughout the inter-war years. The British government under Lloyd George paid lip-service to the League's ideals, but most Cabinet ministers and senior Foreign Office officials continued to view it privately with a degree of scepticism. The French government proclaimed that it was ready to accept a major international role for the League, even if it impinged on national sovereignty, but such apparent open-mindedness merely reflected the hope of politicians in Paris that the organization would act as a 'policeman' preventing Germany from breaking the shackles of Versailles. The political tensions that surrounded the League during its formative years were, however, little known among the wider public. The Methodist press was throughout 1919 and 1920 full of articles and letters expressing confidence in 'the most magnificent instrument of peace ever seen'. The *Methodist Times* and the *Primitive Methodist Leader* both conducted a vigorous campaign in support of the League, criticizing any hint that politicians and diplomats might be trying to circumvent it, by returning to the pre-war tradition of secret diplomacy.[12] A.S. Peake contributed articles to the *Leader* attacking 'old-time statecraft' and declared that 'thoughtful men are driven to see that the security of peace must be sought on the moral plane'.[13] 'Historicus' in the *Methodist Times* waged a veritable war on Lloyd George's 'ramshackle government' for not doing more to promote the League.[14] Both papers argued that the religious press had a major responsibility for putting pressure on politicians to stand by the internationalist principles that they articulated so freely in public.[15] The annual conferences of the various connexions also continued to pledge themselves during these years to 'use every means' at their disposal to support the development of collective security.[16]

The League attracted widespread support in part because there was little real popular understanding about the problems that were bound to face any such organization. The mantra of collective security seemed to offer an easy formula for subordinating traditional national egoisms and animosities to a quasi-legal process that would prevent conflict and promote international justice. The apparent consensus among British Methodists in favour of the League, manifested in the large number of affiliations by individual chapels and churches to the League of Nations Union,[17] in fact concealed some important differences. The logic of collective security rested on the ultimate willingness of member states to use force to prevent aggression and 'safeguard the peace of nations'. The Wesleyan Minister A.W. Harrison – himself a veteran of the First World War – almost certainly reflected the views of most Methodists when he argued in his 1928 book on *Christianity and the League of Nations* that the use of military means was acceptable when it was undertaken for a clear moral purpose in accordance with agreed international procedures.[18] Two years earlier, he had written in his book on *Christianity and Universal Peace* that 'men must learn to apply the new morality in their own way to the peculiar needs of their time'.[19] Harrison's 'realist' views were not universally shared. Some leading Methodists were even reluctant to accept that the League had the right to impose economic sanctions, arguing instead that the organization should seek to exert its influence simply by trying to mobilize world opinion, shaming the aggressor into retreat. Although the end of the First World War led to a decline in membership of such organizations as the Wesleyan Pacifist Fellowship, a significant number of Methodist ministers remained committed to an unconditional pacifism, pledging their support to the inter-denominational Fellowship of Reconciliation.[20]

The tensions within British Methodism on international affairs were nevertheless subdued during the 1920s, masked by a shared commitment to the shibboleths of collective security, and support for disarmament initiatives of the kind discussed at the Washington Naval Conference of 1921–2.[21] The annual conferences of the various connexions passed resolutions throughout the decade committing themselves to work in support of the League, while the Methodist press published repeated demands for new political initiatives and administrative reforms designed to allow the organization to operate more effectively. Both the *Leader* and the *Methodist Times* warmly endorsed proposals to give the League more power to act in case of international aggression, and welcomed the moves that took place in the autumn of 1924 to create a new system of binding international arbitration, via the so-called Geneva Protocol.[22] The Locarno accords of the following year, by which Britain effectively guaranteed the existing boundaries of western Europe in an effort to resolve the long-standing Franco-German animosity, was also welcomed by the Methodist press. The Principal of Hartley Victoria College argued in the *Leader* that Locarno was 'the most substantial instalment toward world peace that has yet been offered',[23] although one or two voices did warn that the agreements might drag Britain into a war that was not of its own making. The Locarno agreements were welcomed in

84

part because they presaged a return of Germany to the mainstream of international life. All the main Methodist newspapers looked increasingly askance at the Versailles settlement by the mid-1920s, echoing a growing public sense that Germany's semi-pariah status was both unacceptable and potentially destabilizing, since it served only to compound the country's sense of bitterness. It was for this reason that the Methodist press responded positively to proposals to reschedule Germany's reparations payments, as well as supporting the country's eventual admission to the League of Nations in 1926.

The commitment of the Methodist connexions and the Methodist press to the internationalist spirit embedded in the League was extended to support for the international ecumenical movement that developed between the wars. Although there were no Methodist representatives on the two COPEC commissions that produced reports on questions of international politics and war, discussed earlier, there were a significant number of Methodists among the 1,500 delegates at the main Conference in Birmingham.[24] Representatives from the Methodist connexions were also active in such forums as the Universal Christian Conference on Life and Work that was held at Stockholm in 1925.[25] A.W. Harrison took part in the 1925 conference of the World Alliance for Promoting Friendship through the Churches, which had been set up before the First World War, in order to improve the international atmosphere at a time of growing belligerence. While Harrison was like many of his fellow Methodists convinced that 'the work of pacification is a distinctly Christian work',[26] with the result that the churches had a moral duty to involve themselves with the search for world peace, he was disappointed with the 'vague generalities on Christian brotherhood' that dominated proceedings at Geneva.[27] The Revd F.L. Wiseman took a more positive view of the proceedings at the 1927 Lausanne Conference on Faith and Order, which focused more narrowly on relations between the churches, and returned home confident that in future 'we shall look less exclusively on our own things and more charitably on the things of others'.[28] He was, though, too optimistic in his assessment both of the strength of the ecumenical impulse in general and of the significance of the Lausanne Conference in particular.[29] While the main Protestant churches in Britain supported greater international co-operation in both the political and religious arenas, their leaders were always uncertain about how best to translate vague aspirations into more concrete results. The threatening developments of the 1930s, memorably described by the poet W.H. Auden as the 'low honest decade', posed a set of dilemmas that demanded something more than a vague commitment by the churches to the principle of world peace.

## The Crisis of the 1930s

In November 1929 a meeting was organized at the Kingsway Hall in London on the subject of 'Methodism and World Peace', including among its main speakers the Foreign Secretary Arthur Henderson, a life-long Wesleyan and an enthusiastic supporter of the League of Nations.[30] During the weeks leading up to the meeting, the *Methodist Recorder* carried a number of articles on questions of peace and war, prompted in part by a recent debate on the subject within the Congregationalist Church. The author of an editorial published in the *Recorder* in late October firmly sided with those who believed that there were occasions when a resort to war could be justified, rejecting pacifism as 'a counsel of despair' more suited to a debating society than the world of practical affairs. The acerbic tone of the editorial aroused criticism from the young Wesleyan Minister the Revd Leslie Weatherhead,[31] who contributed an article to the *Recorder* two weeks later expressing his views on the whole question. Weatherhead fretted that the younger generation knew little 'of the wickedness and waste of war', which he condemned as 'utterly unchristian', and then proceeded to suggest that the medals awarded in war signified 'murder and mutilation, tears and treachery, lust and lies'.[32] The atmosphere at the Kingsway Meeting held a few days later was predictably 'electric', while in the weeks that followed the *Recorder* carried numerous letters from readers outraged by Weatherhead's apparent slur on those who had been decorated during the 1914–18 war. One correspondent described such views as 'slander'.[33] Another accused Weatherhead of causing great pain to the families of those who had died.[34] Weatherhead himself was chastened by such reactions, but he still responded with a staunch declaration that 'no nation has yet been Christian enough to try Christ's way. If it did and even the worst happened – which I do not think possible – then a crucified nation would do for the world what a crucified Christ did and is doing. If a whole nation is determined to take Christ's way [and renounce the use of force] it may have to give up its life for its beliefs.'[35]

The furore caused by Weatherhead's letter died down in the months that followed, since the intellectual and organizational energy of British Methodism was inevitably taken up during 1930–1 by preparations for union. A number of Methodists, including the young Donald Soper, were involved in an initiative that took place in 1932 to establish a 'Peace Army' of volunteers who were ready to go to the Far East to place themselves between Chinese and Japanese troops after the outbreak of war in the region.[36] Although the men and women who flocked to the banners of the 'Peace Army' never got any further than Tilbury, many of them were active in protests against the sale of armaments to Japan. The question of disarmament acquired a high international profile at the start of 1932, when the Geneva Disarmament Conference opened following seven years of detailed preparations. The Methodist press held out high hopes for the Conference,[37] not least because it was to be chaired by Arthur Henderson, who had left the Foreign Office six months earlier following the collapse of the second Labour government. It soon became apparent, though, that agreement was never going to be achieved given the longstanding mistrust between the governments in Paris and Berlin. The divisions became still worse following Hitler's rise to power at the start of 1933. Although its supporters were reluctant to admit the fact, it was clear to most participants that the Conference was effectively doomed once the Nazi regime had established itself in power, given its commitment to rearmament and the pursuit of a more aggressive German foreign policy.

The controversial decision by the Oxford Union in February 1933 to support a motion that 'This House will in no circumstances fight for its King and Country' focused public attention in Britain firmly on the rights and wrongs of pacifism. The victory of a Labour candidate in the East Fulham by-election a few weeks later, on a platform that among other things opposed British rearmament, was widely interpreted at the time as evidence that public opinion was also unwilling to countenance any policy that might increase the risk of war.[38] A few weeks after the Oxford Union passed its celebrated 'King and Country' motion, an article appeared in the *Recorder* by the Revd Henry Carter roundly declaring his view that 'the abolition of war . . . is dependent upon the absolute renunciation of war and the war-spirit by the Christian because he is a Christian'. He went on to add that in the case of a future conflict 'I should reason, preach and write against it, and should use any lawful means to dissuade others from recourse to fighting'.[39] Carter's bold language aroused a storm of fury, not least because as Secretary of the Temperance and Social Welfare Department in the new church, he played a pivotal role in discussions shaping its position on key questions of policy. A.W. Harrison responded in the same publication with an article suggesting that the distaste for war shared by all Methodists should not undermine a reasoned attempt to grapple with the complexities of international life. Harrison argued that the principal challenge facing Christians was to ensure that the League of Nations commanded the resources to promote collective security and defeat any possible challenges to international law. He concluded his piece with a claim that 'Christian statesmen . . . [should] not throw up the difficult and laborious tasks of constructing international peace and disarmament at the bidding of some emotional appeal to drop the complicated machinery of civilisation and leave all to Divine Providence.'[40] The charge that pacifism was essentially an emotional rather than an intellectual position was made many times in the years that followed.

Numerous letters poured into the offices of the *Recorder* and the *Methodist Times and Leader* during the weeks that followed (the latter newspaper as the name suggests was formed from a merger of the *Methodist Times* and the *Primitive Methodist Leader* following Methodist union). Some contributors agreed with Carter that 'the only thing that can end war is the determined refusal to fight',[41] while one even urged men working in the munitions industry to walk out of the factories so as to prevent the production of armaments. Other contributors argued that in a world where 'there are Hitlers and Chinese war-lords . . . we must have protection'.[42] Such was the ferocity of the debate that one letter-writer plaintively warned that Carter's strictures were in danger of splitting 'our new Church in twain' almost as soon as it had been created.[43] While there was something hyperbolic about such language, the expression of such powerful sentiments in the correspondence columns of the Methodist press showed the strength of emotions on the subject. Both papers took a firm line on the subject. The *Recorder* under the editorship of Frederick Wiseman carried a leading article in May 1933 arguing that pacifists 'do not have any monopoly of hatred of war or enthusiasm for peace', and added that 'the argument that pacifism finds its justification in the Cross . . . fails to carry conviction when it is examined'. It concluded with a plea for a realistic approach to international affairs that was not blind to practicalities: 'The one supreme task which confronts the Christian Church is to explore the meaning of love *in the manifold and complex relations of life*' (emphasis added).[44] The *Times and Leader* also criticized the position taken by those who wrote to the paper calling on Conference to launch a crusade in which Methodism would take the lead in seeking to save 'the peace of the world' as it had once taken the lead in seeking 'to save souls'.[45]

The Conference that met in London in July 1933, six months after Hitler's rise to power, adopted a 'Declaration on Peace and War' that was carefully designed to be acceptable to *all* its members. The Declaration condemned war as 'a crime against humanity',[46] and committed the Methodist Church to 'press for world-wide reduction of armaments, together with the limitation and control of their manufacture and use', a topic of particular sensitivity given the ongoing Disarmament Conference at Geneva. On the vexed question of 'individual participation in war', the Declaration explicitly acknowledged the existence of divisions between those 'whose inward conviction and loyalty to Christ compel them to oppose war in all cases', and others who 'with equal sincerity ... [accept] obligations, commitments and loyalties of a national or international character which they deem binding on the body politic and themselves within it'.[47] The proposed formula, which echoed the one reached at the COPEC Conference some years earlier, proved broad enough to be acceptable both to unconditional pacifists and to the advocates of collective security. The Conference debate nevertheless revealed the depth of the underlying differences within the Methodist Church on questions of peace and war. The months and years that followed showed that even an agreement to acknowledge that church members held different views on the subject was not going to prevent further discussion and debate.

In February 1934 the *Recorder* published a letter by five leading Methodist pacifists, including Henry Carter and Donald Soper, setting out the rationale for the Methodist Peace Fellowship (MPF) that had been set up the previous year. The letter set out the terms of the MPF Covenant, which condemned war as 'contrary to the spirit, teaching and purpose of Jesus Christ our Lord', especially in the modern era when it 'involves the destruction of human life without mercy or limits'.[48] Reaction was once again divided. In the week following the publication of the letter, the *Recorder* carried a reply by the Anglican priest the Revd E.N. Porter Goff, noting that 'I am a little puzzled as to what exactly Mr Carter and his friends are aiming at'. Porter Goff was Secretary of the Christian Organisations Committee of the League of Nations Union, and his commitment to the principle of collective security made him wary of a pacifism that refused help to 'a country which is wantonly attacked by another'.[49] Some Methodist ministers were more outspoken in their criticism. The Revd F. Norman Charley spoke for a good number of correspondents when he wrote that 'I cannot by any stretch of the imagination' understand the approach to questions of peace and war characteristic of the MPF.[50] Carter tried valiantly to defend himself against such attacks but, like many pacifists in the inter-war years, he struggled to relate his commitment to an unconditional pacifism with the complex realities of international politics. He was reluctant to reject outright the ideal of collective security, presumably because it had penetrated so deeply into the consciousness of most critics of traditional diplomacy in the inter-war years,[51] but he struggled to explain how a thorough-going pacifism could be reconciled with a commitment to the League of Nations Covenant that rested on the ultimate readiness of states to use force to prevent unprovoked aggression.

The tension between the pacifists and the proponents of collective security was revealed starkly at the 1934 Methodist Conference held in Leicester. Henry Carter had always been determined to use his position as Secretary of the Temperance and Social Welfare Department 'to face the new generation of Methodists with the relevance of the Christian gospel to all areas of life'.[52] It was therefore hardly surprising that some of the proposals drafted by the Department's Industrial and International Relations sub-committee caused considerable consternation when they were discussed at Conference. The mood of the Conference was radical enough to endorse a statement deploring 'H.M. Government's recent decision to increase immediately the Air Forces of this country'.[53] It also approved a statement on 'The Private Manufacture and Sale of Arms', which noted that there was 'incontrovertible evidence that the sale and manufacture of arms for private profit constitute a serious menace to international peace'.[54] There was, though, considerable dismay about a draft 'Programme of Peacemaking for the Methodist Church' which contained a derogatory reference to the role of Officer Training Corps in schools, condemned by one critic as an attempt by Carter to dragoon Conference to 'his particular point of view'.[55] The reference was eventually deleted after a vote on the issue, with the result that the approved Programme merely committed the church to a 'persistent educational process' designed to encourage young people to reject militarism.[56] There was also considerable unease at Conference about a proposal by the Revd Percy Carden for a reconsideration of the relationship between the War Office and Methodist chaplains serving in the armed forces.[57] Carden's passionate claim that Methodism's 'proclamation of the redeeming love of Christ' should lead its adherents to reject any formal relationship with a department charged with preparing for war was rejected by a large majority, after the Revd Owen Watkins argued that the chaplains performed a vital task in promoting the spiritual welfare of the men under their care. Such controversies predictably provoked a strong response in the columns of the *Recorder* and the *Times and Leader* in the weeks following Conference. The Revd J. Ernest Rattenbury used his 'Conference Reflections' in the *Recorder* to condemn the minority who sought to bully their colleagues into 'extreme Pacifism', and argued that Conference should in future 'limit the scope of fervent but unilateral people'.[58] One contributor to the same paper's correspondence page condemned pacifists for their 'arrogance and intolerance', while another observed that 'If Carden and his friends had their way, England would be defenceless in the event of another war.'[59] A letter-writer in the *Leader* suggested that it was time for the 'pacifists to come down to earth'.[60] Carden himself replied that the pacifists were 'unrepentant' and declared that 'In future Conferences we hope to be heard more and more.'[61]

Senior figures within the Methodist hierarchy were perturbed about the depth of the divisions visible at the Leicester Conference. It was for this reason that a sustained attempt was made to ensure that the events at Leicester were not repeated the following year. At the 1935 Conference in Bristol, Henry Carter sponsored a joint resolution on international affairs with A.W. Harrison, the man who had criticized his original 1933 pacifist *credo* in the *Recorder*. Harrison acknowledged that some members of Conference might be surprised that two men with such contrasting views should be able to sponsor a resolution, but went on to remind his audience that all Methodists were firmly united in their 'detestation of war'. This effort to bind together the proponents of absolute pacifism and the advocates of collective security was predictably well-received by

Conference. The resolution was 'carried unanimously, amid great cheers', a striking testimony to a widespread sense of relief that the divisions of the previous year had been avoided.[62]

The passionate debates on peace and war that took place in Britain during these years claimed one unlikely victim, a middle-aged Methodist minister by the name of J. Whittaker Bond, who at the end of 1934 found himself the subject of a writ for libel issued by the Foreign Secretary Sir John Simon.[63] Simon was held responsible by many activists in the peace movement for the slow pace of events at the Disarmament Conference, following its first meeting in January 1932, and he consequently fell victim to numerous false rumours that his supposed reluctance to push proceedings along in Geneva was due to his (non-existent) shareholdings in arms firms. The Foreign Secretary became increasingly angry at the circulation of such claims, but as a trained lawyer he was shrewd enough to understand that he could do little to prevent them without firm evidence that would allow him to take the appropriate legal action. His chance finally came in November 1934, when Bond told a Free Church Council meeting in Norfolk that the reason Simon had been attacking the Peace Ballot, currently being organized by the League of Nations Union, was 'because his money is invested in armaments firms'. Simon had certainly been critical of the Peace Ballot, a mass propaganda exercise that involved circulating millions of ballot papers asking for responses to such questions as 'whether the manufacture and sale of arms for private profit [should] be prohibited by international agreement', and Bond was not the first person to suggest that the Foreign Secretary's private financial interests governed his views on policy. He was, though, unfortunate (or foolish) enough to repeat the claim at a meeting that was attended by a local newspaper reporter. Simon was in due course notified of what had taken place, and immediately seized the chance to begin proceedings for slander.

Bond's support for the peace movement seems to have been inspired by his memory of the horrors of the First World War. He was certainly unaware of the potential sensitivity of his remarks.

Simon for his part would doubtless have taken no action under normal circumstances, but he was by the end of 1934 facing widespread criticism for his performance at the Foreign Office, and the Foreign Secretary's own judgement seems to have deserted him. Simon was himself the son of a Nonconformist minister, and he had profound worries about the public response to any possible legal action. Bond's solicitors advised their client to apologize unreservedly, but the Foreign Secretary was determined that the case should come to court in order to give him an opportunity to clear his name once and for all. The strain on Bond was enormous. He wrote to Simon pleading with him to 'accept my . . . apology', and asked others to intervene on his behalf, although to no avail. The Foreign Secretary did however ask the Revd J. Scott Lidgett – a long-standing critic of pacifism – to write to Bond emphasizing that he had no desire to be 'vindictive or indifferent to the defendant's manifest embarrassment'. The strain on Bond was so great that he was too ill to attend in person when the case came to the High Court in January 1935, instead sending a written apology acknowledging that 'I am now convinced that it was entirely untrue to say that Sir John had any interest in armaments firms, and that there was no ground whatever for my statements'. There is no doubt that Bond's original statement to the Free Church Council meeting in Norfolk was slanderous, but he was far from alone in believing that the private manufacture of armaments made war more likely, since the 'merchants of death' had a vested interest in preventing any attempts to create peace.[64] It has in any case been seen that the Methodist Church was already committed to the view that the manufacture of arms for profit was likely to promote international tension. Although the Methodist press took a decidedly censorious tone when reporting on Bond's foolhardiness in making specific claims against Simon, there is little doubt that many other Methodists – both ministers and lay people – shared his fundamental views on questions of war and peace.

## The Development of Methodist Pacifism in the 1930s

Christian organizations represented a major strand in the British pacifist movement during the inter-war years.[65] Groups organized along similar lines to the Methodist Peace Fellowship were set up in most of the major denominations,[66] including the Anglican Pacifist Fellowship and the Baptist Peace Fellowship, while the Fellowship of Reconciliation continued to draw support from Christian pacifists of all denominations (and sometimes from those without firm religious convictions at all).[67] Numerous books appeared during the period arguing that pacifism was the only logical position for any Christian who sought to follow faithfully the teachings of Christ. The Cambridge academic Professor Charles Raven argued in his 1934 Halley Stewart Lecture that the evolution of human society had rendered war obsolete, with the result that new ways needed to be found to settle international conflict.[68] The Glasgow University professor G.H.C. MacGregor wrote a book setting down *The New Testament Basis of Pacifism*, designed to show that war 'cannot under any conditions be brought within the orbit of the Christian ethic'.[69] The Peace Pledge Union (PPU) that developed under the inspirational leadership of Canon H.R.L. ('Dick') Sheppard during the mid-1930s provided the most effective forum for the pacifist movement to articulate its views to a wider public, particularly once membership soared to more than 100,000 in the tense years immediately before the outbreak of the Second World War.[70] Although the appeal of the PPU extended far beyond those with a well-developed religious belief, attracting support from the likes of Bertrand Russell, a significant proportion of its leading members were active in one of the Christian denominations. Donald Soper became one of its most tireless supporters, travelling up and down the country making passionate speeches in which he argued that an unconditional commitment to peace and non-resistance represented the best way to defuse international tension and avoid disaster.[71] Henry Carter also served as one of the PPU 'sponsors', speaking at meetings with other leading pacifists such as the Labour politician George Lansbury, and urging his audience to sign the 'pledge' committing themselves to 'renounce war and never again to support another'.[72]

A brief review of the biographies of some prominent Methodists active in the pacifist movement during the 1930s can help to illuminate their contribution to the peace movement both in their own church and beyond. The Methodist Peace Fellowship enjoyed the support of more than five hundred ministers when it was first established in 1933, a number that had risen by more than 50 per cent just six years later, when there were in addition some 3,000 lay members as well.[73] The literature produced by the Fellowship emphasized that its members sought to promote links 'with similar bodies in other communions' in order to promote 'effective witness and work for peace'.[74] The monthly magazine *Reconciliation*, published by the Fellowship of Reconciliation, served as an important focus for all the main Christian pacifist groups (including the MPF). The indefatigable Henry Carter continued to play a pivotal major role in the Methodist Peace Fellowship, despite his other duties as Secretary of the Temperance and Social Welfare Department, eventually leading to complaints in some quarters that he was taking advantage of his official position to promote his views on peace and war.[75] He also worked hard to promote links with the broader pacifist movement, speaking frequently at mass meetings such as the one that took place at Central Hall in November 1934, when he told an audience of young university peace activists that they should seek to 'accept the absolute supremacy of the Christian standard' rather than compromise their principles.[76] Carter also accompanied George Lansbury on some of his 'Embassies of Reconciliation' to central Europe, missions which were designed to 'carry the Christian witness for peace' to the region in which it seemed most threatened.[77] Carter was convinced that such trips provided an effective 'new method of promoting peace', since they fostered personal ties that helped to break down the barriers of suspicion and fear. He also placed great emphasis on the need to address the underlying problems that caused international tension, writing a number of articles in 1938 praising proposals made by the erstwhile Belgian

Prime Minister Paul Van Zeeland for an international conference to restore economic confidence.[78] The previous year he took part in a visit by senior churchmen to Spain, to investigate claims of anti-clerical violence there, an experience that led him to exonerate the Republicans and attack the nationalist General Franco as the main instigator of the Spanish Civil War.[79] Although Carter was not as effective a public speaker as Dick Sheppard or Donald Soper, and never developed such a high public profile, his enormous energy and organizational acumen made him an important figure in the inter-war pacifist movement.

Carter's pacifism was based above all on a profound sense that the horrors of war were utterly incompatible with the values of Christianity. The same was true of Donald Soper, who roundly declared in his 1935 book *Question Time on Tower Hill* that 'I know that war is absolutely contrary to the spirit and teaching of Jesus Christ',[80] a sentiment he repeated in numerous articles published in both the religious and secular press.[81] Neither man was particularly interested in grounding their position in detailed scriptural exposition or abstruse theological debates about the criteria for a just war, an approach that made it easier for them to co-operate with individuals active in other strands of the pacifist movement, both religious and secular. They nevertheless found it difficult to escape from the problem that bedevilled British pacifism in the late 1930s: namely, showing *how* pacifist ideas offered a viable response to the complex international situation. While Carter and Soper both professed that their commitment to an unconditional pacifism was rooted in a belief that organized violence was contrary to Christ's teaching, they also hoped that the act of renouncing violence could actively transform social and political relationships, an approach characterized by Soper's claim that 'pacifism contains a spiritual force strong enough to repel any invader'.[82] Such principles were, though, difficult to translate into practice. Carter and Soper, like many pacifists, found it hard to move beyond support for such gestures as the PPU's campaign to encourage its members to send postcards to Hitler expressing their desire for peace. Although Soper became interested in the ideas of non-violent resistance being developed by Gandhi and his followers in India, he only really began to think more systematically about the whole subject at a later stage in his career, and in the years before the Second World War his articles and speeches owed most to the motifs of the radical Nonconformist tradition to which he so obviously belonged.[83] In the 1930s he remained, like many pacifists, a strong believer in the powerful force of personal example. Soper hoped that the development of a strong peace movement in Britain would place pressure on the British government to adopt new policies, in particular unilateral disarmament, that would in turn fundamentally change the dynamic of world politics.[84]

Leslie Weatherhead broadly shared the views of Soper and Carter during the mid-1930s, although his ideas later changed sharply once he began to recognize the scale of the challenge posed by Nazi Germany. Weatherhead like Soper became a familiar voice on the airwaves during the 1930s, and his charismatic public persona played a major part in his appointment to the pulpit of the City Temple in 1936, which gave him a still higher profile. Weatherhead aroused a storm of protest in 1935, at a time when Italy was threatening military action against Abyssinia, by arguing that Britain's possession of numerous colonies meant that its government was in no position to criticize Mussolini's attempts to develop an empire in East Africa. Three years earlier he had vividly expressed his horror of war at a rally held to celebrate the start of the Geneva Disarmament Conference, fretting that after 13 years of peace few young people really understood what it was to see 'boys of nineteen . . . blown to pieces'.[85] Weatherhead was also dismissive of politicians for failing to find ways of resolving the tensions that bedevilled the world during the 1930s, and frequently reiterated the familiar pacifist dictum that closer personal contacts between the people of the world would make war unthinkable. As war approached, though, Weatherhead began to rethink his commitment to unconditional pacifism, expressing some perturbation about the fate of Czechoslovakia in the wake of the Munich agreement. In his book *Thinking Aloud in Wartime*, written in the final weeks of 1939, he frankly acknowledged that it was 'retrogressive *at this stage* to abandon the final appeal to force'. He went on to argue that 'it would be wrong not to resist' the challenge of Nazi Germany, and argued that Britain and France were effectively just acting as policemen in seeking to restrain Hitler's ambitions. In a telling statement he noted that 'I used to think that it might be better to be invaded than to fight, but a realisation of the doctrines which those hold who now threaten us makes me feel that it would be wrong not to resist that for which they stand.'[86] Weatherhead's pacifism never had such deep psychological roots as the pacifism of Carter and Soper, with the result that he was able to make an emotional and intellectual shift that the other two men would have found impossible. While he certainly never reconciled himself to the kind of Christian realism being espoused across the Atlantic in the late 1930s by Reinhold Niebuhr, which questioned the value of applying an ethical code devised for individuals to the behaviour of states,[87] he became increasingly ready to accept that decisions about international affairs should be grounded in an assessment of immediate circumstances as well as by reference to universal abstract principles.

Active involvement in the pacifist movement was not limited to Methodist ministers. Charles Coulson, who in later life became a distinguished mathematician and sometime Vice-President of Conference, was still an undergraduate at Cambridge in the early 1930s. Although he was raised in a Methodist family, it was only with his arrival at Cambridge that Coulson became active in the church, becoming in due course a local preacher. He also became a central figure in the burgeoning student pacifist movement, developing links with distinguished scholars like Charles Raven, as well as working closely with undergraduates from other churches who committed themselves to the pacifist cause. He was also active in the Cambridge Scientists Anti-War Group which drew its membership from both Christians and non-Christians. Coulson's enormous energy and enthusiasm made him an important figure both at Cambridge and in the wider peace movement. He contributed to pamphlets which claimed that if all Christians followed the teaching of the Sermon on the Mount then a future war would be impossible. Coulson's views were based on the assumption that 'the Kingdom of Heaven isn't something that will happen, it's something that has happened; it is within me, and the life I live is to be no less than perfect'.[88] He was as a result clear that his pacifism was not just a matter of 'peace and war' but 'symbolic for the whole approach to life'.[89] In 1935 he made it clear that 'I'm a pacifist because I'm a Christian and I'm a supporter of the Unemployed and against Capitalism because I'm a Christian and they are all part and parcel, for me, of the one great desire to do His will on this poor old earth'.[90] Not all Methodist pacifists were necessarily committed to social and political radicalism, but many of the most active members of the MPF were certainly much exercised by existing inequities and injustices in British society, which they believed helped to create the kinds of tension that led to conflict both at home and abroad. The conviction that the will of Christ represented an absolute injunction necessarily fostered a radical stance in the face of the world. It also helped to foster tensions within the Methodist Church itself.

## British Methodism on the Eve of the Second World War

The deteriorating global situation of the late 1930s meant that the accommodation reached at the 1935 Bristol Methodist Conference between the pacifists and their critics was always likely to prove fragile. Both the *Times and Leader* and the *Recorder* continued to nail their colours firmly to the mast of a collective security system that relied on the use of force as the ultimate sanction to deter aggression. The French government was the target for particular attack by the *Recorder*, which repeatedly blamed Paris for failing to honour its international obligations under the Covenant. The paper reminded British politicians that they were pledged 'to sustain the collective organisation of security centring in Geneva', and lamented the 'quality ... in French diplomacy which seems so often to allure British statesmen away from the path of common-sense'.[91] The *Recorder* also displayed a concomitant tendency to view attempts by Hitler to challenge the Treaty of Versailles with a degree of equanimity, reflecting a widely held view in British society that the settlement of 1919 had imposed unduly harsh restrictions on Germany. In the week following the remilitarization of the Rhineland, in March 1936, the author of the *Recorder*'s 'Notes of the Week' observed that 'sometimes the only method of procuring an amendment of an unjust law is simply and with forethought determination to break the law', adding that the German government's action at least meant there was now 'a clear way forward'.[92] The paper was, though, consistently critical of the domestic regime of Nazi Germany, a position that was echoed by the *Leader*, which had shown a sustained interest in the whole question more or less from the time Hitler came to power in 1933.[93] In the late 1930s, articles began to appear regularly in both papers on the problems faced by Jewish refugees who had fled Germany, while an editorial published in the *Recorder* on 'Christian Civilization' in August 1938 was typical in arguing that Christians should not ignore persecution and suffering simply because it was not taking place in their own society.[94] Although the *Leader* ceased publication in 1937, the deteriorating internal situation in Nazi Germany increasingly coloured the analysis of international developments put forward on the pages of the *Recorder* over the following two years.

The correspondence page of the *Recorder* continued to echo the divisions within Methodism in the second half of the 1930s about the best way of securing international peace. The decision by the British government to begin large-scale rearmament was condemned by leading members of the Methodist Peace Fellowship, one of whom condemned the move as a 'purely pagan' policy.[95] The Revd F. Brompton Harvey, by contrast, argued that potential aggressors would only be deterred if Britain were better armed, while another correspondent suggested that too much emphasis was being placed in contemporary debate on the value of 'the gentleness of the Christian character'.[96] One correspondent even condemned the pacifist movement as 'one of the most mistaken and mischievous of our day'.[97] The 1936 Conference in Newcastle appointed a committee of ministers and laymen to report back the following year on the whole issue of Methodism's attitude towards questions of war and peace (a committee which included the erstwhile Foreign Secretary Arthur Henderson). This committee in turn produced a report that once again observed that war was 'essentially contrary to the Gospel of the Lord Jesus Christ', while recommending that the Church continued to uphold 'liberty of conscience', since there was no agreement among Methodists on the vexed question of 'the participation of the Christian in war'.[98] Although this approach helped to prevent a major split within Methodism during the late 1930s, it could not disguise the continuing differences. The *Recorder* carried a debate in February 1938 on the subject 'Are Armaments Consistent with Christianity' which showed that divisions on the subject were as deep as ever. Some contributors argued that there was 'nothing incompatible with Christian faith' in the policy of rearmament, while others claimed with equal passion that the policy constituted 'a direct antithesis to all that Christianity stands for'.[99] Although the agreement to respect 'liberty of conscience' helped defuse some of the tensions visible a few years earlier at the 1934 Conference, effectively ruling out a struggle to commit the Methodist Church to a particular position on the rights and wrongs of unconditional pacifism, it did little to resolve the underlying differences among ministers and their congregations.

The *Recorder* made no secret about its scepticism towards the policy of appeasement pursued by Neville Chamberlain once he became Prime Minister in May 1937. When Anthony Eden resigned as Foreign Secretary in February 1938, ostensibly in protest against Chamberlain's reluctance to take a harder line towards the dictators, the *Recorder* made it clear where its sympathies lay.[100] The paper warned that if Britain took too soft a line towards the dictators, 'she will find herself compelled into alignment with their reaction',[101] and condemned the German *Anschluss* with Austria that took place in early March as an attack 'on the very root of international law'.[102] By the end of March 1938, the *Recorder's* Notes column condemned the Prime Minister for not 'recognizing the extreme jeopardy in which international law and order now stand'.[103] As the fateful crisis loomed in Czechoslovakia a few months later, the paper warned against any proposals that would condemn the country 'to probable destruction'.[104] Perhaps the best-known critic within Methodism of the drift towards appeasement during these years was Isaac Foot, a life-long Methodist local preacher, who served as Vice-President of Conference during 1937–8. Foot had been a member of the Liberal Party since his youth, and had served in the National Government in 1931, before resigning the following year over the Cabinet's decision to prioritize imperial preference over free trade. In 1937 he narrowly lost a by-election at St Ives in which he repeatedly inveighed against the National Government for its recent failure to push for firm action by the League of Nations to defend Abyssinia against Mussolini. The following year Foot launched a bitter tirade against the government's behaviour in the Munich crisis, which was resolved when the British and French effectively endorsed Germany's seizure of large swathes of Czechoslovak territory, arguing in his local newspaper that relief over the avoidance of war should be tempered by 'a sense of shame' at the measures that had been taken to achieve such a goal.[105] He also gave a long interview to the *Recorder* questioning the value of a peace that condemned the only democracy in central Europe to life under a regime of 'arbitrary power'. Foot lamented the Chamberlain government's surrender to a pessimism that led it to react to events rather than shape their development. He told readers of the *Recorder* that the Methodist community had a 'special responsibility . . . to make a contribution that is needed by this stricken world', adding pointedly that 'We have higher standards to observe than any Cabinet or Parliament.' The worldwide membership of the church meant that Methodists must not 'become subservient to any dictator', but should instead identify with all those who were victims of tyranny and aggression, seeking to find ways of resisting the forces of militarism and destruction.[106]

British public opinion was remarkably fluid in the wake of the Munich crisis that erupted in September 1938. The *Recorder*'s own immediate response was somewhat confused. The author of the

'Notes' column lamented that 'The Czech nation has been treated with an indignity which is unworthy of Britain', although the editorial in the same issue took a more positive line, its author doubtless caught up in the collective sigh of relief that swept through British society following Chamberlain's return to London waving his infamous scrap of paper and declaring the dawn of 'peace in our time'.[107] The sermons preached by leading Methodist ministers on the Sunday following the end of the crisis displayed a similar ambiguity.[108] The Revd J.F. Reed told a congregation at Central Hall 'that God had put his hand upon Neville Chamberlain', while the Revd E.C. Urwin preaching in Bristol praised the Prime Minister for his determination to preserve peace. Leslie Weatherhead, though, urged his congregation at the City Temple to remember that there was little rejoicing in Czechoslovakia, a position echoed by a number of other ministers around the country. Such sentiments became more evident in the months that followed, as unease about both the ethics and the efficacy of Chamberlain's foreign policy grew sharply within the Church, a view that found increasing echoes both in Parliament and the secular press. The *Recorder* published numerous letters questioning whether the agreement with Hitler could conceivably be called 'peace with honour'.[109] The editorial notes in the paper pointedly argued that the merits of appeasement depended 'entirely upon the constructive purpose behind it. As an end in itself it is sheer opportunism.'[110] The paper also began to publish more articles than ever before on the relentless persecution of German Jews, as well as on the problems facing the German churches, in the face of attacks by the Nazi regime on churchmen like Martin Niemöller. There were nevertheless still many voices within Methodism continuing to espouse the cause of non-resistance, even when confronted by such a ghastly regime as the one presided over by Hitler. Few members of the Methodist Peace Fellowship showed any desire to follow Weatherhead's lead and rethink their views in the light of the moral challenge posed by fascism, while far more ministers and lay people joined the organization in the months leading up to the outbreak of war than resigned from it.[111] The organization continued to circulate literature and co-operate with other pacifist groups, even after the German invasion of Prague in March 1939 finally signalled Hitler's desire to expand his power beyond the German-speaking populations of central Europe.[112] Some pacifists in the Methodist Church even opposed the introduction of new Air Raid Precaution measures, on the grounds that such preparations could make war more likely. There was no greater agreement among Methodists on the correct attitude to war in the fateful summer of 1939 than there had been at the founding Conference of the united church seven years earlier.

There was by the late 1930s a powerful sense among many leading British churchmen that they could not hope to speak with authority on the international crisis unless serious attempts were made to improve inter-denominational relations at home and develop closer ties with other churches abroad. This was in turn bolstered by a growing sense that the Church had to play a pivotal role around the world in countering the ideologies of German Nazism and Soviet-style Communism, which both in their different way challenged traditional Christian belief by demanding complete commitment to human institutions and values that left little room for private religious conviction. The Methodist press carried many articles and letters placing high hopes on the international Conference on Church, Community and State, which convened at Oxford in July 1937, along with the Conference on Faith and Order that met at Edinburgh the following month. The *Recorder* published an editorial shortly before the Oxford Conference suggesting that most people had little interest in abstruse theological divisions, but instead wanted to see the churches co-operate together in a practical effort to promote international harmony and friendship.[113] It was a theme taken up by delegates from the Methodist Church who attended the Conference, including W.F. Lofthouse, who noted that 'We Methodists . . . can never forget that we are bidden to be the friends of all, the enemies of none.'[114] Although the detailed coverage of the Oxford Conference was partly eclipsed by coverage of the annual Methodist Conference at Bradford, which was taking place at the same time, the *Recorder* still found time to praise the delegates for their attempts to draw closer together 'in thought and sympathy'.[115] The *Leader* also took a positive line, carrying articles suggesting that 'the possibility of world peace hang on our knowing the mind of God and obeying His will'.[116] Both papers warmly welcomed the 'Message to the Christian Churches' issued at Oxford, which challenged nationalist ideology that acknowledged no higher authority than the interest of the state. They also supported proposals for a World Council of Churches designed to provide a stronger institutional foundation for the ecumenical impulse.[117] They did not, however, make much comment on the conclusion reached by the sub-commission on 'The Church and War' that pacifism was a legitimate position for a Christian. The Methodist Conference that met at the same time as the Oxford Conference reiterated its strong commitment to the international ecumenical movement, passing a resolution calling on 'Christian people everywhere' to promote 'the unity of Christ's Church as an instrument of reconciliation between the divided nations'.[118]

The Methodist press also gave considerable attention to the Edinburgh Conference on Faith and Order,[119] presided over by the Archbishop of York, William Temple. Most of the Methodist delegates from Britain – including Lofthouse, Wiseman, Flew and Pyke – were assigned to a study group dealing with questions relating to the nature of the Church and the sacraments. Pyke and Wiseman, who had both attended the first Faith and Order Conference in Lausanne ten years earlier, wrote a number of articles recording their positive impressions of the Edinburgh Conference, which was attended by delegates from all the main churches apart from the Roman Catholics. Wiseman regarded the Conference as 'a remarkable assembly and a remarkable experience'.[120] Pyke suggested that the mood had been much more open and magnanimous than was the case at Lausanne, and spoke with particular warmth of the improving relationship between the Orthodox and Protestant churches, suggesting that 'the East has a great deal to teach the West, as certainly it has much to learn of us'.[121] The resounding 'Affirmation' issued by the Conference, which acknowledged that 'our divisions are contrary to the will of God', predictably received general acclaim among the Methodist hierarchy across Britain. There were nevertheless some notes of uncertainty about the real significance of the developments that took place at Oxford and Edinburgh. Richard Pyke recalled in his autobiography that the various ecumenical conferences he attended in the 1920s and 1930s 'made little impression on either my mind or my heart . . . It was evident that there was great seriousness of purpose among the leaders, but no one could compare the theological affirmations of the Eastern Church with our convictions as Free Churches without the sorrowful thought that . . . the differences are so deep that not in the time of any living person will there be an agreement which can result in reunion.'[122] The passage of years may have clouded Pyke's memory, leading him to forget his more optimistic contemporary assessment of the Edinburgh Conference, but his comments highlight the defining tension faced by the international ecumenical movement between 1919 and 1939: namely, how best to mobilize general expressions of goodwill and mutual understanding between the churches into a more concrete influence on relations between states. The forces of ecumenicalism proved powerless – at least in the short term – in the face of the passions and tensions facing the world in the late 1930s.

## Conclusion

Some reference was made in Chapter 3 to the distinction made by Martin Ceadel in his work on the British peace movement between 'pacifists', who were absolutely opposed to the use of violence to resolve international crises, and 'pacificists' who accepted that there were occasions when it might be justified to use force in order to prevent aggression or defeat gross injustice. The term helps to illuminate the tensions within inter-war Methodism over such issues as rearmament and collective security. All Methodists were happy to support resolutions declaring that war was 'a crime against humanity', but there were marked differences as to whether this meant that there were no circumstances under which a resort to war might prove to be justifiable. It was a division that was visible in the other main Protestant churches throughout the inter-war years, manifested as early as 1924 in the COPEC resolution on 'Christianity and War', as well as in the wider peace movement with its division into pacifist organizations like the Peace Pledge Union and pacificist organizations such as the League of Nations Union. These divisions were comparatively subdued during the 1920s, but once the scale of the challenge posed by Nazi Germany became clear during the following decade, the whole question of the correct Christian response to war became much more pressing.

The 1930s saw the development among some members of the Christian pacifist movement, such as Charles Raven, of increasingly sophisticated attempts to relate the principles of Christian faith to the rights and wrongs of war. Most prominent pacifists within the Methodist Church preferred, though, to engage in action rather than reflection. Many of them were by instinct social and political radicals who doubted whether Christian principles could be reconciled with the values and practices of modern capitalism. The pacifism of individuals like Soper and Carter was part of a broader ethical perspective that remained hopeful about the potential for changing the world around them. It was for this reason that they were able to co-operate so easily with all those who were critical of the *status quo*, whether in the Methodist Church or beyond, in the belief that fundamental reform could only come about as part of a broader 'reorientation' of public policy in all its manifestations. Leading Methodist 'pacificists' were also slow to couch their discussion of questions of war and peace in a well-honed theological or philosophical language. Even so erudite a figure as R. Newton Flew, who found it hard to relate to the pacifist-minded students he taught at Wesley House,[123] was reluctant to use his considerable knowledge of the work of theologians like Karl Barth to construct a critique of attempts to apply uncritically a transcendent ethic to the complex realities of everyday life.[124] It is indeed striking that Methodists on both sides of the debate seem to have been surprisingly impervious to the broader theological and philosophical arguments on war and peace that were being advanced in Europe and America during these years. Although the name of Reinhold Niebuhr was occasion- ally mentioned in some of the discussions that took place within British Methodism, there was little real engagement with the ideas he put forward in works like *Moral Man and Immoral Society*, which argued that the ethical imperatives that applied to individual behaviour did not necessarily hold true at the collective level. It is perhaps even more surprising that so little of the discussion was couched in the more familiar theological framework of the 'just war'.[125] The absence of a strong tradition within Methodism of analysing issues of peace and war in such terms meant that many of the debates that took place were all too often articulated in a language that merely echoed the mantras of the broader secular debate beneath a patina of Christian rhetoric.

The tensions that emerged within British Methodism on the question of war and peace in the 1930s posed a real challenge to the newly unified church, although the decision to invoke the principle of 'liberty of conscience' helped to take at least some of the sting out of the disagreements. It is clear with hindsight that the division between pacifists and non-pacifists was not simply about questions of war and peace alone. It also reflected a deeper tension between the rights of private conscience and the practical need for the Church to operate as something more than a simple aggregation of its members. It was possible under conditions of peace for the 'truce' to operate reasonably well. The outbreak of war fundamentally changed the situation, though, once the question of national survival came to the fore. Despite the grim developments of the 1930s, it was still possible right down to 1939 to hope that war might somehow be averted. Once such hopes proved illusory, the divisions within the Church were always likely to become more intractable. The following chapters examine how the outbreak of the Second World War raised a new series of challenges, both for pacifists who rejected war unconditionally, and for their critics who believed that the defeat of Nazism was necessary to prevent the triumph of barbarism.

# 5

# British Methodism and the
# Second World War

## Introduction

The Second World War that erupted in Europe in the autumn of
1939 claimed at least three times as many victims as the conflict of
1914–18. Even the horrors of trench warfare and poison gas, which
had once so exercised the world's moral imagination, faded in com-
parison with the barbarism of Auschwitz and the agony of Dresden.
The vast majority of violent deaths between 1939 and 1945 were
those of civilians, whose lives were snuffed out either by bombing
and starvation, or by the ruthless techniques of murder associated
with the concentration camp and the killing squad. Although survivors of even the worst savageries have recalled how some form of
moral life continued to flicker among the horrors,[1] it is telling that
the agonies of the Second World War still linger in the popular and
academic imagination, more than sixty years after the defeat of
Hitler's Nazi regime in the rubble of Berlin. The First World War
was seen at the time – and is often still seen today – as evidence of
the folly and obstinacy of mankind. The events of the Second World
War, by contrast, appear to require a different order of vocabulary to
explain them. The premeditated horrors of the concentration camp
suggest a capacity for human evil that cannot easily be reduced to
prosaic discussions of cultural preconceptions and administrative
conflicts.

The grotesque character of the Nazi regime helped to simplify
the ethical dilemmas posed by the Second World War, since it was

no longer possible to make a serious case for 'moral equivalence' between the two sides, as some critics of the First World War had tried to do a generation earlier. Christian pacifists who opposed Britain's involvement in the struggle against the axis powers could only do so on the grounds that the ethical imperative not to take up arms was so compelling that it 'trumped' any duty to help those facing persecution by one of the most appalling governments in history. Many pacifists did in fact rethink their views when confronted with the stark reality that a position of non-resistance might help strengthen a government in Germany that revelled in its adherence to a brutish ideology of racial supremacy and subordination. It is of course true that Britain's co-operation with the tyrannical regime of Stalinist Russia in the war against Hitler constitutes one of the tragic ironies of human history, helping to set in motion a chain of circumstances that was to lay the foundations for the division of Europe, and the development of a Cold War that lasted down until 1989. Such a law of unintended consequences has indeed been put forward on many occasions as one of the most compelling grounds for supporting unconditional pacifism. The ethical challenge posed by the Second World War did not, though, simply revolve around the choice of *whether* to support the war against Germany and the other axis powers. Equally important was the question of *how* the war should be waged. Traditional reflections on the conditions required for the just war, going back to Augustine, have argued that the means used in fighting an enemy should be proportionate to the ends for which a war is fought. They also set down strict limits on the circumstances under which it is permissible to injure and kill non-combatants.[2] It is hard to see how the fire-bombing of Dresden or the dropping of nuclear weapons on Japan could ever be justified in terms of such ideas, a stark reality that posed a problem for the leaders of all the main British churches during the Second World War, who had to face the unpalatable fact that military success might only be won at the cost of almost unbearable suffering among 'innocent' enemy civilians.[3] The ethical dilemmas of total war proved even more intractable in 1939–45 than they had in 1914–18. So too did the practical demands of responding to the needs of a population facing the dislocation and destruction of their ordinary patterns of life.

The Methodist Church of Great Britain was as much affected by the moral and material challenges of war as any other British church. The Luftwaffe's bombing of major cities like London and Liverpool not only destroyed numerous chapels and missions; it also created massive suffering and chaos for huge swathes of the civilian population. The church was forced to respond to the problems posed by ministering to a 'nation at arms', providing chaplains for troops stationed at home and abroad, as well as authorizing the transformation of many of its premises into canteens and camp-homes to meet the physical needs of the men and women in the forces. Even so, while the practical demands of war commanded most attention between 1939 and 1945, the broader ethical questions still loomed large. The following pages once again explore the perennial tension within British Methodism between a pacifist minority and a majority that rejected the views of those who questioned the justice of a war even when waged to defeat so palpably dreadful a regime as the one presided over by Adolf Hitler. They also examine how leading members of the Methodist Church responded to the ethical dilemmas raised in the latter stages of the war by a military strategy that was effectively predicated on destroying enemy civilian lives by the tens of thousands. The emotional and organizational legacy of British Methodism played an important role in determining the practical and ethical response of the Methodist Church to the crisis of 1939–45. The crisis, in turn, helped to determine the evolution of British Methodism long after the cities of Germany and Japan had been reduced to ashes and rubble.

## Responses to the Outbreak of War

The six months following the Munich Crisis of September 1938 witnessed a shift in British public opinion on international affairs, marked by growing popular scepticism about both the ethics and the logic of appeasement, a change that was echoed by a number of ministers within the government.[4] It was widely recognized that war was imminent in the wake of the German invasion of Prague in March 1939, followed a few weeks later by the Italian invasion of Albania, although feverish attempts continued over the next six months to avert such a cataclysm. The Revd Maldwyn Edwards noted hopefully in the pages of the *Recorder* soon after the seizure of Prague that 'the pacifist controversy in Methodism has died down for the present', a sentiment that was proved wrong just a few weeks later, when the British government announced that it intended to introduce a limited form of conscription for men aged 20 and 21. The *Recorder* was immediately inundated with letters and articles debating how the Methodist Church should react to such stark evidence of 'war preparation', while the Annual Conference that took place in Liverpool in July expressed its doubts about the wisdom of peace-time conscription. A meeting of the Methodist Peace Fellowship held at Liverpool during the Conference heard that the organization had acquired 180 new members during the previous two months alone, including 15 ministers, a figure that grew rapidly throughout the following year. By the spring of 1940 the MPF had some 5,000 members, a thousand of them ministers, which meant that the organization was the largest of the denominational pacifist groups. The MPF committed itself in 1939 to helping young men who planned to appear before the tribunals to seek exemption from military service on the grounds of conscience.[5] Its leaders also made considerable effort during this time to improve its somewhat chaotic organization, and launched a *Bulletin* that was circulated with the *Christian Pacifist*, a monthly news-sheet produced by the Fellowship of Reconciliation on behalf of all the main Christian pacifist groups.

The actual outbreak of war in September 1939 crystallized still further the tensions between pacifist and non-pacifist members of the Methodist Church. The President of Conference, Richard Pyke, made it clear in a 'Message to the Methodist People' that he believed the defensive nature of the war gave it an essentially just character: 'If ever there was a war where only a desire to resist aggression and to save freedom for the world were the reasons for which it was waged, it is this war.' He also suggested that most young men who were of an age to fight for their country would be happy to do so, although he committed the Methodist Church 'to give our protection to those whose conscience will not allow them to bear arms'. He went on to argue that:

> The evils of the world have to be fought; and if in fighting them we fail, it were better so to complete our work in the world than to escape into a safe place, while wickedness continues to afflict and ravage those who have not deserved the aggression, the persecution, and the imprisonment which is now the lot of thousands.[6]

The first editorial published in the *Recorder* following Britain's declaration of war agreed that 'We are profoundly thankful that the moral issues of the present hour are so clear.'[7] A number of letters were sent to the paper challenging such a view, expressing anxiety 'that the Church should publicly proclaim her sympathy with the national cause',[8] but the paper continued to insist in its editorials that 'no other honourable course was open to this country than that which ... has been taken'.[9] The echoes of the debate that had taken place within Methodism in 1914 about the rights and wrongs of war were unmistakable.

The outbreak of war against Nazi Germany posed a considerable challenge to the pacifist conscience, both Christian and non-Christian alike, given the nature of Hitler's government.[10] Many of those who had once spoken fervently in favour of the unconditional renunciation of force by the state now began to reconsider their views, particularly when the fall of France in May 1940 raised the prospect that the horrors of Nazism might soon become an all-too-present reality for the British people. The writer Margaret Storm Jameson, a long-time PPU activist, issued a pamphlet arguing that any pacifist who continued to hold true to their convictions had to accept that national submission might imply 'the concentration camp, the death of our humblest with our best, the forcing of our children's minds into an evil mould'.[11] The journalist and children's writer A.A. Milne similarly abandoned his earlier pacifism, articulated in such works as *Peace with Honour*, and published a book urging others to do likewise.[12] Pacifists who based their rejection of war on a 'deontological' Christian ethic that allowed no compromise were less inclined to change their position under the strain of war, although a large number still did so, including the long-time Anglican peace activist Maude Royden who resigned from the PPU in September 1939.[13] The best-known Methodist pacifist to change his views was Leslie Weatherhead, who wrote in his book *Thinking Aloud in War-Time* that he had come to believe that international order still required an 'appeal to force as its final authority', if it were not to allow the triumph of such horrors as Nazism. He went on to question the wisdom of treating Christ's words as simple commandments that should be followed unconditionally:

> It must be remembered that the rule of doing what Jesus would do is not the charter which He Himself provided for the conduct of our lives. We are in no way commensurate with him. There is something approaching blasphemy in the assertion that Calvary is the basic pattern of the Christian life. That sublime offering could be made only by one such as the Son of God . . . Force cannot make a bad man good, but it can and I think ought to limit the scope and extent of the evil he pleads . . . I used to think that it might be better to be invaded than to fight, but a realisation of the doctrines which those hold who are now threatening us makes me feel that it would be wrong not to resist that for which they stand.[14]

Although a close look at Weatherhead's numerous pronouncements during the 1930s suggests that his pacifism had always been more conditional in character than that of men like Carter and Soper, the change of heart of such a high-profile figure caused considerable ripples within Methodism. The membership of the MPF nevertheless continued to grow, probably peaking at some point early in 1940, before declining gently at a time when a German invasion of Britain seemed an increasingly likely prospect in the wake of the evacuation from Dunkirk. Around a quarter of ministers who had been members in the six months or so following the outbreak of war had left the organization two years later, suggesting that a considerable number of them had come to accept that war could be morally acceptable when fought for a cause such as the defeat of Nazism in Europe and Japanese aggression in the Far East.

All the main British churches were of course forced to confront the ethical challenge posed by a war fought on a scale never before experienced.[15] The position taken by the Church of England during the Second World War was markedly different from 1914–18. While the commitment of leading Anglicans like Charles Raven to the pacifist cause created some tension on occasions, it also encouraged dialogue of a kind that would have been unimaginable in the First World War.[16] William Temple, who served as Archbishop of York during the first years of the war, before moving to Canterbury in 1942, was a staunch theological critic of unconditional Christian pacifism, but he was passionate in defending the rights of conscientious objectors. He was also cautious about any attempts to present the war as 'fighting for Christianity', arguing that war was at best a necessary evil that existed 'on the political plane, where all judgements are relative' (a position that clearly owed a good deal to the influence of Niebuhr).[17] Temple even fell out with the then Archbishop of Canterbury, Cosmo Lang, on the question of praying for victory.[18] Nor was Temple alone among senior Anglican clergy in refusing to return to the uncritical patriotism that many felt had disfigured the Anglican Church in the First World War. George Bell, the Bishop of Chichester, became the most vocal critic of the strategy of saturation bombing of Germany during the Second World War, claiming that a policy predicated on the destruction of tens of thousands of enemy civilian lives could never be reconciled with the ethics of Christianity. It is perhaps striking that some of the most eloquent reflections on the moral questions thrown up by the conflict of 1939–45 came from the pens of Anglicans, rather than those who might have been expected to reflect the more critical traditions of the Nonconformist conscience.

## Methodism and the Practical Challenge of War

The Methodist Church's extensive presence in the heart of the major British industrial cities meant that its premises and members were particularly vulnerable to massive aerial bombardment by the Luftwaffe and, later on, the depredations of the V1 and V2 flying bombs. It was also, though, well-placed to respond to the human misery that was the inevitable concomitant of such horrors. The practical challenges proved to be very great. The destruction of Methodist churches and other premises such as meeting places and book-rooms took place on a vast scale. During the second half of 1940–1 the *Recorder* regularly carried photographs of wrecked buildings in which the local minister had bravely set up his desk as a symbol of his congregation's determination to continue their work. Nor was it only the depredation of German bombers that created problems. During the first few months of the war there were numerous complaints that the local authorities, particularly under Air Raid Precaution measures, had requisitioned Methodist premises without the necessary authority.[19] The evacuation of children of Methodist families from the cities to so-called 'safe areas' threatened to break up the close family networks that were still a feature of many congregations. The war eventually saw a drop in the membership of the Methodist Church of around 10 per cent. Although the *Recorder* carried countless letters and articles fretting about the decline, particularly at a time when many in the churches hoped that the dreadful experience of war would lead the British people back to God, the comparatively modest drop was in reality testimony to the continuing vigour of the Methodist Church in the face of the challenge of total war.

One of the most immediate challenges facing the Methodist Church was to respond to the needs of the large number of men and women joining the armed services. The Army, Navy and Air Force

Board asked for Methodist ministers aged forty or less to volunteer for service as full-time chaplains, while its Secretary contributed numerous articles to the *Recorder*, calling on local chapels to welcome men posted to their area.[20] Around 240 ministers were eventually appointed as commissioned chaplains in the armed forces, of whom a number lost their lives, often while helping the sick and wounded on the battlefield. Some 1,500 other Methodist ministers were appointed 'officiating chaplain' with special responsibilities towards servicemen and -women based in Britain.[21] A number were also selected to deal full-time with the growing number of casualties in hospital. Two ministers from the Liverpool District visited some 2,500 people each year in local hospitals (including Methodist soldiers from as far away as Canada and West Africa).[22] Methodist 'camp homes' were set up on many of the larger military bases, to provide a place where services could take place on a Sunday, and in which for the rest of the week the troops could read or play billiards and cards. Numerous local Methodist halls were turned into makeshift canteens, staffed by members of the local church, in order to provide refreshments to those serving in the forces or other organizations such as the ARP and the Home Guard.[23] All these attempts to mobilize the energies of Methodist ministers and lay people were not simply designed to respond to the religious and material needs of troops and civilian defence forces. They were also motivated by the traditional Methodist concern about the evils of drink. The emphasis on providing 'tea and sympathy' was governed at least in part by a forlorn hope that camp homes and canteens might provide an attractive alternative to the public house.

The experience of Methodist chaplains serving in the armed forces naturally varied according to the situation in which they found themselves. The Annual Conference that took place at Sheffield in 1940 was told that four of the fifty chaplains who had gone with the British expeditionary force to France were missing in the wake of the retreat from Dunkirk. A number of chaplains were interned in German Prisoner-of-War camps, where they played an important role in ministering to the religious needs of their fellow prisoners, as well as helping to improve general morale in the face of considerable privation and fear.[24] Most Methodist chaplains working in the armed forces interpreted their role in a broad and flexible manner, doing far more than simply holding religious services, seeking instead to promote the welfare of the troops around them. Chaplains serving with British forces in Egypt set up a Wesley House at Alexandria, while the Wesley Hall that was later established in the Suez Canal zone seated 500 people, and contained a chapel that could accommodate 30. It was also surrounded by an elaborate garden designed to provide a place of retreat from the strife of the war.[25] Similar institutions were set up in Italy as the British Eighth Army moved northwards following their advance from North Africa, each containing a chapel and a meeting room where troops could gather and play cards or read. Such initiatives were again put in place following the Normandy landings in the summer of 1944, although the intense fighting and the rapid movement on the battlefield meant that the work of chaplains from all the denominations was by now focused on the more traditional roles of tending to the wounded and providing reassurance to the fit. Both the exigencies of war and the organization of chaplaincy work meant that Methodist chaplains, like their counterparts from the other churches, spent much of their time offering practical support and counselling to soldiers who did not belong to their own (or any) denomination.

The energies of the Methodist Church were not only directed towards helping those who served in the armed forces. The physical destruction suffered by many British cities during the German bombing raids of 1940–1 created numerous opportunities for the kind of practical service that had always formed a central plank in Methodist witness. The evacuation of millions of children from the cities upon the outbreak of war posed the most immediate problem for Methodist congregations, both in the major conurbations, and in the towns and villages to which evacuees were sent. Some ministers in the big cities fretted about the situation of children from local Methodist families who were placed in 'far-from-Christian' homes.[26] In other cases the problems were more mundane. One young girl from London later recalled how the local Anglican vicar in the Surrey village to which she was evacuated tried to have her confirmed into his church even though she was from a staunch Methodist family.[27] Ministers in areas that received evacuees complained that attendance at services had fallen because regular members of the congregation were unwilling to leave at home unsupervised children who had been billeted upon them. Some local circuits faced the additional problem of finding their premises turned into makeshift schools for the evacuee population. The circuits in big cities like Birmingham sought to ensure that children who had been sent away remained in touch with their home churches,[28] while Methodist churches in towns like Blackpool worked hard to identify arriving evacuees from Methodist families. It was nevertheless difficult for even the most determined congregation to help youngsters evacuated to their area to overcome the trauma of such a dramatic rupture with the familiar routines of their previous life.

A great deal was written in the Methodist press during the early years of the war about the new Forward Movement, officially launched at the 1939 Conference, designed to combine social witness and religious commitment in much the same way that Hugh Price Hughes had done during the closing decades of the nineteenth century. Although the inner-city Methodist Missions were heavily damaged in the bombing raids that took place in 1940–1, they responded heroically to the crisis, distributing bedding and food to thousands of civilians who had lost their homes and possessions. During the height of the Blitz in London, for example, Methodist missions in the city provided temporary accommodation for large numbers of people, helping relatives to locate one another, and even on occasion reuniting children with their pets. Donald Soper established a canteen at the West London Mission catering for those forced to take refuge in the nearby Holborn deep shelter.[29] The Liverpool City Mission, serving an area that was heavily bombed by the Luftwaffe in the spring of 1941, regularly dispatched its missionaries to help those whose homes and families had been ripped apart in the raids. Perhaps the most celebrated mission to help the victims of the Blitz was the one managed by the Revd William Sangster at Methodist Central Hall in Westminster. When the Blitz began in September 1940, large numbers of families and individuals flocked to the cellars of the building, which remained open every night until May 1945. More than 450,000 people passed through its doors during the period the shelter was in operation. Sangster himself worked tirelessly to manage the human flood, spending his evenings and nights offering help and advice, and organizing the practical work of distributing food and blankets. Sangster was deeply committed to the new Forward movement, and was convinced that the 'grim necessity which has driven the citizens of London to the shelters has provided the Church with her finest opportunity to capture the people that she has had for a generation'.[30] He was nevertheless shrewd enough to realize that organized 'religion' meant little to many Londoners, and deliberately avoided formal preaching in the cellars of Central Hall, instead merely responding to those who approached him for advice about how best to make sense of the horrors going on around them. Sangster was convinced that the most effective way of engaging in Christian witness under the conditions of war was through practical service, and he avoided becoming too closely involved in the wider debates that took place within Methodism about the rights and wrongs of the conflict. For other members of his church, though, the suffering raised more urgently than ever before the familiar question of how the traditional Christian emphasis on peace should shape reactions to a world that was being ripped apart by the bloodiest conflict in history.

## The Development of Pacifism in the Methodist Church during the Second World War

Both pacifists and non-pacifists belonging to the Methodist Church played an active role in the relief work designed to bring help to those suffering from the traumas of war. Although a small number of pacifists in Britain were concerned that providing support to men and women engaged in such duties as fire-watching could be interpreted as an indirect way of helping the war effort, such views had little support within the Methodist Church. Donald Soper worked closely with Sangster at Central Hall, while the canteens set up by the West London Mission served all those who came to them, whether they were in uniform or not. The tensions over the broader question of the rights and wrongs of the war nevertheless continued to rumble on throughout the early years of the conflict. It became clear in the months following the outbreak of war that support for unconditional pacifism was strongest among the younger generation of Methodists, both ministerial and lay.[31] More than 200 individuals joined the MPF in the two months before the retreat from Dunkirk, most of them young, while more than 600 people attended the annual Fellowship rally held at Wesley's Chapel in London in April 1940. The reaction of the Methodist 'establishment' to this activity was at best equivocal. The formal commitment to defend the rights of conscientious objectors proved to be more than simple rhetoric in the years that followed, and although letters were occasionally published in the *Recorder* attacking COs, the vitriol never came anywhere close to the level of 1916.[32] The President of Conference in 1939–40, Richard Pyke, was nevertheless on occasion sharply critical of pacifists within his church. He attacked ministers who used the pulpit to promote their pacifist views,[33] and made it clear that he believed it was reasonable to pray 'sincerely and confidently' for victory on the battlefield. Some contributors to the *Recorder* took a still more robust position, lamenting that Methodism was becoming 'a refuge for pacifists, peace-cranks and conscientious objectors'.[34] Others demanded that no men should be recruited to the ministry who held pacifist views. As a result, many COs felt that there was 'little sympathy' for their position among their fellow members.[35] The *London Quarterly and Holborn Review* occasionally carried some more sophisticated reflections on the whole subject of peace and war, including one by Charles Wright on the dangers of a 'pietistic escapism' that sought to flee from the travails of the world,[36] but there were surprisingly few attempts in the main Methodist publications to locate discussion of the rights and wrongs of pacifism in a broader theological or ethical context.

Pressure grew within the Church during the first eighteen months of the war for Conference to take a stand on the whole question of pacifism. Some district synods such as Sheffield and Liverpool passed resolutions arguing that the conflict was being waged in the interests of 'freedom' and 'civilization', while a number of Quarterly Meetings sent memorials to Conference demanding a firm declaration of support for the war.[37] The tension came to a head at the 1941 Annual Conference, which after much debate approved by 136 votes to 16 a 'Statement on the Foundations of Peace', which was inspired by a recent joint resolution from the leaders of the major churches. The most controversial part of the statement consisted of a sentence claiming that 'Conference is confident that the Methodist People will steadfastly uphold this *sacred cause* until its complete victory has been achieved by a righteous and lasting peace' (italics added). Members of the MPF felt 'ambushed' by this apparent breach of the principles set down by Conference during the 1930s. Henry Carter made a passionate speech opposing the resolution, but was frequently heckled from the floor, and failed to win many supporters with his emotional attack on 'the blotting out of human life on a wholesale scale'.[38] The new President of Conference, the Revd Walter Armstrong, made it clear that he was perturbed by the 'general impression ... that the Methodist Church has committed itself to pacifism', and was determined to send a signal that Methodists were as committed to the war as the members of any other major denomination.[39]

The *Recorder* predictably welcomed the 'stronger attitude' set in motion at Conference, and pointedly refused to print letters protesting against the decision, although some letters did appear by Methodist ministers in national newspapers attacking the new line.[40] The paper offered staunch support to the war effort during the years that followed, including a propaganda visit by Isaac Foot to the United States in 1943, which was designed to mobilize the support of American Methodists in marginalizing the incipient isolationist tendencies that were evident in some quarters.[41] At the time of the 1941 Conference, the MPF itself still had around 5,000 members (including more than 800 ministers).[42] The character of the ideas expressed by many members of the Fellowship nevertheless went through some changes in response to the threat to national survival posed by the war. Until the outbreak of hostilities in the autumn of 1939, leading MPF activists such as Soper and Carter were confident that pacifism was a viable political strategy that could transform the international landscape, a belief summed up in Soper's familiar dictum that pacifism contained a spiritual force that could repel any invader.[43] Such optimism about the political efficacy of pacifism faded rapidly in the face of the German onslaught, though, encouraging the development of a more 'inward-looking focus amongst many pacifists'.[44] Soper himself noted towards the end of the war in *Peace News* that 'The utilitarian argument for non-violence breaks down under the overwhelming pressure of brute fact . . . I am alone sustained by the Christian faith which assures me that what is morally right comes with the ultimate resources of the universe.'[45] Men like Charles Coulson had argued in the 1930s that their pacifism meant that they would feel impelled to 'stand by' even in the face of overwhelming evil, but there was always something rather naive about such sentiments, which failed to comprehend the horrors of a totalitarian system of the kind that was being established by Hitler in Nazi Germany. The pacifist sentiments articulated by many in Britain during the 1920s and 1930s were forged above all by a pervasive sense that millions had died for no good reason on the battlefields of the First World War, which led them to the view that there could *never* be any cause so vital that it could justify military action with all its concomitant destruction and misery. The wilful horrors committed by the totalitarian regimes of Europe strained the imaginative capacity of those who instinctively believed that the way to resolve international conflict was by a reasoned attempt to identify and remove its causes. All those who maintained their pacifist position during the war years, in the face of endless revelations of the horrors taking place in Europe and Asia, were forced to do so in full knowledge of the potential consequences of their position.

The discussions at the meeting of the annual MPF Conference

in September 1943 represented something of an apogee of the 'sect-like' ethos of Methodist pacifism during the war years. Delegates discussed a series of issues including such vexed questions as whether the Christian life could be led in the wider world, or instead required a retreat to 'Christian communities', detached from the broader culture.[46] Many leading Methodist pacifists had always looked sceptically at the development of too inward-looking a focus, fearing that it would serve to limit their influence, and it was partly for this reason that men such as Henry Carter favoured the development of closer links among the various Christian pacifist groups. Carter was largely responsible for the establishment in 1943 of an informal committee charged with reviewing the matter in greater depth. In the first half of the following year, members of the Council of Christian Pacifist Groups agreed a constitution for a new Pacifist Council of the Christian Church, to be chaired jointly by Carter and Charles Raven.[47] Other leading members of the MPF such as the Revd Leslie Keeble, the son of Samuel Keeble, also played an important role in the organization. It was, though, difficult for the new Council to exert much influence on public opinion, beyond issuing some rather general statements calling for a peace based on clear principles of social and political justice. Although members of pacifist organizations were banned from broadcasting on the BBC during the war, and sometimes had problems finding distributors for their publications as well, they were given a fair degree of latitude by the authorities so long as they did not engage in activities that directly damaged the war effort. They were not, though, able to make much headway in winning popular support at a time when public opinion overwhelmingly supported the war against Nazi Germany and its allies.

The treatment of conscientious objectors was – as in the First World War – an issue of considerable concern for pacifists within the Methodist Church. Henry Carter published an article in the *Recorder* on 'The Conscientious Objector, the Church and the Tribunal' within weeks of war breaking out, but the paper only published it in a severely truncated form that eliminated the sympathetic tone of the original.[48] The treatment of COs by the tribunals was far better than in the previous war, although accounts did appear from time to time in publications such as the Bulletin of the Central Board for Conscientious Objectors (CBCO), complaining about the behaviour of some tribunal members. Some 60,000 individuals registered as conscientious objectors during the war. Most were granted exemption, typically on the condition that they engaged in agriculture or some other productive activity not directly related to the war effort. Others were granted non-combatant status, which meant that they were required to wear uniform, but not expected to carry out any duties that forced them to carry weapons. A number of 'absolutists' were still sent to prison, though, either for refusing to submit to the bureaucratic process required of those seeking exemption or because they would not accept the terms under which it was given. Nor were matters easy even for those whose claims were accepted by the state. Arthur Smailes, a Methodist local preacher who was later to become one of the most distinguished geographers of his generation, was dismissed by Portsmouth Council from one of its colleges when he declared himself to be a CO.[49] The proportion of COs who had some meaningful association with the Methodist Church is no easier to determine than in the First World War. One of those involved in helping conscientious objectors subsequently noted that just because an individual gave their religious affiliation when seeking exemption from military service, it did not mean that their faith was a major factor in their decision to register as a CO.[50] It is nevertheless striking that several of those who served on the tribunals were convinced that Methodists were disproportionately represented among those who came before them. Judge Wethered of the South-Western Tribunal noted in 1942 that almost 3,000 of the 4,056 men who appeared in front of him based their appeal on religious grounds. Some 662 of these were Methodists – more than any other denomination – and a strikingly high figure even when allowing for the traditional strength of Methodism in the region.[51] A similar pattern was visible in Lancashire. Wethered himself was struck by the unsophisticated views expressed by many aspiring conscientious objectors, noting that 'their position is the result of simple Bible teaching operating on a mental background of almost complete ignorance of the external world, outside a very small circle of home, friends, work and Chapel'.[52] Although there may have been some truth in this claim, a closer look at the background of some of the COs belonging to the Methodist Church reveals the danger of over-generalization. The Secretary of the CBCO was right when he observed that there was 'no such thing as a typical Conscientious Objector'.[53]

Cecil Davies was the son of a Methodist family from Cornwall, who had identified himself as a pacifist and supporter of the PPU even as a young teenager, before subsequently moving to London to study at university. A reporter from the *Daily Express* found out that he was likely to be among the first wave of potential conscripts intending to register as a conscientious objector and, after taking the young man out for drinks, wrote a damning story about 'Conchie No. 1', complete with a photograph showing his subject posed nonchalantly with a cigarette in front of an ornate fireplace. Davies subsequently received a good deal of vitriolic hate-mail, as well as bringing opprobrium on his friends and family back in the west country, where one of his like-minded Methodist acquaintances was even barred from teaching in the local Sunday school. When Davies eventually made his case for exemption at the South-Western Tribunal before Judge Wethered, he articulated his position in abstract intellectual terms rather than by reference to his religious views, highlighting the problem of determining with precision the underlying motivations of individual COs. He was however given unconditional exemption, and spent the rest of the war in a variety of occupations, ranging from working with evacuated children in Devon through to acting in plays to entertain the crowds in the bomb shelters of London.[54]

The case of another Methodist conscientious objector, Robert Foster, was very different from that of Davies. Foster was already in the armed forces during the 1930s, and was serving in Singapore when war broke out, by which time he already had growing doubts

about the compatibility of his religious views with his chosen profession.[55] Since Foster was in the army, his case was not eligible to
be heard by a tribunal in the normal way, and he was sentenced to
prison for one year (later remitted) in October 1939 for refusing an
order to type a letter. He was eventually transferred back to Britain,
contacting Donald Soper, who provided him with extensive help
and advice when he was released from Maidstone jail at the end of
1940. After carrying out a number of odd jobs, Foster began to work
for the Revd David Mace, who was later to become one of the most
important figures in relationship counselling during the post-war
years, helping to convert a derelict house into a Marriage Guidance
bookshop. Although Mace was critical of 'absolutist' conscientious
objectors who refused to accept alternative service, he was a confirmed pacifist who believed that 'the renunciation of violence is a
Christian principle', and he gave considerable help to a number of
Methodist COs throughout the war.[56] Foster himself later applied
to become a Methodist minister in the 1950s. His 'conversion' to
pacifism at the outbreak of war was probably less of a Damascene
conversion and more a step on a road that he had been taking since
childhood, when he was greatly influenced at school by a Quaker
teacher, and at home by the memory of two family members killed
in the First World War. Despite his difficult experiences, Foster
went to great lengths in his unpublished memoirs to praise those in
the army who dealt with him. It was a sentiment echoed by a surprisingly large number of COs, including the grandson of George
Lansbury, who later recalled how he always remained grateful for
the respect shown to him by the authorities when he realized that
his conscience precluded him from taking part in war.[57]

The case of Bill Wilkins from Brighton nevertheless shows that
considerable difficulties could still face those whose conscience led
them to reject military service. Wilkins had expressed concerns about
the ethics of military service to his local Methodist minister before
he was called up in 1943, but nevertheless accepted conscription into
the army, later serving in Italy and witnessing at first hand the carnage of Monte Cassino. His father and uncles had been COs in the

First World War, and the memory of their stand finally gave him the courage to follow their 'splendid example', and refuse to follow any future orders that might lead him to 'to kill another'. Wilkins was sent to prison, later escaping, but he was recaptured after being shot by an Italian civilian who mistook him for a German soldier. After a number of further hearings, at which he was sentenced to various terms of imprisonment, the authorities finally gave him permission to plead his case before a civilian tribunal. By this time, though, the war had already been over for more than a year. Wilkins's case was, like Foster's, made more complicated because he was already in uniform when he realized that his conscience would not allow him to accept military service. His readiness to spend more than two years fighting his case showed, though, the depth of his determination to follow the dictates of his conscience even when it came at the cost of much personal distress.

Some Methodist conscientious objectors carried out alternative duties that placed them in considerable danger. A number joined the Friends Ambulance Service Unit whose members operated on the front line of the battlefield.[58] Others worked in the Bomb Disposal Squad, a job that necessarily had a high fatality rate, which tested the faith of those unlucky enough to be involved in such work.[59] A small number of Methodist COs were sent to prison during the Second World War – more than eighty by the summer of 1942 – usually because they refused to accept the alternative service specified by the tribunals when granting conditional exemption.[60] Sympathizers sent them books and letters designed to keep their spirits up at times of great stress. The MPF also continued to offer help and advice to those facing call-up, leading to accusations in some quarters that they were 'coaching' young men in how to make the best impression before the tribunal. The most elaborate attempt to help Methodist COs was, however, the establishment of the Christian Pacifist Forestry and Land Units.[61] During the first few weeks of the conflict, Henry Carter was asked on a number of occasions to find productive work for conscientious objectors, 'but the problem was too large and the opposition too intense to be met solely by a one-to-one method'.[62] Following a meeting with the Minister of Labour Ernest Brown (himself a practising Nonconformist), Carter was put in contact with an official at the Forestry Commission, who said that his organization would be happy to offer work on one of its plantations in Kent if some other body would provide the necessary accommodation.[63] Over the next few months, with the close co-operation of other pacifist groups, a derelict house was turned into a hostel providing accommodation for a number of men at the Kent plantation. Other units quickly followed, sometimes on land owned by sympathizers (often Methodists), and sometimes in response to a local demand for agricultural and forestry labour. Many individuals were also placed on farms run by the county War Agricultural Committees. By July 1940 some 200 men were working under the aegis of CPFLU; twelve months later the figure was around 600 (of whom 350 were working in one of the dedicated units), swollen in part by an influx of COs who had been dismissed by their employers for their views.[64] By 1944, more than 900 men were working in one of the dedicated units or belonged to the Kingsway Unit (an umbrella organization designed to forge bonds between conscientious objectors working in isolation on the land up and down the country).[65] The logistical problems were considerable. As CPFLU grew it gradually developed a more sophisticated administrative infrastructure, as well as practical experience in setting up and equipping hostels under war-time conditions, but it remained perennially short of the money needed to carry out its work. Although Henry Carter tried on one occasion to obtain government funding to support the organization's activities, the money was never forthcoming, perhaps hardly surprising given the strain placed on the public purse by the cost of the war.[66]

More than 90 per cent of those who found work through the activities of CPFLU belonged to a Christian denomination, hardly surprising given that the avowed aim of the organization was 'to enable religiously-minded conscientious objectors to find employment in agreement with their desire to serve human welfare'.[67] Some 44 per cent were Methodists and 17 per cent Anglicans, while the rest belonged to such denominations as the Congregationalists and the Baptists.[68] A number of prominent Methodist pacifists played a leading role in managing the development of the organization. Many of the units made a conscious attempt to live together in fellowship, identifying their task as the creation of a new kind of Christian community, echoing the various attempts to set up Tolstoyan communities in the closing years of the nineteenth century.[69] A number of informal conferences held in 1942 came to the conclusion that 'the Units should so order their life as to become "nuclei" of the spiritual church of the future'.[70] There was considerable agreement that 'work and character are to some extent interdependent',[71] helping to give many units a quasi-monastic ethos, although some found it difficult in practice to forge a common identity. The members of one Scottish unit noted honestly that they had been forced 'to develop habits of toleration, unselfishness, good humour in time of stress – habits which require careful cultivation'.[72] In 1943 Carter wrote that some members had found their experience so positive that they wanted the units to continue after the end of the war as 'pioneers in a new Christian social experiment', while plans were also put in place to send men abroad to help with European reconstruction once the war had ended. A project that began as a practical attempt to find meaningful work for men who refused to join the armed forces became for a time a veritable experiment in alternative living.

The CPFLU was despite its successes looked on with some scepticism by many senior figures within Methodism throughout the war. It may indeed not be exaggerating to suggest that pacifists within the Methodist Church found themselves more marginalized during these years than pacifists who belonged to the Anglican Church. Although William Temple was sharply critical of pacifists during his time as Archbishop of Canterbury, arguing that they failed to acknowledge a 'theology of the State which involves obligations for Christian citizens',[73] he was ready to acknowledge that pacifist witness remained a valuable reminder of the Christian ideal in a world of compromise. It was for this reason that he was able to co-operate both with Anglican pacifists such as Raven and non-Anglican pacifists like Carter in thinking through the ethical challenges posed by war.[74] Carter himself was in some ways more honoured beyond Methodism during the war years than he was in his own church. The 1942 Annual Conference in Manchester offered a generous tribute to him on his retirement as Secretary of the Temperance and Social Welfare Department, praising his 'consistency and loyalty to conscience', but his role in the CPFLU and the MPF were largely passed over in a presentation that took place some months later.[75] The position of pacifists at the 'grass roots' level was often still harder than that of well-known figures like Carter and Soper, whose reputation and position both within Methodism and beyond provided them with a degree of public respect. Many ministers who were committed pacifists faced sharp criticism from their congregations, while Methodist COs often found it hard to integrate into the churches located in the area to which they were sent to carry out alternative service. Members of the Methodist Church who questioned the morality of fighting against the axis powers were tolerated; they were not necessarily always respected or treated with particular graciousness.

## The Ethics of War Fighting

The ethical challenge posed by the war was in a sense straightforward for pacifists who believed that support for the war effort was incompatible with their Christian faith. The situation was more difficult for those who accepted the justice of the cause for which Britain was fighting, but recognized that the massive bloodshed inherent in modern warfare raised difficult moral questions over such policies as the carpet bombing of German cities. The *Recorder* carried many letters and articles in the early years of the war discussing whether it was right for Methodists to pray for victory,[76] although the validity of such prayers became far less controversial when the 1941 Conference declared victory to be a 'sacred cause'. The London Blitz also triggered a lengthy correspondence in the paper over the challenges posed by forgiveness in the face of such horrors, a topic that recrudesced from time to time in the years that followed, usually revolving about the relative priority to be given to 'forgiveness' versus 'justice'.[77] There was, however, surprisingly little sustained debate within the Methodist Church about the relationship between means and ends in modern warfare. The same was not true in the Anglican Church, perhaps because of a deeper familiarity with the just war tradition, with its sense that the rights and wrongs of particular conflict could not be considered without examining the destruction to which it would lead. William Temple's recognition that killing in war could be morally justified in a world where the 'law of love' was not yet triumphant seems to have governed his reflections on such questions as the bombing of civilian areas.[78] The Archbishop was, however, rather naive in accepting the assurances of leading British politicians that the main purpose of allied bombing raids on Germany in 1943–5 was the destruction of military targets, a claim that led him to insist that such raids represented an acceptable attempt to destroy the German war machine.[79] The strongest challenge to such a view within Temple's own church came from the Bishop of Chichester, George Bell, whose calls in the early part of the war for a ban on night bombing later escalated into an attack in the House of Lords on the carpet-bombing of German cities as 'threatening the roots of civilisation'.[80] There was indeed something decidedly redolent of the Nonconformist Conscience in Bell's repeated demand that the Church had to avoid becoming 'the State's spiritual auxiliary with exactly the same ends as the state'.[81]

Bell's attacks on the saturation bombing of German cities were welcomed by a number of leading figures in the MPF, such as Henry Carter, but they do not seem to have made a great deal of impression beyond the ranks of convinced pacifists within the Methodist Church. When allied planes bombed Rome in July 1943, the *Recorder* firmly denied that it constituted 'an act of vandalism',[82] since it had been carried out with such care that it provided 'an outstanding vindication of the Allies' claim to be fighting for civilisation'. It is telling that the paper offered no reflections on the massive bombing of Hamburg that took place the same month, even though the raids received considerable coverage in the national press. Nor did it pay much attention to Bell's outspoken comments on the whole subject. It did however publish a letter by the Revd G.E. Hickman-Johnson in February 1944, shortly after one of the bishop's speeches in the House of Lords, denouncing 'the increasing practice of bombing towns and cities out of existence'.[83] His words in turn provoked a sharp response from other contributors to the *Recorder*, who believed that 'the issue of bombing towns is only part of a whole evil which the Nazi barbarians compelled us, in the interests of our Christian civilisation, to confront'.[84] W.F. Lofthouse contributed a piece in August 1944 to the paper's 'What's Puzzling You' column, arguing that the bombing of German cities could be reconciled with the Christian injunction not to do evil, since 'the innocent must and do often suffer with the guilty in this world of inter-twined human relations'.[85] The *Recorder* was, however, reluctant to give much coverage to the difficult moral questions that were raised by allied bombing of enemy cities. The same was true of the other main Methodist publications, including those like the *London Quarterly and Holborn Review*, which might have offered the most natural forum for the discussion of such matters. It is striking that the *Recorder* contained almost no mention of the huge raids that destroyed Dresden in February 1945.

The shortage of newsprint and paper was doubtless in part responsible for the sparse discussion within the Methodist press about the morality of such practices as the fire bombing of civilian areas. There was however a deeper sense that once the church had committed itself to the position that the war against the axis powers was, in the words of one prominent Methodist historian, a 'war of righteousness',[86] then the question of 'means' was relegated below the fundamental 'end' of securing victory. Leading figures in the Church showed no great wish to step outside the prevailing assumptions that governed the British war effort, in order to ask searching questions about the moral perplexities that were endemic in modern warfare. If the weakness of the pacifist case rested on its reluctance to engage with the stark reality that the rejection of the military 'means' might lead to a grotesque 'end', then too many of their critics failed to face the equally stark fact that the horrors of modern warfare were so profound that they were bound not merely to shatter the lives of those who were caught up in the violence, but also to change the fundamental moral calculus by which the justice of a particular war was assessed. There were periodic paeans of praise in the Methodist press for the heroic resistance of the Soviet people on the Eastern Front, but even the briefest reading of articles and letters by leading Methodists suggests that the sheer horror of so much that unfolded in Europe and the Far East was not really fully grasped by contributors, perhaps because it strained the imaginations even of a generation who had been familiar with the horrors of the Somme. Even the ghastliness of the London Blitz paled in terms of its sheer destructiveness with the scale of the bloodshed on the continent. The distance from the horrors taking place in cities like Hamburg and Dresden provided such events with a patina of acceptability that would have been smashed if the destruction was taking place in Manchester or Birmingham.[87] Leading members of all the main British churches, including the Methodist Church, were well aware that the passions of war made it only too easy to demonize opponents in a way that made their slaughter easier to accept. There nevertheless remained a sense in which the neat formulations developed by many churchmen who supported the war had the effect of distancing and perhaps diminishing the sufferings of those on all sides.

It is perhaps not surprising that British public opinion was muted in its response to what in retrospect appears as the most dramatic moment of the Second World War: the dropping of two atomic bombs on the Japanese cities of Hiroshima and Nagasaki in August 1945. The event was widely seen at the time in terms of its significance in ending the war in the Pacific rather than as a quantum leap in the destructive potential of humanity. And, in any case, a warweary population had little sympathy for the plight of their enemies when they had so much destruction at home to deal with. The discussions about war that had taken place in the *Recorder* during the previous five years had revolved most closely around the conflict with Germany, the country whose forces posed the main threat to the British mainland, although the situation in the Pacific had been followed with some care at such critical times as the loss of Singapore. The *Recorder* received a number of letters protesting against the dropping of the bomb, but the author of its 'Notes' column suggested that it was 'war that is wrong', and argued that 'the use of an atomic bomb to kill thousands is not more immoral than the use of a molecular bomb to kill hundreds'.[88] An editorial published in the paper similarly argued that 'There is no point in this arithmetic of inequity which makes an atomic bomb a hundred thousand times more sinful than a rifle bullet.'[89] The Peace Message issued by the President of Conference following Japan's surrender made no mention of the bomb. While there was some logic in the argument that it was the *fact* rather than the *scale* of war that presented the greatest challenge to humanity, there is little doubt that these sentiments failed to engage fully with the realities of the new nuclear age, which raised more urgently than ever the relationship between means and ends in the military arena. More prescient were those like Donald Soper, who heard the news of Hiroshima while sitting on a beach in Cornwall, and realized immediately that the advent of atomic weapons made the search for a peaceful world more imperative than ever before.[90] Within a few months of the explosion, it had become obvious to every sentient person that future wars might turn out to be far more ghastly than anything that had gone before, raising the vital question of how humanity was going to adjust to the grim realities of the nuclear age. If a major conflict was bound to lead to the destruction of large parts of the world, then it seemed difficult to justify such an outcome either in terms of the just war tradition, or in the more mundane calculus of a common-sense belief that there were times when the means simply did not justify the ends.

## Conclusion

Senior figures in the Methodist Church were anxious from the start of the war to promote new thinking about the post-war domestic order.[91] The Beveridge Report of 1942, which laid the foundations for the welfare state, was welcomed on the pages of the *Recorder* and by Conference. The structure of the post-war international order also attracted a good deal of attention. Conference was as early as 1941 receiving memorials from some circuits demanding the establishment of a Commission 'to consider the requirements, from a Christian point of view, of a new world order'.[92] The future of Germany attracted particular attention, particularly in the light of the widespread belief that the harsh clauses of the Treaty of Versailles had helped to foster the rise of Nazism in the 1930s. The Revd F. Brompton Harvey wrote a pamphlet early in 1944 asking 'Should Germany be Forgiven?', an issue subsequently taken up by the *Recorder*, which printed an editorial suggesting that the German people should accept responsibility for the war since they had 'marched into battle with both eyes open'.[93] The subject aroused considerable passion on the paper's correspondence page, as debate raged between those who warned against a peace based on revenge, and others who attacked the 'sentimentalists' for failing to acknowledge the harsh realties of power politics.[94] In the final year of the war, the paper began to give more attention to the plans for a new international organization that were hammered out by allied representatives at Dumbarton Oaks in Washington. While acknowledging that the failure of the League of Nations had shown how difficult it was to establish an organization capable of preserving world peace, the *Recorder* continued to insist that 'the good seed sown five and twenty years ago has a new promise'.[95] It was a sentiment that found an echo in many articles appearing in other Methodist publications,[96] as well as in the various recommendations set before Conference by the Temperance and Social Welfare Department during the final years of the war.[97]

This continuing commitment to the virtues of internationalism was reflected in the lengthy 'Statement on the International Situation' agreed by the 1945 Annual Conference in Nottingham, which took place a few weeks after the end of the war in Europe. The Statement called for a peace that was based on 'justice and restitution', yet which held open the door to those among the defeated nations who 'with penitence . . . seek to retrieve their place in the community of nations'. It also called for protection for 'small nations, and minorities within nations, along with care for, and advancement of, the backward nations'. Although the Statement was cautious on such politically sensitive questions as decolonization, it was strident in its call for a more just and equitable international order based on 'freedom from want', a development that it accepted would require the rich nations to make sacrifices in favour of the 'economically handicapped'.[98] This recognition of the intimate connection between questions of global economic justice and world order was to become a far more pronounced theme in the decades that followed, as questions ranging from decolonization through to third-world debt came to the fore in discussions at Conference and in the Methodist press. More radical members of the church, such as Donald Soper, believed that the development of a peaceful world would require still more far-reaching changes. In the Christmas Message he published in *Peace News*, at the end of 1944, he told his readers that, 'There is a false simplicity in the idea that we can concentrate upon the renunciation of war without at the same time concentrating on the abolition of capitalism and nationalism and power-politics.'[99] Henry Carter echoed these thoughts with his own claim in a BBC broadcast that the post-war world had to see more than 'a mere rebuilding on the old foundations'.[100]

The debate within British Methodism about the rights and wrongs of war was less bad-tempered during 1939–45 than a generation before, although this may partly have been due to the constraints that the church placed on free debate, despite its commitment to the principle of 'liberty of conscience'. Following the decision by the 1941 Conference to declare the war a 'sacred cause', it became very difficult for those who questioned the morality of the conflict to obtain access to publications such as the *Recorder*. One senior Methodist minister justified such an approach on the grounds that in war-time 'luxurious extensions of liberty must be given up . . . we must put first things first, maintain a sense of proportion, and make our unstinted contribution to national unity, determination and endurance'.[101] Such 'unseasonable truths' reflected the extent to which most Methodists in Britain were happy to endorse a language of patriotism that committed their loyalties to the government and the wider community during a time of crisis. It was those who opposed the war who continued to articulate their views in terms of the kind of rhetoric traditionally associated with the Nonconformist Conscience, with its characteristic suspicion of any attempt to subordinate individual freedom to the dictates of the state. These tensions were to continue into the post-war period when the world was divided into two great competing power blocks, each armed with massive stocks of nuclear weapons, capable of destroying the world many times over. The era of the Cold War raised a new set of challenges for all the British churches, as they sought to engage with the ethics of a defence policy that rested *in ultimo* on a readiness to use force on a scale that would effectively destroy the created world.

# 6

# The Shadow of the Bomb

## Introduction

The mood of national optimism that swept through Britain following the allied victory in Europe was reflected among the delegates to the 1945 Methodist Conference, who assembled in Nottingham a few weeks before the first atomic bomb was exploded at Hiroshima on 6 August 1945. By the time Conference met a year later in London, though, the international outlook had become a good deal less benign. The war-time Grand Alliance between Britain, the USA and the USSR had disintegrated into shrill disagreement over such vexed questions as the future of a defeated Germany, while the dawn of the atomic age had shown all too graphically the horrors that could result from any future conflict. The Special Resolution on 'A Call to World Peace' that was passed by the 1946 Conference fretted over the growth of international 'distrust and suspicion', and lamented the prospect of 'another and still more devastating war', in a world where 'Man's moral control of affairs . . . has fallen far behind his mastery of physical power.'[1] Delegates who attended the Conference left in no doubt that their church would in the years ahead have to respond to a new set of international problems that were likely to prove as complex and potentially catastrophic as any that had gone before. The devastation of the Second World War had shown all too graphically the capacity of humanity for destruction and barbarism. It was difficult in the post-war world to believe that the defeat of Nazi Germany and its allies would easily usher in a new era of peace and prosperity.

140

The challenges posed to Britain by the burgeoning Cold War were both international and domestic in character. The expansion of Soviet power across eastern and central Europe after 1945, along with the triumph of Mao's Communist Party in China at the end of the decade, created a powerful new threat to British interests around the world. Communist ideology also attracted support in many West European countries, including Britain, both within the labour movement and among a considerable section of the intelligentsia. A good deal of attention has recently been given by historians to the attempts made by the main western powers to wage a 'cultural Cold War' in the years after 1945, in order to marginalize the ideological challenge of Soviet Russia, and bolster the social and political status quo.[2] The American Central Intelligence Agency funded numerous organizations and journals in an effort to secure the commitment of the West European intellectual elite to the values that were the supposed hallmark of western civilization.[3] The churches had an important role to play in the minds of those charged with waging the cultural Cold War, both as symbols of the Judaeo-Christian heritage that was threatened by Soviet communism, and as institutions capable of mobilizing large swathes of public opinion. The Vatican's part in countering the ideological appeal of communism in large parts of continental Europe is a story that has been told on a number of occasions.[4] Considerable attention has also recently been given to attempts by the Anglican establishment to promote the idea that 'Marxian Communism is contrary to Christian faith and practice'.[5] Far less research has been carried out on the role played by the Nonconformist churches in Britain during the Cold War.[6] The dense network of ties that bound the Church of England to the wider social and political elite made it comparatively easy for the Foreign Office to engage senior Anglicans in its periodic efforts to mobilize all 'the ethical and spiritual forces inherent in this western civilisation of which we are the chief protagonists'.[7] Senior civil servants and diplomats were less inclined to consider how they could line up the Nonconformist churches behind the cause of 'civilization'. The situation was ironic given that the Foreign Secretary in the 1945–50 Labour government was Ernest Bevin, a former Baptist lay preacher, who was not himself averse to arguing that the western alliance required a profound 'spiritual' foundation if it were to defend itself against the Soviet threat.[8]

There was always something a little half-hearted about the Foreign Office's attempt to foster the support of church leaders in Britain for the struggle against Soviet communism during the years after 1945. The religious motifs that occurred from time to time in speeches by ministers such as Bevin were largely designed to reassure a sceptical American administration that the Labour government's support for democratic socialism at home would not make it an unreliable ally in the struggle against Soviet communism abroad. The powerful religious imagery that informed President Truman's crusading Cold War rhetoric in America would have been almost unthinkable on the lips of any British politician hoping to be taken seriously by his audience. While Foreign Office officials made considerable efforts to influence the views of senior figures in the Church of England on international politics, their attempt to mobilize support among religious leaders was subtler than the one adopted by members of the Truman administration, who took a far more direct approach when seeking to persuade church leaders to offer their support 'in this critical passage of history'.[9] The presentation of the Soviet threat as an enemy to the distinctive way of life of 'one nation under God' was consonant with the deepest traditions of American history in a way that was less obviously true in the case of Britain. Some ministers in the Labour government were in any case sceptical about providing a religious validation for British traditions and culture at a time when they were anxious to make profound social and economic changes. None of this undermines the argument that the churches in Britain were 'caught up' in a cultural Cold War during the decades that followed the defeat of Nazi Germany. All the churches were forced to define their position on issues ranging from the ideological challenge of communism through to the ethics of war in the nuclear age. They were not, though, simply passive actors vulnerable to manipulation by a government hoping to make use of them for its own objectives.

*the 1950's for a new light
-i- f- newbody?*

The previous chapter showed how the Second World War marked
a key staging post in the organizational and cultural development
of British Methodism, as the conflict accelerated the destruction of
traditional patterns of residence and religious observance, eroding
still further the role of the chapel as a central focus in the daily lives
of its members. The process was continued in the post-war world by
a whole host of pressures – cultural, economic, political and scientific – that together helped to foster a rapid process of secularization
across British society.[10] The development of new communications
technologies ranging from television through to the telephone
broadened the horizons of millions of Britons beyond the immediate world of family and community. Growing social mobility
eroded traditional patterns of communal and family life, as well as
having an inevitable effect on patterns of religious observance. The
decline in levels of church attendance since 1945 is of course a notoriously complex and multi-faceted phenomenon,[11] and it is generally accepted that the bald figures may underestimate the extent to
which millions of people continue to have some kind of commitment either to 'Christianity' in general, or to one denomination
in particular.[12] It nevertheless remains impossible to question the
diminishing significance of organized religion in post-war Britain.
The process of secularization may, however, have had the paradoxi-
cal benefit of improving relations between the various churches, as
church leaders responded to the challenge of decline by seeking to
foster closer co-operation at both the national and local levels. The
traditional boundaries between denominations have become much
weaker in the years since 1945.[13]

The attitude of the Methodist Church on questions of peace and
war during the post-war period was influenced by all these changes
both at home and abroad. The pressures of secular modernity were
not only critical in facilitating a shift towards a theology that increasingly emphasized questions of 'social holiness and justice' over more
traditional concerns with such questions as temperance and personal behaviour.[14] They also helped to engender what might loosely
be termed a more 'modern' outlook among Methodists. The rest of

143

*This was late C19...
not 'traditional' !!*

this chapter will examine the discussions and arguments that took place within British Methodism during the first part of the Cold War on such questions as the ethics of nuclear deterrence and the relationship between economic justice and global conflict. These issues provoked enormous concern across British society during the 1940s and 1950s, which was echoed within the Methodist Church, leading to passionate debate about how best to respond to the challenges posed by a complex and dangerous international environment. The growing co-operation between the main churches after 1945 meant that the formal response of the Methodist Church on questions such as nuclear weapons was increasingly influenced by developments in other denominations. Although it would be wrong to suggest that there was a co-ordinated response among the main Protestant churches in Britain to international affairs during the early years of the Cold War, there was a growing desire to work beyond denominational boundaries when addressing *all* major social and political questions, not least because such a strategy increased the chances of being heard by those in positions of power. The growing permeability of denominational boundaries also influenced the activities of those who continued to believe that war – and preparations for war – were under all circumstances incompatible with the ethics of Christian teaching. The previous few chapters have shown how pacifists within the Methodist Church sought to establish close ties with other pacifist organizations in the years before 1945. Although this pattern continued in the years after the end of the Second World War, there was no return to the kind of bitter divisions between pacifist and non-pacifist that had threatened to rip apart British Methodism during the 1930s. The advent of nuclear weapons encouraged both sides to engage in a more sustained and thoughtful dialogue about the practical and ethical challenges of peace and war than had ever proved possible in the years before the Second World War.

## Methodism and the Challenge of Communist Ideology during the Early Cold War Period

The Methodist Church devoted a good deal of energy in the immediate post-war period to considering how best to respond to the problems faced by the tens of millions of people on the continent who were facing destitution. Henry Carter in particular played a pivotal role in supporting initiatives to help the flood of refugees that spread across the continent in the wake of the final allied victory. It was nevertheless clear from the moment hostilities ended that a new ideological divide was emerging between East and West, which was bound to have a deep impact on the future of Europe, and threaten to create future conflicts that would create even greater misery. In March 1947 the American President Harry S. Truman made a speech to both houses of Congress, in which he grandiloquently committed his country to 'the defence of free peoples everywhere'. One of Truman's principal aims in making his speech was to persuade audiences at home and abroad that the Soviet Union represented a major threat to the long-term existence of the western democracies, with the result that any lingering hopes of preserving the war-time alliance with Moscow should be consigned to history. The author of the *Methodist Recorder*'s 'Notes of the Week' column echoed this line just a few weeks later, commenting that 'there are now two worlds – the Russian and the Western – so different in conceptions of human values as that they are never likely to become one except through the absorption of one by the other – that is by conquest, whether military or ideological'. The column went on to suggest that western 'appeasement' of the Soviet Union had failed to work over the previous two years, merely leading to the 'sacrifice of smaller nations' such as Hungary, with the result that the new hard line emanating from Washington was the most appropriate policy to adopt under the circumstances.[15] The paper pursued this line even more strongly following the communist coup that took place in Czechoslovakia sixth months later, in February 1948, arguing that:

145

As a creed, Communism may be held, in a free society, by those who believe in it, and may be displayed for consideration by all the forms of legitimate propaganda. As a practice, which by chicanery and force destroys human liberty, it must be resisted if life is to continue in the world on any tolerable terms . . . The claim that Communism seeks the elevation of mankind is the merest claptrap. It is politics in their most naked and shameless manifestation. Its weapon is not reason but the machine gun and the bludgeon.[16]

The *Recorder* continued to devote a considerable amount of attention throughout the following years to the Communist threat, frequently articulating the kind of Cold War rhetoric that characterized much of the secular press during this period. In the late 1940s the paper published a number of articles by an Anglican priest, the Revd Cecil Rose, arguing that 'The Third World War is already in progress, though its weapons and strategy are so new that men fail to recognise them until it is too late.' He suggested that communist saboteurs in Britain were attempting to undermine the economic recovery by promoting labour unrest in the factories, a process that he feared might 'tip the balance against recovery'.[17] Rose was a strong admirer of the burgeoning Moral Rearmament movement, based in Switzerland, and he repeatedly praised its efforts to promote a campaign of moral renewal designed to provide a spiritual bulwark against communism.[18] The *Recorder* also carried numerous letters lamenting the rise of communist influence in British industry, including one from the General Secretary of the Tobacco Workers Union, himself a Methodist local preacher, who suggested that there was 'ample evidence' for claims that the trade unions were subject to communist influence and infiltration.[19] Although the paper did publish a few letters expressing the view that communism was 'more Christian than any other form of government',[20] the general tone of the paper was uncompromising in its approach, typified by an article it carried by a Methodist minister in April 1949 deploring the 'rapidly spreading cancer of Communism' that was eating away at the heart of British life.[21]

Although the *Recorder* was still widely considered to represent the

146

authoritative voice of Methodism in the post-war world, its construction of the communist threat both at home and abroad was not necessarily representative of broader currents of thought within the Methodist Church. Methodist ministers based in the large industrial cities were often struck by the widespread sympathy expressed by many workers for the USSR, while those who worked with students in universities and training colleges were impressed by the high level of interest in radical ideas of various kinds. The attention given to questions of atomic weapons in 1946–7, both by the British Council of Churches and by a Commission appointed by the Methodist Conference, also helped to direct attention to more fundamental questions about the nature of international conflict in the modern world. There was by the spring of 1948 a growing recognition among some leading Methodists of the need to engage more systematically with the ideological challenge of communism – a realization that was increasingly true in the other main denominations as well. One of the earliest attempts to do this took the form of a brief pamphlet by the Revd Edward Rogers, published in 1948 under the title *A Christian Looks at Communism*, which was designed to provide a guide for a general readership that was not well-versed in the intricacies of Marxist dogma or Soviet history:

> What is this Communism about which there is so much fuss and argument? Is it a good thing or a bad thing? . . . To hear some people talk you would think all the Communists were wicked criminals who revelled in robbing and destroying and killing, and hated everybody else. I know several Communists, and they are not a bit like that. Many of them are sincere and hard-working men who are ready to suffer bitter persecution for the cause in which they believe.[22]

Despite his sympathetic opening comments, though, Rogers went on to tell his readers that the communist search for 'a better world' was doomed to failure since 'It is impossible to make a *good* world out of *bad* men.' In order to build a better society, he suggested, 'We must change conditions but we must change people as well.' Despite its somewhat platitudinous tone, *A Christian Looks at Communism* marked the beginning of a sustained attempt by a number of influential figures in the Methodist Church to think through the new challenges posed by the changing domestic and international climate.

The Methodist Conference that met in Bristol during the summer of 1948 held a formal debate on 'The Challenge of Communism'. It also passed a resolution instructing the relevant divisions of the Church 'to consider the nature of the challenge, to make practical recommendations to meet it, and, if Conference approve them, to communicate them to all responsible for the leadership of youth throughout the Church'.[23] The Conference pointedly adopted a statement on 'Human Rights and Religious Freedom' that was inspired by growing concern about the difficulties facing the churches behind the Iron Curtain, particularly in the wake of the Prague coup of 1948, which had come to symbolize for many the irredeemably aggressive nature of Soviet foreign policy. The interim statement produced by the working group on 'The Challenge of Communism', in time for the 1949 Conference, made a great effort to locate the whole question in the broadest possible social and economic context. The authors of the report were agreed that 'the next phase of human society will be collectivist' – a development which they considered need not 'unduly alarm the Christian'. They did, however, warn that while 'capitalist individualism of sinful and unregenerate men has stimulated the sin of avarice . . . it does not follow that the collectivist organisation of men *still sinful and unregenerate* will solve our problems'. The committee acknowledged the scale of the material advances that had been achieved in the Soviet Union during the course of the previous thirty years, but maintained that Marxist doctrine was not able to offer any satisfactory understanding of such vexed issues as the nature of personality. Its warped understanding of the human condition had instead led inevitably to 'the tyrannical rule of a minority party' and the 'ruthless suppression of opposition' in countries where communists had taken power.[24] The formal discussions authorized by Conference were echoed by an increasingly

148

sophisticated discussion of the whole question in Methodist publications. The *London Quarterly and Holborn Review* carried a piece in 1949 on 'Christianity and Communism' by a Methodist minister from the Isle of Wight, warning that Christians must respond constructively to the ideological challenge of Marxism by showing that they were not simply the 'self-deluded upholders of a decaying and unjust order'.[25] Another contributor writing in the same year warned against the concentration of economic power 'in the hands either of the few or the state', and somewhat gnomically urged the churches to 'march with the events of history' if they wanted to 'play their part in guiding the destiny of mankind'.[26] The editor of the *Review*, the Revd Leslie Church, also entered the fray with an article arguing that the communist challenge could not be met simply by 'economic reconstruction' or 'atomic warfare', but instead required a response that addressed the more fundamental illusion that the human condition could be transformed by material means alone.[27]

Church noted in his article on 'The Challenge of Communism' that a series of pamphlets on the subject was being prepared under the auspices of the Beckly Trust on Social Service, which were designed to help Methodists understand the question more fully. The five pamphlets that were subsequently published in 1950 represented a co-ordinated attempt to provide an intellectual framework for thinking through the relationship between Christianity and Communism.[28] They were far more sophisticated in tone than the pamphlet *A Christian Looks at Communism*, published two years before by Edward Rogers, and were intended primarily for an audience of Methodist ministers and educated Methodist lay people. There were marked differences in the approaches and sympathies taken by the various authors. Henry Carter wrote on the subject of 'How Soviet Rule Came to Russia', attributing the 1917 Revolution to a popular desire to overthrow the 'corrupt' and 'oppressive' tsarist regime.[29] Although he acknowledged that ruthlessness and bloodshed had often been a feature of Soviet history, Carter was unable to disguise a degree of admiration for the way in which Stalin had mobilized the population behind the process of massive industri-

Urwin was an able man.

alization, brought about by the celebrated five-year plans to expand industry. Nor did he say anything about the Great Terror that ripped apart Soviet society in the mid-1930s, even though he had at the time been General Secretary of the Temperance and Social Welfare Division, responsible among other things for helping the Methodist Church shape its response to international developments. The Revd E.C. Urwin, the current General Secretary of the Division, took a much more critical line in his pamphlet on 'Communism and Violence'. While Urwin was happy to admit there was 'a large substratum of truth' in many of Marx's critiques of capitalist society, he questioned Marx's views about the nature of historical development, and accused Lenin of creating a 'Red Fascism' that gloried in a veritable cult of violence. He went on to condemn the economic system created by Stalin as the 'worst kind of state capitalism', which he believed was as exploitative in character as the nineteenth-century *laissez-faire* capitalism against which Marx had inveighed so powerfully. Urwin told his readers that wherever communists came to power, they quickly abandoned any pretence of co-operating with other parties, and instead sought to cement their position by 'purges, expropriation of landlords, rigid regimentation of life, suppression of minorities, forced labour and unceasing police supervision'.

The remaining three pamphlets took a rather different approach to their subject matter. The distinguished Methodist historian Maldwyn Edwards contributed a pamphlet on 'The Communist Millennium'. He argued that the apocalyptic tone which characterised Marx's work owed much to his Jewish background, and suggested that the determinism inherent in his philosophy of history provided those who accepted his ideas with the psychological assurance of believing that they were 'on the winning side'. Edwards's attempt to identify a quasi-religious core in Marxism had been articulated by critics of the radical Russian intelligentsia for many years, perhaps most notably in Nikolai Berdyaev's book on *The Origins of Russian Communism*, and it became a staple theme in such classic western 'Cold War' works of the 1940s and 1950s as *The God that Failed*.[30] The pamphlet by W.F. Lofthouse, on *The Philosophy*

150

of *Communism*, focused by contrast on the ideas of those who had been in power since 1917. Lofthouse argued that Soviet leaders were serious in claiming dialectical materialism as the foundation of their world-view, with the result that their ideas had to be studied carefully by those who sought to understand the challenge posed by communism to the 'West' in general and Christianity in particular. His analysis of the subject ended with a repudiation of the idea that there was anything genuinely 'scientific' about the philosophical ideas that held sway over the minds of those in the Kremlin. Edward Rogers' pamphlet on 'The Economics of Communism' took a very different approach, offering its readers a well-informed account of the intricacies of surplus value that formed the basis of Marx's economic theory. While acknowledging the ingenuity of the theory, Rogers continued to insist that there was something profoundly naive about Marx's belief that a fundamentally new economic order could ever be constructed in a world cursed by 'the sins of men'. He argued instead that 'the failings of the mid nineteenth century economic order' studied by Marx had 'a deeper cause than the necessities of surplus value economics'. Such language was far-removed from the simplistic language that had characterized Rogers's own earlier pamphlet *A Christian Looks at Communism*, but the underlying sentiments were remarkably similar, challenging both Marxist theory and Soviet practice for believing that a perfect society could be built without first changing the character of the men and women who comprised it. All five pamphlets taken together provided a serious attempt to think through the nature of the challenge posed to Christianity by communism both at home and abroad.

One of the most thoughtful attempts to consider the challenge of Soviet communism in the international arena was developed during these years by the distinguished Cambridge historian Herbert Butterfield, a life-long Methodist and sometime local preacher, whose Beckly Social Service lectures were published by Epworth Press in 1953.[31] Butterfield developed in his lectures a sophisticated and historically informed Christian realism, which rested on the belief that governments were most likely to promote international order when they pursued a pragmatic foreign policy designed to manage the tensions between states, rather than pursue a 'war of righteousness' aimed at eliminating and destroying their rivals. Although there is no space here to examine Butterfield's ideas in any depth, it is worth noting the obvious relevance of such ideas to the period of the Cold War. While critical of the ideological diplomacy waged by Moscow, Butterfield also cautioned against a virulent anti-communism that refused to seek accommodation with the Soviet government on the grounds that such a policy was immoral. He cited the celebrated dictum of the historian Lord Acton that 'absolute power tends to corrupt absolutely', arguing that in diplomacy this implied the need for a response based on steady containment rather than ideological shrillness. Butterfield sought to argue that his position – which at first glance appeared to represent little more than a commitment to the balance-of-power politics that had emerged in the eighteenth century – was profoundly Christian in character. He suggested that a foreign policy that refused to assume that any state had a monopoly of moral virtue recognized the simple truth that every political system had its foibles and could not alone redeem the failings of sinful human beings. While he was sharply critical of the government that had developed in Russia since 1917, he remained equally convinced that its leaders were in some sense the heirs of their tsarist forerunners, and could therefore be dealt with in much the same way by a mixture of firmness and fairness. Butterfield also cast doubt on those who believed that the United Nations could alone form the basis for a new international order, arguing instead that it represented at most a useful extra forum for governments to talk to one another. The complexity of Butterfield's views perhaps explains why they failed to attract much attention among his fellow Methodists, since his argument was difficult to follow for those who were not well versed in the historical examples that he used to illustrate his position. The lack of response was regrettable. Butterfield's ideas provided an intellectual framework that could have paved the way for a more sophisticated discussion of the problems that had exercised the Church for many years.

The debate about the challenge posed to Christianity by communism continued to rage within the Methodist Church during the early 1950s, at a time when the Korean War and the McCarthy 'witch-hunts' in America kept the international spotlight firmly directed on the issue. The Commission set up by Conference in 1948 to report on 'The Challenge of Communism' met several times a year, reporting back annually on its activities, although never again in so much detail as in its 1949 interim report. Conference also approved proposals to ensure that the subject was placed on the curriculum of the Methodist training colleges. Edward Rogers produced a lengthy work in 1951 published under the title 'A Commentary on Communism', based on his own Fernley Hartley Trust lectures, which traced the communist ideal from the philosophy of Plato right through to the post-war period.[32] Articles also continued to appear from time to time in the *London Quarterly and Holborn Review*. Some of these pieces articulated the line taken by the *Methodist Recorder*, warning that Soviet communism posed a profound threat to civilized values in the western world, both through internal subversion and external aggression. The Revd D.R. Davies, an Anglican priest from Sussex, contributed an article on 'The Great Lie of Communism' to the *Review* in 1951, in which he claimed that the challenge posed to western civilization by communism was greater 'than the Saracen conquest of Southern Europe in the eighth century'. He went on to reject the widespread view that the best way to counter communism was to improve social and economic conditions, arguing instead for a 'moral and spiritual' campaign designed to counter the dominant secular ethos, based on the assumption that 'the potentialities of existence are confined within time and matter'.[33] Davies's passionate views – which he repeated two years later in a second article on 'Communism: The New Islam' – were not representative of most articles on the subject that appeared in the *Review*.[34] Far more typical were those like the one contributed by the Methodist minister Revd T.J. Foinette, who urged his readers not simply to condemn Marxism for its unabashed materialism, but rather to learn that effective mission required ministers to recognize the 'whole need' of their fellow men and women both spiritual *and* material. Other articles published by the *Review* discussed the treatment of communism in the work of theologians and philosophers such as Barth and Berdyaev.[35] Most contributors identified the challenge of communism as both a spiritual *and* material phenomenon, which the churches had to meet through supporting 'progressive' social and economic policies, as well as offering an alternative vision of the human condition to the one provided by Marxism-Leninism. It was an approach that had already been articulated in the Anglican Church at the 1948 Lambeth Conference, at which a resolution was passed noting that 'the challenge of the Marxian theory of Communism' had to be opposed both by 'sound teaching' and through 'fearless witness against political, social and economic' injustice.[36]

The debate within Methodism after 1945 over the challenge posed to Christianity by communism was part of a broader attempt to rethink the Methodist Church's position on many social and political questions, at a time when the nationalization of industry and the creation of the Welfare State seemed to represent a fundamental break with many of the assumptions and practices of the past. The Temperance and Social Welfare Department spent a good deal of time in the months leading up to the 1949 Conference in Liverpool preparing a new 'Declaration of the Methodist Church on Christian Social and Political Responsibility'. The Department was at this time headed by the Revd E.C. Urwin, who also chaired the Commission on the Challenge of Communism, so it is hardly surprising that there was a marked symmetry in the two bodies' analysis of the changes taking place in post-war British society. The authors of the draft Declaration on Social and Political Responsibility deliberately sought to build upon 'the genius of Methodism, which from its foundation has sought to exhibit the social consequences inherent in the Christian message'. They also defended a 'theology of politics' that attributed to governments a duty both to prevent 'evil doing' *and* to promote 'the conditions under which men can live as the redeemed children of God'. The draft Declaration praised liberal democracy as 'an instrument of liberty and self-government', but it also acknowledged that 'democracies are as liable to err In judgement as other forms of government', given the fallibility and moral frailty of human beings. It then turned its attention to economic matters, warning that private enterprise if unchecked by state control could 'easily degenerate into avarice and exploitation', while public ownership of the means of production 'may carry within it limits on individual personality with a depression of human effort'. Urwin and his colleagues attributed the challenge posed by the growth in popularity of Marxist ideas both in Britain and abroad to a popular hunger for justice and brotherhood, but warned that even the most radical attempts to transform society were likely to fail, since men and women might 'still be moved by avarice and lust for power'.[37]

The commitment to a mixed economy and a political system that allowed for a degree of public control of private property was not far removed from the principles that informed the economic programme of the 1945–50 Labour government. Nor did the discussions at Conference suggest that many delegates found anything particularly controversial about the new Declaration on Christian Social and Political Responsibility, even though it was in some ways decidedly at odds with much of the Liberal tradition that had once resounded so powerfully within Methodism. There had in fact always been something contradictory about the values associated with the Nonconformist Conscience of the late nineteenth and early twentieth centuries, resting as it did on a passionate desire to infuse social and political life with a renewed moral significance, while simultaneously preventing the state from encroaching into areas deemed to be the preserve of private conscience. A similar tension was perhaps still visible in Conference in the late 1940s, as delegates endorsed the principle that the state had a positive role to play in social and economic life, but still opposed the continuation of peace-time conscription as an unnecessary assault on civil liberties. The 1949 Declaration nevertheless reflected a strong and growing commitment within Methodism to search for a social and economic order capable of providing a 'third way' between the extremes of Soviet collectivism and American capitalism.

It was perhaps easier for the Methodist Church to develop a new 'theology of politics' than it was to identify a coherent strategy for promoting in a practical way the principles articulated in the various Conference resolutions and statements outlined above. Many Methodist ministers made a sustained attempt to establish closer links with local factories during the late 1940s and early 1950s, hoping to engage with workers who did not regularly attend services of worship, and might otherwise be tempted by the lure of radical ideologies. One minister in Sheffield, who was attached as padre to a large engineering firm, certainly found that much of his time was spent fielding questions about the Church's attitude to communism in general and Soviet Russia in particular.[38] Several Methodist ministers in Glasgow joined a city-wide initiative by the Protestant churches to engage with the workers in the city's shipyards and factories, in the belief that 'where a Christian witness is given the Communist is not a source of political danger'.[39] Ministers in the east end of London held street meetings that were deliberately timed to coincide with open-air meetings held by members of the Communist Party. There was however concern in some quarters about the whole attempt to establish the new 'theology of politics', responding to the demands of men and women in their 'whole need', which some ministers and lay people feared was taking their church too far from its traditional evangelical mission. One Methodist minister wrote an angry letter to the *Recorder* in the spring of 1951 warning that his church had in recent years given too much attention to 'the claptrap of human dignity', with the result that 'the dynamic of the gospel was dissipated in the elaboration of themes of human welfare, and evaporated in every conceivable form of social and cultural activity'.[40] The charge was not really fair, given that Conference resolutions invariably sought to emphasize that social and economic reforms could not alone transform society, but it did echo a long-standing tension within Methodism between the proponents of a social gospel and those who preferred to emphasize the role of 'grace' in the redemption of individuals and humanity.

## International Politics and the Debate on Nuclear Weapons

The divisions within the Methodist Church about how best to respond to the ideological challenge of communism were mirrored by disagreements about the extent to which communist powers like the Soviet Union and China really posed a threat to Britain. The *Recorder* continued to comment at length in its editorial columns on international developments throughout the post-war period. During the early years of the Cold War, its coverage of foreign affairs was governed by an assumption that the USSR and other communist countries were ruled by governments driven by the 'single clear objective' of spreading their power across the globe with 'the precision and promptitude of a machine'.[41] The paper predictably condemned the North Korean invasion of South Korea in the summer of 1950 as evidence of deep-seated 'imperialist designs' on the part of the USSR and China.[42] Communist leaders such as Khrushchev and Mao were repeatedly criticized for 'posturing in front of the world', while failing to show any goodwill or flexibility in diplomatic negotiations, using them instead as a mask to advance their own national interests. The *Recorder*'s recommendations on questions of policy flowed logically from its analysis of the character of the main communist governments. Its editorials repeatedly argued that the task of containing communism required a firm diplomatic and military policy by the main western powers. Such ideas did not receive universal support within British Methodism. There was certainly still widespread hope that the United Nations could provide a mechanism for establishing a workable system of international relations based on the principles of co-operation and negotiation. The General Committee of the Department of Christian Citizenship voted by a large majority to support the UN 'police action' in Korea in 1950, against the vocal opposition of pacifists within the Church, precisely because its members identified the invasion of South Korea as an 'act of aggression' that should be dealt with by the mechanisms of collective security.[43] Although the UN repeatedly showed itself deadlocked and impotent throughout the 1950s, it continued to exercise considerable sway on the loyalties of British Methodism, just as the League of Nations had done for a previous generation.

The Temperance and Social Welfare Division of the Methodist Church – renamed the Department of Christian Citizenship (DCC) in 1950 – played a critical role in shaping the Methodist Church's response to international questions throughout the early years of the Cold War. The two men who served as General Secretary of the Division during the period, E.C. Urwin and Edward Rogers, were both well-informed observers of the international scene, who travelled abroad regularly in order to obtain first-hand knowledge of the problems they had to deal with. The same was true of Kenneth Greet, a long-standing pacifist, who served as the second Secretary in the Department for much of the 1950s and 1960s. The DCC also included as part of its organizational machinery an International Relations committee, chaired for many years by the Revd R.D. Moore, who used his 'extraordinarily comprehensive' knowledge of developments abroad to frame the resolutions on international affairs that were regularly submitted by the Department to Conference for approval.[44] The staff of the Department worked hard to maintain close links with the British Council of Churches and the World Council of Churches, reflecting the powerful ecumenical impulse within British Methodism, as well as a more practical recognition that the churches were likely to exercise most influence if they spoke with one voice. It remained difficult, though, to identify effective strategies to translate broad declarations of principle into practical initiatives of the kind that could capture the attention of policymakers. Senior politicians did occasionally address meetings of the various committees of the Department of Christian Citizenship, while copies of Conference resolutions on international topics were routinely sent to the Foreign Office or Number 10 Downing Street. The same was true of many resolutions passed by district synods and circuits. Even the most cursory perusal of the official Foreign Office files does not, however, provide much evidence to suggest that ministers or civil servants read them with great attention.

The complex international political and military manoeuvres that characterized the early years of the Cold War were all made in the shadow of Hiroshima. While it took some time for the full significance of the bomb to sink in, the main British Protestant churches had within a few months come to recognize that atomic weapons posed a new and profound ethical challenge above and beyond those posed by conventional weaponry. The British Council of Churches set up a 'Commission on the Era of Atomic Power', which included among its members the distinguished Methodist minister R. Newton Flew, who had been one of the leading figures in the inter-war ecumenical movement. The report of the Commission, which was issued in 1946, warned against a 'secular futurism' that believed technology could solve all human problems. It also cautioned members of the churches not to withdraw from political life, instead calling on them to engage in a systematic attempt to influence the public debate over armaments policy. The authors of the report trod carefully when talking about the sensitive question of British policy on nuclear weapons. They acknowledged that a decision by the government to renounce unilaterally any attempt to develop atomic weapons would effectively end Britain's claim to great power status – but also carefully pointed out that such a position 'can by no means be dismissed as absurd'.[45] The Methodist Conference of 1946 appointed a special Commission to examine the significance of the BCC report, which duly reported back the following year.[46] The members of the Commission, which was chaired by Maldwyn Edwards, confessed to being 'deeply perplexed' by the complex ethical decisions raised by the creation of the atomic bomb. They also carefully avoided drawing any hard-and-fast conclusions about whether Britain should develop its own nuclear weapons. The Commission's members were nevertheless convinced that the country faced a 'momentous' choice in deciding whether it should seek to remain a major international power, or instead renounce the development of nuclear weapons in an effort to 'offer to the world an example of a truer and better way of being'. The whole question of atomic weapons became a subject of fierce debate within British Methodism during the years that followed, reaching a crescendo in the second half of the 1950s, at a time when the Campaign for Nuclear Disarmament was putting the nuclear issue at the heart of British politics. Nor did the discussions simply revolve around the familiar disagreement between pacifists and non-pacifists. The sheer scale of the devastation that would result from any future conflict fought with nuclear weapons raised important new questions even for those who believed in principle that there were times when it was legitimate for the Christian to support the state's use of armed force.

The allied victory over Nazi Germany and Japan in the summer of 1945 led to the relaxation of the formal and informal constraints that faced the pacifist minority within the Methodist Church during the war. Although the Methodist Peace Fellowship lost around 20 per cent of its membership following the evacuation of British troops from Dunkirk in 1940, it still had around 3,700 members in 1946, including some 600 ministers. The MPF leadership made strenuous efforts in the immediate post-war years to streamline the organization and foster debate about its role and strategy in the light of the changing international situation. Donald Soper told an MPF rally at Kingsway Hall in 1946 that the organization should become 'a spearhead of evangelism', seeking to win round other Methodists to the view that 'the pacifist message is an integral part of the Christian faith',[47] a position that was echoed at Fellowship meetings up and down the country over the following years. There was also a general recognition that the Fellowship needed to form an integral part of the broader pacifist movement, both Christian and non-Christian, in order to win the greatest possible support for their programme. The MPF had by the start of 1947 developed an 'organizational union' with the Fellowship of Reconciliation, sharing offices in London, and establishing a subscription system that bound the finances of the two bodies closely together.[48] Close links were also maintained with the other denominational peace movements, including the Anglican Peace Fellowship, while the monthly journal *Reconciliation* provided an important forum for disseminating information across the whole Christian pacifist movement. The membership of the MPF rose slightly during the second half of the

1940s, but some of its members still felt that it was losing the 'sense of mission' that had been its hallmark in the 1930s, when there were still hopes that 'all Methodism' might be converted to the pacifist cause. The Fellowship's Annual Meeting was listed in the Conference handbook for the first time in 1949, but there remained a powerful sense among the leadership that more effort was required 'to make Christian pacifism a live issue in Methodism'.[49] Some local MPF groups held public meetings on such themes as 'The Era of Atomic Power', in order to provoke debate, but they seldom attracted significant audiences from beyond the ranks of those who already had strong views on the whole subject. It was only really with the outbreak of a 'hot war' in Korea, in 1950, that the question of pacifism once again became a major theme for debate within Methodism.

The 1950 Conference that took place in Bradford just a few weeks after the start of the Korean War provided the setting for some sharp debates about international affairs in general and nuclear weapons in particular. In the course of the debate about a special resolution on 'World Peace and the Hydrogen Bomb',[50] Donald Soper warned against the tendency in some quarters to blame the Cold War on the USSR, arguing instead that 'there was intransigence and concepts of violence in the hearts of the USA and its satellites just as disreputable'. He went on to add that 'I would rather see the world overrun by Communism than plunged into a third world war.'[51] Soper's remarks were received in silence according to the report in *The Times*, while the President of Conference, W.E. Sangster, noted somewhat archly that 'there were no grounds for assuming they reflected the opinion of Conference'.[52] Following the publicity generated by Soper's words, the journal *Picture Post* asked him to visit the farm run by the erstwhile pacifist and editor of *Peace News*, John Middleton Murry, who had changed his views on peace and war following the revelations of the horrors of the Nazi death camps. Soper's defence of his views displayed the distinctive mixture of moral fervour and occasional naivety that characterized many of his pronouncements throughout his long and distinguished life. He argued that there was a 'better chance of overthrowing communism . . . with the moral and spiritual forces that are embraced by Christianity than with guns', and added that 'the moral and spiritual harm' that would result from a third world war would be worse than the harm that would result from 'the overrunning of the world by communism'. Soper told Murry that if the Russians invaded 'I would welcome them with cups of tea . . . You may think this is crazy but it is no more crazy than blowing the whole universe to pieces with hydrogen bombs.' He added that if American flying fortress bombers were used to drop supplies of food and clothing on the Russians, it would make an 'overwhelmingly penetrating impression upon the Russian mind', and help to break down the mistrust between East and West.[53]

There was some tension in Soper's position. While he was anxious to assert that his commitment to pacifism was an absolute conviction that required him to preach against all forms of violent resistance, regardless of the consequences, he also sought to convince his readers that such a course of action if practised at a national level could unravel the knots of hatred and tension that led to war. Soper was shrewd enough to recognize that all pacifists faced a perennial danger of underestimating the power of evil in the world, in order to make it psychologically easier to defend the morality of a policy of unconditional pacifism,[54] but there were times when he himself came close to falling into the trap. He was too ready to defend Communist China in the early 1950s, despite ample evidence that Mao's new regime was behaving with a terrible brutality towards its own people. He was also far too slow to question many of the things he was told when visiting Russia in November 1954, in company with a number of other British churchmen, during which time members of the party attended several Orthodox and Baptist services. Soper contributed a series of articles to the communist *Daily Worker* newspaper praising the Soviet government for its efforts to raise the living standards of its people. He also – and far more tendentiously – told a press conference at Heathrow Airport following his return home that he had seen no evidence of religious repression in Russia. Soper was inclined at times to assert a kind of

*Soper became an Hon Fellow of Wds College — Lightly esteemed — although often criticized — visit any libertt!! Naïve. I was a member of OCW.*

moral equivalence between East and West, which led him in turn to emphasize the many injustices and bellicosities of western societies, while downplaying those found in countries like the USSR and China. Such a tendency was doubtless in part a response to a crude western Cold War rhetoric that viewed the struggle between East and West as a Manichaean conflict between light and darkness, but it remained something of an 'achilles heel' for Soper himself (and perhaps for the pacifist movement more generally), reflecting a reluctance to engage with the manifest horrors taking place behind the Iron Curtain. While Stalin had died by the time Soper visited the USSR in 1954, the Soviet Communist Party continued to maintain its position by the systematic use of violence to repress any challenge to its monopoly of political power.

Soper was chosen as President of Conference at a time when the Korean conflict was still raging, but there is little evidence to support his claim that his election was evidence of a growing willingness among Methodists 'to listen to the pacifist case'.[55] A good deal of Soper's own peace work continued to take place outside the Church in the first half of the 1950s. He was elected as chairman of the national H-Bomb Campaign established in 1954, following the British government's announcement that it intended to manufacture thermo-nuclear weapons, and spoke at anti-nuclear rallies with leading political figures such as the Labour MP Nye Bevan. Although there was only limited support in British Methodism for the kind of unconditional pacifism promoted by Donald Soper and the MPF, it became increasingly clear in the second half of the 1950s that the nuclear question was reconfiguring the traditional debate between 'pacifists' and 'non-pacifists' into a more complex pattern. Many of those within the Church who came to take a 'unilateralist' position did not do so because they thought that the use of force in the international arena was always in principle wrong. They instead believed that damage resulting from nuclear war would be so devastating that there were no circumstances that could make the use of nuclear weapons acceptable.

## Methodism and the Anti-nuclear Movement in the 1950s

The Methodist Conference approved in 1954 a 'Positive Peace Policy', prepared by the Department of Christian Citizenship, which identified the 'new weapons of destruction' that had been developed during the previous decade as the greatest threat facing humanity. While acknowledging that 'morally these bombs may be no better and no worse than any other instrument by which man slays his fellows', the Policy roundly declared that the ecological consequences of nuclear war meant that 'the weapons [are] too powerful for this small earth'. It also called on the governments of Britain, the United States and the USSR to renounce the first use of such weapons.[56] The Conference that met the following year in Manchester reaffirmed its commitment to the Peace Policy, at a time when public unease about the British government's nuclear programme was growing sharply, manifested among other things in the growth of Soper's own H-Bomb campaign. The memorials and resolutions sent to the 1955 Conference by local circuits and districts also showed a huge rise in concern about the issue at the 'grass-roots' level within Methodism. The Pontypool Quarterly Meeting voted by 27 to 9 to ask Conference 'to make the strongest protest to Her Majesty's Government against the decision to manufacture thermo-nuclear weapons', a request echoed by the Quarterly Meeting in Goole. The Jarrow Circuit wanted Conference to issue a declaration that the scientific discoveries should only be applied 'in accordance with Christian morality'.[57] Conference once again responded to these concerns by calling on the nuclear powers to make a joint declaration renouncing the first use of nuclear weapons. It also announced the establishment of a Commission to investigate a possible revision of the 1937 Declaration of the Methodist Church on Peace and War, in order to see whether traditional Christian teaching on 'the just war' was still valid in the light of the changes in weapons technology that had taken place over the previous twenty years.

The growing concern within Methodism about nuclear weapons was echoed in the other main churches, while the British Council of Churches continued to review the whole subject throughout the second half of the 1950s. The issue of British nuclear tests in the Pacific was a particularly sensitive topic in the first half of 1957. The *Recorder* carried letters expressing fears about the 'appalling risks' that might result from radioactive contamination, although the paper's own editorial notes generally supported politicians and scientists who publicly defended the safety of atomic testing,[58] while the Department of Christian Citizenship called on the British government to put forward international proposals to ban tests.[59] Many of the May synods demanded an end to plans for nuclear tests at Christmas Island in the Pacific Ocean, and urged the Prime Minister and his colleagues 'to forgo any further experiments with nuclear weapons'.[60] Other Nonconformist churches also called for an end to H-Bomb tests.[61] By the time the 1957 Conference met in Nottingham to discuss a new draft 'Declaration of the Methodist Church on Peace and War', it was clear that opinion was aroused more strongly than at any point since 1945.

The Declaration presented for approval echoed its predecessor in acknowledging the existence of a division within Methodism between those who were convinced that war should 'in every case be rejected' and others who believed 'that there are situations in which the waging of war . . . is the lesser of two evils'.[62] It continued with a summary of the theological foundations of both positions, arguing that the first rested on a 'theological interpretation of the Cross' which assumed that direct practical obligations flowed from the ethical injunctions of the Sermon on the Mount, while the latter rejected the notion that it was possible to apply in a simple manner 'an individual ethic to a collective situation'. The Declaration went on to examine at some length traditional notions of what constituted a 'just war'. The language used in the Declaration was far more sophisticated than the language that characterized its 1937 predecessor. The close attention devoted to the concept of the 'just war' also represented a marked innovation, given the lack of interest in the subject that had characterized debates on peace and war within Methodism in previous decades, and perhaps signalled the

*'Just War'*

degree to which growing ecumenical contacts had encouraged leading Methodists to engage with ideas that had always been a staple in
Anglican and Roman Catholic discussion of the subject. The most
controversial aspect of the draft Declaration was, though, its stark
claim that nuclear weapons added 'a new dimension to the terror of
war'. Since the consequences of a nuclear war were bound to outweigh any possible benefits, it was 'impossible' to imagine that a 'war
waged with such weapons' could ever be just.

The draft Declaration attracted a good deal of debate on the floor
of the Conference.[63] Donald Soper wanted a still clearer statement
that the use of atomic weapons could never be acceptable, apparently
concerned by a rather curious sentence that seemed to imply that a
nuclear war fought in a 'graduated and controllable' manner might
be considered to meet the traditional criteria for a just war. Another
speaker said that he took the Declaration to mean that Methodists
should now oppose the manufacture of nuclear weapons altogether.
The final agreed Declaration did not unequivocally oppose the possession of nuclear weapons, presumably on the grounds that they
could act as a deterrent, but a moment's reflection indicates that
their value as a deterrent rested inescapably on the prospect that
they *might* be used. As Soper and others were quick to point out, if
it could never be right to use nuclear weapons, then it was not clear
that it could ever be right to threaten to use them. And, under those
circumstances, it seemed logical to conclude that the only morally acceptable course of action was to give up the weapons altogether. The 1957 Declaration on Peace and War did not commit the
Methodist Church to support the cause of British unilateral nuclear
disarmament. It did make it harder for those who were opposed to
unilateral nuclear disarmament to articulate a clear and acceptable
rationale for their position.

The ambiguities and tensions visible at the 1957 Methodist
Conference became still clearer during the years that followed. The
Department of Christian Citizenship continued to monitor the
whole issue with some care, and in the spring of 1958 its Executive
Committee passed a resolution reiterating that 'thermo-nuclear

warfare would be a crime against humanity, not justified in any circumstances'. It also called on the British government to press for talks with the other nuclear powers and to declare its readiness to suspend any further nuclear tests while the talks were in progress. When the resolution was presented for approval to the 1958 Conference, Edward Rogers (who was still General Secretary of the DCC) made it clear that no British government would at the present time accept a programme of unilateral nuclear disarmament. Soper responded that such an approach was too cautious, and argued that unilateral disarmament by the British government was required to help break the deadlock between the main powers. He was supported by George Thomas, the Labour MP, who had played a big role in the recent debates on unilateral disarmament within the Labour Party. Soper eventually agreed to accept the resolution in its present form, in order to avoid a potentially damaging division, although other delegates continued to push for an amendment that would have made it stronger.[64] There was even greater confusion during the 1959 Conference, at which the President and long-time MPF member, the Revd E.W. Baker, rejected a policy of nuclear deterrence as 'a blatant denial of everything that we believe about God's purpose for man'. When Edward Rogers presented the DCC Report to Conference for approval, in the process commending a recent report by the British Council of Churches on 'Christians and Atomic War', there were a number of calls from the floor for a full debate on the subject.[65] Soper subsequently moved an amendment proposing that 'Conference calls upon Her Majesty's Government unilaterally to renounce the further manufacture and testing of nuclear weapons as a practical step towards [international] agreement'. The amendment was passed by 'an overwhelming majority'. Soper told the *Scotsman* newspaper the following year that his resolution had called for the unilateral abandonment of nuclear weapons, and that he was astounded when it went through.[66] The terms of the amendment were in fact more modest than he implied, focusing on a ban on the future manufacture and testing of weapons, but the debate had certainly shown that there was a good deal

167

of support at all levels of the Methodist Church for British unilateral nuclear disarmament.

When Edward Rogers became President of Conference in 1960, he used his opening address to call for 'honest discussion' within the Methodist Church over questions of peace and war, before going on to provide his own characteristically sophisticated examination of the contemporary international scene. He warned against the idea that the East–West conflict was 'a simple melodrama of villains and heroes', instead suggesting that it was a struggle between 'centralised state capitalism and large-scale managerial capitalism'. Rogers deliberately avoided talking too much about nuclear weapons in his speech, not least because he was shrewd enough to realize the danger of raising a subject that had become such a sensitive issue. The formation of the Direct Action Committee against Nuclear War in 1957, along with the establishment of the Campaign for Nuclear Disarmament a year later, represented a major change in the pattern of political protest in Britain.[67] Although many leading figures in CND initially believed that they were most likely to influence government policy by working through the established political process, the subsequent growth of large-scale public demonstrations, such as the celebrated Aldermaston marches, in practice represented a marked challenge to the political *status quo*. Many individuals who had previously shown little interest in politics were galvanized into taking part in order to express their anxieties about the risk posed to humanity by nuclear weapons. The ideological and organizational profile of the nuclear disarmament campaign of the late 1950s and early 1960s was extremely complex. Organizations such as CND included within their membership middle-class socialists and old-style trade unionists, committed Christians and resolute atheists, absolute pacifists and 'pacificists' who were worried about the devastating consequences of nuclear war. Some activists in the disarmament movement were firmly committed to a programme of 'civil disobedience', picketing military bases and munitions factories, while others placed their hopes on lawful protests as the most effective way of putting pressure on governments. Members of the Methodist Church who

168

were committed to taking their struggle for nuclear disarmament beyond the confines of their own church therefore had to orient themselves within this new 'politics of protest'.

Some ministers active in the Methodist Peace Fellowship fretted from time to time that the 'eclectic anti-H bomb witness' was leading to 'a watering-down of the full Christian pacifist case'.[68] Most senior figures in the Fellowship nevertheless believed that the growing public concern over nuclear weapons represented an opportunity rather than a threat. The chairman of the MPF for 1958, the Revd L.T. Jarvis, argued that Christian pacifists should build links with the broader peace movement in order to impress on as many people as possible that renouncing war was 'the only satisfactory' response to the crisis facing the world.[69] Soper put the case even more strongly a few months later, arguing that 'the issue of immediate war is so vital and peremptory that on balance I am satisfied that it is far better to make an impact on even one element in this cosmic peril, even if those who feel this impact cannot at present travel the whole way to total disarmament'.[70] Soper himself remained a pivotal figure in the broader campaign for nuclear disarmament, appearing on platforms up and down the country with luminaries such as Bertrand Russell, and was a prominent participant in the Aldermaston marches at which he attacked US foreign policy for turning Britain into an 'occupied country'.[71] He also visited factories involved in the manufacture of components used in the nuclear programme, such as the Siddeley Engines factory in Bristol, where he urged the workers to engage in a token strike as a protest against the activities of the plant. Although Soper was ready to support certain forms of direct action, he was opposed to the more extreme tactics that were used by the Committee of 100 when it was established in 1960, hoping instead that the disarmers could achieve their goals through the mainstream political process. He welcomed the vote at the 1960 Labour Party Conference in favour of British unilateral disarmament, just as he was frustrated and disappointed by the reversal of the decision the following year, which effectively signalled that any future Labour government was unlikely to follow a unilateralist agenda. Soper subsequently characterized CND during this period as a kind of 'ecumenical pilgrimage', inspired by 'a vision that went far beyond its practical and immediate aims', and there is little doubt that he was not alone in finding something in the movement that was deeply congenial to his own emotional make-up. Soper himself acknowledged that pacifism was never altogether a rational creed, adding that 'what a man thinks depends on what he feels', but he also never tired of arguing that pacifism represented a considered and realistic response to the challenge of the nuclear world. His pacifism was always part of a broader creed that assumed the final abolition of war could only be achieved by the 'dismantling of the social and economic structure which not only encourages it but also demands it'.[72] In the short-term, though, Soper was willing to countenance the idea of unilateral nuclear disarmament as a 'practical action' that would mobilize popular support for peace and act as a springboard for broader change.

Soper's energy gave him an important role in the MPF, but the organization continued to develop its own distinctive organizational structure and identity throughout the 1950s. One of its most prominent figures was the distinguished Oxford mathematician and chemist Professor Charles Coulson, who had belonged to the Fellowship since 1935, and served as Vice-President of Conference in 1959–60. Coulson was an enthusiastic supporter of atomic energy when used for peaceful purposes, fervently denying that 'nuclear knowledge [was] . . . the fruit of some forbidden tree'. He contributed an article in 1957 to the *London Quarterly and Holborn Review* looking forward to a time when atomic power could be used to fuel such grand schemes as the desalination of seawater for use in irrigating the arid regions of the world.[73] He was also, however, convinced that scientists needed to become more sensitive to the ways in which their work might be used in less constructive ways. A few years earlier, he had contributed another piece to the same journal on the complex relationship between science and religion, warning against any attempt to separate them into two distinct spheres,[74] an argument that he subsequently developed at length in his celebrated book on *Science and Christian Belief*. Coulson's distinctive combination of scientific expertise and passionate commitment to nuclear disarmament made him a popular speaker both within and beyond Methodism. He also regularly contributed articles to the *Recorder* on the subject. Nor was he alone in lending his academic prestige to help bolster the cause. Professor Harold Miller from Sheffield University, a long-standing MPF member, contributed numerous articles to the pacifist press on such questions as the likely impact of atomic tests on public health. A number of well-known Methodist politicians also played an important role in the nuclear debate that took place within the Church, most notably George Thomas, who was a frequent speaker at MPF rallies and Conference meetings in support of unilateral disarmament.[75]

The public campaign to 'ban the bomb' had little impact on the size of the MPF's membership, which was perhaps not surprising given that so many unilateralists were not pacifists, and therefore unable to 'sign up' to the MPF Covenant. The Fellowship did send several hundred members to each of the Aldermaston marches – the largest organized denominational presence from any of the main churches – who marched behind banners proclaiming that 'We Say No to War' and (rather less pithily) 'H-Bombs make Just War Impossible'.[76] The MPF was also responsible, along with the Fellowship of Reconciliation, for instituting 'The Cross and the Bomb Campaign' that held public meetings up and down Britain throughout 1959 and 1960 to encourage public reflection on the moral dilemmas posed by nuclear weapons. The MPF also co-operated with the Department of Christian Citizenship in producing information targeted at young members of the Church who wished to seek conscientious objector status exempting them from National Service.[77] Some ministerial members of the MPF made a systematic attempt during the second half of the 1950s to think through whether there were any specifically *Methodist* foundations for their pacifist commitment – a question that had received surprisingly little attention in the past. The Revd J.C. Jacobs from Sheffield contributed a piece to *Reconciliation* in 1959 linking his pacifism to the Wesleyan

doctrine of Christian Perfectionism.[78] A few months earlier, the Revd
John Newton from Richmond College argued at an MPF meeting in
West London that pacifism was inherent in Wesley's emphasis on
'the universality of the gospel', which 'implies to a Methodist [that]
all wars are civil wars'.[79] The MPF produced a number of publications designed to show readers how 'The Christian Pacifist case is
rooted in a theological interpretation of the Cross and the practical obligation to act on that belief.'[80] There nevertheless remained
a pervasive sense among many MPF members that their activities were not doing much to influence opinion within their own
church. As the Campaign for Nuclear Disarmament began to fade
in the early 1960s, despite the huge public anxiety that surrounded
the Cuban Missile Crisis of October 1962, it seemed clear that the
cause of unconditional pacifism had not advanced much within the
Methodist Church. The developments of the late 1950s were, by contrast, instrumental in reshaping attitudes within the church towards
nuclear weapons. The debates that took place in the second half of
the 1950s forced many members from across the Methodist Church
to engage in a sustained reflection about how best to confront the
challenge of war at a time when technological advances meant that
it might result in the annihilation of human civilization.

## British Methodism and the End of Empire

Although the Cold War and the threat of nuclear destruction
dominated discussion about international affairs within British
Methodism following the end of the Second World War, a good
deal of attention was also given to other developments, including
the gradual fragmentation of the main European empires and the
concomitant emergence of a large number of independent states in
Asia and Africa. The withdrawal from empire was almost universally welcomed within British Methodism (although concern was
occasionally expressed about the impact of the process on missionary work). The jingoistic imperialism that had been such a feature
of Wesleyan Methodism half a century before had faded almost

entirely by the 1950s. The idea that the population of countries like India could benefit from the benign tutelage of white Europeans had by the post-war years come to seem almost as preposterous to many Britons as it had long appeared to the subject peoples themselves. The retreat from empire nevertheless created numerous challenges, given the poverty of many former colonies, and the existence of ethnic and religious divisions that led to bitter civil war in countries like India and Cyprus. The fact that so many members of the Church had a personal knowledge of life in the former colonies, via mission work or some other form of service in a field like education, helped to stimulate a sense that British Methodism should take a particular interest in their transition to independence. The *Recorder* carried countless articles throughout the 1940s and 1950s on developments taking place across Africa and Asia, recognizing that many of its readers were keen to follow events in areas of the world with which so many of them were familiar.

The Methodist Conference that met at Nottingham in July 1945 called for policies to promote 'the care for, and advancement of, the backward nations'. It also demanded action to ensure 'freedom of want' for people across the world.[81] The 1949 Conference in Liverpool called on its members to respond to 'the cry of human suffering and wrong', and argued that the worldwide Church should strive to become 'a symbol of world unity, transcending divisions of race, nationality, colour and creed'.[82] The 1952 Conference issued a 'Special Resolution on World Affairs', which fretted among other things about the impact that 'fear of hunger' and 'frustrated national aspirations' were having on international harmony.[83] The 1955 Conference in Manchester approved the Department of Christian Citizenship report which included the suggestion that money spent on armaments could better be spent on helping poor countries to 'overcome the evils of hunger, poverty and disease'.[84] The DCC itself was preoccupied throughout the 1950s by questions of global justice. Its report to the 1951 Conference made it clear that it viewed demands for 'self-government' with sympathy in cases where they were a natural response to 'racial discrimination' and 'economic impoverishment and exploitation'.[85] There was neverthe-less something rather vapid about many of the pronouncements made by the Methodist Church on the question of poverty in the developing world during these years. A few senior figures, includ-ing Edward Rogers, had a good grasp of the complex economic and political factors that created and perpetuated poverty in the former colonies. The prevailing rhetoric, however, focused above all on the *fact* of poverty without devoting much sustained attention either to its causes or to possible responses. It was only in later decades that the Methodist Church really started to give serious thought to the mechanisms through which global economic structures created a gulf between the rich and poor nations.

Rather more attention was given during the 1950s to the whole question of racial conflict in the various countries that comprised the British Commonwealth. The region that attracted most atten-tion was predictably southern Africa (where Methodism had a strong presence given both its long missionary activity and formal links to the local Methodist churches). The *Recorder* carefully fol-lowed the development of apartheid in South Africa from the 1940s onwards, making a particular effort to keep its readers informed about the situation of the Methodist Church there, and carrying numerous interviews with senior ministers from the country.[86] The paper also periodically carried articles and letters criticizing the British government for its reluctance to lead international protests against apartheid, and gave short shrift in its editorial notes to claims that such interference with the internal affairs of another state was not compatible with normal diplomatic traditions. The Methodist Conference for its part passed a number of resolutions condemning developments in South Africa, while efforts were made to offer prac-tical support to Methodists in the country who were condemned by the government for engaging in supposedly subversive activities.[87] The British government's creation of the Central African Federation in 1953, bringing together Southern and Northern Rhodesia along with Nyasaland, also created concern among many Methodists back in Britain. The move was unpopular with a large majority of the African population, who feared that the existing race laws in Southern Rhodesia would be extended to the rest of the Federation, an anxiety that was echoed by many contributors to the *Recorder*. Although some Methodist ministers from the region argued that the violence that erupted from time to time was the product of communist agitation among African workers,[88] such views attracted little support among the church hierarchy back in Britain. It is not, however, altogether clear that the issue yet aroused such strong passions at grass roots level. Local district synods certainly passed far fewer resolutions and memorials on the subject than they did on questions of nuclear weapons. The abstract ideals of global justice seemed to loom less strongly in the minds of many 'ordinary' Methodists during the 1950s than the threat of impending apocalypse. It was only in the 1960s and 1970s that the debate within British Methodism about international affairs placed questions of global justice at the very heart of discussions.

Although there was a reasonable consensus within British Methodism about the most important questions relating to the 'end of empire', there was still on occasion sharp disagreement about Britain's 'imperial' role. The fiercest debate took place in the autumn of 1956 during the Suez crisis, which erupted when Anthony Eden's government decided to use force to regain control of the canal-zone, following the decision by the Egyptian leader Gamal Abdel Nasser to nationalize the canal in order to raise funds to finance the Aswan dam.[89] The circumstances surrounding Britain's decision to launch a military intervention (in tandem with France and Israel) were decidedly opaque, but the final decision was widely interpreted both at home and abroad as a breach of international law. Even before the invasion began, Donald Soper was involved in organizing protests about possible British military action, at one stage leading 500 members of his Kingsway congregation in a protest march against the 'gunboat diplomacy' being pursued by the British government in an effort to force Nasser to back down.[90] The outbreak of hostilities magnified concerns. The report subsequently submitted to the 1957 Conference by the Department of Christian Citizenship was hardly

175

exaggerating when it observed that the Suez affair had 'presented very serious problems for Christian judgement'.[91] The General Committee of the DCC warned against any attempt to resolve the crisis unilaterally by force rather than through the United Nations, while the President of Conference issued a statement urging the British government 'to withdraw from situations and avoid policies which will stir up and lead to wider conflicts'.[92] Soper meanwhile called on his congregation at Kingsway to engage in acts of civil disobedience in protest at the actions of the British government.[93] The *Recorder* by contrast expressed strong support for Britain's military intervention, arguing in its Notes column that the British government and its allies had acted in order 'to stem the rising flood of danger' in the Middle East.[94] The following week's edition was predictably full of letters on the subject. Some contributors argued that 'nothing justifies our armed action against Egypt' since it had blackened Britain's name abroad and 'dealt a blow to the United Nations which could prove fatal'. Others praised the *Recorder* for its 'sane and balanced' views on the subject.[95] The difference between the two sides was not for the most part about the rights and wrongs of using force *per se*. Critics of the Suez adventure usually opposed it on the grounds that it broke faith with the United Nations and smacked of an old-style heavy-handed imperialism. Supporters claimed that the action was necessary to preserve international law. In the event, the reluctance of the US government to offer firm backing to the British government precipitated a financial crisis that forced the Eden government to end operations in the Canal Zone, leading to a humiliating withdrawal that signalled both at home and abroad the extent of Britain's decline as a global power. The Suez crisis led to a sharp division of public opinion. It is hardly surprising that it split opinion within the Methodist Church as well.

## Conclusion

The determination of the Eden government to prevent Nasser from seizing the Suez Canal has often been explained by the Prime

Minister's belief that the 1930s had shown the importance of acting to defeat dictators before they became too powerful to resist. The Suez crisis was in reality, though, a thoroughly modern conflict rooted in the end of empire and the rise of nationalism in the developing world. It was also in part a Cold War conflict, given that the reluctance of the American government to support Britain was largely due to its fear of alienating many of the newly independent states, and driving them into the Soviet sphere of influence. The challenges of the Cold War that erupted after 1945 were nevertheless not so new as they sometimes appeared to contemporaries. There had long been a concern in countries like Britain about the possible impact of radical Marxist ideas on the development of western 'civilization'. Publications had already begun to appear in English by the middle of the nineteenth century reviewing the vexed relationship between communist ideas and Christian values,[96] while the creation of the Soviet Union in the wake of the 1917 Russian Revolution prompted a veritable cascade of books and pamphlets on the subject. William Temple gave an address at York in 1933 in which he suggested that communism was 'the most serious menace which has threatened the Christian faith in the civilized world for some hundreds of years'.[97] A few years later, the *Spectator* magazine published a series of essays by prominent authors, including Reinhold Niebuhr and John Strachey, which sought to answer such vexed questions as whether communism should itself be regarded as a faith.[98] The rise of the USSR to superpower status in the wake of the Second World War made the whole question more urgent, given that the 'communist challenge' was now geopolitical as well as ideological. The debate that took place within Methodism in the 1940s and 1950s over the nature and significance of the issues at stake in the Cold War was therefore part of a broader discourse that resonated through the other main churches and indeed across British society more generally. The same was true of the Methodist Conference's repeated support during these years for a social and economic policy that rejected the extremes of both free market capitalism and collective socialism. The declarations and statements adopted by Conference were not only in harmony with the tradition of social activism that had been a feature of Methodism for many years. They also reflected the broader changes that were taking place in British political culture during the post-war period.

The general consensus within Methodism in favour of the mixed economy and the politics of consensus was not reproduced when nuclear weapons formed the subject of debate. The whole question of Britain's possession of atomic and hydrogen bombs posed no particular problems for unconditional pacifists who believed that their Christian commitment required them to renounce violence whatever the consequences. Nor did it pose difficulties for those who accepted uncritically the Cold War 'view' that Britain and the other western powers required nuclear weapons to deter the USSR and its allies from seeking global domination. The question of the nuclear deterrent was, by contrast, more complex for those who could not accept either of these positions uncritically. There is little evidence to suggest that there was much increase in support within British Methodism in the 1950s for unconditional pacifism. There is a great deal of evidence to suggest that many thousands of Methodists were convinced that the possession of nuclear weapons by their country was immoral and dangerous. All these perplexities fostered the development of competing perspectives that resulted in a vigorous debate about how the Methodist Church should respond to the nuclear issue. The arguments that were advanced often proved to be incoherent and unconvincing. They certainly failed to lead to any general agreement. It is nevertheless striking that the debate on nuclear weapons was for the most part conducted during these years with a good deal of fair-mindedness. The following chapter examines how some of these themes developed in the second part of the Cold War. The challenge posed by the Soviet Union and other communist countries to the security of the western world continued to attract a good deal of concern within British Methodism during the 1960s and 1970s. There was, though, a growing recognition that the 'western' economic and political order was itself responsible for much of the poverty and exploitation of the developing world.

The inevitable result was the emergence of a chorus of voices within Methodism calling for the Church to take a more critical view of the international status quo.

Perhaps
Soper was not so
dominant as Higher
suggest.

# 7

# Methodism and International Politics during the Later Cold War

## Introduction

The poet Philip Larkin once famously observed that sexual intercourse began in 1963. While some historians might question his choice of date for the start of the 'permissive society', it is difficult to question the claim that the 1960s marked a fundamental change in the character of British society, ranging from the rapid decline of social deference through to the growing acceptance of new forms of sexual relationships. In the words of one distinguished historian of the period, the 1960s 'rouses strong emotions ... for some it is a golden age, for others a time when the old secure framework of morality, authority and discipline disintegrated'.[1] The main churches could not remain untouched by such upheavals. All the principal denominations had to respond to a new set of demands that forced them to reconsider their values and practices in the light of the changes taking place around them. The reforms introduced at the second Vatican Council in the 1960s reshaped the character of the Catholic Church both in Britain and abroad. The publication of books such as John Robinson's *Honest to God* signified that some of those at the heart of the Anglican establishment were prepared to engage in open debate even about the fundamentals of Christian belief.[2] The Methodist Church of Great Britain for its part possessed a particular constellation of strengths and weaknesses when seeking to confront the avalanche of change set in motion during these years. Since the church had a long tradition of responding to the

180

problems faced by a changing society, from the early days of the Industrial Revolution through to the chaos of the Second World War, it was at least as well placed as the other churches to confront the demands placed on it by a new set of challenges. It is no accident that Methodists were closely involved in debates and actions over many of the issues that began to come to the fore during this period: abortion, homosexuality, racism, and so forth. At the same time, though, even the most sympathetic observer cannot doubt that the Methodist Church was by the 1960s struggling to define its mission and maintain its membership at a time when organized religion in Britain faced so many challenges.

The tensions that resulted from these developments could not be masked altogether either in the pages of the Methodist press or in debates among those who attended such events as the Annual Conference and district synods. The 1960s witnessed the rise to prominence of a number of Methodist ministers with radical views about the role and responsibilities of British Methodism. John Vincent, who had studied for his doctorate under Karl Barth in Switzerland, published a book in 1965 on *Christ and Methodism* that tartly criticized many of his fellow ministers for repeating 'the theological simplicities of the nineteen-thirties and the pastoral principles of the eighteen-nineties'. Another Methodist minister, Colin Morris, noted acerbically in his book *Include Me Out* (1968) that 'I am a son of a prophetic movement which became an institution by mistake.'[3] Nor were Vincent and Morris lone voices. The broader social changes that took place during the 1960s convinced many Methodist ministers and lay people of the need to think more seriously than ever before about the organization of their church and its role in the world. Nor, of course, were all these debates and challenges confined to the heady days of the 1960s. The 1970s witnessed a level of industrial militancy and political instability in Britain that raised fundamental questions about the future of the country's economic and political system. The 1980s saw the emergence of the new social and economic phenomenon of 'Thatcherism' that, despite its rhetorical challenge to many of the developments of the

1960s, actually helped to entrench the individualism and consumerism that were such powerful hallmarks of the earlier decade. Britain changed radically as a country during the years between 1960 and 1985. It is hardly surprising that the Methodist Church changed as well. The process was nevertheless both painful and controversial.

The Methodist Church's response to developments beyond Britain also went through a marked evolution in the decades following the Cuban Missile Crisis of 1962, which seemed for a few dreadful days to presage exactly the kind of global nuclear annihilation that had caused so much public anxiety over the previous few years. Although mass protests in favour of unilateral nuclear disarmament declined surprisingly quickly in the first half of the 1960s, the Cold War and the arms race continued unabated, providing a profound challenge to Christian pacifists and non-pacifists alike. The Department of Christian Citizenship, which was renamed the Division of Social Responsibility in 1974, continued to report to Conference on such controversial questions as the future of the British nuclear deterrent. It also carefully followed the numerous conflicts that disfigured the world during these years, ranging from the wars in Vietnam and Afghanistan through to the bloodshed in the Falkland Islands and Northern Ireland. The whole issue of nuclear weapons became particularly important during the early 1980s, following the British government's decision to buy Trident missiles, and authorize the stationing of American intermediate range nuclear weapons in the United Kingdom. There was nevertheless a significant change in the focus of debate during these years away from the drama of East–West relations and towards the challenge of poverty and racial injustice in the developing world. Although this development was not always universally welcomed within the church, the growing preoccupation with North–South issues was in effect just a logical transfer of Methodism's perennial concern with economic and social questions from the domestic to the international arena. If the church had a duty to speak out on matters of justice, then it was not clear why this obligation should end at the national frontier.[4]

## The Continuing Challenge of War: Vietnam and the Falklands

The Cuban Missile Crisis of October 1962 represented the single most dangerous moment of the Cold War.[5] While historians sometimes disagree about how close the world came to a full-blown conflict between the two superpowers, the brinkmanship between Kennedy and Khrushchev dramatized the challenge posed to humanity by the prospect of a nuclear conflagration. The two superpowers subsequently made some effort to avoid situations in which they might find themselves 'head to head' with one another, but this simply exported the conflict to the developing world, with the result that many 'hot' wars were fought between client states of the USA and the USSR. The political leaders in both Moscow and Washington worked assiduously to increase their influence on foreign governments via means ranging from the provision of foreign aid through to the supply of armaments. It would be too simplistic, though, to assume that the superpowers were always able to dominate 'their' clients. The crises that rocked the Middle East in the 1960s and 1970s showed that so-called client states were often adept at manipulating those who sought to control them. The intricacies of the conflicts that disfigured the world during the 1960s and 1970s defied easy analysis at the time – and continue to do so today even at a time when the benefit of hindsight and access to archives has allowed historians to rethink many of the crucial episodes of the Cold War.

The next few pages focus on the response within British Methodism to two major conflicts of the period: the wars in Vietnam and the South Atlantic. Although British forces were not directly involved in the Vietnam War, global media coverage ensured that the intervention of the US military in the region created almost as much public furore in Britain as it did in the United States. Many on the left of the political spectrum viewed the conflict as an attempt by the greatest military power on earth to defend its interests by any means, regardless of the misery that resulted for millions of ordinary Vietnamese. This interpretation aroused a good deal of sympathy among a significant number of prominent Methodists, who came to view the conflict less as a defence by the free 'West' against the challenge of the communist 'East', and more as an attempt by the richest power of the 'North' to assert its interests regardless of its impact on one of the poorest countries of the 'South'. The Falklands War, by contrast, raised a different set of dilemmas. Although nobody could defend the morality of the Argentinian junta that seized the islands in 1982, the invasion raised important questions about how best to respond to such aggression, not least because any military response by the British government was likely to appear as little more than a desperate attempt to preserve the vestiges of empire. The wars in South-East Asia and the South Atlantic were precisely the kind of complex conflicts that could not be reduced to a simple matter of black and white. Both the American and British governments argued that they were taking military action in order to promote the greater good. Their critics instead believed that the politicians were either masking their real motives beneath a bogus moralistic rhetoric, or fooling themselves into thinking that the use of force could resolve complex political problems, in a world that was crying out for new and more imaginative ways of resolving conflict.

The military intervention by American forces in Vietnam was designed by the US government to defend the South Vietnamese government against attacks both from its communist neighbour to the North and from guerrilla (Vietcong) forces in the South.[6] It was also part of a broader strategy to 'contain' Soviet and Chinese communism that had been central to US foreign policy since the 1940s. By the late 1960s, more than half a million US servicemen were serving in the region, while almost sixty thousand eventually lost their lives. The Vietnam War rapidly became a catalyst for protests across the western world, prompted both by widespread anger about the morality of American policy, as well as by a more pervasive anti-establishment ethos that formed part of the 1960s *Zeitgeist*. The graphic reports that appeared in the western media following such events as the slaughter of hundreds of unarmed Vietnamese villagers at My Lai, in 1968, attracted outrage around the world.[7] So too did the deployment by US forces of chemical weapons like phosphorous rockets and defoliants such as Agent Orange. Although successive British governments refused to send troops to help American forces in Vietnam,[8] the conflict still provoked numerous demonstrations in London and other major cities. The rights and wrongs of US policy in South-East Asia inevitably began to attract attention both in the Methodist press and in debates at Conference. The DCC's Annual Report for 1965 noted somewhat acerbically that American policy was designed to sustain the corrupt South Vietnamese government so as 'to preserve a base for the military containment of Chinese communism'. It added that the 'minimum aim of British policy must be to dissuade her American ally from extending and intensifying the range of the conflict'.[9] Three years later, the department's Report confirmed its view that the 'tragic war' was mistaken and that American attempts to win the conflict by military means were doomed to failure. Criticism of US policy in Vietnam was also frequently voiced on the floor of Conference. Donald Soper proposed a resolution at the 1966 Conference condemning the recent American bombing of the North Vietnamese capital Hanoi, while the Revd Harold Morton told delegates that many people in the developing world saw 'the West as the real threat to peace'.[10] The resolution was passed by a large majority, despite sharp opposition from speakers critical of its 'glaring errors and false foundations'. The *Recorder* was deluged with letters protesting against the resolution. One correspondent condemned Conference for being 'overwhelmed by Lord Soper's gushing eloquence', adding that 'The Church ... has no moral right to decide on political questions on which so many members hold diverse views.' Another condemned the 'smug pomposity' of Conference, and went on to note that 'many Methodists (including myself) prefer to choose the lesser evil of war than allow the free world to be engulfed by Communism or Hitler's form of National Socialism'.[11] The debate over Vietnam predictably recrudesced at the 1967 Conference. Donald Soper complained that the DCC's Report appeared to blame North Vietnam for sabotaging recent efforts to promote peace talks, while the Chairman of the Bristol District argued to loud cries of dissent that North Vietnam was being bullied by 'the greatest military power in the world'. Although the Report was eventually approved, the debate once again showed the extent to which the war in Vietnam had come to divide opinion within the Methodist Church.[12]

Some of those within Methodism who opposed the Vietnam War were, like Soper, unconditional pacifists who did not believe that the use of force could ever be justified in the international arena. The Methodist Peace Fellowship continued to issue literature arguing that the injunction to 'love your enemy' could never be reconciled with the practice of dropping bombs on them.[13] Most critics of US policy focused their attention, though, on the American government's readiness to use force as part of its broader strategy of containing communism without apparent reference to the human cost. Although the Vietnam War was seldom discussed in the Methodist press or at Conference in terms of the just war tradition, many of those who attacked the US military presence in South-East Asia effectively based their argument on the claim that the devastation wrought by the conflict far outweighed any possible benefits. Other members of the church took a more radical line altogether, echoing anti-war demonstrators who proclaimed that their opposition to the Vietnam War was part of a broader challenge to the established global and domestic order. The *Recorder* periodically published articles from Methodist students who earnestly sought to explain how demonstrations of the kind that took place in London's Grosvenor Square, in front of the American Embassy, were fuelled not just by anger over Vietnam but also by frustrations over a whole range of other issues as well.[14] The paper's editorials did not, though, exhibit much sympathy for the huge street demonstrations that became such a hallmark of British life in the late 1960s.[15]

The Vietnam War dragged on into the 1970s, ending only when the last US forces were withdrawn in 1975, although by that time American military strategy had for some years rested on the use of air power rather than ground troops to offer support to its South Vietnamese ally. The critical pronouncements of the DCC on US policy during the war ensured that its role remained controversial for many Methodists, a phenomenon that continued after it was renamed in 1973 as the Division of Social Responsibility, as part of a broader administrative restructuring of the church. The Division played a pivotal 'behind-the-scenes' role in shaping the Methodist Church's response to all the major international questions that erupted throughout the years between 1960 and 1985. The Arab–Israeli wars of 1967 and 1973 naturally attracted a good deal of attention in the church, although at this stage the whole Middle East question proved comparatively uncontroversial for British Methodists, merely prompting somewhat bland Conference resolutions that called on both sides to seek a peaceful solution based on a recognition of the need for mutual security. Nor was the wider Middle East imbroglio seen primarily as a religious conflict, at least until the overthrow of the Shah's government in the Iranian Revolution of 1979 introduced the world to the phenomenon of so-called 'Islamic Fundamentalism'. The issues that raised greatest passion within the church were predictably those in which Britain was most directly involved. The Methodist press gave considerable coverage to the violence that erupted in Northern Ireland in the late 1960s, although the issue was raised at Conference rather less than might have been expected. Nor did the *Recorder* give much sustained attention to the efforts made by the Irish Methodist Church, and most notably the Revd Eric Gallagher, to launch a series of initiatives designed to bring together the Catholic and Protestant communities. While Gallagher's work showed how the churches could play a key role in building confidence between the two sides, rather than acting as a source of division, such tireless work was all too easily drowned out by the endless stream of bad news emanating from the province.[16] The accession of Britain to the European Community in 1973 also aroused some concern from Methodists fearful that the country would become a subordinate member of an organization in which Catholics formed a majority (an echo of those members of the Protestant community in Northern Ireland who bitterly opposed any prospect of a united Ireland on the grounds that it would turn them into a minority). Such voices were, however, drowned out by those who believed that West European unity was helping to make a future war less likely. The eruption of hostilities in the South Atlantic in 1982 by contrast raised a veritable furore within the Methodist Church, as the British government's decision to react with military force to the occupation of the Falkland Islands led to sharp debate over the circumstances under which a country should go to war. As was to prove the case twenty years later, during the second Gulf War, discussions about international politics always proved most controversial when they involved immediate issues of life and death.

The Falklands War caused sharp divisions across British society.[17] The Conservative government's decision to dispatch a naval taskforce in response to the Argentinian invasion was seen by many commentators both in Britain and abroad as the knee-jerk reaction of a fading empire wedded to an unrealistic sense of its importance in the world. The resulting conflict cost more than 900 lives (some 650 Argentinians and 250 Britons). Margaret Thatcher and her ministers defended their decision to go to war by arguing that the invasion was a gross breach of international law by a dictatorial regime.[18] The government's critics responded by arguing that the sovereignty issue was less clear-cut than ministers implied. All the main churches in Britain became involved in the public debate over the rights and wrongs of the conflict. The Falklands War posed no particular ethical conundrums for unconditional Christian pacifists who refused to accept that the use of armed force could ever be reconciled with the fundamental values of their faith. While there had been some attempts since the 1960s to rethink the theological foundations of pacifism in the language of situational ethics,[19] which avoided the kind of 'black and white' language that had traditionally informed most reflections on Christian pacifism, the best-known pacifists within the Methodist Church continued to base their argument on the claim that the Sermon on the Mount represented an absolute ethic that should be accepted as a guide to Christian conduct.[20] The war in the South Atlantic did, however, pose a dilemma for all those who accepted the principle that war could be reconciled with the Christian conscience when it was shown to be the lesser of two evils. The junta that ruled Argentina had been responsible for thousands of deaths among its own civilian population during the previous years, raising the question of whether it could ever be right to surrender British subjects to such a brutal jurisdiction. At the same time, though, it was not immediately clear whether a persuasive moral defence could be mounted in support of a war fought to maintain the international *status quo* in a remote and sparsely populated part of the world some eight thousand miles away from the British mainland.

The Division of Social Responsibility liaised closely with the other main churches during the early stages of the Falklands crisis, endorsing the British Council of Churches' call on the British government to refrain from using force to resolve the situation in the South Atlantic.[21] The Secretary of the Division, the Revd Brian Duckworth, argued in the *Recorder* that no military action should be taken without specific permission from the United Nations Security Council.[22] The President's Council of the Methodist Church also sent a telegram to the Prime Minister urging restraint.[23] The *Recorder* carried numerous letters and articles attacking the decision to deploy the naval task force,[24] including a number by the Revd Kenneth Greet, a life-long pacifist and veteran of the Division of Social Responsibility, who was by now serving as Moderator of the Free Church Federal Council.[25] Such sentiments were not, though, shared by all contributors to the paper. One minister from Exeter took issue with all those whose opposition to the war was based on an unconditional pacifism, putting forward an argument that bore the clear imprint of the Christian realism of Reinhold Niebuhr: 'The beautiful and elevated moral maxims of the Sermon on the Mount are for the personal guidance of those who are walking by the Spirit, and cannot be applied to the laws of a secular state, most of whose citizens do not possess the mind of Christ.'[26] Other correspondents preferred to focus on the more practical dangers of appeasement. One warned that the DSR was, in questioning the British government's decision to dispatch the task force to the South Atlantic, 'taking us back again to 1938 and all we are hearing is a play-back of the sentiments their predecessors were then uttering'.[27] Another criticized those who 'undermine the great majority who are opposed to the evil regimes of the world'.[28] A Methodist chaplain who sailed with the task force argued that British policy towards the Falklands was designed to restore 'a way of life . . . usurped by force of arms'.[29] The *Recorder* also published some very sharp letters of complaint from readers condemning the reaction of Methodist leaders to the conflict. One contributor pointedly praised the Archbishop of Canterbury Robert Runcie for supporting military action, and criticized senior Methodists who took a more equivocal stand, or engaged in outright criticism of British policy.[30] Another contributor writing just after the war ended noted tartly that 'there seems to be a general assumption by those in positions of authority in our Church that what they have to say must necessarily be a true reflection of Methodist thinking across the Church. This has never been wholly so, and in the recent military situation even less than usual, I suspect.'[31]

The end of the South Atlantic conflict in June 1982, following the surrender of Argentinian forces, prompted a debate at Conference a few weeks later which once again revealed tensions between a section of the Methodist hierarchy and more 'grass-roots' sentiment. The DSR sponsored a resolution for approval by Conference welcoming the end of the war and offering condolences to the bereaved. The resolution also more controversially called on the British government to identify 'other ways than the use of force to maintain international security', and went on to urge that after a period of 'calm reflection' the government should open negotiations with Argentina about the long-term future of the Falkland Islands. During the debate on the resolution, Greet repeated his unconditional opposition to the use of military force, and deplored the recent events in the South Atlantic as 'a victory for militarism'. Brian Duckworth as Secretary of the DSR expressed the view that the 'victory would not last'. There was, however, disquiet among some delegates both

190

about the tone of the resolution and the statements by Greet and Duckworth. The Revd Gordon Wakefield from Queen's College told Conference that most Methodists had supported the war. The Revd Harry Warne noted that the tone of the resolution did not reflect the views of ordinary church members, and unsuccessfully sought to propose a motion that 'Conference expresses thankfulness for the liberation of the Falkland Islands and dependencies.'[32] The proceedings at Conference attracted some particularly sharp comments in the *Recorder* during the weeks that followed. One local councillor from Plymouth described Greet's comments as 'a slap in the face . . . for those who, in this and other conflicts, have bravely given themselves in the interests of a greater freedom'.[33] Other contributors attacked the refusal of Conference organizers to allow discussion of the thanksgiving motion proposed by Warne as a constraint on free discussion. The *Recorder* itself took a fairly equivocal editorial line on the subject, but in fostering such open debate the paper inevitably provided a stark insight into the scale of the tensions within the church over the conflict.

The sharp divisions among British Methodists over the Falklands War were echoed across the other main denominations. There was nevertheless a general reluctance across the churches to see the war as anything other than a tragic conflict that created enormous misery for all the casualties and their families. It was for this reason that so much controversy surrounded the Thanksgiving Service that was held at St Paul's Cathedral towards the end of July, a few weeks after the British recaptured Port Stanley and secured the surrender of Argentinian forces. Kenneth Greet was instrumental in ensuring that prayers for the dead of both sides were included in the service (a decision that attracted a good deal of media controversy). He was also asked by Cardinal Basil Hume to express concern to the Archbishop of Canterbury about the possibility of Margaret Thatcher reading one of the lessons, since it might make the service appear as an overtly 'political' act.[34] The religious affairs correspondent of *The Times* noted that the preparations for the service were 'the most striking demonstration in recent years of the fundamental tension between Church and State', adding that 'a service entirely designed in Downing Street' would have been far more triumphal in tone than the one that actually took place at St Paul's, which instead emphasized the need for reconciliation and repentance.[35] Many Conservative MPs were furious about the character of the Thanksgiving Service, believing that it failed to honour the sacrifices made by British servicemen who had died during the war. The disagreement in fact reflected a more profound division between the main churches and the government about many aspects of public policy during the 1980s, a subject that erupted again a few years later, when the *Faith in the City* report sharply rebuked the government for failing to deal with the problems of urban poverty. The Thatcher government was seen by many in the churches as a confrontational administration committed to policies that were bound to create division both at home and abroad.

## The Continuing Challenge of Nuclear Weapons

Although the level of public protest against nuclear weapons declined sharply in the mid-1960s, the following twenty years or so witnessed the publication of countless books and articles on the ethical questions raised by the possession and possible use of weapons of mass destruction. The British Council of Churches also regularly reviewed the issue. Three Methodists sat on a BCC working group that produced a report in 1963 on 'The British Nuclear Deterrent', most of whose members agreed that a unilateral renunciation of nuclear weapons by the British government would not advance multilateral disarmament, and might even represent a 'perilous reversal of policy'.[36] Among the minority who questioned this conclusion was John Vincent, a Methodist minister and Vice-President of the North-West Region of CND, as well as the author of a recent book on *Christ in a Nuclear World* (1962). Vincent's book provided a sophisticated attempt to think through some of the moral and political challenges posed by the existence of nuclear weapons to Christians who were not committed to an unconditional pacifism (as Vincent himself was not). *Christ in a Nuclear World* sought to develop a fresh approach by arguing that God's will was not a 'static' doctrine, that could be defined in straightforward and unchanging terms, but was instead only to be found in 'the singular and unique situation confronting man at a given time'.[37] Such an attempt to think through the challenge posed by nuclear weapons in the language of situational theology was far removed from the kinds of debates that had taken place within Methodism, and indeed across most of the other churches, during the previous fifteen years or so. Vincent sought to move beyond the 'black and white' language that had so often been used to discuss the question, arguing instead that 'Christ is where his deeds are done', even if that was in the USSR or China.[38] While some of Vincent's more traditional critics were unhappy with the tone of these arguments, which seemed at first glance to challenge many traditional Christian ideas and values, *Christ in a Nuclear World* performed a valuable service in seeking to confront the issue of nuclear weapons in a concrete fashion. Instead of referring to traditional arguments relating to the ethics of pacifism and just war, the book sought to transcend the barren categories that had so often previously characterized discussion on the subject. In a subsequent publication, written after the publication of the BCC report on 'The British Nuclear Deterrent', Vincent tried to ground his argument more firmly in the contemporary historical situation. While reiterating his claim that Christ had to be found 'in the pattern of politics', he made it clear that he believed it unlikely that Russia would seek to invade Britain if it renounced nuclear weapons, with the result that nuclear disarmament should be considered both 'morally and politically prudent'.[39]

A further and perhaps more surprising contribution to the debate over nuclear weapons was provided by the life-long Methodist and Cambridge historian Herbert Butterfield. It was seen in the last chapter that Butterfield had in the early 1950s espoused a form of Christian realism which assumed that international conflict could only ever be managed rather than resolved in an imperfect world.[40] In an essay published a few years later, on 'Human Nature and the

Dominion of Fear', he applied some of his ideas to the contemporary nuclear debate. The essay was in turn published in a slightly modified form in 1964 by Christian CND. In a sophisticated argument, Butterfield suggested that 'the destructiveness which some people are now prepared to contemplate, is not to be justified for the sake of any conceivable mundane object, any purported religious claim or supermundane purpose or any virtue that one system of organization can possess against another'.[41] Since the destruction of humanity would represent the end of any form of society altogether, it was absurd to claim 'that the world must perish rather than that justice should fail'.[42] There was in fact a clear consistency between such ideas and Butterfield's earlier reflections on international politics, in which he argued that any attempt to pursue a total war aimed at destroying an opponent could only serve to undermine the compromises that were necessary in the search for peace. The same 'realism' that had urged him to caution against placing international politics on too moralistic a foundation led him to believe that there were no causes so important that they could justify the use of nuclear weapons. *y Ay article on H.A.*

A rather different view of the challenge of maintaining peace was offered by the Revd E. Gordon Rupp in his 1965 Alex Wood Memorial Lecture on 'The Dilemmas of Peacemaking', in which he sharply criticized the 'pessimism' of modern continental theology, which 'denied any religious or theological significance to the hope of social or political amelioration'. He went on to add that if it was 'in history where Christ died, it is also where he rose again'.[43] Rupp's critique of a 'realism' that questioned the wisdom of applying Christian ethics directly to practical human problems articulated the instincts that had inspired Methodism since the time of Wesley. The church itself set up a 'Moral Theology Group' in 1970 to review the vexed problems involved in relating the principles of the New Testament to the complex realities of modern society, although the interface between 'theology' and 'society' necessarily remained an area of challenge and controversy, not least in the context of international politics. The DCC repeatedly condemned the slow pace of the various efforts made by governments around the world to promote disarmament, lamenting in its 1965 Annual Report that politicians and soldiers were unwilling to think outside their 'familiar ways' and imagine a world without weapons.[44] The Division's Executive Committee subsequently endorsed a proposal by the International Department of the BCC that Britain should consider forgoing the possession of nuclear weapons if it would help to 'secure a satisfactory non-proliferation' agreement (a rather futile suggestion given that the first British Polaris submarine went on patrol just a few months later). There was, though, still no shortage of voices challenging anything that could be seen as support for unilateral nuclear disarmament.[45] The debate began to fade somewhat in the 1970s, as discussion within the church on international affairs began to focus more on questions of international justice, although the DCC (and later the DSR) carefully followed the Strategic Arms Limitation Talks that began in the late 1960s. The *Recorder* also continued to print occasional articles and letters on nuclear weapons, including a heated debate on the rights and wrongs of the decision to drop atomic bombs on Japan, which was published on the 25th anniversary of Hiroshima. It was only with the election of the Thatcher government in 1979, though, that the issue of the British independent nuclear deterrent once again became a central focus of discussion and debate within the Methodist Church.

The new Prime Minister and her colleagues were determined to bolster Britain's defences against the threat which they believed the USSR posed to the values and interests of the western world.[46] It therefore moved quickly to authorize the replacement of Britain's Polaris nuclear deterrent with new submarines equipped with Trident missiles. Ministers also responded positively to requests by the American government to station intermediate-range cruise missiles in Britain, which the Ministry of Defence claimed was necessary to counter the threat posed by Soviet SS 20 missiles based in Eastern Europe. These decisions provoked a hostile response across large sections of British society, a reaction that was for many bound up with a wider anger about the controversial social and economic policies pursued by the Thatcher government, which were blamed for creating a massive rise in unemployment and social deprivation. The Soviet invasion of Afghanistan in December 1979 also helped to polarize public debate in Britain about both international politics in general and nuclear weapons in particular, as the deteriorating international situation seemed to raise the possibility of a more serious conflict. The rapid revival of CND and the establishment of peace camps outside military bases like the one at Greenham Common in Berkshire attracted huge attention in the media,[47] while the decision of the 1980 Labour Party Conference to commit itself to unilateral nuclear disarmament placed the future of Britain's independent deterrent firmly on the political agenda. The divisions within British society over nuclear weapons were once again echoed in all the main churches. In 1980 the BCC adopted a resolution declaring that 'the doctrine of deterrence based upon the prospect of mutually assured destruction is increasingly offensive to the Christian conscience'.[48] Two years later, a Church of England working party chaired by the Bishop of Salisbury produced a report on 'The Church and the Bomb', which questioned whether the use of nuclear weapons could ever be reconciled with the doctrine of the just war or the Christian duty of stewardship for creation, and recommended that the Church should urge the government to abolish the British nuclear deterrent. The 'Church and the Bomb' predictably attracted enormous attention in the press, since it was widely seen as evidence of the worsening relationship between the government and the established church, although in the event the General Synod voted against supporting unilateral British disarmament in February 1983.[49] The United Reformed Church, by contrast, expressed its support for scrapping the British nuclear deterrent.[50]

The debate about nuclear weapons also erupted within the Methodist Church during these years. The new editor of the *Recorder*, Michael Taylor, introduced a regular 'Peace Platform' column that provoked wide-ranging discussion on a whole host of issues relating to disarmament and security. Some ministers used their weekly sermons to encourage congregations to think about the issue and not 'bury our heads in the sand'.[51] The early 1980s also witnessed a sharp increase in the number of circuits and districts submitting suggestions and memorials to Conference calling for reductions in defence expenditure and the abolition of the arms trade, reflecting renewed concern on such issues at the 'grass-roots' level of the church.[52] Concern about the arms trade became particularly pronounced following the publication in 1982 of Kenneth Greet's book *The Big Sin: Christianity and the Arms Race*, which powerfully attacked 'the most cynical and unprincipled trade the world has ever seen'.[53] The decision by the British government to purchase the Trident missile system and authorize the deployment of new American missiles in the UK served as a particular focus for concern. The 1980 Conference in Sheffield supported a DSR Resolution that Polaris submarines should not be replaced when they came to the end of their operational life. Two years later Conference duly criticized the British government's decision to purchase Trident. Conference also approved on a number of occasions a nuclear freeze, effectively rejecting the deployment of intermediate cruise and Pershing missiles in Britain. Such decisions were far from universally popular within the wider church. The *Recorder* published many letters from contributors who condemned critics of the British government's defence strategy for relying on 'emotive language' to bolster their case.[54]

Some critics of nuclear pacifists within the main British churches believed that the revitalized peace movement was primarily an expression of a long tradition of political radicalism, which failed to offer 'a specifically Christian contribution with respectable theological credentials' to the debate about nuclear weapons.[55] A number also suggested that too many of the pronouncements issuing from the churches 'merely echo the contentions of the secular order'.[56] There was certainly unease among delegates at the 1981 and 1982 Methodist Conferences that debate about nuclear weapons within the church had become too focused on 'technical' issues rather than fundamental principles. It was for this reason that the Division of Social Responsibility was instructed by the 1982 Conference to prepare a report reviewing the theological arguments for unilateral and multilateral nuclear disarmament. The furore that followed its eventual publication bore an uncanny resemblance to the row created within the Church of England over 'The Church and the Bomb'. The DSR report took as its starting-point the principle that the use of nuclear weapons would represent 'a denial of the stewardship over the world to which God has called us'.[57] It then went on to review the 'widely polarised' arguments put forward in favour of both multilateral and unilateral disarmament. The authors suggested when reviewing the case for unilateral disarmament that nuclear weapons perverted 'the very building blocks of creation' in order to 'undo that which was done, to put God's purposes into reverse', and added that a decision to renounce them could be defended in theological terms as an example of 'the politics of forgiveness' at the level of the state. The discussion of the theological foundations of the case for multilateral disarmament was less positive in tone, and focused primarily on the practical reasons for such an approach, rather than seeking to define a more specifically theological foundation for the possession of nuclear weapons. It is not surprising given the tone of the report that its most striking conclusion was support for 'a decision to discontinue the British nuclear deterrent'. The authors were keen to stress that such a unilateral initiative should be understood as a staging post in the search for wider multilateral disarmament, an approach that was doubtless designed to carve out some common ground, but their recommendation nevertheless raised enormous controversy at the 1983 Conference. The report had already provoked considerable criticism in the *Recorder* before Conference assembled, facing attack for favouring dramatic gestures rather than serious thought, while some contributors even argued it was dishonest for seeking to blur the distinction between multilateral and unilateral disarmament.[58] The attacks continued when the report was discussed. One ministerial delegate condemned the report for being 'neither fair, honest, reliable nor whole'. Another suggested that the biblical foundations of the report were 'weak'. Although many voices were also raised in favour of the report, at the end of the debate Conference voted narrowly that it should be received rather than welcomed. Like the Church of England General Synod a few months before, the Methodist Church refused to put its collective weight behind the unilateralist cause, recognizing that the division of opinion among its members precluded such a controversial move.

The decision by Conference highlighted the thorny question of determining how the Methodist Church should react to the activities of those who were ready to engage in acts of non-violent civil disobedience in order to express their dissent from the British government's policies on nuclear weapons. The early 1980s saw a sharp rise in the number of incidents among demonstrators at such military installations as the nuclear submarine base at Faslane and the US airbase at Lakenheath in Suffolk, where protestors frequently tried to block roads and scale perimeter fences. The best-known setting for such protests was the American airbase at Greenham Common, which became the site of the celebrated women's peace camp, established in 1981 to provide a visible symbol of protest against the deployment of cruise missiles there. Members of all the main churches were represented among those who participated in various forms of non-violent direct action, including the present Archbishop of Canterbury Rowan Williams, who was arrested in 1985 for breaking into an American air base and reading psalms on the runway. The organization Christian CND (whose national chairman in 1983 was a member of the Methodist Church) sought to bring together all those who believed that 'the wholesale destruction threatened by these weapons makes their possession and use an offence against God and humanity'. An ordained Catholic priest, Bruce Kent, played a pivotal leadership role in the main CND organization itself. The ethical questions surrounding the whole business of civil disobedience continued, though, to prove a divisive issue for the churches. Since the British government was democratically elected it could legitimately claim a formal mandate for its decisions. Nor do opinion polls taken at the time suggest that public opinion was uniformly opposed to the deployment of Trident and cruise. Those who engaged in acts of civil disobedience were in effect claim-

ing that their absolute conviction about the immorality of deploying new nuclear weapons 'trumped' their obligations to abide by the
law and the outcome of the democratic process. The situation was
not of course a novel one. The conscientious objectors who refused
to fight in the two world wars also based their claim to exemption
from conscription on the grounds that they could not accept the
'official' view that it was morally correct to use force to defeat an
enemy of the state. Most COs were however motivated by a desire
to assert their *own* right not to fight; they seldom advocated civil
disobedience to stop others from fighting. Those who challenged
the deployment of Trident and cruise were by contrast claiming that
acts of civil disobedience were justified where the existing laws were
being used to protect an immoral and unfair status quo. The potential ramifications of such a doctrine for public order in a democratic
society were dramatic.

The whole question of civil disobedience attracted a good deal of
discussion in the Methodist Church during the early 1980s. Many
Methodists were themselves involved in the protests that took place
up and down the country at places like Greenham Common and
Lakenheath. One former female local preacher, herself the daugh-
ter and granddaughter of pacifists, played a prominent role in the
Greenham Common camp from the moment it was first established
in 1981.[59] The motivations expressed by Methodists who engaged
in non-violent civil disobedience were predictably diverse. Some
viewed it as an inevitable concomitant of their commitment to an
unconditional pacifism, inspired by an understanding of Christ's
command to 'turn the other cheek' as an absolute ethical injunction. For others it was part of a broader rejection of the militarist
values that supposedly dominated western society. A number of
Methodists who engaged in non-violent direct action during the
early 1980s acknowledged that their experience led to an erosion
of their Christian faith, although others found that it helped to
deepen beliefs that had previously been remote from the problems
of the world. The issue of civil disobedience aroused a particularly
passionate debate in the *Recorder* in 1983 when the President of

Conference, the Revd N.E. Denny, visited Greenham Common and announced that he believed it was 'sometimes necessary to break the law in the struggle for peace'.[60] He added that he would himself be ready to sit in the road in order to block the movement of cruise missiles. His words provoked a stormy response in the letters column of the paper. One minister said that it should be made clear that the President was speaking in a private capacity; another contributor attacked those who provided support for the 'troublesome women' at Greenham.[61] Many correspondents pointed out that there would be anarchy if every individual chose to break the law according to the dictates of their own conscience, while one of them suggested that the Greenham peace camp was sponsored by 'the Soviets, the Communists and other extremists of this country'.[62] The *Recorder* also received many letters, though, noting that civil disobedience had 'an honourable place in the history of Christian and moral protest movements'.[63] The issue predictably attracted attention at Conference in 1983, not least because one district had recently passed a motion noting that 'Christian obedience can lead in some circumstances to non-violent disobedience.' As there was a general recognition that the complex theological and political questions surrounding the whole subject could not be easily resolved – this was also the Conference at which there was such a stormy debate about the British nuclear deterrent – the issue was referred to the DSR for further discussion. The Division for its part appointed a working party charged with eliciting opinion from across the church and devising some form of statement to be reviewed at a future Conference.

The interim report presented to Conference the following year was based on a putative exchange of letters between a church member who was considering whether to break the law and two correspondents who believed that such an approach could not be justified. This unusual format proved surprisingly effective at dramatizing the complex issues involved. The letter-writer who was contemplating civil disobedience in protest against Britain's possession of nuclear weapons based their position on the principle that 'back to New Testament times there have been Christians who have disobeyed the law for conscience's sake'. The author added that those who shared such views were convinced that 'democracy doesn't end with expressing [an] opinion in a general election', but instead required a more active and sustained engagement in political activities, in order to prevent governments from becoming disengaged from those who elected them. The respondents urged that any decision to engage in civil disobedience should involve careful reflection, given the potential for such acts to undermine 'the fragile nature of the contract by which we all agree to live and let live within the law'. They also argued that since there was 'a democratic way of changing things' in Britain, there was a duty to 'accept the will of the majority', expressing dissent through lawful channels rather than through direct action that involved breaking the law. The working party that produced the interim report refrained from adjudicating on such irreconcilable positions, contenting itself with noting that Conference had already committed the church to pastoral support of those who 'may in conscience be compelled to refuse work on certain military projects, with consequent loss of employment'.[64] The whole question of non-violent civil disobedience began to fade away in the mid-1980s, once the appointment of Mikhail Gorbachev as Soviet leader in 1985 held out the prospect of a relaxation of international tension, with the result that the issue began to attract less attention in the Methodist press and at Conference. Many individual members of the Methodist Church nevertheless continued to engage in various forms of direct protest, arguing that the possession of nuclear weapons was not only immoral, but also undermined global peace by creating a climate of suspicion and uncertainty.

## The Focus on the South

The debate within the Methodist Church over nuclear weapons during the early 1980s came after a period in which most attention had concentrated on a very different set of international questions:

those relating to the establishment of a more equitable international economic system and the defeat of racism in southern Africa. This focus on North–South issues was at times controversial. The DCC/DSR often received letters accusing it of publicizing the iniquities of the apartheid regime in South Africa while ignoring the abuses of power that took place behind the Iron Curtain. The Division's staff in fact spent a good deal of time monitoring the human rights situation in Eastern Europe, particularly after the Helsinki Final Act was signed in 1975, and regularly made representations to the Soviet Embassy in London on behalf of dissidents facing imprisonment or persecution in the USSR. They also monitored the situation of the churches behind the Iron Curtain (a subject that commanded the sustained attention of the British Council of Churches).[65] In 1980 the President of Conference and members of the DSR joined a deputation to the Soviet Embassy to protest against the invasion of Afghanistan by Soviet troops. The DSR also served as a focus during the 1980s for extensive discussions designed to identify and articulate the theological foundations of human rights.[66] There was nevertheless a degree of truth in the suggestion that some prominent members of the Methodist Church were by the 1970s convinced that poverty and racism in the developing world represented the greatest challenge to the international community. Nor was such a position untenable given the depth of the difficulties that plagued the poor countries of the world. The attempt by all the main churches to raise awareness of the problems faced by the developing nations represented a valid attempt to highlight a subject that often failed to attract great attention in wealthy places like Britain.

The shift from an East–West to a North–South perspective can be seen in the writings of Edward Rogers, the long-serving Secretary of the Department of Christian Citizenship. Although the previous chapter showed that Rogers played a significant part in shaping the response of the Methodist Church to the ideological challenge of communism during the 1940s and 1950s, he was by the early 1960s convinced that global conflict was no longer mainly a matter of 'an ideological division between the Communist and non-Communist world', but was instead fuelled by 'a basically irrational division between the rich and the white and the coloured and the poor'.[67] He was not alone in expressing such views. Many other scholars and churchmen were also starting to focus their attention during this period on the causes of poverty in the developing world. Rogers himself published a book with SCM Press in 1964, under the title *Living Standards: A Christian Looks at the World's Poverty*, in which he began to think through some of these issues in a sustained manner. While he acknowledged that relieving poverty in the developing world would require major cultural and political changes in many poor countries, he also argued that the countries of the developed world needed to do far more to help, both by opening their markets and by stabilizing the prices of key exports from the South. Perhaps the most dramatic part of Rogers' book focused on his attempt to convince his readers that the struggle against global poverty was a central part of the wider struggle for world peace. He argued that the era of 'old fashioned power politics and half-baked ideologies' was coming to an end, and that 'the kaleidoscope of international relations is settling to a new pattern', in which glaring international inequality was the most likely source of conflict between nations. There was as a result a need for 'a serious urgent campaign against poverty' that represented 'the alternative to war'.[68] The strength of Rogers' book rested in its attempt to understand the economic forces that were driving the growing division between the 'haves' and the 'have nots'. Although he was wrong in claiming that the ideological and political divisions between East and West were fading away, as the countries of the communist bloc became wealthier, Rogers provided his readers with a valuable reassessment of the challenges facing the main churches when dealing with the international environment.

The issue of global poverty soon began to resound more loudly within the institutional apparatus of the Methodist Church. The 1966 Annual Conference endorsed the conclusions of a recent British Council of Churches document on 'World Poverty and British Responsibility', which roundly declared 'that as long as a part of the human family live in misery no part of the Universal Church ought to remain undisturbed'.[69] Two years later, a report by the Methodist Church's Joint Overseas Christian Citizenship Committee called for an increase in international aid, and an overhaul of rich countries' trade policies, in order to benefit farmers in the poor world. There was also extensive discussion about more practical steps the church could itself take. The *Recorder* carried articles debating whether a proportion of the funds raised by the sale of church property should be donated to Christian Aid,[70] a proposal that actually met strong opposition in some quarters, while campaigns were also launched from time to time to convince 'rank and file' church members to give a day's pay to the Methodist Development Fund. A number of Methodist authors penned passionate books and articles seeking to persuade their readers that questions of poverty and justice should be placed at the heart of their church's activities. Colin Morris, who had for many years worked in Zambia, wrote in 1968 that the real 'obscenity' of the modern world was 'the jewelled ring on a bishop's finger ... the flash of my gold wrist watch from under the sleeve of my cassock as I throw dirt on the coffin of a man who died of starvation'.[71] He also sought to provide his readers with a theological basis for such dramatic views, arguing that 'the saving work of Jesus is in the concrete deed', rather than in the proclamation of barren formulae or dry biblical texts. Nor was he alone in expressing such views. The *Recorder* was by the late 1960s publishing many articles calling for the rich world to address the problem of global poverty.

The focus on development issues became still more pronounced during the 1970s. A dedicated World Development Desk was set up in the DCC in 1971, charged with handling a range of associated issues, while the growth in its work partly accounted for a subsequent Conference decision to assign a third secretary to the Division. The memorials and suggestions submitted to Conference by districts and circuits suggested that interest in development questions was also growing at the 'grass roots' level. In 1972, for example, one district synod submitted a memorial calling on the British government to adjust its trade policies and allow greater access to the

British market for exports from developing countries. A few years later, the language used in church reports was becoming still more radical, as discussion of 'charity' and 'aid' continued to give way to a focus on the mechanisms through which rich countries exploited their poorer neighbours. The section on World Development in the DSR's 1979 Annual Report stated baldly that 'the root causes of poverty [in the South] lie mainly in the acquisitive style of life lived by the industrial peoples'. It also announced that members of the Division intended to spend some time exploring the ways in which multinational companies exploited the poor countries where they had operations (a theme that was becoming increasingly important at this time in the academic literature on development). The DSR's Annual Report for 1980 went even further, seeking to provide its readers with some theological reflections on the whole question of underdevelopment and aid:

> Our involvement in World Development has enabled us to realise more clearly that we are being harnessed to the process of 'redemption' – a word rooted in economics and still implying, we believe, an economic and political as well as a spiritual meaning. Christ 'buys back' His world from the thraldom of its old order, the unredeemed order to which we subscribe so long as we share in its acquisitive goals and its opportunist and sensual manner of living.

The report went on to note that the Bible called on its readers to 'express our compassion in efforts not simply to alleviate the symptoms of recurring distress but to right the wrongs which ensure their recurrence'. Its authors added for good measure that Wesley's concern with the poor meant that all Methodists had a key role to play in 'combating the basic causes of world injustice'.[72] Such language was very different from the language in which development and poverty had been discussed within Methodism just twenty years earlier. By 1980 responsibility for world poverty was firmly placed with the wealthy of the world.

The second major issue that attracted debate within the Methodist

Church on the problems facing the developing world was the question of racism. The close historical ties of British Methodism with
southern Africa, which dated far back into the nineteenth century,
meant that developments in Rhodesia and South Africa attracted
particular attention. The crisis in Rhodesia had been brewing for
many years before the government headed by Ian Smith took the
decision in 1965 to issue a Unilateral Declaration of Independence
from Britain, in order to avoid pressure from London to hand over
the country 'to irresponsible rule', a phrase that was in effect code
for black majority rule.[73] The DCC Report submitted to the 1964
Annual Conference firmly opposed independence for Rhodesia – in
contrast to the Department's usual positive position on decolonization – since it would 'perpetuate government by a minority group'.[74]
The following year a former chairman of Conference, the Revd H.J.
Lawrence, wrote to the *Recorder* noting that 'If disaster in Rhodesia
is to be avoided the British Government must act decisively and
speedily to give Africans the political and personal freedom to which
they are entitled.'[75] When the Rhodesian government finally made
its Unilateral Declaration of Independence, a few months later, the
Methodist Church's General Purposes and Policy Committee quickly
issued a statement 'deeply deploring' the move. The Revd H.O.
Morton, who was at the time Secretary of the Methodist Missionary
Society, wrote an article in the *Recorder* arguing that the crisis over
Rhodesia confronted Britain with a profound 'moral issue', and went
on to urge the British government to refuse to accept the de facto
'creation of a second South Africa'.[76] A few voices were raised in the
Methodist press suggesting that the African population was not yet
'civilized' enough for democracy – an opinion that was also heard
in some other quarters during this period – but they were very few
in number. There was rather more criticism of church leaders for
failing to match their condemnation of the Rhodesian government
with equally sharp denunciations of the Berlin Wall.[77]

The British government's decision to impose economic sanctions on Rhodesia following the Smith government's Unilateral
Declaration of Independence was extensively discussed (and

approved) by the British Council of Churches. The Methodist Conference also passed a resolution in 1968 supporting sanctions, although some of the letters printed in the *Recorder* questioned whether it was morally justified 'to inflict hardship on a people in an attempt to coerce them in their political belief'.[78] The subject was discussed again at Conference the following year, while in 1970 Rupert Davies emphasized in his Presidential Address that the Methodist Church remained staunchly opposed 'to racism in any form whatever and to the policy of the Ian Smith Government in Rhodesia in particular'. There was, though, a further development in the region that posed a difficult challenge for all the churches. The guerrilla war that was launched against the Smith government, which received considerable logistical support from 'front-line' states such as Zambia and Mozambique, raised the problem of determining when (if ever) it was acceptable to use force to promote a desirable political objective. One Methodist minister who took a particular interest in this question was Colin Morris. In his book *Unyoung, Uncoloured, Unpoor*, published in 1969, Morris roundly declared that 'I believe a Christian is justified in using violence to win freedom in Rhodesia: I know of no other way to win it.' He went on to note that 'Non-violent revolution is like non-alcoholic wines a symbol of sorts but a poor substitute for the real thing.' Morris also argued that 'Terrorism is the only means by which desperate men can dramatize their grievances in a system which controls all the media of education and communication and uses them without scruple to distort the truth about human suffering.'[79] Morris was a long-standing friend of Kenneth Kaunda, the President of Zambia, who had himself become a supporter of the armed struggle in Rhodesia despite his earlier commitment to the principle of non-violent resistance. Kaunda was well-aware of the ethical dilemmas that bedevilled the question of 'whether Christians can themselves use force in the service of justice or actively encourage others to do the same'.[80] The answer for unconditional pacifists was on the face of it unambiguously negative, although a surprising number of pacifists within the Methodist Church seemed reluctant to say so very forcefully, doubtless reflect-

What Does Morris in 2008 think of Mugabe??

ing the competing imperatives involved.[81] The question was more complex for those in the churches who accepted the principle that war could sometimes be justified. Was it possible – either practically or theologically – to make a distinction between a 'defensive' war fought to deter aggression and an 'offensive' war designed to promote the cause of justice? The question was not of course a new one. It was seen in a previous chapter that it posed a significant dilemma in the final quarter of the nineteenth century, when there was extensive debate within Methodism over the rights and wrongs of supporting military action to prevent the slaughter of Christians in the Ottoman lands of south-east Europe. The dilemma also later re-emerged in the 1990s, at a time when the British government launched its 'ethical foreign policy' in response to the wars that erupted in former Yugoslavia. The negotiated solution of the Rhodesian issue in the late 1970s, which came about when a mixture of internal changes and external pressure led to regime change and the creation of the new state of Zimbabwe, resolved the immediate crisis but not the broader moral issue. In November 1979, the Revd David Haslam, who was closely involved in the anti-apartheid movement, noted in a letter to the *Recorder* that 'It seems to me now perfectly clear that the real agent for change in Southern Africa is the armed struggle . . . That is the only way that the whites will be forced to face up to the deep and far-reaching changes that are necessary.'[82] Many of the paper's other correspondents did not welcome such strong views.

Many of the sharpest disagreements about support for the 'liberation movements' of southern Africa were provoked by the question of the church's contributions to the World Council of Churches' Fund to Combat Racism. It was widely claimed in the British press that money donated by the Fund to charitable causes was diverted to groups involved in the armed struggle, leading one delegate at the 1971 Conference to suggest that the Methodist Church was in danger of 'taking up a position of support for violent methods'.[83] The issue continued to bubble away in the years that followed. The decision of the Overseas Division to donate an extra £1,000 to the Fund to Combat Racism, in the spring of 1974, led to a number of memorials being submitted to Conference suggesting that such an action was 'incompatible with the Gospel we preach'.[84] The church hierarchy refused to respond to such demands. Edward Rogers dismissed press reports that money from the Fund to Combat Racism was being diverted to guerrillas in southern Africa as 'politically-motivated'. The response of the Memorials Committee was similarly cautious, noting that the 1972 Annual Conference had declared its support for donations to the WCC Fund. Such responses in turn provoked a good deal of anger, not least because of a sense that the church leadership was not being even-handed. The Revd J.M. Turner from Queen's College had already complained the previous year that although Methodists should never forget the victims of the 'satanic system of apartheid', there were equally vile regimes elsewhere in the world acting 'in the name of Marx and Lenin',[85] while correspondents in the *Recorder* complained that their church did not pay enough attention to the iniquities of non-white regimes in countries like Pakistan and Nigeria.[86] The issue of contributions to the WCC Fund to Combat Racism rumbled on for a number of years, leading some members to threaten resignation from the church,[87] while in 1979 it was proposed that payments to the WCC Fund should not be given out of general funds in order to allow 'a freeing of the consciences of the Methodist people'.[88] The whole issue was unexpectedly resolved when the Charity Commissioners ruled that donations to the Fund were not permitted under the current regulations, apparently on the rather curious procedural basis that eliminating racial inequalities was not strictly speaking a charitable activity.

The apartheid regime in South Africa provoked even more discussion within Methodism than its counterpart in Rhodesia, particularly after the Soweto riots of 1976 concentrated the attention of the world's media on the country. During the 1970s, staff in the DCC/DSR opposed sporting links with South Africa, rejecting the argument that they could foster a multi-racial approach to sport.[89] The Division also put pressure on the British government to retain its arms embargo on the country.[90] Such activities were not always appreciated by a small minority of church members, one of whom complained in the *Recorder* that he was sick of being lectured 'by the ungrateful Asians and the non-whites of Africa'. Another pointedly noted that the church's grass roots was not generally 'comprised of starry-eyed, heads-in-the-sand socialists'.[91] The DCC was aware that its critics believed it gave 'too much attention' to developments in southern Africa,[92] and sought to offer reassurance that it was also concerned with human rights abuses in Eastern Europe,[93] but the focus on South Africa continued to provoke sharp exchanges in the *Recorder*. One of the main objectives of anti-apartheid campaigners in Britain and across the western world was to prevent external investment in South Africa. Since the Methodist Church itself had considerable funds invested in companies with activities that were linked in some way to South Africa, it is hardly surprising that the Central Finance Board began to face criticism for not doing more to change its investment portfolio. Pauline Webb, who served at the time as Vice-Moderator of the World Council of Churches, complained at the 1973 Conference that 'British firms exceeded the apartheid regime in their zeal for repression'.[94] Her sentiments were echoed by Colin Morris. The chairman of the Finance Board responded by arguing that the black population would suffer most from disinvestment, and added that by maintaining its investments in companies active in South Africa, the church might have the opportunity to exercise some leverage over their operations.[95] The dilemma was summed up in the Annual Address of the 1973 Conference to the Methodist Societies, which acknowledged that divisions rested on a 'genuine dilemma as to whether the ills of the world are better healed by dramatic gestures of unequivocal witness or by persistent, unheralded diplomacy'.[96]

The question of church investment in South Africa exploded most dramatically at the 1974 Conference, when a number of protestors shut down the microphone while the Revd Derek Farrow from the Finance Board was addressing the delegates. Farrow had again attempted to point out that the Methodist Church only had investments in companies that were active in South Africa as part of their general operations, rather than as the core of their busi-

*How important was Haslam?*

ness, but his critics argued that 'polite conversations' with company boards would never force profit-driven organizations to reconsider their *modus operandi*. The protest was organized in part by David Haslam, who in a charged letter to the *Recorder* argued that the decision to block out the sound system was designed to make delegates realize what it was like for black South Africans to be silenced in their own land. He also criticized the 'insensitivity' of the response of Conference delegates, most of whom responded angrily to the protest, a reaction that Haslam suggested 'smacked more of the white oppressors ... than the blacks oppressed'.[97] Although the views of the protesters on South Africa were shared by a considerable number of delegates, there was general repugnance at the way in which the normally staid proceedings of the Annual Conference were disrupted so dramatically. The tradition of Methodist radicalism had for countless decades been articulated in an essentially conservative fashion. The 'happening' at the 1974 Conference showed how changes in the wider political culture were starting to impact deeply on the life of the Methodist Church itself.

## Conclusion

Every generation believes it faces challenges and upheavals that are greater than those that confronted its predecessors, and historians may in years to come suggest that the changes that took place across the world between 1960 and 1985 were no more far-reaching than in any other recent 25-year span of history. There can nevertheless be little doubt that the period was a challenging one for all the main churches in Great Britain. The ongoing process of secularization continued to erode church attendance, as well as exercizing a profound influence on the opinions and activities of those who claimed some kind of allegiance to the Christian faith. It was also accompanied by radical new departures in theology that – for many – challenged fundamental beliefs about the purpose and the nature of the world-wide Church. A central paradox rested at the heart of the situation faced by the major churches in Great Britain. All of them were conservative institutions whose values and *modus operandi* seemed increasingly archaic in a changing world. While there was a widespread rhetorical acknowledgement that they needed to 'modernize' in order to engage fully with the contemporary situation, there was much less consensus about what form such 'modernization' should take. The Methodist Church of Great Britain was not immune from these pressures. Although the church had from its earliest days proved effective at preaching a 'social gospel' predicated on the need to respond to the demands of the world, its activities had as often as not been framed within a moral (and perhaps moralistic) framework that seemed increasingly outmoded by the 1960s. The Methodist Church was in reality a curious amalgam of the contemporary and the archaic. The views of some of its younger and more intellectually dynamic ministers and lay members were undoubtedly attuned to the demands of the age, but they also explicitly or implicitly challenged much that passed for traditional Methodism. Nor can this schism be reduced to something as simple as a generational difference over mere customs and conventions. More fundamental questions both about the meaning of the gospel and the nature of mission were at stake. Many 'traditionalists' were perfectly happy to concede that new styles of worship were required to engage with a changing 'audience', but they insisted that the 'message' itself remained unchanging and eternal. 'Radicals' were by contrast convinced that there was a need for a more fundamental re-evaluation of the gospel that emphasized the inherent dynamism of faith and belief. The distinction was hardly new – but it became more obvious at a time of such massive social and political change. There was perhaps a note of ruefulness in the words of the 1971 'Address of the Methodist Conference to the Methodist Societies', which noted that 'Conflicting ways of thought, attitudes of mind and conviction of heart make modern Methodism a mosaic of most variegated pattern.'[98]

There was a marked change in the international concerns of the Methodist Church during the years between 1960 and 1985. While the discussions that periodically erupted over nuclear weapons echoed the debates that had taken place in the 1950s, there was by the end of the period a growing recognition that the Methodist Church needed to make a sustained attempt to engage systematically with the theological questions that flowed from the existence of weapons of mass destruction. The outbreak of the Falklands War in 1982 similarly encouraged renewed reflection on the vexed question of whether even a non-nuclear war could ever do more good than harm in the modern world. It nevertheless remains the case that the most striking innovation in discussion of international questions within the Methodist Church during these years was the rapidly growing concern with questions of international poverty and economic justice. While the development of a practical theology that emphasized the need for hard thinking about the structure of global economic and political power was influenced in part by the emergence of liberation theology, in all its manifold forms, it also represented a real attempt to rethink the traditional concerns of British Methodism on a larger scale. Although there was no shortage of voices within the church expressing reservations about the process, it seems clear that many 'rank and file' Methodists were themselves greatly influenced by the scenes that periodically appeared on their television screens, depicting the horror of famine and the bloodshed in places like Soweto. It does, though, remain true that such issues were still of more concern to the church hierarchy than they were to the ordinary member. There is certainly no doubt that any historian who tried to reconstruct the texture of international politics during these years purely from the records of the Methodist Church would receive a distinctive view of the major issues and conflicts of the day. The East–West issues that preoccupied politicians and the secular media were increasingly 'swamped' by the issues of North–South inequality in the internal dialogue of British Methodism. There is of course a potential justification for such a phenomenon. Many church leaders believed that they had a duty to speak out on a subject that was too often marginalized in the mainstream political discourse of the wealthy nations of the world. It is not clear from this distance in time that they were wrong to do so.

# 8

# Facing a New World

## Introduction

The second half of the 1980s witnessed the dramatic unravelling of the international order that had been established in Europe at the end of the Second World War. The appointment of Mikhail Gorbachev as General Secretary of the Soviet Communist Party, in March 1985, put in motion a process of radical domestic reform that led in time to the implosion of the Soviet Union and the decline of the bipolar division of the world.[1] The collapse of the Berlin Wall in November 1989 prompted a general euphoria in the West, a sentiment articulated by the first President Bush in 1992, when he told an audience in Washington that 'By the grace of God, America won the cold war.'[2] There were, though, exceptions to this triumphalist tone. Many on the left in Britain expressed anxiety about the prospect of a new era in which the ideology of the free market would prove rampant. The response of the major churches to the collapse of communism in Eastern Europe was also quite muted. The Archbishop of Canterbury, Robert Runcie, reflected the views of many senior churchmen when he wrote at the end of 1989 that 'The nearer capitalism comes to triumphing totally, the more questions are raised about its capacity to be magnanimous in victory, to heed the cries of the poor at home and abroad, to seek the paths of peace and to care tenderly for the earth.'[3] Runcie's concerns were echoed by many in the Methodist Church, which was hardly surprising given that numerous resolutions approved by Conference in the 1970s and 1980s had argued that poverty in the developing world was a consequence of the operation of the global market economy. The political changes that took place in Eastern Europe and the USSR during the 1980s were welcomed by Conference, and in the Methodist press, but more attention was given to the continuation of apartheid in South Africa and the challenge of poverty in Africa and Asia. While there was concern in some quarters that senior figures in the church were reluctant to acknowledge the 'bankruptcy of Marxism-Leninism',[4] manifested in the collapse of the Soviet bloc, it is hard to know whether such voices echoed deeper grass-roots unease about the leadership's concern with what one prominent figure called 'a fashionable mess of political pottage'.[5] It is certainly the case that the end of the Cold War did not resolve the massive global disparities of wealth and power that had come to determine the Methodist Church's international agenda over the previous two decades or so.

The collapse of communism did not in the event mark the 'end of history' or the triumph of liberal capitalism across the globe.[6] It instead heralded the transition to a new world *disorder* in which ethnic conflict and religious hatred became the defining motifs of international politics. The first Gulf War that broke out in 1991, following Iraq's invasion of Kuwait, was not itself the product of religious conflict. It did nevertheless fuel new patterns of geopolitical instability and ideological antipathy that fostered greater suspicion between the 'Christian' and 'Muslim' worlds in the years that followed. The eruption of the Yugoslav wars in the early 1990s, which led to hundreds of thousands of deaths, was the consequence of deep-seated legacies of ethnic and religious hatred. So, too, was the genocide in Rwanda. It is equally possible to identify an ethnic or religious dimension to conflicts in areas as diverse as Haiti, East Timor and Eritrea. The main western governments faced enormous problems when deciding how to respond to the breakdown of the old international order. Should they use their military forces to intervene abroad to prevent bloodshed and slaughter? And, if so, did they have the moral authority and political resources to ensure that such action did not create more problems than it resolved? Even more importantly, perhaps, could western governments make an

honest distinction in their own minds between the need for humanitarian intervention and the temptation to advance their narrow
national interests under the cover of a convenient moral rhetoric?[7]
The challenges faced by the international community during these
years was made more complex by the rise of a whole set of further
issues, ranging from environmental decay through to economic and
financial globalization, which together created a world in which it
was hard for governments to calculate the consequences of their
actions.[8] Policy-makers had to engage in a 'paradigm shift' in order
to develop the ideas and concepts needed to comprehend the global
changes taking place around them.

The debates that took place in the Methodist Church following
the end of the Cold War provided a curious echo of the ones that
had erupted in the late nineteenth century, when the proponents
of the Nonconformist conscience agonized about how best to help
Christians facing persecution in the Ottoman Empire. The rest of
this chapter focuses on reactions within Methodism to the challenges posed by the increasingly interventionist policies adopted
by the main western governments following the end of the Cold
War. Senior figures in the Methodist Church sought to work more
closely than ever in this period with representatives from the other
main denominations, via such organizations as the Council on
Christian Approaches on Disarmament (CCAD) and the Council
of Churches in Britain and Ireland (CCBI), recognizing the need to
share expertise and co-operate in seeking to influence government
policy. There were for example three members of the Methodist
Church on the Balkans Working Group set up by the CCBI, while
Brian Duckworth from the Division of Social Responsibility played
a significant role on the Management Committee of the CCAD,
which gave a good deal of attention during this period to determining the conditions that justified outside military intervention to
relieve humanitarian suffering.[9] The following pages also pay some
attention to the ongoing focus of the Methodist Church on North–
South issues as the fundamental leitmotiv of international politics.
The duty to apply Christian principles to the complex problems of

international politics continued to foster substantial divisions in the church during these years – divisions that were rooted both in competing interpretations of global developments *and* in more fundamental disagreement about how to implement Christian teachings on peace and war in the arena of practical politics. The years following the Cold War graphically showed the need for some fresh thinking about the problem of determining when and how it might be possible to reconcile the use of force in the international system with the dictates of the Christian conscience.

## The First Gulf War

Any hope that the end of the Cold War would lead to a new era of global peace was brutally destroyed at the start of August 1990, when Iraq invaded its small oil-rich neighbour Kuwait.[10] The invasion was a clear breach of international law. It also posed a major threat to the oil supplies of Western Europe and the United States. The determination of the international community to respond to the challenge, which led to a rapid deployment of American-led forces to the region, was governed by a range of motives. Many Arab countries were anxious to rein in the ambitions of the Iraqi leader Saddam Hussein, while western governments wanted to uphold the edifice of international law, a desire that dovetailed neatly with their more hard-headed concern to secure the flow of oil from the Middle East. The breach of international law committed by Iraq, when combined with the unsavoury character of the regime, meant that it was possible to mount a plausible legal and moral defence of the coalition's motives. At the same time, though, the manifest concern about oil supplies made it easy for cynics to suggest that the United States and its western allies were simply acting out of narrow economic self-interest. The response of the churches in Britain to the Gulf crisis was governed by the need to disentangle the political and moral aspects of a tortuously complex conflict. To oppose the war was, at least in the short term, effectively to advocate appeasing a ruthless dictator with scant concern both for the rights of his own people and for those of the people in countries surrounding his own. To support the war was to endorse the principle that the use of force could be justified even in a situation when clear economic self-interest was one of the motivating factors inspiring those determined to resort to military action. The Gulf crisis led to extensive discussion within the main churches.[11] The Methodist Church of Great Britain was no exception. From the moment that Iraq invaded Kuwait, through until the end of hostilities, the conflict commanded a good deal of attention both in the Methodist press and in the relevant church committees.

There was no shortage of 'grass-roots' voices in the Methodist Church worrying about the possibility that the Iraqi invasion of Kuwait would allow the British and American governments to find a new enemy to replace the old communist adversaries.[12] The Methodist Peace Fellowship held a number of vigils to encourage church members to seek a way out of what seemed to be the start of an impending cycle of violence. Leading pacifists within the church spoke out both to condemn the action of Iraq and to warn against any military response by the British government.[13] In October, the Board of the Division of Social Responsibility issued a statement condemning Iraq's occupation of Kuwait, but arguing that it should be seen within the wider context of instability within the Middle East, with the result that any solution to the crisis needed to form part of a broader peace effort that would deal with such issues as the Palestinian question. The reaction of all the British churches during the early autumn was comparatively subdued, in part because the recent demise of the British Council of Churches hindered their co-operation, and made it difficult for them to speak out 'with an effective overall voice'.[14] A more vigorous debate began in the national press in late September. Rowan Williams, at that time still an academic at Oxford, and Philip Crowe, the Principal of Salisbury and Wells Theological College, argued in an open letter to the House of Bishops that no war in the Gulf could be considered just since it would not be fought with a 'right intention' (presumably an implication that the West's real concern was with oil rather than international law). The Bishop of Oxford, Richard Harries, responded with a piece in *The Independent*,[15] arguing that the 'most relevant of the just-war criteria is that all peaceful means of achieving a resolution must first have been exhausted'. He went on to suggest that the imposition of sanctions showed a real determination on the part of the British and Americans to resolve the situation by non-military means, adding that only governments had the knowledge to decide when 'peaceful means' had been exhausted.

These exchanges in the national press prompted extensive debate across all the main churches. The Archbishop of Canterbury Robert Runcie argued that a long-term solution to the Middle East was required, adding that sanctions should be given at least a year to take effect,[16] although he was careful not to exclude the possibility that military action might in principle be compatible with the requirements of a just war.[17] His view was rejected at the end of November by a large number of leading church figures and theologians, who issued a declaration that any resort to war would not satisfy 'the last resort' criteria.[18] Members of the Methodist Church also frequently made use of the conceptual vocabulary associated with the just war tradition when debating developments in the Gulf. The Division of Social Responsibility issued material in October that discussed possible military intervention from a just war perspective. The Revd John Hastings argued in the *Recorder* the following month that sanctions alone should be used against Iraq, since the catastrophic consequences of military conflict would outweigh any good that might be achieved. Kenneth Greet wrote in December that the whole notion of a just war was outmoded in the modern world, given the scale of destructive power of modern weaponry.[19] The responses within the Methodist Church to the eventual launch of military action in January 1991, which came after several months of preparation, were similarly negative. Brian Duckworth as General Secretary of the DSR wrote a piece for the *Recorder* a few days before the start of the war arguing that 'the case against sanctions and diplomacy is not yet proven', adding that the use of force was likely to create more problems than it solved.[20] In the same week, another member of the DSR formed part of a CCBI delegation that met the Foreign Secretary Douglas Hurd to express concern that the government now only seemed interested in the military option. The DSR itself issued a statement at the beginning of the war expressing 'grave disappointment and sorrow' at developments, while the first editorial to be published in the *Recorder* after the start of hostilities observed that 'Our judgement, not easy to reach, is that envisaging the consequences of war would be the greater evil.'[21] Lord Soper was inevitably at Tower Hill the moment the UN Deadline ran out on 15 January, declaring that he would 'rather have a sell-out than a kill-out', while the MPF was represented at a Stop the War march that took place a few days afterwards.[22] Although some church members who took part in such marches felt uncomfortable at participating in events organized by political extremists who called for the defeat of coalition troops, they concluded that by cultivating 'inner calmness' they were able to bear witness to the desire for peace, without giving undue support to those whose motives and values might be very different.[23]

It has been seen time and again in this book that war polarized division within the Methodist Church throughout the twentieth century. The response was at least on the surface more one-sided in 1991. The *Recorder* received numerous letters condemning military action from both pacifists and non-pacifists alike. David Haslam fretted over the 'fog of war' that had descended on the nation, and condemned Britain and the United States for dropping thousands of tons of high explosives on a 'rather small, if well-armed nation'.[24] The Revd R.A. Milwood condemned an 'unjust and immoral war'.[25] Other contributors attacked religious leaders like Runcie for refusing 'to accept the clearly pacifist teachings of Christ'.[26] Kenneth Greet attacked the euphemistic language that treated civilian deaths and massive destruction under the euphemism of 'collateral damage'.[27] The critical stance of the DSR was generally applauded (and was subsequently approved by Conference). The situation had certainly changed since the Falklands War, nine years earlier, when there had been many voices in the Methodist press and at Conference supporting the war. Had there been a marked shift among members of the Church on questions of peace and war during the previous few years? Or was it simply that those who supported the war were for some reason less ready to speak out than those who opposed it? The extent of the criticism within the Methodist Church towards western intervention in the first Gulf War was certainly striking, given that the coalition put in place to liberate Kuwait was acting under the auspices of the United Nations. Most of those who opposed military action did so on the grounds that it was premature since economic sanctions had not been given time to work. A few took a different line, though, suggesting that the UN itself could no longer be seen as an independent organization since it was dominated by the western powers. Such an argument inevitably raised difficult questions. The United Nations with all its imperfections still had a better claim to represent the will of the international community than any other institution. If its right to authorize military action was called into doubt, then the world was likely to become a less safe place, in which individual governments would be even more inclined to act as the final arbiter when deciding how best to act in order to advance their interests. It was for this reason that most Methodists who spoke out against the first Gulf War remained firmly committed to the principle of internationalism embedded in the UN, even as they questioned the wisdom of the military intervention that it authorized.

## The Yugoslav Crisis

The end of the hostilities in the Gulf allowed global attention to switch to the burgeoning crisis in the Balkans. During the years after 1945, the government of communist Yugoslavia had been surprisingly successful at managing the divisions between the country's three main religious communities: Catholic, Orthodox and Muslim. These tensions began to recrudesce during the 1980s, though, following the death of the veteran Yugoslav leader Josip Tito, in 1980, and the final disintegration of the communist bloc ten years later.[28]

*remember Tito was a (roat)*

The boundaries between ethnic and national identity in Yugoslavia were notoriously complex (religion was indeed one of the defining motifs by which individuals constructed their own ethnic identity). The Catholic population was mostly located in the northern provinces of Croatia and Slovenia. The Orthodox population formed a large majority in the province of Serbia, but there were large minorities across most other parts of the country, including the provinces of Croatia and Bosnia. The Muslim population was concentrated in Bosnia and the southern district of Kosovo (where the population was overwhelmingly ethnic Albanian rather than Slavic). The ethnic mosaic that had characterized Yugsolavia during the period of communist rule meant that any disintegration along ethnic lines was almost bound to be fractious and bloody. The British media gave comparatively little attention to the Yugoslav crisis in the early 1990s, perhaps because the inherent complexity of the conflict made it a bewildering subject for its audience, while the early struggle between Croats and Serbs was less violent and therefore less newsworthy than subsequent developments in Bosnia.[29] The attention of the British public only really began to grow in 1993, as the Muslim majority in Bosnia started to face an increasingly bitter struggle with the Serb minority and its supporters in the Belgrade government, headed by the former Yugoslav communist leader Slobodan Milošević. The constant bombardment of the Bosnian capital of Sarajevo, along with the slaughter of large numbers of Muslim civilians at Gorazde in 1994 and Srebrenica in 1995, were simply the most visible horrors of a brutal civil war in which atrocities were committed on all sides. Although television helped to shape public opinion by bringing home to a foreign audience the horrors of the situation, the European countries failed to intervene forcefully to end the fighting, instead simply co-operating with the United Nations to provide forces designed to carry out limited humanitarian missions and peace-keeping duties.[30] It was only the deployment of American military and diplomatic power in 1995 that effectively brought the Bosnian conflict to an end, via the so-called Dayton accords, although four years later US-led forces once again had to use their massive firepower to defend ethnic Kosovars who were facing a massacre by Serbian forces. The wars in Yugoslavia once again raised important moral questions about the responsibility of the international community to intervene to prevent aggression and restore peace.[31] Although the Balkans may have long held a reputation for violence and chaos, the region was close to the heart of 'civilized' Europe, with the result that the suffering of its people had an immediacy for the governments and publics of Western Europe that was not necessarily true of conflicts in other parts of the world.

There was universal support among the main churches for attempts to provide humanitarian relief during the Bosnian War of 1993–5. The Methodist Church itself was closely involved with a variety of initiatives designed to provide support for those suffering 'on the ground', while a number of church members played a pivotal role in establishing projects to help civilians whose lives had been destroyed by the war. The United Nations deployed thousands of troops in an effort to ensure that supplies from the outside world reached beleaguered civilians in towns and villages across Bosnia, a move broadly welcomed by the *Recorder*,[32] when it reviewed moves to ensure that aid convoys got through to the places where they were needed. There was rather less agreement in the churches over the vexed question of deciding whether military force should be used more actively to deter Serbian aggression in Bosnia. The Bishop of Barking called for the use of air power to attack Serbian forces that were laying siege to Sarajevo, but he was opposed by many leading figures in the Church of England, who feared that such a policy would simply cause more bloodshed.[33] The response within the Methodist Church on the subject was also somewhat uncertain. The 1992 Conference approved a resolution welcoming the growing UN role in providing humanitarian aid, while the Annual Report of the DSR for 1993 described the UN as 'the best instrument' available to the international community when dealing with such crises, although without specifying in detail what role it should play. The DSR Report also called for a War Crimes Tribunal to be set up when the conflict was over to prosecute those guilty of atrocities.

The 1993 Conference expressed some concern about efforts by the international community to resolve the crisis, in particular the so-called Vance-Owen Plan, which sought to divide Bosnia into various cantons defined according to ethnic identity (an approach that was widely criticized for rewarding those who had promoted 'ethnic cleansing').[34] Conference instead called for a peace based on the 'multi-ethnic principle'.[35] The *Recorder* by contrast took a somewhat more '*Realpolitik*' line in its commentaries, reluctantly accepting that some kind of division along ethnic lines represented the only plausible way of achieving peace in the region.[36]

The whole issue was without doubt a difficult one. The European countries were ready to put troops on the ground to support the transport of humanitarian aid, but their governments lacked the political will to provide enough forces to stop the massacres of Bosnian civilians, or to engage Serbian forces in direct conflict to prevent and reverse ethnic cleansing. They were also reluctant to lift the arms embargo on Bosnia in order to allow the Bosnians to obtain the wherewithal to defend themselves. The weakness of UN forces was graphically illustrated in the summer of 1995, when Dutch troops proved powerless to stop the Bosnian-Serb army's slaughter of thousands of Muslim civilians at Srebrenica, in one of the most horrifying moments of the whole Bosnian war. A few months earlier, the DSR had released a statement calling on the western powers 'to make every effort, military and political, to protect the innocent victims of this war', a position that seemed rather more definite than some of its earlier statements. Such calls had little impact on the British government of John Major, though, given its caution about committing troops to carry out actions that might lead to significant casualties. It was only towards the end of 1995 that the US government's threat to use its massive airpower to destroy Bosnian-Serb forces led to peace talks between the Serb, Croat and Bosnian leaders. It is hard to avoid the conclusion that outside countries were only really able to influence developments inside former Yugoslavia when they were ready to use military power to enforce their will. The stark reality demonstrated in the Bosnian War was that 'humanitar-

225

ian intervention' might demand something more than the simple protection of aid convoys and the provision of 'peace-keepers' if it were to be effective in preventing disaster.

The NATO bombings of Serbia in 1999 once again raised the vexed question of determining whether outside military intervention could be justified to protect innocent civilians from persecution. The government in Belgrade had for some years taken a harsh line towards the ethnic Albanians who lived in the semi-autonomous region of Kosovo, to the south-west of Serbia proper, an area that occupied an important part in the national mythology of the Serbs. By September 1998, some quarter of a million Kosovars had been driven from their homes by Serbian troops, in a blatant attempt at ethnic cleansing. The intense international diplomatic efforts to resolve the crisis ground to a halt following lengthy meetings at Rambouillet in the first few weeks of 1999.[37] The scale of the humanitarian crisis again raised considerable issues of principle for the international community. The desire of the outside world to take action to stop the Serbs from their aggressive policy towards Kosovo came into conflict with the simple fact that the province was formally subject in international law to the rule of the Serbian government. The decision of the international community to start a large-scale bombing campaign against Serbia, which began in March 1999, was therefore always likely to prove controversial (not least because of a lack of explicit UN authorization for such action).[38] The controversy was all the greater because the dropping of bombs by American and British planes inevitably caused civilian deaths and made life harder for the survivors by destroying large parts of the transport infrastructure in cities like Belgrade. The British Labour government headed by Tony Blair had from its arrival in office two years earlier committed itself to an 'ethical foreign policy' inspired, in the words of the Foreign Secretary Robin Cook, by a sense that 'We are instant witness in our sitting rooms through the medium of television to human tragedy in distant lands, and are therefore obliged to accept moral responsibility for our response.'[39] Although the concept of an ethical foreign policy was always more notable for its rhetoric than

its substance, it set out a possible basis for justifying military intervention abroad in cases where it could help to prevent or alleviate
suffering, even if such action infringed traditional notions of state
sovereignty. The apparently benign notion of a foreign policy that
sought to harness military force to a clear ethical objective might in
principle have sounded attractive to all those in the churches who
were not committed to an unconditional pacifism. There was certainly a good deal of debate in the 1990s about the possible need for
'just intervention' by the international community in cases where
it could avert humanitarian crises or promote greater international
security. The practical implications of such a policy nevertheless
raised difficult ethical conundrums.

Richard Harries was once again among the most prominent voices
arguing that the decision to launch bombing raids on Kosovo could
be reconciled with the criteria required for a just war, although he
rightly noted that the phrase was itself something of a misnomer,
since 'all wars are a tragic expression of an injustice that has eaten into
the very fabric of human society'.[40] The Archbishop of Canterbury,
George Carey, took a more cautious line, suggesting that the use of
force was always regrettable and could only be acceptable if it helped
to promote a just and lasting peace. All the main Scottish churches
issued a statement calling for NATO to make a public declaration
about the objectives of the air strikes (in order to clarify whether
such action could really be said to be taken in a just cause).[41] A
similar ambivalence was visible within the Methodist Church. The
*Recorder* broadly expressed support for the bombing in its editorials,
noting (perhaps rather acerbically) that 'the over-riding question
for Christian pacifists is: Can Milošević's thugs be restrained other
than by force of arms?'[42] The Revd Leslie Griffiths, who had served
as President of Conference in 1994–5 (and later became a Labour
peer), argued that Milosevic was 'an evil man', and went on to criticize the World Council of Churches for its negative reaction to the
NATO bombing campaign. He added that 'the short-term suffering,
dreadful as it is, must not now deflect us from the goal of ridding
the Balkans once and for all from the insidious nationalism of a

fascist Serbian regime'.[43] Another contributor to the *Recorder* noted that although 'Jesus told his disciples to turn the other cheek ... I do not think he meant that we should do so vicariously on behalf of all those little children ... who are now fleeing for their lives from Kosovo.'[44] One senior figure in the Church noted that the dispatch of troops would also be necessary to bring about 'a rapid and lasting cessation of violence', since missiles and laser-guided bombs were too blunt an instrument to exercise real influence on the ground. Such sentiments were, however, stridently questioned by other members of the Church. Some letters to the *Recorder* were very sharp in their criticism of the US President George W. Bush and the British Prime Minister Tony Blair, condemned by one correspondent for making 'sanctimonious statements about a "just war" as he breaks the charter of the United Nations as well as the very terms of the North Atlantic Treaty'.[45] Kenneth Greet took a more measured tone, but he too was critical both of the British government and of the churches for failing to be guided in their response to the crisis by a well-articulated theology.[46] Perhaps most strikingly, the President of Conference, Peter Stephens, fretted that the NATO bombing campaign was 'simply adding to the evil and suffering'. Although he acknowledged that there were occasions when the international community had a moral duty to intervene in the internal affairs of a particular country, in order to relieve human suffering, he remained anxious that the use of force in Kosovo would do more harm than good.[47]

The military intervention to protect Kosovo against Serbian aggression was presented by western governments as an attempt to avert a humanitarian disaster. It was also designed to prevent instability in south-east Europe from spreading to neighbouring states. While it might be possible to see the action as an attempt by the British and American governments to embed the values of liberal capitalism in the region, as some commentators have suggested,[48] it is hard to discount the claims by politicians that they were concerned above all to alleviate human suffering and injustice. The same was true of the earlier intervention in Bosnia. It is easy to dismiss the commitment of the British government to an 'ethical foreign policy' as mere rhetorical language designed to justify military intervention to promote its own objectives. It would certainly be naive to imagine that governments do not act to promote their own national interests when developing their foreign policies. It nevertheless remains true that if respect for state sovereignty is treated as the sacrosanct principle of the global order, then the international community will necessarily struggle to justify any form of military intervention in cases where a government is behaving barbarically towards its own people. It does indeed appear from this distance in time that the real failure of the international community in the mid-1990s was its refusal to intervene early enough to prevent the slaughter in Bosnia. It seems fair to suggest in the customary language of the just war that outside intervention in both the Bosnian and Kosovan conflicts was on balance positive in reducing the sum of evil in the world.

## Towards a New Century

The focus on the conflicts in the Gulf and Yugoslavia did not preclude continued debate about 'North–South' issues that had commanded so much concern within the Methodist Church during the previous twenty-five years. There was certainly no shortage of voices suggesting that the main western governments were acting hypocritically in refusing to contemplate military intervention in countries like Rwanda and Haiti, given their claims to be acting in the name of humanitarianism and international law when using force to influence developments in the Gulf and former Yugoslavia, where they had vital national interests at stake. The reports issued by the Division of Social Responsibility in the years after 1985 reflected a pervasive sense that the end of the Cold War had done nothing to ease the plight of the developing world. The 1992 report declared roundly that although liberalism was 'capable of a more effective self-criticism' than Marxist historical materialism, 'the force of Marxism's political and economic analysis cannot be disregarded'. The DSR itself exemplified such a critical approach when reviewing the prevailing structures of the international economic and political order. Its 1988 report called for 'radical change' to the organization of the global economy in order to reduce Third-World debt and promote higher prices for the exports of developing countries. The 1994 report argued that the work of relieving poverty in the developing world required a fundamental rethinking of 'the issues of justice, peace and the environment'. The environment itself began to figure much more prominently in DSR reports from the late 1980s onwards, both because environmental degradation was most damaging in the developing world, and because long-term solutions could only be devised on a global basis. The 1993 Report noted that both communist and capitalist countries had a poor record when dealing with the environment, and expressed a hope that the 'commonality' of the issue might provide a new agenda that could unite the international community in an effort to tackle the problem. The Division predictably continued to give a good deal of attention to the problems in South Africa, both before the disintegration of the apartheid system in the early 1990s, and during the following years as the new government headed by Nelson Mandela began to confront the baneful legacies of the past. The 'International Relief and Development' section of the 1987 report called for the boycotting of Barclays, given its failure to disinvest in the country, while the report submitted to Conference two years later welcomed moves to promote Namibian independence. The 1992 Report noted somewhat drily that 'the Division is well-known, some would say notorious, for taking stands on a wide range of issues'. This was certainly true of its approach to North–South issues throughout the last ten years or so of the twentieth century. The DSR worked tirelessly to maintain the Methodist Church's focus on questions of international poverty and injustice, at a time when the world's attention was all too often diverted elsewhere.

The *Recorder* also devoted a good deal of space to North–South issues, as well as the disintegration of the apartheid regime in South Africa, a development that was naturally welcomed with great enthusiasm across the Methodist Church. There were occasional

hints, though, that a number of the paper's readers were still concerned about the radicalism of the Church's pronouncements on a
variety of issues relating to the developing world. Some contributors to the *Recorder* continued to criticize those who focused on the
crimes of the apartheid regime in South Africa while ignoring the
suffering of people at the hands of authoritarian regimes elsewhere
in the world.[49] Other contributors pointed out that the imposition
of sanctions on South Africa was often opposed by sections of the
black community in the country itself. A number of contributors
to the *Recorder* also voiced concerns about growing 'sectarianism'
within the Methodist Church between radicals and traditionalists.
Most of the concern over what was perceived as the drift towards
an undue political correctness focused above all, though, on domestic issues ranging from poverty through to race. There was much
less concern about calls for the wealthy countries of the world to
address the problem of Third-World debt and an unfair trading system. While there were often sharp divisions within the Methodist
Church over British intervention in the Gulf and former Yugoslavia,
support for a restructuring of North–South relations proved less
controversial, although a gentle scepticism might suggest that this
was because many in the church did not really understand the full
implications of such a move for the wealthy countries of the world.
The rights and wrongs of the international terms of trade were less
controversial than starker questions about peace and war.

There was by the end of the twentieth century a widespread
acceptance within the Methodist Church that global poverty and
injustice were a potent cause of violence around the world, a point
that Edward Rogers had made as early 1964 in his book on *Living
Standards*, in which he argued that the rich countries of the world
should address the problem in order to ensure their own security in
the years ahead. The events that took place on 11 September 2001
seemed to confirm in the most dramatic way how easily conflict
and violence could become a global phenomenon in the modern
world. When two planes smashed into the World Trade Centre in
New York, killing thousands of people, governments around the

world quickly realized that a new era in international politics had begun. The deaths of hundreds more people in hijacked aircraft in Washington and Pennsylvania emphasized the organizational 'reach' of those determined to bring mayhem to the world's only super-power. The government of George W. Bush interpreted the attack as a major challenge to national security at home and abroad. The start of the 'war on terror' marked the beginning of a new phase in the history of American foreign policy. The National Security Strategy published in 2002 made it clear that the United States would act, unilaterally if necessary, to prevent the development of any poten-tial threat to its status as the world's greatest power.[50] It was of course such arguments that provided the rationale for the military intervention in Afghanistan and Iraq. The Al Qaeda movement that provided the financial and logistical support for those who carried out the attacks in New York and Washington had been given shelter by the Taliban regime in Afghanistan. Saddam Hussein in Iraq had no direct links to those involved in the 9/11 attacks, but Washington was convinced that he provided support to other terrorist groups active in the Middle East, as well as being engaged in the develop-ment of weapons of mass destruction that could in time threaten the security of other nations. American foreign policy in the months and years after 9/11 was fuelled in part by a 'neo-conservatism' that was convinced that US power could be used to reshape large areas of the world.[51] It was an ambitious policy that continues to have a powerful legacy down to the present day.

A number of scholars had predicted before the 9/11 attacks that future conflicts would in the post-Cold War world take place between 'civilizations',[52] fuelled as much by differences of values as by competing national interests. It is, though, seldom easy to dis-tinguish between conflicts of values and conflicts over such matters as national boundaries and access to scarce resources. The much-vaunted rise of Islamic 'fundamentalism' since the 1970s has been a response both to the challenges of secular modernity and the endless crises in the Middle East, which has over the course of half a century created a well of resentment and anger against the outside world, condemned for offering support to Israel and a series of corrupt Arab governments. The term Islamic fundamentalism is itself in any case something of a misnomer, given the enormous differences in perspective and belief within the Islamic world.[53] The appearance in western countries of young Muslims willing to sacrifice themselves and others in the name of their religion shows how ideologies that develop in one setting can gain influence in areas far away from where they originated. The rise of religiously inspired terrorism at the start of the twenty-first century raised particularly difficult issues for the main churches in Britain. Most of them had over the previous few decades not only sought to promote a Christian ecumenicalism, designed to ease the inter-denominational tensions that had disfigured church relations in the past, but also tried to build closer links with other faith communities. The events of 9/11 and the developments that followed raised a new series of challenges at a time when questions of religion were once again put back in the centre stage of political debate.

The terrorist attacks on the twin towers and the Pentagon created a sense of trauma and devastation far beyond the United States itself. The television images of aeroplanes smashing into the World Trade Centre against the backdrop of a clear late summer sky had an almost surreal character that exercised a profound influence on all those who viewed them. The rapid commitment by Tony Blair to stand 'shoulder to shoulder' with the American government and people was at the time widely seen in the British media as a statesmanlike response to the horrors on the other side of the Atlantic, albeit that such words were later to come back to haunt the British Prime Minister, when he faced accusations that he was being too uncritical in supporting Washington's 'war on terror'. It has often been pointed out that in a modern secular society it is hard for people to find the rituals or the language to articulate their response in the face of such horrors. Many British churches opened their doors in the days following the attacks in order to give people a place where they could reflect on the events in the United States, lighting candles or entering their name in a book of remembrance, in an echo of the events that had taken place following the death of Princess Diana four years before. Three days after the attack, more than two and half thousand people attended a service at St Paul's Cathedral in London to remember the dead, while many thousand more clustered outside to show their solidarity with the victims. The Archbishop of Canterbury, George Carey, told the congregation that a 'senseless evil had been perpetrated against America and the world'. Carey also touched more tangentially on the vexed question of how the US government and its allies should respond to the atrocities, noting that 'Those responsible for such barbaric acts must be held to account. But we must be guided by higher motives than mere revenge.'[54] The Archbishop of Wales, Rowan Williams, echoed this cautious note a few days later. He suggested that although it was sentimental to assume that Christianity was concerned only with forgiveness rather than justice, any military response to the events of 9/11 should be informed by some careful thought about what it was designed to achieve.[55] The remarks of both Carey and Williams represented an attempt to find a language that was appropriate to the scale of the crisis, and yet helped to define the values that should shape a distinctively Christian response to the recent events in America. Their approach was echoed by the debate that took place in the Methodist Church in the aftermath of the attacks on the twin towers.

The President of Conference, the Revd Christina Le Moignan, responded to the events of 9/11 by calling in the *Recorder* for prayers to remember the victims and their families. A number of senior figures in the Methodist Church expressed concern about the possible impact of the events in America on inter-faith relations within Britain itself. It became clear within a few days, though, that there were some marked differences of perspective about how best to respond to the terrorist attacks across the Atlantic. The President herself contributed a piece to the *Recorder* expressing her anxiety that any military attack by western governments on Al Qaeda bases in Afghanistan would be 'more likely to create terrorists than destroy them'. She also suggested that the existence of global economic injustice, which condemned 'millions of powerless people at the wrong end of the trading system' to grinding poverty, had helped to create a climate in which terrorism flourished.[56] Another minister wrote to the *Recorder* the following week noting her frustration against claims that America was simply a 'victim' of violence, suggesting instead that the country's enormous military and economic power had in the past helped to perpetuate 'the misery of the world's poor', explaining why it attracted such resentment in the less developed regions of the world.[57] Such arguments were striking for two reasons. In the first place, they implicitly rejected attempts to explain the attacks of 9/11 simply by reference to the evil intentions of those who carried them out, arguing instead that they had to be understood against a backdrop of global inequality and anger, while in the second place they were reluctant to engage with the vexed question of whether there was anything within the tradition of Islam that fostered such acts of appalling violence. In the weeks following the 9/11 attacks, there was widespread criticism in the British media of 'liberal' politicians and other establishment figures who sought to explain the violence by reference to the failings of western society, rather than pinning responsibility firmly on the terrorists themselves. A close reading of the *Recorder* shows that there were echoes of this critique within the Methodist Church itself. One Methodist minister writing in the paper attacked those who put forward simplistic arguments blaming poverty for the attacks on America, pointing out that enormous efforts had been made in recent years by the western powers to increase aid and offer debt relief.[58] Another contributor argued that the attacks 'had nothing to do with world poverty'.[59] A third questioned the claim that world terrorism is 'our fault . . . There are wicked evil men in the world.'[60] Such contributions were nevertheless outnumbered by the ones that saw the assault on the symbols of US economic and military power as an attack on the way in which such power had been 'consistently misused to protect the interests of the world's wealthy at the expense of the poor'.[61] These competing attempts to come to terms with the challenge of 9/11 were in many respects simply an echo of the wider debate in Britain about an event that had quickly acquired an epoch-defining resonance. The fragmentary evidence reviewed here nevertheless suggests that most members of the Methodist Church who were prepared to express their views in print were convinced that the events of 9/11 were indelibly connected to broader questions of international justice.

Once it became apparent that a US-led coalition would take military action against Afghanistan, in order to destroy the Taliban regime that gave shelter to senior figures in Al Qaeda, debate began across all the churches about the moral justification for such an action. In early October, the Bishop of Chester questioned the morality of the bombing campaign that had begun a few days earlier. Despite the public furore aroused by his remarks, Lambeth Palace issued a statement noting that the bishop was simply arguing that 'the existence of a justification for military action should not prevent deep and challenging moral questions from being considered',[62] an approach that reflected ambivalence among many senior figures in the Church of England about the use of force in Afghanistan. The response within the Methodist Church was also somewhat uncertain, as a natural horror at the loss of civilian life in the United States was balanced by anxiety that military action might make the situation worse. The *Recorder* carried many articles detailing the likely suffering of civilians in Afghanistan. One minister suggested that the coalition aircraft should drop food rather than munitions, which would not only relieve suffering but also 'have a terrific effect on the world of Islam'.[63] Other contributors returned to the argument that the United States had paved the way for the terrorist attacks, by failing to address the problems of world poverty, with the result that the use of force against the Taliban would do nothing to ease the resentment and anger felt by many in the developing world. Many of those who criticized the decision to begin military operations were nevertheless uneasily aware of the paradox involved in proposing a response based on the principles of toleration and pluralism to a challenge from those whose ideology was rooted in intolerance and exclusiveness. The immediate

236

response within British Methodism to the events of 9/11 and the subsequent military intervention in Afghanistan was in short one of understandable perplexity and uncertainty.

Many of those who opposed the decision to launch military action in Afghanistan were in effect deploying arguments derived from the just war tradition. Critics believed that the question of 'right cause' was ambiguous, given that the United States could not shrug off responsibility for the global injustice that spawned terrorism, while the likelihood of significant civilian casualties meant that the *jus in bello* criteria could not be met. The passions of the debate were however muted by an understanding of the seriousness of the international situation heralded by the attack on the twin towers in New York. The situation was rather different eighteen months later, when the United States and Britain launched the second Gulf War in order to bring about regime change in Iraq. The government of Saddam Hussein had survived defeat in the first Gulf War, in 1991, since coalition forces had not pursued the Iraq army in its retreat to Baghdad. It also survived the imposition of harsh economic sanctions throughout the 1990s, criticized by many in the West for harming the civilian population more than the government. The administration of President George W. Bush was nevertheless determined to oust Saddam, claiming that the Iraqi dictator was developing weapons of mass destruction, and supporting terrorist groups that were destabilizing the Middle East. The administration's critics believed that the desire to destroy Saddam was simply part of a broader mission to secure energy supplies and strengthen the US position in the Middle East.

The international machinations that led to the second Gulf War are too complex to be reviewed here. Most leading governments were sceptical of US policy, fearing that it represented an attempt by Washington to reshape the international community in its own interests, without seeking to engage in complex multilateral negotiations and discussions. The British government was by contrast ready to follow the US lead, although it sought to put pressure on its American counterpart to ensure that any military action received explicit approval from the UN Security Council (it could be argued that implicit authorization was inherent in existing resolutions if it was true that the Iraqi government was refusing to co-operate with UN inspectors searching for evidence of programmes to develop weapons of mass destruction). The 'public relations' offensive of the two governments varied quite sharply in character and content. The US government sought to foster in the mind of the American public a sense that destroying the Iraqi regime would help to create a safer world whose fragility had been so starkly demonstrated by the events of 9/11. The British government by contrast tried to suggest that any military action against Iraq would take the form of a preventative war, defeating Saddam Hussein before he could deploy his weapons of mass destruction, or pass them on to various terrorist groups who might then use them with devastating effect. It was for this reason that London released a detailed document supposedly providing evidence about Iraq's WMD programmes (the celebrated 'dodgy dossier' that was to be the cause of so much political controversy in the years that followed). It was clear from the start of the second Gulf crisis that, despite the best efforts of the government's propaganda campaign, there was widespread public opposition in Britain to the prospect of war. It is therefore hardly surprising that the conflict that eventually broke out in March caused enormous controversy across British society.

The churches in Britain were naturally preoccupied by the burgeoning crisis. A statement released by the Methodist Church in August 2002 noted that military action 'should always be used as a last resort' and 'must be explicitly authorised by resolution of the UN Security Council'.[64] The President of Conference, the Revd Ian White, sent a letter to the Prime Minister the following month noting that 'war in itself is not to be justified on moral grounds', and once again emphasized that a new UN resolution would be required to authorize any use of force.[65] Two months later, White warned in a second letter of the dangers that would result from military action against Iraq, not least the damage to Christian–Muslim relations in Britain itself. In a separate letter written at the same time to a leading Muslim, he carefully set down the stringent conditions that defined the criteria for a just war. In February 2003, when the Gulf Crisis was entering a critical stage, the President released a pastoral letter calling for diplomacy to continue since military action could only be a 'last resort'. He also called on Methodists to listen to one another and reflect on whether a conflict was likely to do more harm than good.[66] The response of the leaders of the other main churches was broadly similar. Both the outgoing Archbishop of Canterbury, George Carey, and his successor, Rowan Williams, made it clear in the closing months of 2002 that they had doubts whether a war against Iraq could be justified. The same sentiments were echoed in the Catholic Church, both by Pope John Paul II, and by the Catholic bishops in Great Britain. Some Anglican and Catholic bishops were nevertheless ready to consider the possibility that a war of 'anticipatory' self-defence might be justified. Richard Harries speaking in the House of Lords argued that traditional notions of just war did not only permit self-defence, narrowly interpreted, but could also be invoked to encompass action designed to forestall an attack. The formal position of the Methodist Church seemed to represent a kind of half-way house, accepting that anticipatory self-defence might represent a valid cause justifying an invasion of Iraq, but only if given explicit legal sanction in the form of a new UN resolution.[67] The political dynamics that prevailed at UN Headquarters in New York means that such a resolution was never passed.

The concern amongst British Methodists about the situation in the Gulf was not confined to formal statements by leading figures in the Church hierarchy. Many individual Methodists were involved in the demonstrations and protests that took place in the weeks and months leading up to the outbreak of hostilities. One Methodist minister who attended a huge demonstration that took place in London in February 2003 told *The Independent on Sunday*, when asked why he was taking part, that 'It comes down to the convictions of my Christian faith. This focus is so much on our own security. The greatest weapon of mass destruction is Aids in Africa. I wonder where our priorities are'.[68] Other ministers led discussions in their local churches about the rights and wrongs of the situation in the Gulf. Some 'grassroots Methodists' who joined in demonstrations were doing so for the first time, motivated both by unease over the way that Britain and United States were approaching the conflict, and by a sense that money was better spent on tackling poverty than fighting wars.[69] Many of those who attended the London demonstration were confident that 'Blair can't ignore this. The people have spoken out against the war – support will not be given'. Others focused on the reaction within their own church, complaining in the pages of the *Recorder* that the Methodist leadership had been too cautious in its reaction to the build-up to war.[70] There were, though, always some voices warning against too simplistic a reaction to a potential conflict. One minister wrote to the *Recorder* in early March noting that 'It must be heartening for Saddam Hussein that he has many friends and supporters', adding that he was concerned that the Iraqi dictator would shortly be able to strike at the West, allowing him to 'annihilate tens of thousands of people'.[71]

The outbreak of hostilities in March 2003 inevitably changed the *de facto* terms of the debate from a focus on '*jus ad bellum* to '*jus in bello*', although one student of the subject has noted that comment from within the churches on the actual conduct of the war was surprisingly limited.[72] A few letters to the Methodist press expressed support for the decision to go to war. One minister from northern Britain articulated an almost Augustinian view of the situation when he told the *Recorder* that 'We live in a fallen and imperfect world ... There are occasions when reason and negotiation are inappropriate and evil must be confronted by force.'[73] Another fretted that opposition to war stemmed from a 'political correctness' that had become 'the yardstick of Christian behaviour'. Such voices were for the most part isolated. A large majority of letters and articles published in the *Recorder* claimed that Britain and America had embarked on a course of action that was morally wrong and legally suspect. The church leadership itself emphasized the need to minister to all regardless of their views. The notes distributed to preachers at the start of the war stressed the need to pray for all those caught up in the conflict, whether in government or the forces, adding that it was important not to allow sermons to become 'an opportunity for pointed criticism of individuals in government'.[74] The conflict posed particular dilemmas for Methodist chaplains who had to minister to troops in a war that faced such strong opposition within the mainstream churches. One of them told *The Times* that his job was to support the troops 'wherever they find themselves in whatever they are ordered to do'. He added that 'When young guys stop me and ask me what it will be like when the fighting starts, I tell them I don't know but I'm as scared as the next man.' The chaplain also reflected on how the abstractions of the debate over the rights and wrongs of war back home faded in the front line where there were 'true life and death issues'.[75] Such sage words found little echo, though, among those who were convinced that the Gulf War represented a tragic episode in the history of British foreign policy.

The rapid victory of the coalition forces in the Second Gulf War meant that the actual period of hostilities was comparatively short-lived, although the civilian casualties on the Iraqi side were still quite high, despite the ability of the Americans and their allies to make use of 'smart' weapons supposedly capable of hitting their targets without causing huge civilian deaths and injuries. The subsequent failure of American and other coalition forces to establish order, following the collapse of the regime of Saddam Hussein, was partly due to a lack of serious planning in Washington about the complex problems involved in institution-building. This failure in turn seems to have reflected a naive belief among many neo-conservative policy-makers that democracy and a working economy would spontaneously emerge from the chaos. The latent divisions in Iraq between Shia and Sunni Muslims were in reality always likely to explode into violence once the central state institutions began to disintegrate, while western military forces were destined to be seen before long as 'occupiers' rather than 'liberators'. The civil war that erupted following the overthrow of Saddam Hussein, which at the time of writing has cost tens of thousands of lives, has cast a retrospective shadow on the earlier debates within the churches about whether military intervention was likely to cause more problems than it solved. While the absence of an explicit UN resolution authorizing the use of force can certainly be interpreted as casting doubt on the 'lawfulness' of the action, it is perhaps of more significance that military intervention does not seem in retrospect to have reduced the sum of evil in the world, apparently confirming the instincts of those who did not believe that the second Gulf War could ever be considered 'just'. It is indeed hard to imagine that any modern conflict can ever be reconciled with traditional Christian teaching on the just war, if that tradition is reduced to little more than a small number of set criteria, to be applied in a simplistic manner to the complexities of international politics. It is for this reason that new and more imaginative ways of thinking are needed to help make difficult judgements about the rights and wrongs of using military force in a particular situation.

## Conclusion

It would at first glance seem churlish to question the value of humanitarian military intervention when it is designed to prevent the slaughter of unarmed civilians who cannot for one reason or another secure the protection of their own government. The customary objection that it undermines the principle of national sovereignty can all too easily appear under such circumstances as little more than a callous refusal to act by those who have the wherewithal to help. A moment of reflection reveals, though, that the situation is more complex than it may at first seem. After all, Adolf Hitler claimed to be intervening in Czechoslovakia in 1938 to protect the German minority in the Sudetenland against repression by the Czech majority. If the phenomenon of humanitarian military intervention is to be seen as anything more than a potential cloak for the pursuit of narrow national interests, then it must take place within an established legal and political framework, which at the minimum would appear to require UN authorization and a wide consensus that any action is likely to do more good than harm.[76]

242

Even then, however, there remain enormous questions of both practice and principle. As one commentator has recently noted, it is false
to assume 'that humanitarian intervention is morally, if not legally,
valid because the ends justify the means employed . . . in practice
these ends are never so clear and the means are rarely so closely
bound to them'. The sharp disagreement between the western powers and the Russians over the various interventions in Yugoslavia
graphically showed the scope for disagreement about the whole
issue. The second Gulf War demonstrated even more starkly how
little agreement there may be even among democratic governments about the efficacy and morality of military intervention. The
situation in this case was made more complex by the fact that the
over-arching rationale articulated by the British and American governments did not just focus on the plight of ordinary Iraqis under
the regime of Saddam Hussein, but concentrated as much on the
potential threat that the Iraqi dictator posed to the stability of the
Middle East and perhaps the wider world. The rights and wrongs
of a 'preventative war' raise as many difficult questions as military
intervention to promote humanitarian relief.

It is no wonder that all the main British churches, including the
Methodist Church, faced confusion when determining how best to
respond to the international crises that erupted in the period following the Cold War. The collapse of the Soviet Union required
some fundamental rethinking about how to react at a time when the
global security architecture was in a state of flux. The development
of a 'postmodern' world demanded reconsideration of old assumptions about how the international order could and should operate.
The most striking aspect of reactions within the Methodist Church
to the two Gulf Wars and the collapse of Yugoslavia was not the
long-standing division between 'pacifists' and 'non-pacifists'. It was
instead the extent to which so many people had become sceptical
about the motives put forward by the US and British governments
when defending their foreign policies. This scepticism may have
reflected an 'anti-establishment' instinct that can by definition be
traced back to the early days of Methodism. It may more realistically

have been rooted in the growth of cynicism about politics and politicians that has been a striking and unhealthy development in Britain over the past twenty years or so. The doubts expressed by many in the Methodist Church about the wisdom of British foreign policy during these years was above all, though, a result of uncertainty in the face of a new set of challenges that required fresh and imaginative thinking about how to live in an ever more complex world. It is not unreasonable to suggest that the main role of the churches when articulating their views on international affairs should be to remind governments of perspectives and values that may be overlooked by politicians and diplomats when faced with the clamour of events. It nevertheless remains a duty of the churches to seek to understand the inherent complexity of the world.[77] Leading members of all the main churches struggled to grasp the changes that took place in the period following the end of the Cold War. They were on occasion not ready enough to understand that politicians also found it difficult to make sense of a new world demanding new thinking and new policies.

# 9

# Conclusion

The US-led invasion of Iraq in 2003 did little to bring peace to the country, as the failure to establish viable new forms of civilian government to replace the regime of Saddam Hussein led to a bloody civil war between Sunni and Shia Muslims. The political ramifications of the failure of western intervention to promote peaceful political and economic development created enormous political shock waves around the world, damaging the popularity of the Bush administration in Washington, and providing numerous political problems for the government of Tony Blair in London. The Methodist Church of Great Britain took a decidedly critical line towards western policy in Iraq in the wake of the war. The Co-ordinating Secretary for Public Life and Social Justice noted in April 2004 that the escalating violence 'confirms the worst fears' of those who had campaigned against military action.[1] A few weeks later the church's International Affairs Secretary expressed shock about the abuse of prisoners by American forces at the Abu Ghraib prison in Baghdad.[2] Those who spoke for the Methodist Church continued to urge positive ways forward in Iraq, emphasizing the need for greater control by the civilian Iraqi government and a central role for the United Nations, but there was something rather forlorn about such prescriptions given the sheer scale of the violence. Senior figures in the church also condemned the British government for adopting harsh measures in the fight against terrorism back home, both because they undermined individual freedoms, and because they were likely to create new tensions that would lead

245

to the alienation of the Muslim community. The London suicide bombings of July 2005, which killed more than fifty people, were widely interpreted in the media as a direct consequence of the radicalization of British Muslims in response to the bloodshed in Iraq *and* to a lack of integration in Britain itself.[3] The main concern of senior members of the Methodist Church in the wake of the London bombings was to co-operate with other Christian denominations and the leaders of other faiths to prevent the atrocity from fostering further hatred and violence. Many local Methodists similarly redoubled their efforts to promote greater inter-faith understanding.[4] The London bombings – like the previous attacks in New York, Bali and Madrid – showed the extent to which violence in one part of the globe could easily have repercussions across the world in an age of globalization.

A vast amount has been written in recent years about the way in which religion has 'reappeared' in recent years as a significant factor in both domestic and international politics.[5] The roots of this phenomenon are extraordinarily complicated. While there is a danger in oversimplifying the whole subject, it is hardly controversial to suggest that the development of new forms of religious fundamentalism has been intimately bound up with the challenges posed to traditional societies across the world by the forces of cultural and economic change.[6] The dominant response within British Methodism has been to treat the growth of religious violence as the product of poverty and exploitation, leading to the logical conclusion that greater global economic justice will help in time to reduce the phenomenon, an approach that it was seen earlier informed many reactions to the events of 9/11. The involvement of many Methodist churches in local inter-faith initiatives in Britain has in a similar vein been inspired by the conviction that different religious communities have the potential to live together in a spirit of tolerance. Such approaches sit easily with the instinctive liberalism of the contemporary Methodist Church, which fosters the belief that it is possible to foster harmony even between religious groups whose claims exhibit an absolute and exclusive character. The institutional liberalism of the Church has certainly provided a perspective from which to criticize the policies pursued by the British government in the 'war against terror'. It nevertheless remains to be seen whether it can provide an intellectual framework for understanding and responding to the violence associated with particular forms of religious fundamentalism. The paradox of tolerance – that it can provide comfort and influence to those who are intolerant – has not really been addressed by any of the main churches in Britain during the first few years of the twenty-first century.

While the crises in Afghanistan and Iraq have necessarily commanded a great deal of the Methodist Church's focus on international affairs in the new millennium, it has continued to give extensive attention to the whole 'North–South' question, not least because of a recognition that the roots of global terrorism lie at least in part in the poverty of the developing world. Some of its more radical representatives have articulated a sophisticated critique of the international order designed to show how the 'neo-liberal' economic order necessarily creates patterns of exploitation and division.[7] The church itself has endorsed the Jubilee Debt Campaign and called for a new policy towards the developing world based on the biblical 'bias to the poor'.[8] The situation in Palestine has also commanded extensive discussion both at Conference and in the Methodist press, while the question of nuclear weapons has once again become a matter of considerable debate, given the British government's recent decision to replace the Trident missile system. It is perhaps curious in the light of the countless changes that have taken place in the international system over the past fifty years that Conference had not until recently engaged in a systematic review of its attitudes towards questions of peace and war since the mid-1950s. It was for this reason that the Methodist Council in 2004 'endorsed a proposal for a joint piece of work by the Methodist Church and the United Reformed Churches to examine the ethics of war in the current context'. The report on *Peacemaking: A Christian Vocation* was eventually submitted to the 2006 Conference, along with a series of resolutions on 'The Ethics of Modern Warfare', and together they provide a fascinating insight into the way in which attitudes have developed within the church over recent years.

The summary of the *Peacemaking* report submitted to Conference argued that Christian reflection on the challenge of peace and war has often been too parochial, located solely within the context of opposition between the pacifist and just war traditions, whereas peacemaking in the modern world requires a broader dialogue with other faiths and secular traditions.[9] It also argued that there was far more 'common ground' between the pacifist and just war perspectives than sometimes realized, given the agreement that a resort to war can never be seen as anything other than a failure to live up to the ethical teaching of Christ. The report went to great lengths to argue that peace was in the deepest sense 'indivisible' and bound up with questions of economic and racial justice, as well as suggesting that all Christians were called to act as peacemakers, whether in their personal and professional lives or as actors in the political process. It also warned that the search for peace should not descend into an uncritical acceptance of the *status quo*, given the need to struggle against deep-seated and long-standing injustices. The report's authors showed their sensitivity to contemporary ecological concerns by urging all those who were committed to the 'just war' tradition to consider the likely impact of any future military action on the environment when determining whether a resort to force was proportionate.

The full report on *Peacemaking* firmly rejected any attempt to 'stretch' the context in which preventative war could be acceptable, and argued that the United Nations had a pivotal role to play in determining when the use of force was acceptable, a position that can be read as a rebuke to the decision of the British and American governments to invade Iraq in 2003. It also accepted that outside military intervention could be legitimate if it was designed to prevent human rights abuses, and should indeed have taken place earlier and more forcefully in Kosovo and Rwanda (although the Report's authors suggested that there were few occasions when a resort to military action did not create more problems than it resolved). The

*not about Zimbabwe ?!*

Conference debate that took place on the report and the associated resolutions showed that there was a good deal of support for their recommendations. Many of those who spoke praised the report as a 'valuable resource' for discussing the question of peacemaking at district and circuit level. Some speakers argued that the church had a duty to act as a 'protest movement', and speak out when governments were pursuing actions that seemed repugnant to the Christian conscience, an argument that once again had particular salience in the light of the ongoing conflict in Iraq. A small number expressed their regret that the report had not adopted a pacifist position and rejected the use of violence altogether. Conference decisively rejected an amendment questioning the recommendation not to replace Trident. The report on Peacemaking itself was, however, only commended by Conference, rather than adopted, a sign that there was still some residual unease about the far-reaching nature of its more radical proposals.

Although many of the ideas developed in the *Peacemaking* report were not new, but rather brought together themes that had characterized debate within the Methodist Church over several decades, the conflict in the Gulf certainly encouraged fresh discussion on the whole subject. A recent book by Leslie Griffiths and Jennifer Potter takes as its starting-point the two authors' reluctance to endorse the anti-war protests that took place on the streets of Britain in 2003, before developing a sophisticated argument calling for new and imaginative ways of thinking about international politics in a postmodern and postcolonial world.[10] It was suggested in the first chapter of this book that Methodist theology is often better identified in the practice of the church than it is in formal doctrine. This is not to suggest that the Methodist Church of Great Britain has not been interested in thinking through theologically the challenge of war and peace in recent years. The debate that took place at Conference in 2006, and indeed at countless previous Conferences, showed a very real desire to set the church's position on the ethics of war within a clear biblical and theological framework. It does however remain the case that the 'position' of the Methodist Church on many questions can throughout its history be found as much in the action of its members as in Conference resolutions or books by leading Methodist theologians and writers. Some delegates to the 2006 Conference reported on efforts by church members in their districts to promote good community relations and tackle the scourge of gang warfare. Others spoke of fellow church members who had gone to work abroad to help in the practical work of promoting reconciliation in troubled areas of the world. Nor, of course, were such initiatives new. The 2006 report on Peacemaking did not so much state the Methodist position as formalize existing practice and custom. Conference in a sense gave its *imprimatur* to developments that had been taking place over many years or even decades.

The previous chapters have sought to build up a collage of responses within the Methodist Church to the international conflicts that have been an endemic feature of the twentieth century. Despite the difficulties inherent in such an approach, discussed at some length in the first chapter, it has the virtue of acknowledging the inherent 'messiness' involved in seeking to gauge the mind of the Methodist Church on such a vast and complex subject. The huge changes that have taken place during the past hundred years or so naturally raise the question of whether it is even worth trying to make any generalizations. The world that Hugh Price Hughes knew is so far removed from the modern age that there is a danger of assuming that just because Methodism has endured it must therefore be possible to identify some 'essential' doctrinal or institutional character (or at least a coherent pattern of development and change). The era of the Nonconformist Conscience was so intimately bound up with the values and practices of late Victorian society that it hardly seems reasonable to expect it to echo down to the present day. It nevertheless remains the case that the Methodist Church has always remained intensely conscious of its heritage, even as it has sought to re-fashion the values and traditions of the past. It is no accident that John Wesley remains a revered figure even today. Nor is it an accident that so much research on British Methodism

250

focuses on the eighteenth and nineteenth centuries rather than the more modern period. To use the language of the leading British critic of the churches, Richard Dawkins, there is a memetic inheritance, a set of ideas and values, that does not necessarily define Methodism but which has helped to shape the pattern of its evolution.[11]

It is probably fair to suggest that theological debate within American Methodism on questions of peace and war has in recent decades been somewhat richer than in the British church. One of the most noted scholars of the concept and development of the just war, Paul Ramsey, was himself a prominent member of the United Methodist Church.[12] Ramsey was a sharp critic of attempts to define pacifism as a central tenet of the United Methodist Church's identity. When the church debated the subject in 1972 as part of its review of its Social Principles, he argued strongly that war could only be regarded as *ultimately* incompatible with Christian teaching, and that there were circumstances under which it could be reconciled with the Christian conscience. Some years later he provided a detailed theological critique of the United Methodist Bishops' Letter 'In Defence of Creation', arguing that it was flawed both in its understanding of the Bible, and in its tendency to engage in a utopianism that confused (in Augustinian language) the heavenly and earthly cities.[13] Other theologians belonging to the United Methodist Church have by contrast argued that its constitution and principles *are* essentially pacifist in character. Stephen Long has provided a sophisticated defence of this position, which among other things attempts to locate such ideas within the Wesleyan tradition of Christian perfection.[14] The whole issue has indeed sometimes proved a source of bitter controversy within American Methodism. Robert L. Wilson's sharp attack on the radical culture that supposedly prevailed among the 'leadership elite' of the United Methodist Church, published in 1988, was inspired among other things by his rejection of the pacifist ideas held by many of those in positions of authority.[15] The sharpness of the debate is perhaps testimony to the wisdom of the British church in seeking to avoid any definite posi-

251

tion on the whole question in favour of establishing some broad principles to guide its response in specific situations.

The debate on war and peace within British Methodism during the first half of the twentieth century took place primarily between the advocates of an unconditional pacifism and their critics who believed that there were occasions when a resort to war could prove the lesser of two evils. In the second half of the century the debate became more complex, as many members of the church committed themselves to 'nuclear pacifism', while not committing themselves to the position that war could never be justified under any circumstances. It is hard to see a distinct doctrinal base for the strong pacifist strand within Methodism, which can be traced back to the eighteenth century, although the emphasis on 'Christian perfectionism' probably helped to mould a set of values responsive to the notion that commitment to an absolute ethic was both morally necessary and sufficiently powerful to transform society. Methodist pacifism – like most Christian pacifism in the twentieth century – has been informed by an optimistic sense that an individual commitment to oppose war will help in time to transform the world, even if in the short term such a stand may bring ridicule and marginalization. The foundation for such a position has always ultimately been scriptural. Although it is possible to point to profound ambiguities within the Bible on the subject of war, the overwhelming logic of the gospels is clearly a commitment to peace, a love of neighbour, and a forgiveness of those who cause one injury or harm. All the most prominent Methodist pacifists of the twentieth century – men such as Samuel Keeble, Henry Carter and Donald Soper – have based their pacifism on a belief that support for war cannot be reconciled with the ethical teaching of the Sermon on the Mount. The fact that their pacifism has also been woven into a broader critique of the social and economic status quo does not undermine the biblical foundations of their position or simply make it part of a wider radical *Weltanschauung*.

The broad ethical foundation of the views expressed by individuals like Keeble and Soper, not to mention countless other men and women, has always made it easy for Methodist pacifists to co-operate both with pacifists in other denominations and with those whose pacifism is entirely secular in nature. There has from the First World War been a strong tradition of Christian pacifists in Britain coming together in organizations such as the Fellowship of Reconciliation. There has also always been a strong Christian presence in such organizations as the Peace Pledge Union (which draws its members from all backgrounds both religious and non-religious). It is possible to identify at least two reasons for this drive towards 'pacifist ecumenicalism' among members of the Methodist Church. In the first place, generations of pacifists have identified their commitment to pacifism as so important that it requires them to build coalitions with all those who share their basic position. In the second place, the Methodist Church has not for much of the twentieth century provided a particularly congenial 'home' for those of its members who were committed to an unconditional pacifism. While the Methodist Peace Fellowship and its predecessors have certainly helped to bring together like-minded individuals within the Methodist Church, they have not been particularly effective at winning over a majority of its members to the same position. The search for a wider 'pacifist community' has therefore been motivated in part by the need for pacifists to look beyond their own church to build links with others who share their views.

The pacifist tradition within the Methodist Church has throughout the twentieth century been outward-looking rather than sect-like in character. In the early part of the century it was clearly rooted in the radical tradition associated with men like John Bright, while as the years passed it began to borrow a language from the burgeoning socialist movement, seeing war as a product of the capitalist system rather than as a symptom of the human condition. While many leading pacifists such as Soper were keen to reject the claim that their ideas were utopian, it is not unfair to suggest that the perennial pitfall facing *all* Christian pacifists is a kind of 'hyper-moralism',[16] which seeks to judge the messy complexity of the world by the ideal standard of the Sermon on the Mount. At its best, as Archbishop

Temple pointed out in the Second World War, Christian pacifist witness has served as a reminder of the standard to which all Christians are bound to aspire. At its worst, it has failed to confront some harsh realities about the nature of international politics. This tension has on more than one occasion led those who call themselves pacifists to underestimate the tragic condition of the world, in order to reconcile their rejection of war with the hope that the human condition can be changed for the better. It has also led at times to an impatience with the kind of practical negotiations and compromises that often provide the best way of managing the 'international anarchy' that constantly threatens to explode into conflict. Reinhold Niebuhr recognized in his 1940 pamphlet *Why the Christian Church is not Pacifist* that a Christian pacifism which emphasized withdrawal from the world, in order not to become corrupted by involvement with the practical business of power politics, could be valuable in reminding the wider Church of the ultimate values by which man was meant to live.[17] He was by contrast sharply critical of those pacifists who believed that it was possible to develop full human communities based only on 'the law of love', rather than 'the law of sin', since they failed to base their position on a proper theological understanding of man and society. It is not necessary to accept all of Niebuhr's points to acknowledge that there is always a danger for pacifists of downplaying the iniquities of the world, in order to sustain intact the belief that a refusal to fight will not necessarily lead to the triumph of evil.

It is a reasonably easy matter to define the boundaries of 'Christian pacifism', at least if the term is taken as a description of those who argue that a resort to war can never be reconciled with the teachings of Christ, and ignores the more complex question of deciding whether the use of force by a state to maintain domestic order is qualitatively different from using force to defend or advance its interests in the international system. It is much harder to assign a simple label to those who do not accept such a position. It was seen in Chapter 3 that the historian Martin Ceadel has used the word 'pacificist' to describe those who, while seeking all possible means to avoid war, are ready to accept that there may be occasions when it represents the lesser of two evils. This position has in the Christian tradition been articulated most frequently in terms of the just war, as it has developed from the time of Augustine and Aquinas. A vast amount has been written on the idea of the just war during the past fifty years. At the heart of much of this debate has been the question of whether the just war tradition provides a fixed set of criteria for determining the conditions under which it is right to wage war, or offers instead 'a fund of practical moral wisdom, based not in abstract speculation or theorization but in reflection on actual problems encountered in war'.[18] The significance of most recent debate on the subject has rested on the fact that it is virtually impossible to imagine how any modern war can meet the traditional *jus in bello* criteria, given the devastating effect of modern weapons, an argument made by many nuclear disarmers in the churches when calling on governments to give up their weapons of mass destruction. It is for this reason that many of those who seek to preserve the idea of the just war as a useful guide to action in the modern world, rather than as a simple argument for nuclear disarmament, have in recent years stressed the need to prevent injustice rather than war *per se* (in effect emphasizing the traditional focus on 'right intention').[19]

The concept of the just war has always been far more influential in the Anglican and Catholic Churches than in the free churches. The present Archbishop of Canterbury Rowan Williams has himself addressed the whole question on more than one occasion.[20] It is by contrast striking that one senior Baptist could say of the second Gulf War that 'the just war tradition cut[s] very little ice with us Baptists. It is not part of our Christian teaching, and as such it didn't really help us a great deal in determining how we responded to the war'.[21] The situation has been more complex in the case of the Methodist Church. It is notable that members of the church seldom invoked the concept of the just war during the debates that took place during the First and Second World Wars. Although the main Methodist Churches produced a significant number of conscientious objectors during the 1914–18 War, majority opinion was sharply critical of their position, and indeed of those who took a pacifist line more generally. The language used to justify British participation in the war, whether at Conference or in newspapers like the *Methodist Recorder*, was often hard to distinguish from the broader patriotic rhetoric of the period. Numerous letters to the Methodist press cast doubt on the character of those who refused to fight and attacked those who sought to defend them. While the pacifist minority in the Methodist Church was treated rather better during the Second World War, the language that was used in formal church statements when putting its support behind the national war effort was once again suffused with the conventional rhetoric of patriotism, rather than a sustained theological reflection on the issues involved. The morality of the wholesale bombing of enemy cities received less attention in the Methodist Church than it did in the Church of England, where greater familiarity with the *jus in bello* criteria raised considerable qualms about the devastation being wrought on civilian populations. It was only in the post-war period that the idea of the just war began to gain greater currency in Methodist circles. The origins of this change may in part have been found in the burgeoning ecumenical instinct within Methodism, which made it more open to the intellectual influences of other denominations, but it probably owed still more to the new challenge posed by nuclear weapons. The fact that the use of such devastating weapons would lead to total devastation, disproportionate to any conceivable compensating good, was a central factor in leading the church to record its view during the 1950s that the use of such weapons could never be justified (even if, perhaps paradoxically, it did not go one step further and state that maintaining such weapons as a deterrent was also unacceptable).

Many of the opinions expressed by members of the Methodist Church on questions of peace and war during the first half of the twentieth century were articulated in terms of a set of assumptions that can be designated for convenience by the label 'Christian Realism'. A large number of those who wrote letters to the Methodist press during the two world wars were inspired by little more than a vague notion that it was right for Britain to go to war to prevent the triumph of opponents who were uncivilized and brutal. There was inherent in such an argument a sense that it was necessary for Christians to accept that the use of force was sometimes necessary in order to prevent the triumph of evil in the world. Some more thoughtful contributors to Methodist publications sought to put this insight into a definite theological framework, arguing in effect that the biblical injunctions to 'love thy neighbour' and to 'turn the other cheek' were best understood as part of a transcendent ethic, which could not be applied in a simplistic fashion to the complexities of the mundane world. Nevertheless, while a number of Methodists were familiar during the first half of the century with the ideas of theologians like Barth and Niebuhr, their reflections were more often the fruit of their own deliberations, which perhaps helps to explain why in both world wars Methodism failed to articulate a distinctively 'Christian' language to respond to the ethical challenges of total war. Nor did the sophisticated ideas developed in the post-war period by the life-long Methodist and Cambridge historian Herbert Butterfield have much impact on his own church, even though they had extensive influence in academe, with their discussion of the way in which a Christian understanding of the imperfect nature of the world can foster creative attempts to manage international tension via the practical processes of diplomacy.

The era of the Cold War raised a new set of challenges that to a degree superseded the old pacifist–non-pacifist division within the Methodist Church. It has already been noted that the invention of nuclear weapons raised the question of whether the use of such instruments could ever be reconciled with the idea of a just war. The support for 'nuclear pacifism' within the church partly reflected the fact that the Soviet regime, even in the depths of the Cold War, never commanded the degree of antipathy that had previously been directed towards Nazi Germany. There was some sense among many leading Methodists in the 1940s and 1950s that communism as an ideology had certain moral virtues, in the sense that it at least claimed to be on the side of social and economic justice, and that

257

the challenge posed by the USSR resulted primarily from the failure of its government to live up to its own declared values. The manifest problem of justifying the possession of nuclear weapons in terms of the just war tradition has without doubt created problems for all those within the churches – including the Methodist Church – who remain doubtful about criticizing successive governments for their commitment to maintaining an independent British deterrent. Those who have been committed to this position have generally put forward one of two main lines of argument. The first argument is that governments alone have the capacity and knowledge to make such judgements, with the result that the churches need to be wary of becoming involved in areas where they have no particular expertise. The second argument, put with great vehemence by one delegate at the 2006 Conference, is the need to recognize the value of prudence in an uncertain world where it is impossible to predict the future. Both these arguments have force. It is nevertheless hard to see in what sense they are particularly 'Christian'. They instead reflect – as so often has been the case – the broader secular debate. This is not to argue that there is no prospect of reconciling the possession of nuclear weapons with the Christian conscience. If it can be shown that a nuclear deterrent not only protects a country against attack, but actually operates as a factor for stability in the international system, then the case can certainly be made. Even the most determined multilateralist must nevertheless be bound to acknowledge that weapons of mass destruction represent a fundamental challenge to the creation whether understood in theological or simple historical terms.

Another factor breaking down the simple distinction between 'pacifists' and 'non-pacifists' in the post-war era has been the development of a new agenda within the Methodist Church that seeks to locate the causes of war in the persistence of international inequality and injustice. Leading figures in the church were already keen in the 1960s to show how the gap between the rich and poor nations was creating tensions that threatened to undermine world peace. The development of a 'North–South' focus represented a shift to a wider conception of 'peacemaking' that was eventually articulated in the 2006 Report discussed earlier. The emphasis placed by the Methodist Church over the past thirty years on such questions as Third-World debt and the evil of apartheid has reflected a 'one world' ethos that assumes that injustices in any part of the globe will in time foster tensions and instabilities across the international system. The tendency of some leading Methodists to dismiss the significance of the East–West split during the final twenty years or so of the Cold War was, however, sometimes rooted in a failure to understand both the iniquities committed within the Soviet bloc and the extent of the challenge posed to the West by the USSR. Although the Soviet Union of Brezhnev and Andropov was not the Soviet Union of Joseph Stalin, it was still a country that systematically repressed its own people, while creating more misery abroad through its support for some of the world's most unsavoury regimes. The regime imposed by Mao in China was even more brutal.[22] One of the most significant impacts of the Vietnam War was to encourage many in the West to assume there was some kind of moral equivalence between Moscow and Washington, a calculation that was too simplistic, and reflected above all the fact that the United States was an open society whose faults were exposed to the gaze of the world. There was nevertheless always some justice in the argument, put by writers like Colin Morris, that worldwide poverty and disease represented the greatest challenge to the Christian conscience. The new focus within the Methodist Church on the North–South division inevitably generated its own tensions. The support expressed by some senior Methodists for the liberation movements of Africa and Latin America appeared to many more traditionally minded members of the church as a form of political activism that went beyond the boundaries of the permissible. While there was little dissent from the view that the church should encourage greater international aid, and support efforts to eradicate disease, the attempts to challenge the structural foundations of inequality at home and abroad appeared to some as a political obsession that threatened to divert the Methodist Church from its real business. The debates that raged on the subject at Conference and in the Methodist press represented two different views of what the church was 'for'. The first emphasized action and commitment to social and political change as a primary expression of what it meant to live out the gospel. The second took a more traditional view of the church as a place concerned with helping its members live their lives in a Christian community that did not neglect the problems of the world, but which refused to place them at the heart of all its activities. Such a development was of course hardly unprecedented. The tension between the 'conservative' and 'radical' traditions within Methodism can be traced back to the times of Wesley himself.

The end of the Cold War signalled the development of a new pattern of international politics that raised still more difficult questions for all the churches when seeking to define their attitudes towards questions of peace and war. The dispatch of British troops to the South Atlantic in 1982 had been designed to reverse an Argentinian attack on territory for which London was directly responsible. The situation in the first Gulf War was rather different, since British forces were deployed in a coalition acting under the auspices of the United Nations, charged with reversing a clear-cut case of illegal aggression against a member state. Despite the long-standing commitment within Methodism to the principle of collective security, there was strong criticism of the first Gulf War, particularly among those who believed that the real objective of coalition forces was to secure oil supplies rather than liberate the Kuwaiti people. Many of those in the Methodist Church who opposed the war explicitly used the language of the just war when putting forward their views, either questioning the morality of the cause, or suggesting that the devastation caused by the conflict would outweigh any possible good. Although there was greater support for the various British military interventions in Yugoslavia, which were designed to ameliorate the humanitarian crisis there, there was even more passionate opposition to the second Gulf War of 2003. The failure of the British and American governments to obtain an explicit UN resolution permitting their action was widely regarded as evidence that the military

*I supported the first Gulf War but was dubious about the second*

260

intervention was unlawful. While this somewhat legalistic approach was challenged by those who argued that the key point at issue was the despotic nature of the Iraqi government, there is no doubt that many of those in positions of authority within the Methodist Church believed that the position of the British and American governments was unconvincing, and driven more by the desire to advance their own interests in the Gulf rather than to bring peace to the region. The most striking thing about much of the discussion that has taken place within British Methodism on international affairs during the post-Cold War period has been its anti-establishment ethos, characterized by a fundamental scepticism about the actions and principles articulated by successive governments, both Labour and Conservative. Such a development has not been limited to Methodism but has also been visible across all the main churches. It is not of course difficult to comprehend such a position. It can certainly be argued that the role of the churches is to offer a 'prophetic voice', or at least to articulate principled positions designed as a yardstick against which it is possible to measure the morality of the responses proposed by governments to the challenges they face on a daily basis. It nevertheless remains a clear danger that the churches' position on international politics – and indeed political questions more generally – fails to engage with the limitations and complexities that form the warp and woof of the problems that necessarily engage political leaders.

One of the most challenging problems facing all the churches in the twentieth century has been the need to ensure that politicians are made aware of their opinions on a whole range of issues. During the late nineteenth century the 'Nonconformist Conscience' was able to make itself felt through the workings of the political process, given the influence of the Nonconformist churches on the Liberal Party. The political realignments of the twentieth century, along with the elusive but real phenomenon of 'secularization', have demanded new strategies for exerting leverage. The situation has always been easiest for the Church of England. The media provide greater attention to the views of bishops than they do to the chairs of districts, while membership of the House of Lords still provides a forum for influence, both through the formal legislative process and via the more discreet channels of private conversation and networking. The British Council of Churches and its successors have in the post-war world provided new opportunities for the churches to act together to influence government. Many of the reports commended to the Methodist Conference on issues such as nuclear weapons and development aid have been BCC documents produced by working groups composed of members drawn from across the churches. The churches have also often worked together through the BCC and its successors when seeking to influence government on such questions as the Falklands War. The 'lobbying efforts' of all the main churches have certainly become more professional in recent decades. The Methodist Church has not been alone in appointing individuals equipped with the experience and knowledge needed to make their voice heard among the cacophony created by the 'lobbying industry'. It is virtually a truism among political scientists to suggest that the most effective way to influence government policy is by the patient cultivation of networks of influence rather than through public 'grandstanding'. Although third-sector organizations such as aid agencies and the churches were at first much slower than businesses and professional associations in grasping this point, they have made up considerable ground in recent years, recognizing that their authority will always be limited if they simply content themselves with sending resolutions and statements to government.

There is a further dimension to this whole question that touches on the question of how the churches relate to governments and the political process. It was raised in a very articulate manner by Alan Booth, Secretary to the World Council of Churches Commission on International Affairs, in his 1970 Beckly Social Service Lecture on the topic of 'Christian Nonconformity in International Affairs'.[23] Booth had enormous experience of dealing with governments around the world, and he chose in his lecture to articulate some of his thoughts in terms of a crafted Christian Realism, which assumed that the churches could only expect to exercise influence if they thought

262

seriously about their role and strategy. He questioned the view that the churches should operate as 'perpetual critics' of government policy, arguing instead for a more constructive form of engagement, based on the principle of both 'involvement and detachment'. Booth then went on to suggest that the churches needed to spend less time issuing bland statements, and more time seeking to understand the problems faced by governments, so that they could engage with them on the basis of a recognition that political leaders all had to make difficult choices under conditions of uncertainty. Although his words were not directed towards Methodism in particular, they can certainly be helpful when reviewing how the Methodist Church has tried to make its voice heard on international affairs. The Methodist Conference has often issued well-meaning statements that are long on sentiment but short on practical detail, in effect seeking to establish what one writer has called 'a moral viewpoint sufficiently elevated above all the concrete choices to be made in proximate situations in which it never has to pay the costs of given policies'.[24] In other words, criticism is easy; practical recommendations are hard. Governments always listen most carefully to organizations and groups that offer well-crafted policy proposals located within the established political consensus. While it is true that the Division of Christian Citizenship and its successor bodies have been commendably diligent in 'grounding' their recommendations in a detailed study of specific issues, many of the positions taken on international affairs by the Methodist Church over the past forty years have been sharply at odds with official thinking. The price of a prophetic voice is all too likely to be marginalization.

The whole question of the Methodist Church's influence on government decisions about international affairs raises once again the complex question of how it develops its position on key questions. It was already clear in the 1930s that the views of many Methodist ministers on questions of war and peace were out of line with those of their congregations. At least a fifth of all Methodist ministers considered themselves to be pacifists in the late 1930s. The proportion of unconditional pacifists among their congregations was almost certainly much lower. In the post-war period the situation has become still more complex. It seems likely that the political opinions of 'ordinary' Methodists have often been more conservative than might be guessed from a brief perusal of Conference resolutions. Although it is impossible to determine exactly what proportion of Methodists voted for Margaret Thatcher during the late 1970s and 1980s, it is certain that her Conservative government attracted considerable support from members of the church, even though Conference passed numerous resolutions that were in effect sharply critical of her government's policies both at home and abroad. The international agenda that has evolved within the Methodist Church over the past forty years has exhibited a decidedly radical timbre: the need to campaign for economic and racial justice around the world; the need to fight the arms trade, and so forth. There is nothing wrong with such a radical vision. It is certainly not hard to make the case that it represents part of a longer-term rethinking of Christian ethics, a shift in attention away from a traditional focus on individual behaviour, in favour of a more sustained reflection on how the Christian faith can be lived out in the concrete setting of the national and international community. It does nevertheless remain the case that the public 'profile' of the Methodist Church has since the Second World War probably appeared to the outside world as more radical than a sociological and attitudinal survey of its members might lead one to expect. This is not in itself remarkable. Most churches are marked by a degree of disjunction between an articulate 'core', which is not necessarily coterminous with the formal hierarchy, and a more passive mass membership. Robert Wilson noted when writing about the United Methodist Church in America that the focus of most ordinary church members, both lay and ministerial, was on local concerns rather than broader national and international issues. There is certainly no reason to echo Wilson's sharp attack against the 'leadership elite' for ignoring grass-roots opinion when discussing the situation in the Methodist Church in Britain. It is nevertheless fair to suggest that there has for many decades been a difference in perspective between those who have the time and interest to reflect at length on how their church should react to the major challenges of the modern world, and those for whom commitment to their church is more personal, and rooted in day-to-day involvement in the rhythms of local circuit life.

It was noted in the first chapter that a study of the response of British Methodism to the main international challenges of the twentieth century can cast some light on public opinion more generally. This is not to suggest that members of the Methodist Church have always formed a representative 'subset' of the wider population. An examination of the views expressed by its members can nevertheless show how certain key issues of international politics resonated beyond the world of government. It is striking to see how closely discussions within British Methodism on international issues during the first half of the twentieth century echoed those of the wider society. The First World War was for the most part uncritically accepted as a war for civilization; the Second World War was accepted as a moral crusade against a totalitarian foe whose government espoused an ideology based on hatred and violence. The pacifist critique of this majority view was a noisy but essentially peripheral counterpoint. Its proponents were accepted for the most part as legitimate embodiments of a long-standing tradition of dissent who had the right to voice their concerns, and act according to their conscience, but they were generally viewed as an unrepresentative minority within a church that espoused the national cause. In the years since 1945, though, it appears that this pattern began to change. Many senior figures in the Methodist Church resisted the pressure to see the Cold War as a battle between good and evil in which communist states took the role played by Nazi Germany between 1939 and 1945. And a very large number of church members were reluctant to accept the claim that possession of nuclear weapons was a legitimate form of defence against a potential aggressor. The growing emphasis on North–South issues, particularly from the 1960s onwards, reflected an attempt to challenge the dominant paradigm of thinking about international politics away from one in which East–West relations exercised a central position. Some of these positions were sharply opposed by 'ordinary' Methodists, but it remains striking that the Methodist Church, along with the other churches, did seek to provide a distinctive perspective on the changes taking place in the world beyond Britain's shores. The Methodist Church as an institution sought to question many of the central assumptions and values of the policy-makers who shaped the world after 1945. This perspective may at times have seemed irrelevant to demands of the 'real world', but it did at least make an effort to encourage fresh ways of thinking about international politics, inspired by values and commitments distinct from those who held positions in government.

There was a time in the 1960s and the 1970s when the study of religion seemed to be of little more than historical interest in a world moving inexorably towards a world of secular modernity. The whole question of religion and international politics has now become a central topic in scholarly debate, fuelled by the rise of terrorism and the ongoing crisis in the Middle East. Scholars and journalists now all too often see 'religion' as a source of conflict rather than a potential force for peace in the world. The role of religious extremism in fomenting conflict has even led to a slew of books attacking all forms of religion as a malign force undermining the search for rational solutions to the problems facing human society.[25] Many of these accounts fail to master the complexity of the phenomenon that they seek to condemn. There does nevertheless seem to be some truth to the claim that the conditions of postmodernity have, at least in certain cases, marginalized traditional liberal patterns of religious belief in favour of more fundamentalist forms of expression. It has been convincingly argued by many scholars and commentators that religious fundamentalism in all its various guises does not so much seek a return to the genuine forms and beliefs of the past, but is instead a 'modern' response to the challenges of the contemporary world.[26] All these factors have together made it too easy in recent years for a secular audience to elide the whole kaleidoscope of religions into a single category, based on the assumption that 'religion' represents a threat rather than an asset in the search for a more peaceful world.

There is a danger in being overly pessimistic. Every generation tends to fall into the trap of believing that the problems it faces are unprecedented. While at the time of writing it is hard to imagine a successful resolution to the 'war on terror' and the crisis in Iraq, it may well be that in twenty or thirty years' time the concerns facing the world will be very different, perhaps revolving around the threat of climate change and the associated problems of famine and mass migration. The impression that 'religion' is a cause of global conflict is over-simplistic even in the age of Al Qaeda. Although there are countless cases in history where the irreconcilable claims of different religious groups have led to conflict and repression, there is also no shortage of examples where adherents of different faiths have lived together in peace, and even more in which those inspired by religious convictions of whatever kind have taken the lead in bringing reconciliation and healing to communities ripped apart by strife. It is a platitude – but also true – to say that religion in all its guises has throughout history brought out both the best and the worst in human beings. One of the main responsibilities of the churches must therefore be to provide a distinct yet practical Christian witness to the value of peace in a world of conflict, rejecting both a pessimism that argues that nothing will ever change, and a millennial optimism that believes the human condition can be transformed once and for all within the realm of history.

The debates within the Methodist Church about the challenges of war and peace have shown a distinct constellation of strengths and weaknesses. The values of what was once quaintly called 'the social gospel' have fostered recognition that problems of war and peace, conflict and justice, must necessarily engage the Christian conscience. The passionate debates that have taken place over such questions as nuclear disarmament reflect the church's ongoing commitment to engaging with the problems of the real world. The Methodist Church has also been successful down the years at understanding that passionate opinions on such topics can lead to division, and that the best way to forestall such divisions is to recognize the right of the individual to follow the dictates of their conscience, a philosophy rooted both in pragmatism and in the Nonconformist heritage. These strengths have – perhaps unavoidably – on occasion been juxtaposed by certain corresponding weaknesses. There has not always been enough hard thinking – either theologically or 'practically' – about the distinctive contribution that the Methodist Church can and should make to debates about international politics. An 'oppositional mentality' that rejects all the prevailing values and management mechanisms of the international political system is likely both to marginalize its critical impact and to condemn itself to a utopianism that fails to engage with the complex causes of global conflict. A 'mentality of over-engagement' is likely to forfeit a specifically Christian perspective on the problems of war and peace by mimicking the language used by policy-makers and diplomats. Both these mentalities have been seen at work in the course of much of the twentieth century. The role of the Methodist Church – like all the churches – is to develop its role as a critical friend that seeks to understand the situations faced by governments without believing that its members have the answers to detailed practical problems that evade those who are more expert and experienced in the ways of the world. The final word must, though, be one of optimism for the future. The recognition of the complex and fragile nature of peace has become far more widespread in recent years across all the churches. The report on *Peacemaking* published in 2006 recognized that genuine peacemaking needs to look beyond the world of states and focus on all forms of conflict wherever they are found in the world. The future challenge is to harness this optimism to facing the problems encountered in the everyday world, ranging from conflict between states in the international system, through to the racial and religious conflicts that divide communities around the globe. There was time when to be a 'realist' was to accept that the major cause of international conflict was the clash of national interests between different states. To be a realist today is to grasp the full complexity of conflict in a globalized world where civil war and inter-communal strife is more prevalent than war between sover-eign states.

The Russian writer Alexander Solzhenitsyn once wrote that 'The line between good and evil runs through the heart of every human being.' His words offer a salutary reminder that no single social or political system can ever hope to resolve altogether the tensions and contradictions that form part of the human condition. The role of all the churches, the Methodist Church included, must always be to promote the cause of peace even in a world in which the words of the peacemaker are often drowned out by the noise of conflict and strife.

An Important and
WEll written book

# Notes

## 1 Introduction

1 For an interesting discussion on the attitude of the early Church towards war, see C.J. Cadoux, *The Early Christian Attitude to War* (London, 1919).

2 Quoted in Peter Brock, *Pacifism in Europe to 1914* (Princeton, 1972), p. 11.

3 For a useful discussion of Augustine's ideas on 'just war', along with those of some of his modern followers, see William R. Stevenson, *Christian Love and Just War* (Manchester, 1987).

4 Among the vast literature on Christian pacifism, see for example Clive Barrett (ed.), *Visions of Christian Pacifism* (Cambridge, 1987); C.J. Cadoux, *Christian Pacifism Re-examined* (London, 1940); Daniel A. Dombrowski, *Christian Pacifism* (Philadelphia, 1991); G.F. Nuttall, *Christian Pacifism in History* (Berkeley, 1971).

5 See for example A.J.P. Taylor, *The Troublemakers: Dissent over Foreign Policy, 1792–1939* (London, 1993).

6 Among the massive biographical literature on Wesley, see in particular Henry D. Rack, *Reasonable Enthusiast: John Wesley and the Rise of Methodism* (London, 1989).

7 *The Letters of John Wesley*, 8 vols (London, 1931), vol. 6, p. 161.

8 'A Calm Address to our American Colonies', *The Works of John Wesley* (London, 1872), vol. 11, p. 124.

9 'A Seasonable Address to the More Serious Part of the Inhabitants of Great Britain', Wesley, *Works*, vol. 11, pp. 120, 123.

10 Briane K. Turley, 'John Wesley and War', *Methodist History*, 29, 2 (1991), pp. 96–111 (citation from p. 106).

11 Turley, 'John Wesley and War'.

12 'The Doctrine of Original Sin', Wesley, *Works*, vol. 9, p. 221.

13 For a valuable sympathetic critique of Wesley's position from one of the leading Methodist theologians of the twentieth century, see R. Newton Flew, *The Idea of Perfection in Christian Theology* (London, 1934). For some useful comments from one of the leading Methodist preachers of the twentieth century on

the impact of Wesley's ideas on thinking about peace and war, see W.E. Sangster, *The Path to Perfection* (London, 1943), p. 183.

14 *Wesley's Veterans: Lives of Early Methodist Preachers told by Themselves*, 8 vols (London, 1909–14), vol. 3, pp. 120, 146–7, 150.

15 Quoted in the Introduction by Bernard Simmel, to Elie Halévy, *The Birth of Methodism in England* (Chicago, 1971), p. 9. For a recent useful discussion of this theme by a Methodist scholar, see John Munsey Turner, *John Wesley: The Evangelical Revival and the Birth of Methodism in England* (London, 2002), pp. 131–50.

16 Eric Hobsbawm, 'Methodism and the Threat of Revolution in Britain', in Eric Hobsbawm, *Labouring Men* (London, 1964), pp. 22–33.

17 Quoted in John Kent, 'Methodism and Politics in the Nineteenth Century', in John Kent, *The Age of Disunity* (London, 1966), p. 127. The works Kent refers to are Maldwyn Edwards, *After Wesley* and R.F. Wearmouth, *Methodism and Working Class Movements, 1800–1850*.

18 On Hughes, see Dorothea Price Hughes, *The Life of Hugh Price Hughes* (London, 1904); Christopher Oldstone-Moore, *Hugh Price Hughes: Founder of a New Methodism, Conscience of a New Nonconformity* (Cardiff, 1999).

19 Among the vast literature on the impact of Methodism on the development of the British Labour movement, see Robert Wearmouth, *Methodism and the Struggle of the Working Classes, 1850–1900* (Leicester, 1954); Robert Wearmouth, *The Social and Political Influence of Methodism in the Twentieth century* (London, 1957); E.J. Hobsbawm, *Primitive Rebels* (London, 1974).

20 On the history of the Peace Society, see A.C.F. Beales, *The History of Peace* (London, 1931); Peter Brock, *Pacifism in Europe to 1914* (Princeton, 1972), pp. 367–406.

21 Brock, *Pacifism*, pp. 380, 392.

22 Some useful reflections on the changing character of the Wesleyan Church in the nineteenth century can be found in R.B. Walker, 'The Growth of Wesleyan Methodism in Victorian England and Wales', *Journal of Ecclesiastical History*, 24, 3 (1973), pp. 267–84.

23 Quoted in Brock, *Pacifism*, p. 352.

24 Quoted in John Morley, *Life of Richard Cobden* (London, 1903), p. 159.

25 *Methodist Recorder*, 11 July 1876.

26 *Methodist Recorder*, 11 January 1878.

27 *Methodist Recorder*, 8 March 1878.

28 Clive Field, 'A Sociological Profile of British Methodism, 1900–1932', *Oral History*, 4, 1 (1976), pp. 73–95.

29 For some useful comments on this theme, see R. Pinder, 'Religious Change in the Process of Secularisation', *Sociological Review*, 19, 3 (1971), pp. 343–66. Other useful discussions of the phenomenon of 'secularization' include Callum Brown, *The Death of Christian Britain: Understanding Secularization, 1800–2000* (London, 2001); David Martin, *A General Theory of Secularization* (Oxford, 1978).

30  Robert L. Wilson, *Biases and Blindspots: Methodism and Foreign Policy since World War II* (Wilmore, Ky. 1988) focuses on the opinions of what he terms the 'leadership elite' in his study of attitudes within the United Methodist Church. His methodology is, however, very much driven by a desire to illustrate the gulf in attitudes between an elite and the grass roots within the Church. Although this subject is touched on in this book, the different intention here means that the focus is cast more broadly (and less intemperately) than in Wilson's own work.

31  See, for example, the various essays in Clive Marsh *et al.* (eds), *Unmasking Methodist Theology* (Trowbridge, 2004).

## 2  From the Boer War to the First World War

1  Among the vast literature on British foreign policy before the First World War, see John Charmley, *Splendid Isolation? Britain, the Balance of Power and the First World War* (London, 1999); George W. Monger, *The End of Isolation: British Foreign Policy, 1900–1907* (London, 1963). A useful account of international politics before 1914 can be found in James Joll, *The Origins of the First World War* (London, 1984).

2  Some useful reflections on this subject can be found in G.R. Searle, *The Quest for National Efficiency* (Oxford, 1971); Samuel Hynes, *The Edwardian Turn of Mind* (Princeton, 1968).

3  J. Armitage Robinson *et al*, *Hugh Price Hughes as We Knew Him* (London, 1902), p. 79.

4  *Methodist Times*, 8 September 1887 (Editorial on 'The War Madness').

5  *Methodist Times*, 31 January 1889 (Report of Hughes sermon on 'The Deadly Militarism of Lord Wolseley').

6  Quoted in D.W. Bebbington, *Evangelicalism in Modern Britain* (London, 1993), p. 216.

7  For a useful discussion of Nonconformist reaction to the Armenian slaughter, see D.W. Bebbington, *The Nonconformist Conscience: Chapel and Conscience in Modern Britain* (London, 1982), pp. 116–18.

8  See, for example, *Methodist Times*, 14 November 1895 (Editorial on 'Lord Salisbury and the Turk').

9  *Methodist Times*, 17 September 1896 (Notes of Current Events).

10  *Methodist Recorder*, 1 October 1896 (Editorial Notes).

11  *Methodist Times*, 24 September 1896 (Report on a public meeting in Manchester).

12  *Methodist Times*, 1 October 1896 (Editorial on 'The Awakening of England').

13  *Methodist Times*, 17 September 1896 (Letter by W.M. Crook).

14  *Free Methodist*, 1 October 1896 (Notes on Current Events).

15  *Primitive Methodist*, 1 October 1896 (Editorial on 'The Armenian Question').

# Notes

16 *Primitive Methodist,* 8 October 1896 (Report of a public meeting in Middlesbrough).

17 *Primitive Methodist Magazine,* October 1896, p. 717.

18 *Primitive Methodist Magazine,* April 1897, p. 320.

19 *Methodist Times,* 1 April 1897 (Notes of Current Events).

20 For a vivid general account of the Boer War, see Thomas Packenham, *The Boer War* (London, 1979).

21 For a useful discussion of the anti-war movement (including some material on opposition to the war in Methodist circles) see Stephen Koss (ed.), *The Anatomy of an Anti-War Movement: The Pro-Boers* (Chicago, 1973). Also see Arthur M. Davey, *The British Pro-Boers, 1877–1902* (Tafelberg, 1978).

22 Arthur Grimble, *A Pattern of Islands* (London, 1952), p. 1.

23 For some useful reflections on this theme, see the various essays in Eric Hobsbawm and Terence Ranger (eds), *The Invention of Tradition* (London, 1983).

24 For a useful biography of Richard Cobden, including his views on imperial questions, see Nicholas C. Edsell, *Richard Cobden: Independent Radical* (Cambridge, Mass., 1986). On Bright, see Keith Robbins, *John Bright* (London, 1979).

25 William Arthur, *What is Fiji, the Sovereignty of which is offered to Her Majesty?* (London, 1859).

26 *Parliamentary Debates* (1872), vol. 212 (Debate on 25 June 1872).

27 For some general discussions of Hughes's view of empire, see Oldstone-Moore, *Hugh Price Hughes,* pp. 311ff.; Stephen Koss, 'Wesleyanism and Empire', *Historical Journal,* 18, 1 (1975), pp. 105–18.

28 *Methodist Times,* 31 January 1889 (Report of a sermon preached by Hughes at St James's Hall on 27 January 1889).

29 Oldstone-Moore, *Hugh Price Hughes,* pp. 183ff. On the controversy over the Wesleyan Missionary Society, also see Sir Henry Lunn, *Chapters from My Life* (London, 1918), pp. 88–128.

30 *Methodist Times,* 27 October 1887 (Report of meeting of the second and third London districts on Wesleyan foreign missions).

31 'The Command of the Sea', *London Quarterly Review,* 85 (1896), pp. 315, 325, 326.

32 'Europe in Africa', *London Quarterly Review,* 85 (1896), p. 220.

33 A.S. Geden, 'Nigeria', *London Quarterly Review,* 92 (1899), p. 265.

34 Urquhart A. Forbes, 'The Diffusion of Modern Civilisation', *London Quarterly Review,* 92 (1899), pp. 340, 344.

35 Dorothea Price Hughes, *The Life of Hugh Price Hughes* (London, 1904), p. 550.

36 *Methodist Times,* 12 October 1899 (Notes of Current Events).

37 *Methodist Times,* 7 November 1901 (Notes of Current Events). On the concentration camps, see for example A.W.G. Raath (ed.), *The British Concentration Camps of the Anglo-Boer War 1899–1902* (Bloemfontaine, 1999)

38 Davey, *British Pro-Boers,* p. 150.

273

39  The best discussion by far on the subject can be found in H.C.G. Matthew, *The Liberal Imperialists* (Oxford, 1973).

40  E.H. Fowler, *The Life of Henry Hartley Fowler, First Viscount Wolverhampton* (London, 1912), p. 461.

41  Denis Crane, *The Life-Story of Sir Robert Perks* (London, 1909), p. 203.

42  *Methodist Times*, 20 September 1900 (Notes of Current Events).

43  J.M. Turner, 'Methodism in England, 1900–1932', in Rupert Davies *et al.* (eds), *A History of the Methodist Church in Great Britain* (London, 1965–88), vol. 3, p. 349.

44  Hughes, *Life of Hugh Price Hughes*, p. 554.

45  On Clifford's attitude towards the war, see Sir James Marchant, *Dr John Clifford: Life, Letters and Reminiscences* (London, 1924), pp. 145ff. On the role of the Free Church Council in the Boer War, including the role played by some free churchmen in writing a manifesto to serve as the possible basis of peace, see E.K.H. Jordan, *Free Church Unity: History of the Free Church Council Movement, 1896–1941* (London, 1956), pp. 72–6.

46  Koss, *The Pro-Boers*, p. 231.

47  Hughes, *Life of Hugh Price Hughes*, p. 291.

48  Quoted in Maldwyn Edwards, *Methodism and England* (London, 1944), p. 176.

49  *Methodist Weekly*, 1 November 1900 (Editorial on 'Belligerent Christians').

50  *Methodist Weekly*, 6 December 1900 (Editorial Notes).

51  *Methodist Weekly*, 8 November 1900 (Letter by Dr S. Lunn).

52  *Methodist Weekly*, 15 November 1900 (Letter by the Revd Michael Elliot).

53  *Methodist Weekly*, 15 November 1900 (Editorial Notes).

54  *Methodist Weekly*, 27 June 1901 (Editorial Notes).

55  *Methodist Weekly*, 13 June 1901 (Editorial Notes).

56  *Methodist Weekly*, 16 January 1902 (Editorial Notes).

57  *Methodist Weekly*, 29 May 1902 (Editorial on 'The Two Imperialisms').

58  *Primitive Methodist World*, 5 October 1899 (Notes and Comments).

59  *Primitive Methodist*, 25 January 1900 (Editorial on 'The War and Christian Philanthropy').

60  *Primitive Methodist World*, 5 October 1899 (Notes and Comments).

61  *Primitive Methodist World*, 19 October 1899 (Topics of the Week).

62  See, for example, *Primitive Methodist World*, 30 November 1899.

63  For details of Hocking's career, including his activities during the Boer War, see Silas K. Hocking, *My Book of Memory* (London, 1923).

64  *Primitive Methodist World*, 8 March 1900 (Topics of the Week). For a useful description of the violence that could face those who opposed the war, see Hocking, *Book of Memory*, pp. 181, 185.

65  *Primitive Methodist World*, 2 November 1899 (Topics of the Week).

66  *Primitive Methodist World*, 1 February 1900 (Report on a sermon preached by Revd D. Watson at Higher Openshaw, 28 January 1900).

67  *Primitive Methodist World*, 10 August 1899 (Report of speech by Butt in July 1899 at Aliwal North).

68  *Primitive Methodist World*, 31 August 1899 (Letter by the Revd John Smith).

69  *Primitive Methodist*, 17 May 1900 (By-the-Way column).

70  *Primitive Methodist*, 26 July 1900, 2 August 1900 (Letters by the Revd Edwin Smith).

71  *Free Methodist*, 22 March 1900 (Letter by the Revd William Redfern).

72  *Free Methodist*, 12 July 1900 (Report on Free Methodist Conference).

73  *Methodist Weekly*, 29 January 1903 (Editorial on 'Slavery for South Africa').

74  See, for example, *Methodist Times*, 1 February 1906 ('Outlook' by Historicus).

75  Bebbington, *Nonconformist Conscience*, pp. 153–60; see, too, Stephen Koss, *Nonconformity in Modern British Politics* (London, 1975), pp. 100–24.

76  See, for example, E.D. Morel, *Red Rubber: The Story of the Rubber Slave Trade Flourishing on the Congo in the Year of Grace 1906* (London, 1906). For a general discussion of Morel's role in the Congo Reform Movement, see Catherine Ann Cline, *E.D. Morel, 1873–1924: The Strategies of Protest* (Belfast, 1980), pp. 20–67.

77  E.D. Morel, *Morocco in Diplomacy* (London, 1912).

78  For a summary of the various attacks made on the old diplomacy, see Michael Hughes, *Diplomacy Before the Russian Revolution* (London, 2000), pp. 1–19.

79  For details of Guttery's long career, see John G. Bowran, *The Life of Thomas Arthur Guttery* (London, 1921).

80  *Primitive Methodist Leader*, 10 September 1908 (Article by Guttery on 'Who is the Liberal Foreign Minister?').

81  *Primitive Methodist Leader*, 8 August 1912 (Article by Guttery on 'The Price of Peace').

82  See, for example, *Primitive Methodist Leader*, 25 January 1912 (Current Events).

83  For a useful series of essays about Grey's time at the Foreign Office, including his attitudes on a variety of questions, see F.H. Hinsley (ed.), *British Foreign Policy under Sir Edward Grey* (Cambridge, 1977).

84  *Methodist Times*, 28 February 1889 (Report of a sermon by Hughes on 'Arbitration and War').

85  For the background to the decision to call the Conference, see Dan L. Morrill, 'Nicholas II and the Call for the First Hague Conference', *Journal of Modern History*, 46, 2 (1974), pp. 296–313.

86  *Methodist Times*, 22 December 1898 (Editorial on 'England's Supreme Opportunity').

87  Darril Hudson, *The Ecumenical Movement in World Affairs* (London, 1969), pp. 6–7.

88  *Primitive Methodist Leader*, 23 March 1911 (Current Events).

89  *Primitive Methodist Leader*, 6 July 1911 (Article by Henshaw on 'The Splendours of Peace').

90  *Methodist Times*, 16 March 1911 (Notes and Comments).

91  *Methodist Times*, 23 March 1911 (Notes and Comments).

92  *Methodist Recorder*, 23 March 1911 (Editorial Notes).

93  *United Methodist*, 31 October 1907 (Notes on Current Events).

94  A useful account of the Dreadnought issue in Anglo-German relations can be found in Robert Massie, *Dreadnought: Britain, Germany and the Coming of the Great War* (London, 1992). A helpful discussion of the agitation for rearmament during these years can be found in A.J.A. Morris, *The Scaremongers: The Advocacy of War and Rearmament, 1896–1914* (London, 1984).

95  *Primitive Methodist Leader*, 25 January 1906 (Current Events).

96  *Primitive Methodist Leader*, 8 March 1906 (Current Events); 2 August 1906 (Current Events).

97  *Primitive Methodist Leader*, 26 January 1911 (Current Events); 16 February 1911 (Current Events).

98  Bebbington, *Nonconformist Conscience*, p. 154.

99  *Methodist Times*, 16 January 1908 (Notes of Current Events).

100  *Methodist Times*, 13 February 1908 (Notes of Current Events).

101  *Methodist Times*, 16 January 1908 (Notes of Current Events).

102  A useful discussion of the tension between Grey and his critics in the Liberal Party can be found in John A. Murray, 'Foreign Policy Debated: Sir Edward Grey and his Critics, 1911–1912', in Lillian Parker Wallace and William C. Askew (eds), *Power, Public Opinion and Diplomacy* (Durham, NC, 1959), pp. 140–71.

103  On the entente see in addition to the books by Monger and Charmley, cited above, Christopher Andrew, *Théophile Delcassé and the Making of the Entente Cordiale* (London, 1968).

104  *Methodist Times*, 24 March 1904 (Notes of Current Events).

105  *Methodist Times*, 5 September 1907 (Notes of Current Events).

106  Useful material on divisions over Persia can be found in Murray, 'Foreign Policy Debated'.

107  On the dislike of Russia among many on the left of the political spectrum, see for example Max Beloff, *Lucien Wolf and the Russian Entente, 1907–1914* (London, 1951). See, too, the numerous articles that appeared in the newspaper *Darkest Russia* edited by Wolf.

108  *Primitive Methodist Leader*, 8 February 1906 (Current Events).

109  *Primitive Methodist Leader*, 21 May 1907 (Current Events).

110  For a discussion of Anglo-Russian relations during this period see Keith Neilson, *Britain and the Last Tsar: British Policy and Russia, 1894–1917* (Oxford, 1995). For a useful discussion of the same subject focusing more on the relationship between the two powers in Asia, see Jennifer Siegel, *Endgame: Britain, Russia and the Final Struggle for Central Asia* (London, 2002).

111 *Primitive Methodist Leader*, 3 October 1907 (Current Events). On Curzon's policies in the region, see the relevant chapters of David Gilmour, *Curzon* (London, 1995); and Patrick French, *Younghusband: The Last Great Imperial Adventurer* (London, 1994).

112 *Primitive Methodist Leader*, 3 October 1907 (Current Events).

113 *Free Methodist*, 5 September 1907 (Notes on Current Events).

114 *Primitive Methodist Leader*, 21 September 1911 (Current Events).

115 For a brief summary of these events, see Murray, 'Foreign Policy Debated', *passim*. Also see the relevant section of Siegel, *Endgame*.

116 *Primitive Methodist Leader*, 3 August 1911 (Current Events).

117 *Primitive Methodist Leader*, 23 November 1911 (Current Events).

118 *Primitive Methodist Leader*, 14 December 1911 (Current Events).

119 *Primitive Methodist Leader*, 25 January 1912 (Current Events).

120 *Primitive Methodist Leader*, 18 January 1912 (Current Events).

121 *Primitive Methodist Leader*, 23 May 1912 (Article by Guttery on 'Ruthless Russia').

122 For a useful discussion of Anglo-German relations during these years, see the relevant pages of Paul Kennedy, *The Rise of the Anglo-German Antagonism, 1860–1914* (London, 1982).

123 The Methodist theologian R. Newton Flew, for example, studied Protestant theology in Bonn and Marburg during his youth, and was later (ironically) much influenced by a number of German Catholic theologians. For details, see Gordon S. Wakefield, *Robert Newton Flew, 1886–1962* (London, 1971).

124 A useful discussion of co-operation between the churches in trying to improve Anglo-German relations before 1914 can be found in Hudson, *Ecumenical Movement*, pp. 16–29.

125 *Primitive Methodist Leader*, 20 August 1908 (Current Events).

126 On the Agadir crisis, see M.L. Dockrill, 'British Policy during the Agadir Crisis, 1911', in Hinsley, *British Foreign Policy*, pp. 271–83.

127 *Primitive Methodist Leader*, 6 July 1911 (Current Events).

128 *Primitive Methodist Leader*, 19 October 1911 (Current Events).

129 *Primitive Methodist Leader*, 15 February 1912 (Current Events). For an account of Haldane's visit, see Richard Burdon Haldane, *An Autobiography* (London, 1929), pp. 238–46.

130 *Primitive Methodist Leader*, 23 May 1912 (Current Events).

131 *United Methodist*, 14 November 1907 (Notes on Current Events).

132 *United Methodist*, 21 November 1907 (Notes on Current Events).

133 *Methodist Times*, 19 April 1906 (Notes of Current Events).

134 *Methodist Times*, 26 April 1906 ('Outlook' by Historicus).

135 *Methodist Times*, 17 May 1906 (Notes of Current Events).

136 On attempts to improve relations between the English and German churches before the First World War, see Hudson, *Ecumenical Movement*, pp. 16–29.

137 *Methodist Times*, 9 November 1911 (Notes and Comments).

138 For some further reflections on this theme see Hughes, *Diplomacy Before the Russian Revolution, passim.*

## 3 Methodism and the First World War

1 For two excellent if contrasting general accounts of the First World War, suitable for those lacking great knowledge of the period, see Niall Ferguson, *The Pity of War* (London, 1998); David Stevenson, *1914–1918: The History of the First World War* (London, 2005).

2 On Davidson's career during the war, see G.K.A. Bell, *Randall Davidson: Archbishop of Canterbury* (London, 1938), pp. 731–955.

3 A valuable discussion on the subject can be found in Alan Wilkinson, *The Church of England and the First World War* (London, 1978).

4 For a useful summary of the impact of war on the Nonconformist churches, see Stephen Koss, *Nonconformity in Modern British Politics* (London, 1975), pp. 125–44.

5 *Methodist Times*, 26 February 1914 (Editorial on 'The Church and Labour').

6 *Primitive Methodist Leader*, 15 January 1914 (Notes of the Week).

7 *Primitive Methodist Leader*, 22 January 1914 (Article by the Revd R.W. Keightley on 'Ploughshare or Sword?').

8 *Primitive Methodist Leader*, 5 March 1914 (Notes of the Week).

9 For the history of the United Methodist Church, see Henry Smith *et al, The Story of the United Methodist Church* (London, 1932).

10 *United Methodist*, 5 March 1914 (Notes by the Way).

11 Among the vast literature on the origins of the First World War, the best recent synopsis of scholarly work remains Hew Strachan, *The Outbreak of the First World War* (Oxford, 2004).

12 For a useful discussion of attitudes towards the armaments industry before the First World War, see Clive Trebilock, 'Legends of the British Armaments Industry, 1890–1914: A Revision', *Journal of Contemporary History*, 5, 4 (1970), pp. 3–19.

13 *Methodist Times*, 23 July 1914 (Report on Conference Proceedings).

14 On Lidgett's response to the outbreak of war, see Alan Turberfield, *John Scott Lidgett: Archbishop of British Methodism* (London, 2003), pp. 152–3. Some useful information on the subject can also be found in the pages of J. Scott Lidgett, *My Guided Life* (London, 1936).

15 *Methodist Times*, 6 August 1914 (Notes and Comments).

16 *Methodist Recorder*, 6 August 1914 (Notes of the Week).

17 *Primitive Methodist Leader*, 6 August 1914 (Article by Guttery on 'The Madness of Europe').

# Notes

18 *Primitive Methodist Leader*, 13 August 1914 (Article by the Revd W. Younger).

19 *United Methodist*, 13 August 1914 (Notes by the Way).

20 See, for example, Kit Good, 'England Goes to War, 1914–15' (University of Liverpool PhD Thesis 2002).

21 Alan Wilkinson, *Dissent or Conform: War, Peace and the English Churches* (London, 1986), *passim*; also see on this subject, Clive Field, 'A Sociological Profile of British Methodism, 1900–1932', *Oral History*, 4, 1 (1976), pp. 73–95.

22 *Methodist Times*, 6 August 1914 (Letter by the Revd J. Parton Milum).

23 *Methodist Times*, 20 August 1914 (Letter by the Revd W.F. Lofthouse).

24 *Methodist Times*, 8 October 1914 (Letter by the Revd H. Baird Turner).

25 *Methodist Times*, 12 November 1914 (Letter by the Revd F. Warburton Lewis).

26 *Primitive Methodist Leader*, 13 August 1914 (Article by Guttery on 'The Duty of the Empire').

27 *Primitive Methodist Leader*, 24 December 1914 (Article by Guttery on 'Will Europe Hang the Kaiser?').

28 *Primitive Methodist Leader*, 17 September 1914 (Letter by Ben Spoor).

29 *Primitive Methodist Leader*, 24 September 1914 (Letter by 'Pax').

30 *Primitive Methodist Leader*, 26 November 1914 (Letter by the Revd J.J. Reeves).

31 *Primitive Methodist Leader*, 3 December 1914 (Letter by W.J. Osbourne).

32 *Methodist Times*, 17 September 1914 (Editorial on 'Two Manifestoes').

33 *Methodist Times*, 20 August 1914 (Article on 'Three Messages from the President').

34 *Wesleyan Methodist Conference Minutes*, 1915 ('Address to His Majesty the King').

35 *Primitive Methodist Conference Minutes*, 1915 ('The Conference Address to the Churches').

36 For a detailed and sophisticated argument along these lines, see W.M. Crook, 'The War: Its Origins and Causes', in *London Quarterly Review*, 123 (1915), pp. 1–14.

37 On Moulton's life, see W.F. Moulton, *James Hope Moulton* (London, 1919).

38 Prof. J.H. Moulton, 'Christianity and Defensive War', *London Quarterly Review*, 123 (1915), pp. 32–45 (quotations from pp. 37, 41, 42).

39 H.S. Seekings, 'The Morality of the Sermon on the Mount', *Holborn Review* (April 1915), pp. 183–97 (quotations from pp. 194, 195).

40 Arthur Wood, 'Moral Problems Raised by the Great War', *Holborn Review* (October 1915), pp. 417–30 (quotations from pp. 419–20).

41 See, for example, the petition by eight churches in south Liverpool, contained in Liverpool Record Office, 287 LSO 2/8.

42 E.K. Jordan, *Free Church Unity* (London, 1956), pp. 144–5.

43 Similar efforts to respond to the need of servicemen billeted away from

home was made by the other connexions. See, for example, *United Methodist Conference Minutes*, 1915 ('Report of the Chaplaincies and Camp Homes Committee').

44 MARC, Minutes of the Wesleyan Army and Navy Board, 25 November 1914.

45 MARC, Minutes of the Liverpool District Synod of the Wesleyan Church, May 1916.

46 MARC, Minutes of the Nottingham and Derby District Synod of the Wesleyan Church, May 1916.

47 For a general history of the military chaplains during the First World War, see Brigadier The Rt Hon. Sir John Smyth, *In This Sign Conquer* (London, 1968), pp. 153–203.

48 For a discussion of the circumstances surrounding the appointment of Methodist chaplains in the British army, see Ken Hendrickson, 'Victorian Military Politics of Establishment and Religious Liberty: William H. Rule and the Introduction of Wesleyan Methodism in the British Army, 1856–1882', *War and Society*, 17, 2 (1999), pp. 1–23. See, too, Owen Spencer Watkins, *Soldiers and Preachers: Being the Romantic Story of Methodism in the British Army* (London, 1906); MARC, Box 36, G.T. Bigg, 'Notes on the Beginning of Chaplaincy Work'.

49 On the resentment in the non-Wesleyan connexions about the lack of dedicated chaplains on the outbreak of war, see *Aldersgate Primitive Methodist Magazine* (1914), p. 754. A brief discussion of the circumstances leading up to the creation of the new United Board can be found in Jordan, *Free Church Unity*, pp. 141–2. Further information can also be found in Smith *et al*, *Story of the United Methodist Church* (London, 1932), pp. 117–20.

50 A useful first-hand account of the duties carried out by one Wesleyan chaplain can be found in Robert J. Rider, *Reflections on the Battlefield: From Infantryman to Chaplain, 1914–1919* (Liverpool, 2001).

51 Peter Harrison, 'Deaths Among Army Chaplains, 1914–20', *Journal of the Society for Army Research*, 83 (2005), 63–72.

52 Owen Spencer Watkins, *With French in France and Flanders* (London, 1915), p. 17.

53 Useful material relating to the fate of the colleges during the war can be found in W. Bardsley Brash, *The Story of Our Colleges, 1835–1935* (London, 1935).

54 *Methodist Times*, 3 September 1914 (Article by Bateson on 'Methodism and the War'). For useful material on the response of students at Handsworth College in Birmingham, see the introduction to Rider, *Reflections on the Battlefield*, pp. 4–7.

55 *Methodist Times*, 3 December 1914 (Letter by Kingsley East).

56 *Methodist Times*, 10 December 1914 (Letter by F.S. Wrigley).

57 A useful discussion of the whole conscription issue can be found in R.Q.A. Adams and Philip P. Poirier, *The Conscription Controversy in Great Britain, 1900–1918* (London, 1987). For the circumstances surrounding the introduction of the

# Notes

Military Service Act, see John Rae, *Conscience and Politics* (London, 1970), pp. 1–67.

58 David Dutton, *Simon: A Political Biography of Sir John Simon* (London, 1992), pp. 37–9. For Simon's resignation speech setting out his views, see *Parliamentary Debates (Commons), 1915–1916*, vol. 77, cols. 962–78.

59 Koss, *Nonconformity*, p. 133.

60 *Parliamentary Debates (Commons), 1915–1916*, vol. 77, cols. 957–8.

61 For a critical account of the tribunals, see David Boulton, *Objection Overruled* (London, 1967). For a more positive account, see Rae, *Conscience and Politics*. Useful accounts of local tribunals in action include Ivor Slocombe, 'Recruitment into the Armed Forces during the First World War: The Work of the Military Tribunals in Wiltshire, 1915–1918', *Local Historian*, 30, 2 (2000), pp. 105–23; Philip Spinks, 'The War Courts: The Stratford-upon-Avon Borough Tribunal, 1916–1918', *Local Historian*, 32, 4 (2002), pp. 210–17.

62 *Methodist Recorder*, 13 January 1916 (Notes of the Week); 20 January 1916 (Notes of the Week).

63 *Methodist Times*, 6 January 1916 (Notes and Comments).

64 Turberfield, *Lidgett*, p. 155.

65 *Primitive Methodist Leader*, 13 January 1916 (Notes of the Week).

66 *Primitive Methodist Leader*, 20 January 1916 (Notes of the Week).

67 *United Methodist*, 6 January 1916 (Editorial).

68 *Methodist Times*, 20 January 1916 (Letter by W.B. Harris).

69 *Methodist Times*, 27 January 1916 (Letter by S. Fox).

70 *Methodist Times*, 16 March 1916 (Letter by the Revd H.W. Horwill).

71 *Methodist Times*, 27 January 1916 (Letter by G.T. Thorne).

72 *Methodist Times*, 16 March 1916 (Letter by W.B. Harris).

73 *Methodist Times*, 20 January 1916 (Letter by an 'Aberdeen Methodist').

74 *Methodist Times*, 1 June 1916 (Letter by 'a mother').

75 *Methodist Recorder*, 24 February 1916 (Letter by the Revd Joseph Dawson).

76 *United Methodist*, 20 January 1916 (Letter by the Revd J.E. Black).

77 *Primitive Methodist Leader*, 20 April 1916 (Letter by the Revd Arthur Barham).

78 *Primitive Methodist Leader*, 11 May 1916 (Letter by A. Gilbert).

79 *Primitive Methodist Leader*, 17 August 1916 (Letter by John Whittaker).

80 MARC, Methodist Peace Fellowship File.

81 *Methodist Times*, 5 November 1914 (Letter by Keeble)

82 *Methodist Times*, 13 January 1916 (Letter by Keeble).

83 *Methodist Recorder*, 27 April 1916 (Letters by the Revds B.C. Spencer, E. Omar Pearson, E.H. Jackson).

84 *Methodist Recorder*, 18 May 1916 (Article by the Revd James Lewis on 'Quakerism in Wesleyan Methodism').

85 MARC, Methodist Peace Fellowship file.

86 Cited in Thomas C. Kennedy, 'Public Opinion and the Conscientious Objectors, 1915–1919', *Journal of British Studies*, 12, 2 (1973), p. 112.

87 *Primitive Methodist Leader,* 2 March 1916 (Article by Guttery on 'How Britain will Use her Power').

88 *Primitive Methodist Leader,* 25 May 1916 (Article by Guttery on 'The Call of Conscience').

89 *Methodist Times,* 30 March 1916 (Notes and Comments).

90 *Methodist Times,* 30 March 1916 (Notes and Comments).

91 Jordan, *Free Church Unity,* p. 143. Conscientious objectors were, however, looked at with some scepticism across the free churches. See, for example, the statement by the Free Church Council issued in June 1916, quoted in Turberfield, *Lidgett,* p. 156.

92 MARC, Minutes of the Liverpool District Synod (Wesleyan), May 1916.

93 MARC, Minutes of the Norwich District Synod (Primitive Methodist), April 1916.

94 *Primitive Methodist Leader,* 4 May 1916.

95 *Primitive Methodist Conference Minutes,* 1916 (Resolution on Primitive Methodist Soldiers, Loyal Address to the Crown, Resolution on Conscientious Objectors).

96 *United Methodist,* 27 July 1916 (Report of the Proceedings of the United Methodist Conference).

97 Martin Ceadel, *Pacifism in Britain 1914–1945: The Defining of a Faith* (Oxford, 1980), pp. 34–5.

98 On the Fellowship of Reconciliation, see Jill Wallis, *Valiant for Peace: A History of the Fellowship of Reconciliation, 1914–1989* (London, 1991).

99 On Clifford Allen and the No Conscription Fellowship, see Martin Gilbert, *Plough my Own Furrow: The Story of Lord Allen of Hurtwood* (London, 1965).

100 For Snowden's reminiscences of this time, see Philip Snowden, *An Autobiography* (London, 1934), vol. 1, pp. 402–13.

101 Rae, *Conscience and Politics, passim.*

102 A useful discussion of attitudes towards conscientious objectors can be found in Kennedy, 'Public Opinion and the Conscientious Objectors'.

103 Quoted in Ceadel, *Pacifism in Britain,* pp. 50–1.

104 Quotations from Jim Simmons, *Soap-Box Evangelist* (London, 1972), pp. 17, 30.

105 See, for example, the case of the Wesleyan schoolteacher discussed in *The Friend,* 31 March 1916.

106 Friends House, Harvey Papers, TEMP MSS 835/8/1, Harvey to Runciman, 31 March 1916.

107 On the role of the Christadelphians during the First World War, see F.G. Jannaway, *Christadelphians during the Great War* (London, 1929).

108 For material relating to the operation of the Pelham Committee, see Friends House, Harvey Papers, TEMP MSS 835, Box 10. The printed statistics relating to the religious affiliations of the various COs can be found in Rae, *Conscience and Politics,* pp. 250–1.

# Notes

109 *Methodist Times*, 2 March 1916 (Letter by Owen Rattenbury).

110 *The Times*, 20 January 1916 ('The Conscientious Objector' reporting views of Joynson-Hicks).

111 Details of the cases of a number of Methodists, from various connexions, who appealed to the Middlesex Appeals Tribunal can be found in Public Record Office MH 47/67. The cases of a number of Methodist COs in Lancashire can be followed in Friends House, Harvey Papers, TEMP MSS 835/8/1 (Minutes of committee at Blackburn).

112 *Methodist Times*, 20 February 1919 (Letter by the Revd W.H. Barnes).

113 *Primitive Methodist Leader*, 6 November 1919 (Report of meeting of Primitive Methodist Fellowship of Freedom and Peace).

114 For a useful discussion of some of the tensions in a Durham pit village inhabited by a large number of Primitive Methodists, see Robert Moore, *Pitmen, Preachers and Politics* (London, 1974), pp. 199–200.

115 Methodist Studies Centre, John Herbert Brocklesby, 'Escape from Paganism' (unpublished memoirs completed in 1958).

116 *Primitive Methodist Leader*, 5 July 1917 (Article by Guttery on 'Victory: A Moral Duty').

117 *Methodist Times*, 26 July 1917 (Report of the Proceedings of the Wesleyan Conference).

118 *Methodist Times*, 20 September 1917 (Notes and Comments).

119 *Methodist Times*, 29 November 1917 (Article on 'COs and the Francise').

120 *Primitive Methodist Leader*, 28 June 1917 (Letter by the Revd J.W. Richardson).

121 *Primitive Methodist Leader*, 16 August 1917 (Article on 'Civil and Religious Liberties).

122 *Primitive Methodist Leader*, 22 November 1917 (Article by Peake on 'Who is Offended?').

123 *United Methodist*, 13 September 2001 (Editorial by the Revd Henry Smith on 'The Treatment of COs').

124 *United Methodist*, 26 July 1917 (Report of Peace Fellowship Meeting).

125 *Methodist Times*, 22 March 1917 (Notes and Comments).

126 *Primitive Methodist Leader*, 22 March 1917 (Article by Guttery on 'The Rebirth of Russia').

127 *Methodist Times*, 12 April 1917 (Editorial on 'Enter America').

128 *Methodist Times*, 12 April 1917 (Outlook by 'Historicus').

129 *Methodist Times*, 16 August 1917 (Notes and Comments).

130 Lord Newton, *Lord Lansdowne* (London, 1929), p. 467.

131 *Methodist Times*, 13 December 1917 ('Lord Lansdowne's Article: Opinions of Representative Methodists').

132 *Primitive Methodist Leader*, 20 December 1917 (Letter by Joseph Maland).

133 Lloyd George, *War Memoirs of Lloyd George*, 2 vols (London, 1938), vol. 2, p. 1517.

134 *Methodist Times*, 17 January 1918 (Outlook by 'Historicus').

135 *Primitive Methodist Leader*, 31 January 1918 (Article by Guttery on 'Peace in the Offing').

136 *Wesleyan Methodist Conference Minutes*, 1917 (Special Resolution on the League of Nations).

137 *Wesleyan Methodist Conference Minutes*, 1918 (Special Resolution on the League of Nations).

138 *Primitive Methodist Conference Minutes*, 1918 (Resolution on the League of Nations).

139 Ceadel, *Pacifism in Britain*, pp. 1–8.

# 4 British Methodism and the Inter-War Crisis

1 For a brilliantly written account taking such a view see Niall Ferguson, *The War of the World: History's Age of Hatred* (London, 2006).

2 *Christianity and War* (London, 1924), COPEC Commission Report 8, pp. 53, 61, 67. The pacifist members of the Commission did, however, make it clear that they did not believe that 'the use of force upon persons at all times and in all circumstances is anti-Christian; the matter of war stands apart from others'.

3 On the World Alliance, see Hudson, *Ecumenical Movement*; Ruth Rouse and Stephen Charles Neill (eds), *A History of the Ecumenical Movement, 1517–1948* (London, 1967).

4 For an argument along these lines, see Robert Currie, *Methodism Divided: A Study in the Sociology of Ecumenicalism* (London, 1968).

5 *Methodist Times*, 15 May 1919 (Editorial Notes).

6 *Primitive Methodist Leader*, 3 July 1919 (Article by Guttery, 'Is it Truce or Peace?').

7 *Methodist Times*, 26 June 1919 ('Historicus' Column).

8 *Methodist Times*, 22 May 1919 (Letter by Keeble).

9 *Methodist Times*, 20 February 1919 (Editorial Notes on the publication of the Draft Covenant of the League).

10 For a valuable account of the Paris Peace Conference, including differences among the victor powers about the proper role of the League, see Margaret MacMillan, *Peacemakers: The Paris Conference of 1919 and its Attempt to End War* (London, 2001).

11 *Methodist Times*, 19 June 1919 (Editorial Notes).

12 See, for example, *Methodist Times*, 29 April 1920 (Editorial Notes).

13 *Primitive Methodist Leader*, 13 November 1919 (Article by Peake 'Is Peace Secure?').

14 *Methodist Times*, 10 July 1919 ('Historicus' Column).

15 *Methodist Times*, 17 June 1920 (Editorial Notes).

# Notes

16 *Primitive Methodist Conference Minutes*, 1920 (Resolution on League of Nations).

17 Methodist congregations were the most inclined of all the denominations to sign up to corporate membership of the LNU. See Donald S. Birn, *The League of Nations Union* (Oxford, 1981), p. 137.

18 A.W. Harrison, *Christianity and the League of Nations* (London, 1928).

19 A.W. Harrison *Christianity and Universal Peace* (London, 1926).

20 *Methodist Times*, 3 November 1921 (Letter by the Revd F.B. James).

21 On the Washington Naval Conference, see Erik Goldstein and John H. Maurer, *The Washington Conference, 1921–22* (London, 1994).

22 See, for example, *Methodist Times*, 11 November 1924 (Editorial Notes).

23 *Primitive Methodist Leader*, 29 October 1925 (Article by the Revd H.J. Pickett on 'The Significance of Locarno').

24 For a brief discussion of COPEC by one of the most prominent British Methodists of the period, see Samuel Keeble, *COPEC* (London, 1924).

25 For details of the Stockholm Conference (and the Life and Work movement in general) see Hudson, *Ecumenical Movement*.

26 *Methodist Times*, 20 August 1925 (Editorial Notes).

27 *Methodist Times*, 10 September 1925 (Article by Harrison on 'The Stockholm Conference').

28 *Methodist Recorder*, 25 August 1927 (Article by Wiseman on 'World Conference on Faith and Order').

29 For a useful account of the Lausanne Conference, see Rouse and Neill, *History of the Ecumenical Movement*, pp. 420–5.

30 On Henderson see Michael Hughes, *Foreign Secretaries in an Uncertain World, 1919–1939* (London, 2006), pp. 81–98.

31 On Weatherhead see Kingsley Weatherhead, *Leslie Weatherhead: A Personal Portrait* (London, 1976).

32 *Methodist Recorder*, 7 November 1929 (Article by Weatherhead on 'War').

33 *Methodist Recorder*, 21 November 1929 (Letter by the Revd Frederick Brown).

34 *Methodist Recorder*, 21 November 1929 (Letter by the Revd E.T. Smith).

35 *Methodist Recorder*, 28 November 1929 (Letter by Weatherhead). A close reading of Weatherhead's original article in fact suggests that he was not unconditionally committed to pacifism, noting that 'war can only be counted as the right thing to do when the alternative would be an even blacker betrayal of idealism'.

36 For details see Ceadel, *Pacifism in Britain*, pp. 93–8.

37 *Methodist Recorder*, 28 January 1932 (Notes of the Week).

38 On the East Fulham by-election, see Richard Heller, 'East Fulham Revisited', *Journal of Contemporary History*, 6, 3 (1971), pp. 172–96.

39 *Methodist Recorder*, 23 March 1933 (Article by Carter on 'The Churches and the War').

40 *Methodist Recorder*, 30 March 1933 (Article by the Revd A.W. Harrison on 'The Churches and War: Has Mr Carter said the Last Word?').

41 *Methodist Recorder*, 30 March 1933 (Letter by the Revd Leslie Jollie).

42 *Methodist Recorder*, 6 April 1933 (Letter by the Revd E.J.B. Kirtlan).

43 *Methodist Recorder*, 6 April 1933 (Letter by T.W. Cowap).

44 *Methodist Recorder*, 4 May 1933 (Editorial on 'Christianity and War').

45 *Methodist Times and Leader*, 29 June 1933 (Letter by the Revd T.W. Bevan; leading article on 'Should Methodism Go Pacifist?').

46 Most of the other major Christian churches in England issued similar declarations in the early 1930s. See E.N. Porter Goff, 'A Christian Peace Policy', in Percy Dearmer (ed.), *Christianity and the Crisis* (London, 1933), p. 507.

47 *The Minutes of the Annual Conference of the Methodist Church* (henceforth *Conference Minutes*), 1933 (Appendix VI, 'Peace and War: Declaration of the Methodist Church'). For a description of the debate leading up to this resolution, including a pacifist amendment moved by Samuel Keeble, see *Methodist Times and Leader*, 20 July 1933 (Report on Conference Proceedings).

48 *Methodist Recorder*, 8 February 1934 (Letter published under heading 'A Methodist Peace Fellowship').

49 *Methodist Recorder*, 15 February 1934 (Letter by Porter-Goff).

50 *Methodist Recorder*, 22 February 1934 (Letter by Charley).

51 On the relationship between Christian pacifists and the advocates of collective security, see Michael Pugh, 'Pacifism and Politics in Britain, 1931–1935', *Historical Journal*, 23, 3 (1980).

52 Quoted in E.C. Urwin, *Henry Carter C.B.E.: A Memoir* (London, 1955), p. 67.

53 *Conference Minutes*, 1934, Temperance and Social Welfare Division, V (International and Industrial Relations), 4 'Increase of Air Forces'.

54 *Conference Minutes*, 1934 (Appendix III, Addenda to the Declaration of the Methodist Conference on 'Peace and War: Addendum Respecting the Private Manufacture and Sale of Arms').

55 *Methodist Recorder*, 26 July 1934 (Report on Conference Proceedings).

56 For the final version, see *Conference Minutes*, 1934 (Appendix III, 'A Programme of Peacemaking for the Methodist Church').

57 *Methodist Recorder*, 26 July 1934 (Report on Conference Proceedings).

58 *Methodist Recorder*, 2 August 1934 (J. Ernest Rattenbury, 'Conference Reflections').

59 *Methodist Recorder*, 16 August 1934 (Letters by James Peters and John Sayers).

60 *Methodist Times and Leader*, 23 August 1934 (Letter by John Hall).

61 *Methodist Recorder*, 9 August 1934 (Letter by Carden).

62 *Methodist Recorder*, 18 July 1935 (Report on Conference Proceedings).

63 The following two paragraphs are drawn from Michael Hughes, 'The Foreign Secretary Goes to Court: John Simon and his Critics', *Twentieth-Century*

*British History*, 14, 4 (2003), pp. 339–59. For a discussion of Simon's time as Foreign Secretary, see Hughes, *Foreign Secretaries in an Uncertain World*, pp. 99–122. A fuller discussion of Simon's career can be found in David Dutton, *Simon: A Political Biography of Sir John Simon* (London, 1992).

64  For some useful information on this topic, see David G. Anderson, 'British Rearmament and the "Merchants of Death": The 1935–36 Royal Commission on the Manufacture of and Trade in Armaments', *Journal of Contemporary History*, 21, 9 (1994), pp. 5–37.

65  For a useful discussion of the relationship between secular and Christian pacifism during the 1930s, see Ceadel, *Pacifism in Britain, passim*; Mark Gilbert, 'Pacifist Attitudes to Nazi Germany, 1936–45', *Journal of Contemporary History*, 27, 3 (1992), 493–511. For a general account of the peace movement in twentieth-century Britain that tends to downplay the role of Christian groups, see James Hinton, *Protests and Visions: Peace Politics in Twentieth-Century Britain* (London, 1989).

66  The short-lived Church of England Peace Fellowship, for example, was founded in 1934, while the Anglican Pacifist Fellowship was set up in 1937. Alan Wilkinson, *Dissent or Conform?*, p. 129.

67  On the Fellowship of Reconciliation, see Wallis, *Valiant for Peace.*

68  Charles Raven, *Is War Obsolete?* (London, 1935).

69  G.H.C. MacGregor, *The New Testament Basis of Pacifism* (New York, 1954), p. 13.

70  On the PPU, see Ceadel, *Pacifism in Britain*, 242–93; David C. Lukowitz, 'British Pacifists and Appeasement: The Peace Pledge Union', *Journal of Contemporary History*, 9, 1 (1974), pp. 115–27; among Sheppard's writing, see particularly his *We Say No: The Plain Man's Guide to Pacifism* (London, 1935). See, too, R. Ellis Robert, *H.R.L. Sheppard: Life and Letters* (London, 1942).

71  For a useful description of the atmosphere of a PPU meeting at which Soper spoke, see Vera Brittain, *Testament of Experience* (London, 1981), pp. 164–7.

72  For reports of PPU meetings addressed by Carter, see, for example, *Peace News*, 1 August 1936.

73  MARC, Methodist Peace Fellowship file, 'Endorsement of the war by the Methodist conference'.

74  MARC, Methodist Peace Fellowship file, 'The Methodist Peace Fellowship: what it is, how to begin, what to do' (no date, but probably 1938). For a useful account of the MPF's formal status within the Methodist Church, see 'The Methodist Peace Fellowship Bulletin' in *The Christian Pacifist*, 1, 2 (February 1939).

75  *Methodist Recorder*, 23 March 1939 (Letter by the Revd T.A. Roberts).

76  Coulson Papers, Box 133, F1/1, 'Speech by Henry Carter at Central Hall, 9 November 1934'.

77  For first-hand accounts of Carter's visits, see for example *Methodist Recorder*, 6 January 1938, 22 September 1938. For further details of Lansbury's various attempts to promote peace through his visits abroad and his involve-

ment with the PPU, see Jonathan Schneer, *George Lansbury* (Manchester, 1990), pp. 176–95. Further details of Lansbury's Christian socialism can be found in John Shepherd, *George Lansbury: At the Heart of Old Labour* (Oxford, 2002).

78 Henry Carter, 'Battlefield or Council Table: The Van Zeeland Report', *The Christian World*, 17 February 1938; Henry Carter, 'Main Issues for a World Conference', *Peace News*, 19 February 1938.

79 Frederic Hale, 'A Methodist Pacifist and the Spanish Civil War', *Proceedings of the Wesleyan Historical Society*, 54 (2004), pp. 149–69.

80 Donald Soper, *Question Time on Tower Hill* (London, 1935), p. 38.

81 See, for example, Donald Soper, 'Challenge to the Church', *Daily Herald*, 11 January 1937.

82 Quoted in Pugh, 'Pacifism and Politics', p. 645.

83 See, for example, Donald Soper, 'What is Today's Nonconformist Conscience?', *Daily Herald*, 15 October 1936 (in which Soper's panegyric to Hugh Price Hughes perhaps rather conveniently overlooked Hughes's views on war and peace in the final years of his life).

84 Such a position certainly commanded a degree of support within the Methodist Church. See, for example, *Methodist Recorder*, 30 April 1936 (Letter by the Revd J. Napier-Milne).

85 Weatherhead, *Leslie Weatherhead*, p. 81.

86 Leslie D. Weatherhead, *Thinking Aloud in Wartime* (London, 1939), pp. 24, 33, 60.

87 Reinhold Niebuhr, *Moral Man and Immoral Society: A Study in Ethics and Politics* (London, 1933).

88 Coulson Papers, Box 133, F1/2, Coulson to Robson, 3 October 1935.

89 Coulson Papers, Box 133, F1/2, Coulson to Stanley, January 1935.

90 Coulson Papers, Box 133, F1/2, Coulson to Budd, 23 January 1935.

91 *Methodist Recorder*, 13 February 1936 (Notes of the Week); *Methodist Recorder*, 26 March 1936 (Notes of the Week).

92 *Methodist Recorder*, 19 March 1936 (Notes of the Week).

93 The *Leader* had in fact taken a more informed interest than the *Recorder* in German developments more or less from the moment Hitler came to power in 1933. See, for example, the series of articles and letters on the subject that appeared in the *Methodist Times and Leader* throughout 1933.

94 *Methodist Recorder*, 18 August 1938 (Editorial on 'Christian Civilization').

95 *Methodist Recorder*, 19 March 1936 (Letter by the Revd G.E. Hickman Johnson).

96 *Methodist Recorder*, 16 April 1936 (Letter by Harvey); *Methodist Recorder*, 23 April 1936 (Letter by G.P. Dymond).

97 *Methodist Recorder*, 30 April 1936 (Letter by J. Todhunter).

98 *Conference minutes*, 1937 (Appendix IV, 'The Church and peace').

99 *Methodist Recorder*, 10 February 1938 (Articles by the Revd W.J. Hannam and the Revd T.W. Bevan).

# Notes

100  *Methodist Recorder*, 24 February 1938 (Notes of the Week)

101  *Methodist Recorder*, 10 March 1938 (Notes of the Week).

102  *Methodist Recorder*, 17 March 1938 (Notes of the Week).

103  *Methodist Recorder*, 31 March 1938 (Notes of the Week).

104  *Methodist Recorder*, 1 September 1938 (Notes of the Week); *Methodist Recorder*, 29 September 1938 (Notes of the Week).

105  Michael Foot and Alison Highet, *Isaac Foot: A West Country Boy – Apostle of England* (London, 2006), p. 219.

106  *Methodist Recorder*, 20 October 1938 (Interview with Isaac Foot). Note too the interview with Walter Runciman, another veteran Methodist Liberal politician, who had led a mission to Prague in August 1938 designed to resolve the crisis. *Methodist Recorder*, 13 October 1938 (Interview with Runciman). Some further useful reflections on the reaction of the churches to appeasement can be found in Adrian Hastings, *A History of English Christianity, 1920–1985* (London, 1986).

107  *Methodist Recorder*, 6 October 1938 (Editorial on 'The Reign of Right').

108  *Methodist Recorder*, 6 October 1938 (Article on 'Preachers on the New Opportunities for Peace').

109  *Methodist Recorder*, 13 October 1938 (Letters by Moria O'Neill and G.E. Lee).

110  *Methodist Recorder*, 3 November 1938 (Notes of the Week).

111  The figures can be found in the monthly column in the *Christian Pacifist* reporting on developments in the various denominational pacifist organizations.

112  See, for example, *Methodist Recorder*, 30 March 1939 (Letters by the Revd W. Horner and the Revd L.A. Wigley).

113  *Methodist Recorder*, 1 July 1937 (Editorial on 'Economics and Ecumenics').

114  *Methodist Recorder*, 29 July 1937 (Article by Lofthouse on 'Life and Work at Oxford').

115  *Methodist Recorder*, 29 July 1937 (Editorial on 'The Church's Life and Work').

116  *Methodist Times and Leader*, 15 July 1937 (Article by Basil Matthews on 'World Christianity and the New Pagan Faiths').

117  Hudson, *Ecumenical Movement*, p. 160.

118  *Conference Minutes*, 1937 (Resolution on World Peace).

119  A useful analysis of the Edinburgh Conference can be found in Rouse and Neill, *History of the Ecumenical Movement*, pp. 431–5.

120  *Methodist Recorder*, 19 August 1937 (Article by F.L. Wiseman on 'World Conference on Faith and Order').

121  *Methodist Times and Leader*, 19 August 1937 (Article by Pyke on 'The Path to Reunion').

122  Richard Pyke, *Men and Memories* (London, 1948), p. 117.

123  Wakefield, *Robert Newton Flew*, p. 98.

289

124  It is striking that most Methodist pacifists who had read Barth instinctively rejected his ideas as potentially 'very dangerous'. See W.F. Lofthouse, 'Karl Barth and the Gospel', *London Quarterly and Holborn Review*, 158 (1933), pp. 28–37.

125  The most sustained attempt to study the (negative) implications of the just war doctrine by a Methodist writer was probably E.C. Urwin's *The Catholic Doctrine of Just War* (London, 1937), although this was not primarily aimed at a Methodist audience.

# 5  British Methodism and the Second World War

1  For an interesting discussion on this theme, see Tzevtan Todorov, *Facing the Extreme: Moral Life in the Concentration Camps* (London, 1999).

2  For useful review of the 'classical' tradition of just war see, for example, the relevant pages of Jenny Teichman, *Pacifism and the Just War: A Study in Applied Philosophy* (Oxford, 1986). For a recent discussion of the idea of the just war in Augustine, see John Mark Mattox, *Saint Augustine and the Theory of the Just War* (London, 2006). A helpful account of the idea of the just war in the medieval period can be found in Frederick H. Russell, *The Just War in the Middle Ages* (Cambridge, 1975).

3  For an interesting discussion of the moral issues raised by such massive bombing of civilians from the perspective of a contemporary standpoint, see Jonathan Glover, *Humanity: A Moral History of the Twentieth Century* (London, 1999).

4  Among the vast literature on appeasement, see the relevant pages of R.A.C. Parker, *Chamberlain and Appeasement: British Policy and the Coming of the Second World War* (Basingstoke, 1993); R.A.C. Parker, *Churchill and Appeasement* (Basingstoke, 2000). For a rather different view, see John Charmley, *Chamberlain and the Lost Peace* (London, 1989). For a useful article on the Church of England's response to appeasement, see Andrew Chandler, 'Munich and Morality: The Bishops of the Church of England and Appeasement', *Twentieth-Century History*, 5, 1 (1994), pp. 77–99.

5  For a useful discussion of the treatment of conscientious objectors in the Second World War, including details of the tribunals, see Rachel Barker, *Conscience, Government and War: Conscientious Objection in Great Britain, 1939–45* (London, 1982).

6  *Methodist Recorder*, 7 September 1939 (Pyke, 'Message to the Methodist People').

7  *Methodist Recorder*, 7 September 1939 (Editorial on 'With Firmness in the Right').

8  *Methodist Recorder*, 5 October 1939 (Letter from the Revd R.E.C. Johnson).

9  *Methodist Recorder*, 2 November 1939 (Editorial on 'Such a Time as This').

# Notes

10 Richard A. Rempl, 'The Dilemmas of British Pacifists during World War II', *Journal of Modern History*, 50, 4 (1978), pp. 1213–29.

11 Quoted in Ceadel, *Pacifism in Britain*, p. 297.

12 A.A. Milne, *War with Honour* (London, 1940).

13 On Royden, see Sheila Fletcher, *Maude Royden* (Oxford, 1989).

14 Weatherhead, *Thinking Aloud in Wartime*, pp. 23, 28, 31, 60.

15 For a useful discussion of the responses of the churches to the Second World War, see Wilkinson, *Dissent or Conform*, pp. 232–97. See, too, Hastings, *English Christianity*, pp. 355–400.

16 See, for example, *An Agreed Report on a Deputation of Pacifist Clergy to the Archbishops of Canterbury and York, Lambeth Palace, June 11th 1940* (London, 1940).

17 F.S. Temple (ed.), *Some Lambeth Letters* (Oxford, 1963), p. 102 (Letter by William Temple dated 14 August 1943).

18 J.G. Lockhart, *Cosmo Gordon Lang* (London, 1949), p. 436.

19 See, for example, the reports of the various district synods held in September 1939 (a summary of which can be found in the *Methodist Recorder*, 21 September 1939).

20 On the reorganization of the Board following the outbreak of war, see MARC, Minutes of the Royal Navy, Army and Air Force Board, 19 September 1939.

21 *Methodist Recorder*, 7 June 1945 (Report of meeting on the Army, Navy and Air Force Board on 22 May 1945).

22 Merseyside Record Office, 287 IDS/51/4 (Minutes of the Liverpool District Synod, September 1942).

23 See, for example, *Methodist Recorder*, 16 November 1939 (Article on 'A Great Opportunity for Methodism'); 4 January 1940 (Article on 'What the Churches are Doing for Servicemen'). On the organiszational problems involved in defining responsibility for running camp homes throughout the war, see MARC, Minutes of the Royal Navy, Army and Air Force Board, 26 September 1944.

24 *Methodist Recorder*, 19 October 1944 (Article on 'Padre's Work with Prisoners-of-War').

25 *Methodist Recorder*, 8 February 1945 (Article on 'Wesley Hall in Canal Zone').

26 *Methodist Recorder*, 21 September 1939 (Article by the Revd N.F. Hutchcroft on 'War's Effect on Sunday Schools').

27 See, for example, the case of Olive Mary Moir detailed in BBC website, WW2 People's War, Article A7210829.

28 See, for example, *Methodist Recorder*, 21 September 1939 (Letter by the Revd J. Norton).

29 Donald Sóper, *Calling for Action* (London, 1984), p. 40.

30 *Methodist Recorder*, 7 November 1940 (Article by Sangster on 'God in the Shelters'). Further information about Sangster's career during the war can be found in Paul Sangster, *Doctor Sangster* (London, 1962).

31  *Methodist Recorder*, 20 June 1940 (Letter by Mrs E.C. Urwin).

32  For a short but balanced and sophisticated discussion of the ethical problems inherent in the conscription issue, see John T. Newton, 'The State and
the Individual Conscience', *London Quarterly and Holborn Review*, 166 (1941),
pp. 204–8.

33  *Methodist Recorder*, 6 June 1940 (Pyke article on 'Pacifism in the Pulpit').

34  *Methodist Recorder*, 27 June 1940 (Letter by Sir William Letts).

35  Kenneth Greet, *Fully Connected* (Peterborough, 1997), p. 137.

36  Charles J. Wright, 'The Relevance of Christian Faith to Present World
Order', *London Quarterly and Holborn Review*, 166 (1941), pp. 270–81.

37  *Conference Agenda*, 1940 (Memorial from Birmingham Small Heath).
Liverpool Record Office, 287 DIS/51/2 (Liverpool District Resolution of
September 1940).

38  *Methodist Recorder*, 24 July 1941 (Report on Conference proceedings);
*Conference Minutes*, 1941 (Appendix V, 'Conference Statement on the National
Situation').

39  *Methodist Recorder*, 17 June 1941 (Report of Armstrong's opening
address).

40  *Peace News*, 8 August 1941 (summarizing a letter by Revd C. Leslie Brewer
in the *Guardian*).

41  For further details of the visit, see Foot and Highet, *Isaac Foot*, pp. 222–52.

42  *Christian Pacifist*, 3, 8 (1941).

43  Quoted in Pugh, 'Pacifism and Politics', p. 645.

44  I am drawing here on the ideas of Martin Ceadel presented in *Pacifism in
Britain*, pp. 294–315.

45  Quoted in Martin Ceadel, *Thinking about Peace and War* (Oxford, 1989),
p. 147. For some interesting retrospective thoughts by Soper on the ethical problems facing pacifists in war-time, see Soper, *Calling for Action*, pp. 41–5.

46  *Christian Pacifist*, 21 (September 1943).

47  *Christian Pacifist*, 26 (February 1944).

48  For a copy of Carter's original articles see Peace Pledge Union archive
(Henry Carter file).

49  Obituary: Arthur Eltringham Smailes, *Transactions of the Institute of British
Geography*, N.S. 10 (1985), p. 120.

50  Denis Hayes, *Challenge of Conscience: The Story of the Conscientious
Objectors of 1939–49* (London, 1949), p. 27.

51  Barker, *Conscience, Government and War*, pp. 38–9.

52  Barker, *Conscience, Government and War*, p. 38.

53  Hayes, *Challenge of Conscience*, p. 25.

54  Details of Davies' career are taken from Felicity Goodall, *A Question of
Conscience* (Stroud, 1997).

55  On Foster's career, see PPU Archives (Unpublished memoir by Robert
Foster, 'Flashback: The War Years and After from the Life of Robert Foster').

# Notes

56 David Mace, 'An Absolute Pacifist', *Christian Pacifist*, 2, 12 (1940).

57 Oliver Postgate, *Seeing Things* (London, 2000), pp. 97–9.

58 See, for example, the case of Bill Spray detailed in BBC, WW2 People's War, Article A6210992.

59 See, for example, the case of Arthur Marsden detailed in BBC, WW2 People's War, Article A4435652.

60 *Christian Pacifist*, 8 (August 1942).

61 The most complete account of the CPFLU (by a former member) can be found in Lewis Maclachlan, *CPFLU: A History of the Christian Pacifist Forestry and Land Units* (London, 1952). A useful recent memoir can be found in the case of Ronald Smith detailed in BBC, WW2 People's War, Article A3192040.

62 MARC, Division of Social Responsibility Collection, file headed CPFLU: newsletters, etc. (henceforward CPFLU file), Henry Carter article on 'Christian Pacifist Forestry and Land Units: Three Years Record'.

63 Carter's relations with the Ministry of Labour, which insisted that he should lead the whole initiative, can be found in the various documents in: London School of Economics, Fellowship of Reconciliation Archive, FoR 6/2. The documents in this file are used extensively throughout the paragraphs that follow.

64 MARC, CPFLU file (Circular letter by Henry Carter dated August 1941).

65 MARC, CPFLU file (Anonymous article on 'The Kingsway Unit: What is It?').

66 MARC, Division of Social Responsibility Collection, file headed CPF&LU (Letter by Carter dated 5 February 1941).

67 MARC, CPFLU file (Henry Carter, 'Forestry and Land Units: The Record of Six Months Work', an article from the *Christian Pacifist*, July 1940).

68 MARC, CPFLU file (Circular by the Secretary of CPFLU, 4 April 1944).

69 For an interesting insight into life at one of the earliest CPFLU units at Harvington, see the house magazine *Unity* contained in the archives of the Peace Pledge Union.

70 MARC, CPFLU file (Henry Carter report on the first conference of the South Wales district).

71 MARC, CPFLU file (Frank Noble article on 'Ruskin', Kingsway Unit newsletter, 30 April 1942).

72 MARC, CPFLU file (Anonymous and undated article on 'The Christian Pacifist Forestry Units in Scotland').

73 Temple, *Some Lambeth Letters*, p. 138 (Letter by William Temple dated 17 January 1944).

74 William Temple (ed.), *Is Christ Divided?* (London, 1943), includes the chapter by Temple and Raven on 'Pacifists and Non-Pacifists' and the chapter by Carter on 'Citizens and Strangers'.

75 *Methodist Recorder*, 1 October 1942 (Article on 'Presentation to Henry Carter').

76 *Methodist Recorder*, 29 August 1940 (Article by the Revd C.R. Smith on

'Should we Pray for Victory'); *Methodist Recorder*, 12 September 1940 (Letter by the Revd H.R. Hindley).

77 See, for example, *Methodist Recorder*, 17 October 1940 (Letter by G.P. Burns); for later examples see the pamphlet by F. Brompton Harvey, *Should Germany be Forgiven?* (London, 1944) and the letter by the Revd R.H. Lowe in *Methodist Recorder*, 6 April 1944.

78 Alan M. Suggate, *William Temple and Christian Social Ethics Today* (Edinburgh, 1987), p. 158.

79 Temple, *Some Lambeth Letters*, p. 102 (Temple letter dated 14 August 1943).

80 G.K.A. Bell, *The Church and Humanity, 1939–46* (London, 1946), p. 132.

81 Quoted in Ronald C.D. Jasper, *George Bell: Bishop of Chichester* (London, 1967), p. 257.

82 *Methodist Recorder*, 29 July 1943 (Notes of the Week).

83 *Methodist Recorder*, 17 February 1944 (Letter by the Revd G.E. Hickman-Johnson).

84 *Methodist Recorder*, 24 February 1944 (Letter by the Revd Dr C.J. Wright).

85 *Methodist Recorder*, 17 August 1944 (Lofthouse contribution to 'What's Puzzling You?').

86 The words were those of Herbert Butterfield. For a discussion of Butterfield's  intellectual career, see C.T. McIntire, *Herbert Butterfield: Historian as Dissenter* (New Haven, Conn., 2004).

87 For a useful discussion of how 'distance' informs moral judgement see Glover, *Humanity, passim*.

88 *Methodist Recorder*, 16 August 1945 (Notes).

89 *Methodist Recorder*, 23 August 1945 (Editorial on 'Prospects for Peace').

90 Soper, *Calling for Action*, p. 38.

91 See, for example, W.F. Lofthouse, 'To End Hitlerism', *London Quarterly and Holborn Review*, 165 (1940), pp. 31–42.

92 *Conference Agenda*, 1941 (Memorial from the Anstey Circuit in Leicestershire).

93 *Methodist Recorder*, 16 March 1944 (Editorial on 'Should Germany be Forgiven?').

94 *Methodist Recorder*, 21 September 1944 (Letter by the Revd R.B. Wright); *Methodist Recorder*, 5 October 1944 (Letter by the Revd E. Calvert).

95 *Methodist Recorder*, 26 October 1944 (Editorial on 'The New League').

96 See, for example, Percy Carden, 'Building the Temple of Lasting Peace', *London Quarterly and Holborn Review*, 169 (1944), pp. 28–35; R. Martin Pope, 'Peace and World Renewal', *London Quarterly and Holborn Review*, 169 (1944), pp. 193–7.

97 See, for example, *Conference Agenda*, 1944 (Report of the Temperance and Social Welfare Department).

98 *Conference Minutes*, 1945 ('Statement on the International Situation').

99 *Peace News*, 15 December 1944 (Soper, 'Christmas Message').

100 Henry Carter, BBC broadcast on 'Bread and Work', October 1944. See, too, Henry Carter, *Towards World Recovery* (London, 1945).

101 F. Brompton Harvey, 'Unseasonable Truth: Thoughts on the War', *London Quarterly and Holborn Review*, 167 (1942), pp. 335–43.

# 6 The Shadow of the Bomb

1 *Conference Minutes*, 1946 (Special Resolution on 'A Call to World Peace').

2 A valuable and readable discussion of the 'Cultural Cold War' can be found in David Caute, *The Dancer Defect: The Struggle for Cultural Supremacy during the Cold War* (Oxford, 2003).

3 See, for example, Giles Scott-Smith, *The Politics of Apolitical Culture: The Congress for Cultural Freedom, the CIA and Post-War American Hegemony* (London, 2002); Frances Stonor-Saunders, *The Cultural Cold War: The CIA and the World of Arts and Letters* (New York, 2000).

4 See, for example, Anthony Rhodes, *The Vatican in the Age of the Cold War, 1945–80* (Norwich, 1992).

5 See the 'Resolution on Communism', in *The Lambeth Conferences 1867–1948* (London, 1948). On the role of the Anglican Church in the Cold War see, for example, Dianne Kirby, 'Divinely Sanctioned: The Anglo-American Cold War Alliance and the Defence of Western Civilization and Christianity', *Journal of Contemporary History*, 35, 3 (2000), pp. 385–412; Dianne Kirby, *Church, State and Propaganda: The Archbishop of York and International Relations: A Political Study of Cyril Foster Garbett, 1942–1955* (Hull, 1999). A more general (but still very valuable) discussion can be found in Dianne Kirby (ed.), *Religion and the Cold War* (Basingstoke, 2003).

6 For a useful general discussion of the whole subject see Owen Chadwick, *The Christian Church in the Cold War* (London, 1992).

7 National Archives, CAB 129/23, Cabinet Paper on 'The First Aim of British Foreign Policy'.

8 For some useful comments on Bevin's views in this context, see Kirby, 'Divinely Sanctioned', *passim*.

9 Dianne Kirby, 'Harry S. Truman's International Religious Anti-Communist Front, the Archbishop of Canterbury and the 1948 Inaugural Assembly of the World Council of Churches', *Contemporary British History*, 15, 4 (2001), pp. 35–70 (quotation from p. 43).

10 Among the vast literature on this subject, a particularly readable discussion can be found in Michael Burleigh, *Sacred Causes: Religion and European Politics from the Dictators to Al Qaeda* (London, 2006).

11 Among the large literature on this subject of 'secularization' see, for example, Martin, *A General Theory of Secularization*; Brown, *Death of Christian Britain*.

12 See, for example, Philip Richter and Leslie Francis, *Gone but not Forgotten: Church Leaving and Returning* (London, 1998).

13 For some useful comments on this theme, see Pinder, 'Religious Change in the Process of Secularisation'.

14 For an interesting discussion on this theme, see David Clough, 'Theology through Social and Political Action', in Clive Marsh *et al.* (eds), *Unmasking Methodist Theology* (Trowbridge, 2004), pp. 41–7.

15 *Methodist Recorder*, 17 April 1947 (Notes of the Week).

16 *Methodist Recorder*, 18 March 1948 (Editorial on 'Christianity and Communism').

17 *Methodist Recorder*, 11 March 1948 (Article by Rose on 'State of Emergency').

18 *Methodist Recorder*, 7 August 1948 (Article by Rose on 'Spotlight on Hope').

19 *Methodist Recorder*, 8 April 1948 (Letter by P. Belcher).

20 *Methodist Recorder*, 22 April 1948 (Letter by E.W. James).

21 *Methodist Recorder*, 21 April 1949 (Article by the Revd Thomas Metcalfe on 'Christ or Communism?').

22 Edward Rogers, *A Christian Looks at Communism* (London, 1948).

23 *Conference Minutes*, 1948 (Resolution on 'The Challenge of Communism').

24 *The Debate about Communism: An Interim Statement* (London, 1949).

25 T.J. Foinette, 'Christianity and Communism', *London Quarterly and Holborn Review*, 174 (1949), pp. 38–42.

26 Eric Fletcher, 'The Church and International Affairs', *London Quarterly and Holborn Review*, 174 (1949), pp. 43–6.

27 Leslie Church, 'The Challenge of Communism', *London Quarterly and Holborn Review*, 175 (1950), pp. 193–6.

28 The five pamphlets were published together in Maldwyn Edwards (ed.), *Communism* (London, 1952). The quotations in the following two paragraphs are all taken from this edition.

29 Carter's contribution was written before the Second World War, which explains the somewhat outdated nature of his discussion.

30 Richard Crossman (ed.), *The God that Failed* (Washington DC, 1949).

31 Herbert Butterfield, *Christianity, Diplomacy and War* (London, 1953). For a useful intellectual biography of Butterfield, which gives due weight to his Methodist background, see McIntire, *Herbert Butterfield*.

32 Edward Rogers, *A Commentary on Communism* (London, 1951).

33 D.R. Davies, 'The Great Lie of Communism', *London Quarterly and Holborn Review*, 176 (1951), pp. 33–8.

34 D.R. Davies, 'Communism: The New Islam', *London Quarterly and Holborn Review*, 178 (1953), pp. 117–22.

35 Norman Gantze, 'The Church Attitude to Communism: Views of Barth and Berdyaev', *London Quarterly and Holborn Review*, 176 (1951), pp. 319–22.

36 'Resolution on Communism' at the 1948 Lambeth Conference reproduced in *The Lambeth Conferences 1867–1948*. Also see D.M. Mackinnon (ed.), *Christian Faith and Communist Faith* (London, 1953).

37 *Conference Minutes*, 1949 ('Declaration of the Methodist Church on Christian Social and Political Responsibility').

38 *Methodist Recorder*, 1 February 1951 (Article on 'Christian Witness in a Sheffield Factory').

39 *Methodist Recorder*, 15 February 1951 (Article on 'Industrial Chaplains at Work in Glasgow').

40 *Methodist Recorder*, 1 March 1951 (Letter by the Revd F. Ockenden).

41 *Methodist Recorder*, 4 March 1948 (Notes of the Week).

42 *Methodist Recorder*, 21 September 1950 (Notes of the Week).

43 *Conference Agenda*, 1951 (Report of the Division of Christian Citizenship).

44 Kenneth G. Greet, *Fully Connected* (Peterborough, 1997), p. 53.

45 British Council of Churches, *The Era of Atomic Power* (London, 1946).

46 *Conference Agenda*, 1947 (Report of the Commission on 'The Era of Atomic Power').

47 *Christian Pacifist*, May 1946 (MPF Notes); June 1946 (MPF Notes).

48 *Reconciliation* (the new name for *Christian Pacifist*), February 1947 (MPF Notes).

49 *Reconciliation*, December 1949 (MPF Notes).

50 *Conference Minutes*, 1950 (Special Resolution on 'World Peace and the Hydrogen Bomb').

51 *Methodist Recorder*, 20 July 1950 (Report on Conference Proceedings).

52 See, for example, the report in the *The Times*, 18 July 1950.

53 *Picture Post*, 5 August 1950.

54 See, for example, Soper's thoughtful Alex Wood lecture, 'Here Stand I: The Place of Compromise in Christian Life' (London, 1959), in which he acknowledged that 'in a world corrupted by sin' it must necessarily prove impossible to introduce the gospel as 'a full political and sociological programme' in the realm of history.

55 *Reconciliation*, September 1953 (MPF Notes).

56 *Conference Agenda*, 1954 ('Positive Peace Policy').

57 *Conference Agenda*, 1955 (Resolutions and Memorials).

58 *Methodist Recorder*, 11 April 1957 (Letter from Ethel Schofield and Ena Fytche).

59 *Conference Agenda*, 1957 (Report of the Department of Christian Citizenship).

60 See, for example, *Methodist Recorder*, 16 May 1957 (Report on May Synods).

61 *Methodist Recorder*, 4 April 1957 (Article on 'End H-Bomb Tests Urges Free Church Council').

62  *Conference Minutes*, 1957 ('Declaration of the Methodist Church on Peace and War').

63  *Methodist Recorder*, 18 July 1957 (Report on Conference Proceedings).

64  *Methodist Recorder*, 17 July 1958 (Report on Conference Proceedings).

65  British Council of Churches, *Christians and Atomic War* (London, 1959).

66  Quoted in Donald Frost, *Goodwill on Fire: Donald Soper's Life and Mission* (London, 1996), p. 60.

67  For a very useful short history of the anti-nuclear movement in this period, set against the context of wider global developments, see Laurence S. Wittner, *Resisting the Bomb: A History of the World Nuclear Disarmament Movement, 1954–70* (Stanford, 1997), pp. 184–96. Useful sources for the British peace movement in the 1950s and early 1960s include: Christopher Driver, *The Disarmers: A Study in Protest* (London, 1964); Frank Parkin, *Middle Class Radicalism: The Social Bases of the Campaign for Nuclear Disarmament* (Manchester, 1968); Richard Taylor, *Against the Bomb: The British Peace Movement, 1958–1965* (Oxford, 1988).

68  *Reconciliation*, March 1959 (MPF Notes). See, too, the report on the MPF Executive Meeting contained in *Reconciliation*, November 1958 (MPF Notes).

69  *Reconciliation*, June 1958 (MPF Notes).

70  *Reconciliation*, May 1959 (MPF Notes). For Soper's memories of this time, see Soper, *Calling for Action*, pp. 49ff.

71  Constance Willis Papers, 'Soper Address to Aldermaston March in Trafalgar Square', 30 March 1959.

72  Soper, *Calling for Action*, pp. 38, 49.

73  C.A. Coulson, 'Nuclear Knowledge and Christian Responsibility', *London Quarterly and Holborn Review*, 182 (1957), pp. 40–7.

74  C.A. Coulson, 'Science and Religion: A Changing Relationship', *London Quarterly and Holborn Review*, 178 (1953), pp. 87–94.

75  On George Thomas, see his own autobiography *The Memoirs of Viscount Tonypandy* (London, 1985); E.H. Robertson, *George: A Biography of Viscount Tonypandy* (London, 1992).

76  *Reconciliation*, April 1959 (MPF Notes).

77  See for example *Another Kind of National Service* (London, 1956), co-produced by the DCC and the MPF.

78  *Reconciliation*, May 1959 (Article by J.C. Jacobs on 'Holiness and Pacifism').

79  *Reconciliation*, December 1958 (MPF Notes).

80  *I am Persuaded: A Methodist Statement of the Christian Pacifist Case* (London, 1956).

81  *Conference Minutes*, 1945 ('Statement on International Situation').

82  *Conference Minutes*, 1949 (Declaration of the Methodist Church on 'Christian Social and Political Responsibility').

83  *Conference Minutes*, 1952 (Special Resolution on 'Christians in World Affairs').

84 *Conference Minutes,* 1955 (Report of Department of Christian Citizenship).

85 *Conference Agenda,* 1951 (Report of Department of Christian Citizenship).

86 *Methodist Recorder,* 13 January 1955 (Article by the Revd J.W. Watson on 'South Africa and the Way Ahead').

87 *Christian Citizen,* 9, 1 (1955).

88 *Methodist Recorder,* 12 March 1959 (Letter by the Revd F. Mussell).

89 Among the large literature on the Suez crisis see Barry Turner, *Suez, 1956* (London, 2006).

90 *The Times,* 14 September 1956; 17 September 1956.

91 *Conference Agenda,* 1957 (Report of Department of Christian Citizenship).

92 *Methodist Recorder,* 8 November 1956 (Article by Greet on 'Crisis Week').

93 *Methodist Recorder,* 8 November 1956 (Article headed 'A Protest March from Kingsway').

94 *Methodist Recorder,* 8 November 1956 (Notes of the Week).

95 *Methodist Recorder,* 15 November 1956 (Letters by the Revd W.E. Sangster and the Revd Samuel Hulton).

96 See, for example, Anon., *The Communism of Christianity* (Keighley, 1850).

97 F.A. Iremonger, *William Temple: Archbishop of Canterbury* (London, 1948), p. 601.

98 The essays were subsequently published as H. Wilson Harris (ed.), *Christianity and Communism* (Oxford, 1937).

# 7 Methodism and International Politics during the Later Cold War

1 Arthur Marwick, *The Sixties* (Oxford, 1998), p. 3.

2 John A.T. Robinson, *Honest to God* (London, 1963).

3 Colin Morris, *Include Me Out* (London, 1968), p. 90.

4 For a sophisticated secular argument about the way in which ethical responsibilities develop in such a way, see Peter Singer, *Applied Ethics* (Oxford, 1986).

5 For a useful guide to the key developments in the Cuban Missile Crisis see Mark J. White, *The Cuban Missile Crisis* (Basingstoke, 1996).

6 Among the vast literature on the Vietnam War see, for example, Peter Lowe, *The Vietnam War* (Basingstoke, 1998). For a recent account focusing on opposition within the United States to the War see Marc Jason Gilbert, *The Vietnam War on Campus* (Westport, Conn., 2001). For an account focusing on the impact of the war on the US political system, see David L. Anderson, *Shadow on the White*

*House: US Presidents and the Vietnam War, 1945–75* (Lawrence, Kan., 1993).

7 For a recent discussion of the My Lai massacre and its long-term impact on America, see Kendrick Oliver, *The My Lai Massacre in American History and Memory* (Manchester, 2006).

8 On the response of British governments to the Vietnam War (particularly in the 1960s) see Sylvia Ellis, *Britain, America and the Vietnam War* (Westport, Conn., 2004).

9 *Conference Agenda*, 1965 (Report of the Department of Christian Citizenship).

10 *Methodist Recorder*, 7 July 1966 (Report on Conference Proceedings).

11 *Methodist Recorder*, 21 July 1966 (Letters by H.J. Galliford and J.C. Steel).

12 *Methodist Recorder*, 20 July 1967 (Report on Conference Proceedings).

13 *I am Persuaded: A Methodist Statement of the Christian Pacifist Case* (London, 1970).

14 *Methodist Recorder*, 28 March 1968 (Article headed 'Case for the Defence').

15 *Methodist Recorder*, 28 March 1968 (Editorial headed 'Play it Cool').

16 For a valuable account of Gallagher's role in the peace process see Dennis Cooke, *Peacemaker: the Life and Work of Eric Gallagher* (Peterborough, 2005). It is of course worth making the point that much of Gallagher's work was necessarily conducted in secret and therefore hardly likely to form the subject of newspaper reports.

17 Among the large literature on the Falklands War, see for example David Boyce George, *The Falklands War* (London, 2005); Lawrence Freedman, *Britain and the Falklands War* (Oxford, 1988).

18 The 'official' position of the British government on the decision to take military action to regain the Falklands was set down in the various speeches made in the House of Commons on 14 April 1982. See *Parliamentary Debates (Commons)*, vol. 429 (1981–2).

19 For an interesting early pamphlet by a prominent Quaker along these lines, see Richard Ullmann, 'The Dilemmas of a Reconciler' (London, 1963).

20 For a useful statement of views current within the MPF during this period, see 'A More Excellent Way' (London, n.d.). A more sophisticated statement critiquing the boundary between 'pacifism' and 'non-pacifism' can be found in John Stacey, 'Towards a Reconciliation of Pacifism and Non-Pacifism', *London Quarterly and Holborn Review*, 1967, pp. 148–54.

21 *Methodist Recorder*, 13 May 1982 (Article headed 'Falklands: Church Plea for Restraint').

22 *Methodist Recorder*, 29 April 1982 (Article headed 'Falkland UN Call'). For a useful statement of Duckworth's approach to his role as DSR Secretary see Brian Duckworth, 'Faith Working Through Love: Towards a Methodist Theology of Social Action', Southlands College Principal's Lecture, 1984.

23 *Methodist Recorder*, 6 May 1982 (Article headed 'President's Council Message to Premier').

24  *Methodist Recorder*, 22 April 1982 (Letters by the Revd John Hastings and the Revd H.M. Hart).

25  See, for example, *The Times*, 22 May 1982 (Article headed 'Church Leaders and the Falklands').

26  *Methodist Recorder*, 27 May 1982 (Letter by the Revd J. Lawson).

27  *Methodist Recorder*, 13 May 1982 (Letter by Ronald Thomas).

28  *Methodist Recorder*, 29 April 1982 (Letter by Ewart Tamblyn).

29  *Methodist Recorder*, 3 June 1982 (Article headed 'Chaplain Tells of Life at the Front Line').

30  *Methodist Recorder*, 10 June 1982 (Letter by the Revd Harry Warne).

31  *Methodist Recorder*, 24 June 1982 (Letter by the Revd Donald Harper).

32  *Methodist Recorder*, 8 July 1982 (Conference Proceedings). Warne had previously written to *The Times* during the Falklands War attacking some of Greet's pronouncements. See *The Times*, 29 May 1982 (Letter by Warne).

33  *Methodist Recorder*, 15 July 1982 (Letter by T.F.R. Jones).

34  Greet, *Fully Connected*, pp. 150ff.

35  *The Times*, 28 July 1982 (Article headed 'Serving God not Government').

36  *The British Nuclear Deterrent* (London, 1963).

37  John Vincent, *Christ in a Nuclear World* (London, 1962), p. 21.

38  Vincent, *Christ in a Nuclear World*, p. 119.

39  John Vincent, *Christian Nuclear Perspective* (London, 1964), pp. 16, 29.

40  Butterfield, *Christianity, Diplomacy and War, passim*.

41  Herbert Butterfield, 'Human Nature and the Dominion of Fear', in Herbert Butterfield, *International Conflict in the Twentieth century: A Christian View* (London, 1960), p. 92.

42  Butterfield, 'Dominion', p. 94.

43  E. Gordon Rupp, 'Dilemmas of Peacemaking' (New Malden, 1965).

44  *Conference Agenda*, 1965 (Report of the Department of Christian Citizenship)

45  *Methodist Recorder*, 1 July 1965 (Letter by B.D. Clarke).

46  For a useful overview of developments during these years, see Laurence S. Wittner, *Towards Nuclear Abolition: A History of the World Nuclear Disarmament Movement, 1971 to the Present* (Stanford, 2003). For the memories of key figures in the British government of this issue see the relevant pages of Margaret Thatcher, *The Downing Street Years* (London, 1993); Michael Heseltine, *Life in the Jungle: My Autobiography* (London, 2000). For a useful memoir by one leading member of the peace movement see Bruce Kent, *Undiscovered Ends: An Autobiography* (London, 1992).

47  For a history of the activities of the protest movement at Greenham Common see Beth Junor, *Greenham Common Women's Peace Camp* (London, 1995).

48  Cited in Sydney Bailey, *Christian Perspectives on Nuclear Weapons* (London, 1984), p. 14.

49  For a discussion of the debate at Synod, see *The Times*, 11 February 1983

(Article headed 'General Synod Rejects Unilateral Disarmament'). For two useful responses to the debate in the Church of England see Francis Bridger (ed.), *The Cross and the Bomb* (London, 1983), and Robin Gill (ed.), *The Cross Against the Bomb* (London, 1984). A good deal was also written during this period, particularly across the Atlantic, on the question of whether the possession of nuclear weapons could be justified in a just war framework.

50 *Methodist Recorder*, 2 June 1983 (Article headed 'URC Adopts a Policy of Unilateralism').

51 The Revd David Gosling, 'The Nuclear Issue', in *Blessed are the Peacemakers* (London, 1981).

52 *Conference Agenda*, 1980 (Memorial submitted by the Isle of Man Synod).

53 Kenneth Greet, *The Big Sin: Christianity and the Arms Race* (London, 1982).

54 *Methodist Recorder*, 22 January 1981 (Letter by P. B. Yenvell).

55 T.E. Utley, 'Christianity and the Radical Tradition', in T.E. Utley and Edward Norman, *Ethics and Nuclear Arms* (London, 1983), pp. 11–12.

56 Edward Norman, 'The Churches and the Nuclear Debate: The Collapse of Theology', in Utley and Norman, *Ethics and Nuclear Arms*, p. 27.

57 *Conference Agenda*, 1983 (Report compiled under the auspices of the Division of Social Responsibility on 'Nuclear Disarmament – Some Theological Considerations').

58 *Methodist Recorder*, 16 June 1983 (Letter by J.R. Ware).

59 Caroline Moorhead, *Troublesome People: Enemies of War, 1916–1986* (London, 1987), p. 308.

60 *Methodist Recorder*, 10 February 1983 (Article headed 'President at Greenham Common').

61 *Methodist Recorder*, 24 February 1983 (Letters by the Revd W. Jamieson and M.J. Rickard).

62 *Methodist Recorder*, 10 March 1983 (Letter by Alfred Scott).

63 *Methodist Recorder*, 10 March 1983 (Letter by Fiona Lewis).

64 *Conference Agenda*, 1984 (Interim Report compiled under the auspices of the DSR on 'Civil Disobedience').

65 The situation of the churches also commanded the attention of a Working Group set up by the BCC, leading to the publication by Trevor Beeson, *Discretion and Valour* (London, 1974). There was no Methodist representative on the working group.

66 *Conference Agenda*, 1985 ('A Report on Human Rights' compiled under the auspices of the DSR).

67 *Methodist Recorder*, 16 July 1964 (Report on Conference Proceedings).

68 Edward Rogers, *Living Standards: A Christian Looks at the World's Poverty* (London, 1964), pp. 80–1.

69 *Conference Agenda*, 1966 (Report of the Department of Christian Citizenship).

# Notes

70 *Methodist Recorder*, 13 June 1968 (Article on 'World Hunger').

71 Morris, *Include Me Out*, p. 43.

72 *Conference Agenda*, 1980 (Report of the Division of Social Responsibility).

73 Prime Minister Ian Smith: Announcement of Unilateral Declaration of Independence, November 11, 1965. For a brief discussion of Rhodesia at this time see Anthony Verrier, *The Road to Zimbabwe, 1890–1980* (London, 1986), pp. 151–65. For a very detailed discussion see Kenneth Young, *Rhodesia and Independence: A Study in British Colonial Policy* (London, 1969). A useful work on Rhodesia following UDI is Peter Godwin and Ian Hancock, *Rhodesians Never Die: The Impact of War and Change on White Rhodesia, c1970–1980* (Oxford, 1993).

74 *Conference Agenda*, 1964 (Report of the Department of Christian Citizenship).

75 *Methodist Recorder*, 1 July 1965 (Letter by the Revd H.J. Lawrence).

76 *Methodist Recorder*, 18 November 1965 (Article by the Revd. H.O. Morton on 'Rhodesia After UDI').

77 *Methodist Recorder*, 25 November 1965 (Letter by R.H. Thomas).

78 *Methodist Recorder*, 4 July 1968 (Letter by C.H. Thompson).

79 Colin Morris, *Unyoung, Uncloured and Unpoor* (London, 1969), pp. 19, 83, 97–8.

80 Colin Morris (ed.), *Kaunda on Violence* (London, 1980), p. 111.

81 For an interesting debate between Soper and Morris on this question see *Methodist Recorder*, 16 July 1970 (Article headed 'Soper v. Morris'). Soper himself remained unambiguously committed to the position that 'the only thing that will solve problems of southern Africa is the goodness of man to his neighbour'. Constance Willis Papers (Sermon by Soper, dated 1 May 1977).

82 *Methodist Recorder*, 29 November 1979 (Letter by the Revd David Haslam).

83 *Methodist Recorder*, 1 July 1971 (Report on Conference Proceedings).

84 *Conference Agenda*, 1974 (Memorial from the Greenock Quarterly Meeting).

85 *Methodist Recorder*, 20 September 1973 (Letter by the Revd J.M. Turner).

86 *Methodist Recorder*, 19 August 1971 (Letter by A.G. Grey).

87 *Methodist Recorder*, 4 July 1974 (Letter by Leslie Morgan).

88 *Methodist Recorder*, 5 July 1979 (Report on Conference Proceedings).

89 *Conference Agenda*, 1970 (Report of the Department of Christian Citizenship).

90 *Conference Agenda*, 1971 (Report of the Department of Christian Citizenship).

91 *Methodist Recorder*, 6 August 1970 (Letters by H. Hird and W.B. Borrows).

92 *Conference Agenda*, 1971 (Report of the Department of Christian Citizenship).

93 *Conference Agenda*, 1972 (Report of the Department of Christian Citizenship).

94 Webb's discussion of the role of the WCC in South Africa can be found in

Pauline Webb, *A Long Struggle: The Involvement of the World Council of Churches in South Africa* (Geneva, 1994).

95 *Methodist Recorder*, 8 November 1973 (Article by Farrow headed 'Money not the "Big Stick" to Beat Apartheid').

96 *Conference Minutes*, 1973 (Annual Address of the Conference to the Methodist Societies).

97 *Methodist Recorder*, 18 July 1974 (Letter by the Revd David Haslam).

98 *Conference Minutes*, 1971 (Annual Address of the Methodist Conference to the Methodist Societies).

## 8 Facing a New World

1 Among the vast literature on the *perestroika* era, see Martin McAuley, *Gorbachev and Perestroika* (Basingstoke, 1990); Richard Sakwa, *Gorbachev and His Reforms* (London, 1990); Alexander Dallin and Gail Lapidus (eds), *The Soviet System in Crisis: A Reader of Western and Soviet Views* (Boulder, Colo., 1991).

2 *The Guardian*, 29 January 1992 ('Bush Goes on the Offensive').

3 *The Guardian*, 24 November 1989 ('Runcie Doubts Triumph of Capitalism'). ·

4 *Methodist Recorder*, 11 January 1990 (Letter by the Revd J.M. Turner).

5 *Methodist Recorder*, 22 June 1989 (Article by Peter Stephens headed 'On Returning to Conference').

6 Such a belief has been associated, not altogether accurately, with the celebrated work by Francis Fukuyama, *The End of History and the Last Man* (London, 1992).

7 For a succinct discussion of some of these themes, see Vesselin Popovski, 'The Concept of Humanitarian Intervention', in Peter Siani-Davis (ed.), *International Intervention in the Balkans since 1995* (London, 2003).

8 For a lucid discussion of this topic by two Methodist ministers, see Leslie Griffiths and Jennifer Potter, *World Without End: Contours of a Post-Terrorism World* (Peterborough, 2007), pp. 78–121.

9 Archives of the Council for Christian Approaches to Disarmament, Box 44 (various documents). ·

10 Among the voluminous literature on the first Gulf War, see Michael Gordon and Bernard Trainor, *The Generals' War: The Inside Story of the First Gulf War* (London, 2006).

11 For a useful discussion of the responses of the British churches, particularly in the context of Just War thinking, see Charles Reed, *Just War?* (London, 2004), pp. 62–98.

12 *Methodist Recorder*, 23 August 1990 (Letter by Mary Ann Ebert).

13 *Methodist Recorder,* 27 September 1990 (Soper, 'Personally Speaking').

14 *Methodist Recorder*, 1 November 1990 (Article headed 'Gulf Crisis Silence').

15 *The Independent,* 31 October 1990 (Harries, 'The Path to a Just War'). For a further insight into Harries's views on the issues raised by international conflict for the Christian Church, see Richard Harries, *Christianity and War in the Nuclear Age* (Wilton, Conn., 1986).

16 *The Independent,* 16 November 1990 ('Runcie Urges Year's Trial for Sanctions against Iraq').

17 Reed, *Just War?,* p. 74

18 *The Independent,* 26 November 1990 ('Christians Endorse Anti-War Declaration').

19 *Methodist Recorder,* 6 December 1990 (Kenneth Greet, 'Without Portfolio').

20 *Methodist Recorder,* 10 January 1991 (Article by Duckworth headed 'Gulf: Eleventh Hour').

21 *Methodist Recorder,* 17 January 1991 (Editorial, 'Awesome Deadline').

22 *The Times,* 16 January 1991 ('First Lord of the War of Words').

23 *Methodist Recorder,* 31 January 1991 (Article headed 'Dilemma Faces Peace Groups').

24 *Methodist Recorder,* 21 February 1991 (Letter by Haslam).

25 *Methodist Recorder,* 28 February 1991 (Letter by Milwood).

26 *Methodist Recorder,* 31 January 1991 (Letter by Leonard Webb).

27 *Methodist Recorder,* 7 February 1991 (Kenneth Greet, 'Without Portfolio').

28 Among the huge literature on the break-up of Yugoslavia, see the very readable Laura Silber, *The Death of Yugoslavia* (London, 1996). For a more scholarly account see Sabrina Petra Ramet, *Balkan Babel: The Disintegration of Yugoslavia from the Death of Tito to Ethnic War* (Boulder, Colo., 1996).

29 Charalmpos Symvoulidis, 'British and Greek Press Reactions to the Disintegration of Yugoslavia, 1991–1999', University of Liverpool PhD thesis, 2005.

30 For a sharply critical account of British policy towards Yugoslavia in the 1990s, see Brendan Simms, *Unfinest Hour: Britain and the Destruction of Bosnia* (London, 2002). For a somewhat more nuanced account of the dilemmas facing those who favoured intervention, see James Gow, *Triumph of the Failure of the Will: International Diplomacy and the Yugoslav War* (London, 1997). Some further reflections on the failure of UN intervention can be found in William Shawcross, *Deliver us from Evil: Warlords and Peacekeepers in a World of Endless Conflict* (London, 2000). For the perspective of two senior British politicians on the Bosnian imbroglio see John Major, *John Major: The Autobiography* (London, 1999), pp. 277ff. Douglas Hurd's comments on the crisis can be found in Douglas Hurd, *The Search for Peace: A Century of Peace Diplomacy* (London, 1997), pp. 89–110.

31 For a fascinating if idiosyncratic discussion of some of the moral issues surrounding humanitarian intervention see Michael Ignatieff, *The Warrior's House* (London, 1998). Also see Oliver Ramsbottom and Tom Woodhouse, *Humanitarian*

*Intervention in Contemporary Conflict* (Cambridge, 1996), pp. 167–92.

32 *Methodist Recorder*, 20 August 1992 (Editorial on 'Moral Choice'). Members of the Methodist Church also of course played a great role in the dispatch of humanitarian aid to the former Yugoslavia.

33 *The Independent*, 12 August 1993 (Letter by Sheppard).

34 On the Vance-Owen Plan, see David Owen, *Balkan Odyssey* (London, 1996), pp. 94–159.

35 *Conference Minutes*, 1993 (Agreed Motion on 'Former Yugoslavia').

36 *Methodist Recorder*, 26 August 1993 (Article headed 'No Visible Alternative').

37 On the Kosovan War, see Tim Judah, *Kosovo: War and Revenge* (New Haven, Conn., 2002); on the consequences of the war see William G. O'Neill, *Kosovo: An Unfinished Peace* (London, 2002).

38 See David M. Ackerman, 'Kosovo and Nato', in Frank Columbus (ed.), *Kosovo-Serbia: A Just War?* (New York, 1999), pp. 155–66. Also see Martin A. Smith, *Kosovo, Nato and the United Nations*, in Stephen Badsey and Paul Latawski (eds), *Britain, Nato and the Lessons of the Balkan Conflicts* (London, 2004), pp. 153–77.

39 Speech by Robin Cook reprinted in the *Guardian*, 12 May 1997. For a more reflective piece by Cook on the nature of 'ethical foreign policy' see Robin Cook, 'Putting Principle into Practice', *Cambridge Review of International Affairs*, 15, 1 (2002), pp. 45–51.

40 *The Independent*, 2 April 1999 (Harries, 'For a Christian, This is a Just War').

41 *The Scotsman*, 1 April 1999.

42 *Methodist Recorder*, 8 April 1999 (Editorial, 'What Price Peace?').

43 *Methodist Recorder*, 15 April 1999 (Leslie Griffiths: Monthly Column). For a later discussion of Bosnia by Griffiths, see Griffiths and Potter, *World Without End*, pp. 32–9.

44 *Methodist Recorder*, 22 April 1999 (Letter by Frank Chappel).

45 *Methodist Recorder*, 6 May 1999 (Letter by Richard Stainsby).

46 *Methodist Recorder*, 6 May 1999 (Kenneth Greet: Monthly Column).

47 *Methodist Recorder*, 20 May 1999 (Article headed 'President: Stop the War').

48 Mark Curtis, *Web of Deceit: Britain's Real Role in the World* (London, 2003), pp. 134–56.

49 *Methodist Recorder*, 23 March 1989 (Letter by the Revd Norman Valley).

50 *The National Security Strategy of the United States of America*, September 2002.

51 For a series of documents that together set down the (at times inchoate) tenets of 'Neo-Conservatism', see the various documents on the website of the 'Project for a New American Century' (http://www.newamericancentury.org), particularly the 'Statement of Principles'. For an interesting critique by a some-time sympathizer, see Francis Fukuyama, *After the Neocons* (London, 2006). A

further incisive critique from a very different perspective can be found in John Gray, *Black Mass: Apocalyptic Religion and the Death of Utopia* (London, 2007).

52 Samuel Huntington, *The Clash of Civilizations and the Remaking of World Order* (London, 1998).

53 For a useful discussion of the concept of religious fundamentalism as a (paradoxically modern) reaction against modernity, see Karen Armstrong, *The Battle for God: Fundamentalism in Judaism, Christianity and Islam* (London, 2000). See, too, Abdel Salam Sadhammed, *Islamic Fundamentalism* (Boulder, Colo., 1996). For a valuable interpretation of Al Qaeda as an organization both created by – and responding to – the pressures of modernity, see John Gray, *Al Qaeda and What it Means to be Modern* (London, 2004). A critique of fundamentalism from a rather different perspective, emphasizing the value of diversity, can be found in Jonathan Sacks, *The Dignity of Difference* (London, 2002).

54 *The Times*, 15 September 2001 ('Bells of St Paul's Toll for the Dead').

55 *Liverpool Daily Post*, 20 September 2001. Rowan Williams later provided a more developed response to the events of 9/11 in Rowan Williams, *Writing in the Dust* (London, 2002).

56 *Methodist Recorder*, 27 September 2001 (Article by Le Moignan headed 'A World-Changing Event').

57 *Methodist Recorder*, 4 October 2001 (Letter by the Revd Nina Johnson).

58 *Methodist Recorder*, 27 September 2001 (Letter by the Revd Kenneth Walton).

59 *Methodist Recorder*, 8 November 2001 (Letter by Geoff Chapman).

60 *Methodist Recorder*, 15 November 2001 (Letter by Ron Burke).

61 *Methodist Recorder*, 1 November 2001 (Letter by the Revd John Pritchard).

62 *The Times*, 12 October 2001 ('Bishop Questions Allied Bombing Campaign').

63 *Methodist Reorder*, 1 November 2001 (Letter by the Revd P. K. Parsons).

64 Methodist Church Statement on Iraq, 7 August 2002 (Methodist Church website).

65 The Revd Ian White, letter to the Prime Minister, 12 September 2002 (Methodist Church Website).

66 *Methodist Recorder*, 27 February 2003 ('Pastoral Letter').

67 *Methodist Church Statement on Iraq*, 21 March 2003. This paragraph draws heavily on Reed, *Just War?*, esp. pp. 112–13.

68 *Independent on Sunday*, 9 February 2003 ('On the Brink of War').

69 *Methodist Recorder*, 20 March 2003 (Letter by Geoff Chapman).

70 *Methodist Recorder*, 6 March 2003 (Letter by Paul Johns).

71 *Methodist Recorder*, 6 March 2003 (Letter by the Revd Brian Snellgrove).

72 Reed, *Just War?*, pp. 17–20.

73 *Methodist Recorder*, 10 April 2003 (Letter by the Revd Phil Dew).

74 'Notes for Preachers and Worship Leaders during the Iraq Crisis' (Methodist Church Website).

75 *The Times*, 15 March 2003 ('We Don't Love War: Just those Sent to Fight').

76 For a discussion of the possible criteria for intervention, see Popovski, 'Concept of Humanitarian Intervention'.

77 For a superb argument along these lines see Alan Booth, *Christian Nonconformity in International Affairs* (London, 1970).

# 9 Conclusion

1 Statement by Anthea Cox, 15 April 2004 (Methodist Church Website).

2 Statement by Steve Hucklesby (International Affairs Secretary), 14 May 2004 (Methodist Church Website).

3 For an interesting critique of this position, emphasizing instead intra-communal tensions as a main source of disaffection among a section of the Muslim population in Britain, see Shiv Malik, 'The Making of a Terrorist', *Prospect* (June 2007).

4 *Yorkshire Post*, 14 July 2005 (describing activities in the Beeston area of Leeds where three of the bombers lived).

5 For a sophisticated (if controversial) discussion of this phenomenon, see Gray, *Black Mass, passim*.

6 For a lucid discussion of this process see Armstrong, *Battle for God*. For a discussion of Islamic terrorism in these terms see Gray, *Al Qaeda and the Modern*; Bernard Lewis, *The Crisis of Islam: Holy War and Unholy Terror* (New York, 2003).

7 See, for example, David Haslam's article 'Christians on the March', in the *Guardian*, 3 May 2003. See, too, David Haslam, 'Glimpsing the New World Order', also in the *Guardian*, 31 January 2004.

8 Methodist Church Press Release, 22 April 2004 (Methodist Church Website).

9 *Conference Minutes*, 2006 (Report on 'Ethics of Modern Warfare'). The full original report produced by the Methodist–URC group was published under the title *Peacemaking: A Christian Vocation* (Peterborough, 2006).

10 Griffiths and Potter, *World Without End*.

11 Richard Dawkins, *The Selfish Gene* (Oxford, 1976).

12 Among Ramsey's writings on this subject, see Paul Ramsey, *The Just War: Force and Political Responsibility* (New York, 1968); *War and the Christian Conscience* (Durham, NC, 1961).

13 Paul Ramsey, *Speak Up for Just War or Pacifism* (University Park, Pa., 1988).

14 Stephen Long, *Living the Discipline: United Methodist Theological Reflections on War, Civilization and Holiness* (Grand Rapids, Mich., 1992).

15 Wilson, *Biases and Blind Spots*.

16 On the concept of hyper-moralism see David Martin, *Pacifism: An Historical and Sociological Study* (London, 1965).

# Notes

17  Reinhold Niebuhr, *Why the Christian Church is not Pacifist* (London, 1940), pp. 10–12.

18  James Turner Johnson, *Can Modern War be Just?* (New Haven, Conn., 1984), p. 15.

19  See, for example, James Turner Johnson and George Weigel, *Just War and the Gulf War* (Washington DC, 1991).

20  See for example Archbishop Rowan Williams's lecture on 'Just War Revisited' to the Royal Institute of International Affairs, 15 October 2003.

21  Quoted in Reed, *Just War?*, p. 121.

22  For some striking figures relating to the crimes of various communist regimes around the world, see Stéphane Courtois *et al*, *The Black Book of Communism: Crimes, Terror, Repression* (Cambridge, Mass., 1999).

23  Alan Booth, *Christian Nonconformity in International Affairs*.

24  David Martin, *Does Christianity Cause War?* (Oxford, 1977), p. 100.

25  See, for example, Richard Dawkins, *The God Delusion* (London, 2006); Christopher Hitchens, *God is Not Great: The Case against Religion* (London, 2007); Daniel D. Dennett, *Breaking the Spell: Religion as a Natural Phenomenon* (London, 2007).     *Reply by McGrath.*

26  Armstrong, *Battle for God; Gray, Al Qaeda and the Modern*.

# Select Bibliography

Since a list of all the items consulted in writing this book would be enormous, the following bibliography only includes those listed in the notes. In cases where books and articles were published both in Britain and abroad the place of publication in Britain is listed. The date of the edition listed is the one consulted and not necessarily the date of first publication. The list of books and articles is divided between primary and secondary sources, although the division is inevitably somewhat arbitrary in a project of this kind.

## Archives

University of Bradford Library, Special Collections (Constance Willis Papers).
British Library of Economics and Political Science, London School of Economics, Special Collections (Fellowship of Reconciliation Archive).
Friends House, London (Pelham Committee Papers).
John Rylands Library, University of Manchester (Methodist Archives and Records Centre).
King's College London, Liddell Hart Archives (Council for Christian Approaches to Disarmament).
National Archives (Records of the Foreign Office).
Oxford Brookes University, Methodist Studies Centre (Various personal papers and unpublished material).
Oxford University, Bodleian University (Charles Coulson Papers).
Peace Pledge Union, London (Records of the Peace Pledge Union and associated material relating to the history of the British peace movement).

## Newspapers and magazines

*British Weekly*
*Christian Citizen*
*Christian Pacifist*
*Daily Herald*
*Daily Worker*
*DSR News*
*Free Methodist*
*Friend*
*Guardian*
*Independent*
*Methodist Magazine*
*Methodist Recorder*
*Methodist Times*
*Methodist Times and Leader*
*Methodist Weekly*
*Primitive Methodist*
*Primitive Methodist Leader*
*Primitive Methodist Magazine*
*Primitive Methodist World*
*Peace News*
*Picture Post*
*Reconciliation*
*Scotsman*
*Sunday Times*
*The Times*
*United Methodist*
*Yorkshire Post*

## Collections of Documents

*Agenda of the Conference of the Methodist Church of Great Britain*
*Minutes of the Conference of the Methodist Church of Great Britain*
*Minutes of the Primitive Methodist Church*
*Minutes of the United Methodist Church*
*Minutes of the Wesleyan Methodist Church*
*Parliamentary Debates (House of Commons)*

## Websites

Website of the BBC World War II People's Archive
Website of the Methodist Church of Great Britain
Website of the Project for the New American Century
Website of the Royal Institute for International Affairs

## Primary Sources (autobiographies, diaries, contemporary writings, reports, etc.)

Arthur, William, *What is Fiji, the Sovereignty of which is offered to Her Majesty?* (London, 1859).

Beeson, Trevor, *Discretion and Valour* (London, 1974).
Bell, G.K.A., *Randall Davidson: Archbishop of Canterbury* (London, 1938).
Bell, G.K.A., *The Church and Humanity, 1939–46* (London, 1946).
*Blessed are the Peacemakers* (London, 1981).
Bridger, Francis (ed.), *The Cross and the Bomb* (London, 1983).
British Council of Churches, *Era of Atomic Power* (London, 1946).
British Council of Churches, *Christians and Atomic War* (London, 1959).
British Council of Churches, *The British Nuclear Deterrent* (London, 1963).
Brittain, Vera, *Testament of Experience* (London, 1981).
Butterfield, Herbert, *Christianity, Diplomacy and War* (London, 1953).
Butterfield, Herbert, 'Human Nature and the Dominion of Fear', in Butterfield, Herbert, *International Conflict in the Twentieth Century* (London, 1960).

Carden, Percy, 'Building on the Temple of a Lasting Peace', *London Quarterly and Holborn Review*, 168 (1944), pp. 28–35.
Carter, Henry, *Towards World Recovery* (London, 1945).
Church, Leslie, 'The Challenge of Communism', *London Quarterly and Holborn Review*, 175 (1950), pp. 193–6.
'The Command of the Sea', *London Quarterly Review*, 85 (1896), pp. 314–33.
*The Communism of Christianity* (Keighley, 1850).
Cook, Robin, 'Putting Principle into Practice', *Cambridge Review of International Affairs*, 15, 1 (2002), pp. 45–51.
*COPEC Report Number 8: Christianity and War* (London, 1924).
Coulson, C.A., 'Science and Religion: A Changing Relationship', *London Quarterly and Holborn Review*, 178 (1953), pp. 87–94.
Coulson, C.A., 'Nuclear Knowledge and Christian Responsibility', *London Quarterly and Holborn Review*, 182 (1957), pp. 40–7.
Coulson, C.A., *Science and Christian Belief* (London, 1958).
Crane, Denis, *The Life-Story of Sir Robert Perks* (London, 1909).

# Select Bibliography

Crook, W.M., 'The War: Its Origins and Causes', *London Quarterly Review*, 113 (1915), pp. 1–14.

Crossman, Richard (ed.), *The God that Failed* (Washington DC, 1949).

Davies, D.R., 'The Great Lie of Communism', *London Quarterly and Holborn Review*, 176 (1951), pp. 33–8.

Davies, D.R., 'Communism: the New Islam', *London Quarterly and Holborn Review*, 178 (1953), pp. 117–22.

Duckworth, Brian, 'Faith Working Through Love: Towards a Methodist Theology of Social Action', Southlands College Principal's Lecture, 1984.

Edwards, Maldwyn (ed.), *Communism* (London, 1952).

'Europe in Africa', *London Quarterly Review*, 85 (1896), pp. 205–232.

Fletcher, Eric, 'The Church and International Affairs', *London Quarterly and Holborn Review*, 174 (1949), pp. 43–6.

Flew, R. Newton, *The Idea of Perfection in Christian Theology* (London, 1934).

Foinette, T.J., 'Christianity and Communism', *London Quarterly and Holborn Review*, 175 (1950), pp. 38–42.

Fowler, E.H., *The Life of Henry Hartley Fowler, First Viscount Wolverhampton* (London, 1912).

Gantze, Norman, 'The Church Attitude to Communism: Views of Barth and Berdyaev', *London Quarterly and Holborn Review*, 176 (1951), pp. 319–22.

Geden, A.S., 'Nigeria', *London Quarterly Review*, 92 (1899), pp. 262–78.

Gill, Robin, *The Cross Against the Bomb* (London, 1984).

Greet, Kenneth, *The Big Sin: Christianity and the Arms Race* (London, 1982).

Greet, Kenneth, *Fully Connected* (Peterborough, 1997).

Griffiths, Leslie and Potter, Jennifer, *World Without End: Contours of a Post-Terrorism World* (Peterborough, 2007).

Haldane, Richard Burdon, *An Autobiography* (London, 1929).

Harrison, A.W., *Christianity and Universal Peace* (London, 1926).

Harrison, Archibald W., *Christianity and the League of Nations* (London, 1928).

Harvey, F. Brompton. 'Unseasonable Truth: Thoughts on War', *London Quarterly and Holborn Review*, 167 (1942), pp. 335–43.

Harvey, F. Brompton, *Should Germany be Forgiven?* (London, 1944).

Heseltine, Michael, *Life in the Jungle: My Autobiography* (London, 2000).

Hocking, Silas K., *My Book of Memory* (London, 1923).

Hughes, Dorothea Price, *The Life of Hugh Price Hughes* (London, 1904).

Keeble, Samuel, *Industrial Day-Dreams: Studies in Industrial Ethics and Economies* (London, 1896).

Keeble, Samuel, *COPEC* (London, 1924).

Kent, Bruce, *Undiscovered Ends: An Autobiography* (London, 1992).

*The Lambeth Conferences, 1867–1948* (London, 1948).

Lidgett, J. Scott, *My Guided Life* (London, 1936).

Lloyd George, David, *War Memoirs of David Lloyd George*, 2 vols (London, 1938).

Lofthouse, W.F., 'Karl Barth and the Gospel', *London Quarterly and Holborn Review*, 158 (1933), pp. 28–37.

Lofthouse, W.F., 'To End Hitlerism', *London Quarterly and Holborn Review*, 165 (1940), pp. 31–42.

Lukowitz, David C., 'British Pacifists and Appeasement: the Peace Pledge Union', *Journal of Contemporary History*, 9 (1974), pp. 115–27.

Lunn, Sir Henry, *Chapters from My Life* (London, 1918).


MacGregor, G.H.C., *The New Testament Basis of Pacifism* (New York, 1954).

MacLachlan, Lewis, *CPFLU: A History of the Christian Pacifist Forestry and Land Units* (London, 1952).

Major, John, *John Major: The Autobiography* (London, 1999).

Marchant, Sir James, *Dr John Clifford: Life, Letters and Reminiscences* (London, 1924).

Methodist Church, Department of Christian Citizenship, *The Debate about Communism: An Interim Statement* (London, 1949).

Methodist Church, Department of Youth, *Another Kind of National Service* (London, 1956).

Methodist Peace Fellowship, *I am Persuaded: A Methodist Statement of the Christian Pacifist Case* (London, 1956).

Methodist Peace Fellowship, *A More Excellent Way* (London, n.d.).

Methodist Peace Fellowship, *In Quest of Peace* (London, 1994).

Milne, A.A., *War with Honour* (London, 1940).

Moorhead, Caroline, *Troublesome People: Enemies of War, 1916–1986* (London, 1987).

Morel, E.D., *Red Rubber: The Story of the Slave Trade Flourishing in the Congo in the Year of Grace 1906* (London, 1906).

Morel, E.D., *Morocco in Diplomacy* (London, 1912).

Morley, John, *Life of Richard Cobden* (London, 1903).

Morris, Colin, *Include Me Out* (London, 1968).

Morris, Colin, *Unyoung, Uncoloured and Unpoor* (London, 1969).

Morris, Colin (ed.), *Kaunda on Violence* (London, 1980).

Moulton, J.H., 'Christianity and Defensive War', *London Quarterly Review*, 123 (1915), pp. 32–45.

Moulton, W.F., *James Hope Moulton* (London, 1919).


Newton, John T., 'The State and the Individual Conscience', *London Quarterly and Holborn Review*, 166 (1941), pp. 204–8.

Niebuhr, Reinhold, *Moral Man and Immoral Society: A Study in Ethics and Politics* (London, 1933).

Niebuhr, Reinhold, *Why the Christian Church is Not Pacifist* (London, 1940).

*A North–South Programme for Survival* (Cambridge, Mass., 1990).

Owen, David, *Balkan Odyssey* (London, 1996).

*Peacemaking: A Christian Vocation* (London, 2006).

Pope, R. Martin, 'Peace and World Renewal', *London Quarterly and Holborn Review*, 169 (1944), pp. 193–7.

Pope, William Burt, *A Compendium of Christian Theology*, 3 vols (London, 1880).

Porter Goff, E.N., 'A Christian Peace Policy', in Dearmer, Percy (ed.), *Christianity and the Crisis* (London, 1933).

Pyke, Richard, *Men and Memories* (London, 1948).

Raven, Charles, *Is War Obsolete?* (London, 1935).

Rider, Robert J., *Reflections on the Battlefield: From Infantryman to Chaplain, 1914–1999* (Liverpool, 2001).

Robert, R. Ellis, *H.R.L. Sheppard: Life and Letters* (London, 1942).

Robinson, J. Armitage *et al.*, *Hugh Price Hughes as We Knew Him* (London, 1902).

Robinson, John A.T., *Honest to God* (London, 1963).

Rogers, Edward, *A Christian Looks at Communism* (London, 1948).

Rogers, Edward, *A Commentary on Communism* (London, 1951).

Rogers, Edward, *Living Standards: A Christian Looks at the World's Poverty* (London, 1964).

Rupp, E. Gordon, *Dilemmas of Peacemaking* (New Malden, 1965).

Sangster, W.E., *The Path to Perfection* (London, 1943).

Seckings, H.S, 'The Morality of the Sermon on the Mount', *Holborn Review* (April 1915), pp. 183–97.

Sheppard, H.R.L., *We Say No: The Plain Man's Guide to Pacifism* (London, 1935).

Simmons, Jim, *Soap-Box Evangelist* (London, 1972).

Smith, Henry *et al.*, *The Story of the United Methodist Church* (London, 1932).

Snowden, Philip, *An Autobiography*, 2 vols (London, 1934).

Soper, Donald, *Question Time on Tower Hill* (London, 1935).

Soper, Donald, *Here Stand I: The Place of Compromise in Christian Life* (London, 1959).

Soper, Donald, *Calling for Action* (London, 1984).

Stacey, John, 'Towards a Reconciliation of Pacifism and Non-Pacifism', *London Quarterly and Holborn Review* (1967), pp. 148–54.

Temple, F.S., *Some Lambeth Letters* (Oxford, 1963).

Temple, William, *Is Christ Divided?* (London, 1943).

Thatcher, Margaret, *The Downing Street Years* (London, 1993).

Thomas, George, *The Memoirs of Viscount Tonypandy* (London, 1985).

Ullmann, Richard, *The Dilemmas of a Reconciler* (London, 1963).

Urquhart, A. Forbes, 'The Diffusion of Modern Civilisation', *London Quarterly Review*, 92 (1899), pp. 339–57.

Urwin, E.C., *The Catholic Doctrine of the Just War* (London, 1937).

Urwin, E.C., *Henry Carter C.B.E.: A Memoir* (London, 1955).

Utley, T.E., 'Christianity and the Radical Tradition', in Utley, T.E., and Norman, Edward (eds), *Ethics and Nuclear Arms* (London, 1983).

Vincent, John, *Christ in a Nuclear World* (London, 1962).

Vincent, John, *Christian Nuclear Perspectives* (London, 1964).

Watkins, Owen Spencer, *Soldiers and Preachers: Being the Romantic Story of Methodism in the British Army* (London, 1906).

Watkins, Owen Spencer, *With French in France and Flanders* (London, 1915).

Watson, Richard, *Theological Institutes*, 3 vols (London, 1929).

Weatherhead, Leslie D., *Thinking Aloud in Wartime* (London, 1939).

Wesley, John, *The Works of John Wesley*, 14 vols (London, 1872).

Wesley, John, *The Letters of John Wesley*, 8 vols (London, 1931).

*Wesley's Veterans: Lives of Early Methodist Preacers Told by Themselves*, 8 vols (London, 1909–14).

Wood, Arthur, 'Moral Problems Raised by the Great War', *Holborn Review* (October 1915), pp. 417–30.

Wright, Charles J., 'The Relevance of Christian Faith to Present World Order', *London Quarterly and Holborn Review*, 166 (1941), pp. 270–81.

## Secondary Sources

Ackerman, David M., 'Kosovo and Nato', in Columbus, Frank (ed.), *Kosovo-Serbia: A Just War?* (New York, 1999), pp. 155–66.

Adams, R.A.Q. and Poirier, Philip P., *The Conscription Controversy in Great Britain, 1900–1918* (London, 1987).

Anderson, David G., 'British Rearmament and the "Merchants of Death": The 1935–36 Royal Commission on the Manufacture and Trade in Armaments', *Journal of Contemporary History*, 21, 9 (1994), pp. 5–37.

Anderson, David L., *Shadow on the White House: US Presidents and the Vietnam War, 1945–75* (Lawrence, Kan., 1993).

Andrew, Christopher, *Théophile Delcassé and the Making of the Entente Cordiale* (London, 1968).

# Select Bibliography

Armstrong, Karen, *The Battle for God: Fundamentalism in Judaism, Christianity and Islam* (London, 2000).

Bailey, Sydney, *Christian Perspectives on Nuclear Weapons* (London, 1984).
Barker, Rachel, *Conscience, Government and War: Conscientious Objectors in Great Britain, 1939–45* (London, 1982).
Barrett, Clive (ed.), *Visions of Christian Pacifism* (Cambridge, 1987).
Beales, A.C.F., *The History of Peace* (London, 1931).
Bebbington, D.W. *The Nonconformist Conscience: Chapel and Conscience in Modern Britain* (London, 1982).
Bebbington, D.W., *Evangelicalism in Modern Britain* (London, 1993).
Beloff, Max, *Lucien Wolf and the Russian Entente, 1907–1914* (London, 1951).
Birn, Donald S., *The League of Nations Union* (Oxford, 1981).
Booth, Alan, *Nonconformity in International Affairs* (London, 1970).
Boulton, David, *Objection Overruled* (London, 1967).
Brash, W. Bardsley, *The Story of Our Colleges, 1835–1935* (London, 1935).
Brock, Peter, *Pacifism in Europe to 1914* (Princeton, 1972).
Brown, Callum, *The Death of Christian Britain: Understanding Secularization, 1800–2000* (London, 2001).
Burleigh, Michael, *Sacred Causes: Religion and European Politics from the Dictators to Al Qaeda* (London, 2006).

Cadoux, C.J., *The Early Christian Attitude to War* (London, 1919).
Cadoux, C.J., *Christian Pacifism Re-examined* (London, 1940).
Caute, David, *The Dancer Defect: The Struggle for Cultural Supremacy during the Cold War* (Oxford, 2003).
Ceadel, Martin, *Pacifism in Britain, 1914–1945: The Defining of a Faith* (Oxford, 1980).
Ceadel, Martin, *Thinking About Peace and War* (Oxford, 1989).
Chadwick, Owen, *The Christian Church in the Cold War* (London, 1992).
Chandler, Andrew, 'Munich and Morality: The Bishops of the Church of England and Appeasement', *Twentieth Century History*, 5, 1 (1994), pp. 77–99.
Charmley, John, *Chamberlain and the Lost Peace* (London, 1989).
Charmley, John, *Spendid Isolation? Britain, the Balance of Power and the First World War* (London, 1999).
Cline, Catherine Anne, *E.D. Morel, 1873–1924: The Strategies of Protest* (Belfast, 1980).
Clough, David, 'Theology through Social and Political Action', in Marsh, Clive *et al.* (eds), *Unmasking Methodist Theology* (Trowbridge, 2004), pp. 41–7.
Cooke, Denis, *Peacemaker: The Life and Work of Eric Gallagher* (Peterborough, 2005).
Courtois, Stéphane, *et al.*, *The Black Book of Communism: Crimes, Terror, Repression* (Cambridge, Mass., 1999).

Currie, Robert, *Methodism Divided: A Study in the Sociology of Ecumenicalism* (London, 1968).

Curtis, Mark, *Web of Deceit: Britain's Real Role in the World* (London, 2003).

Dallin, Alexander and Lapidus, Gail (eds), *The Soviet System in Crisis: A Reader of Western and Soviet Views* (Boulder, Colo., 1991).

Davey, Arthur M., *The British Pro-Boers* (Tafelberg, 1978).

Dawkins, Richard, *The Selfish Gene* (Oxford, 1976).

Dennett, Daniel D., *Breaking the Spell: Religion as a Natural Phenomenon* (London, 2007).

Dombrowski, Daniel A., *Christian Pacifism* (Philadelphia, 1991).

Driver, Christopher, *The Disarmers: A Study in Protest* (London, 1964).

Dutton, David, *Simon: A Political Biography of Sir John Simon* (London, 1992).

Edsell, Nicholas C., *Richard Cobden: Independent Radical* (Cambridge, Mass., 1986).

Edwards, Maldwyn, *Methodism and England* (London, 1944).

Ellis, Sylvia, *Britain, America and the Vietnam War* (Westport, Conn., 2004).

Ferguson, Niall, *The Pity of War* (London, 1998).

Ferguson, Niall, *The War of the World: History's Age of Hatred* (London, 2006).

Field, Clive, 'A Sociological Profile of British Methodism, 1900–1932', *Oral History*, 4, 1 (1976), pp. 73–95.

Fletcher, Sheila, *Maude Royden* (Oxford, 1989).

Foot, Michael and Highet, Alison, *Isaac Foot: A West Country Boy – Apostle of England* (London, 2006).

Freedman, Lawrence, *Britain and the Falklands War* (Oxford, 1988).

French, Patrick, *Younghusband: The Last Great Imperial Adventurer* (London, 1994).

Frost, Donald, *Goodwill on Fire* (London, 1996).

Fukuyama, Francis, *The End of History and the Last Man* (London, 1992).

Fukuyama, Francis, *After the Neocons* (London, 2006).

George, David Boyce, *The Falklands War* (London, 2005).

Gilbert, Marc Jason, *The Vietnam War on Campus* (Westport, Conn., 2001).

Gilbert, Mark, 'Pacifist Attitudes to Nazi Germany, 1936–45', *Journal of Contemporary History*, 27, 3 (1992), pp. 493–511.

Gilbert, Martin, *Plough My Own Furrow: The Story of Lord Allen of Hurtwood* (London, 1965).

Glover, Jonathan, *Humanity: A Moral History of the Twentieth Century* (London, 1999).

Godwin, Peter and Hancock, Ian, *Rhodesians Never Die: The Impact of War and Change on White Rhodesia, c.1970–1980* (Oxford, 1993).

# Select Bibliography

Goldstein, Erik and Maurer, John H., *The Washington Conference, 1921–22* (London, 1994).

Good, Kit, 'England Goes to War, 1914–15' (University of Liverpool PhD Thesis, 2002).

Goodhall, Felicity, *A Question of Conscience* (Stroud, 1997).

Gordon, Michael and Trainor, Bernard, *The Generals' War: The Inside Story of the First Gulf War* (London, 2006).

Gow, James, *Triumph of the Failure of the Will: International Diplomacy and the Yugoslav War* (London, 1997).

Gray, John, *Al Qaeda and What it Means to be Modern* (London, 2004).

Gray, John, *Black Mass: Apocalyptic Religion and the Death of Utopia* (London, 2007).

Grimble, Arthur, *A Pattern of Islands* (London, 1952).


Hale, Frederick, 'A Methodist Pacifist and the Spanish Civil War', *Proceedings of the Wesley Historical Society*, 54 (2004), pp. 149–69.

Halévy, Elie, *The Birth of Methodism in England* (Chicago, 1971).

Harris, Richard, *Christianity and War in the Nuclear Age* (Wilton, Conn., 1986).

Harrison, Peter, 'Death Among Army Chaplains, 1914–20', *Journal of the Society for Army Research*, 83 (2005), pp. 63–72.

Hastings, Adrian, *A History of English Christianity, 1920–1985* (London, 1986).

Hayes, Denis, *Challenge of Conscience: The True Story of the Conscientious Objectors of 1939–49* (London, 1949).

Heller, Richard, 'East Fulham Revisited', *Journal of Contemporary History*, 6, 3 (1971), pp. 172–96.

Hendrickson, Ken, 'Victorian Military Politics of Establishment and Religious Liberty: William H. Rule and the Introduction of Wesleyan Methodism in the British Army, 1856–1882', *War and Society*, 17, 2 (1999), pp. 1–23.

Hinsley, F.H. (ed.), *British Foreign Policy under Sir Edward Grey* (Cambridge, 1977).

Hinton, James, *Protests and Visions: Peace Politics in Twentieth-Century Britain* (London, 1989).

Hitchens, Christopher, *God is not Great: The Case against Religion* (London, 2007).

Hobsbawm, Eric, 'Methodism and the Threat of Revolution', in Hobsbawm, Eric, *Labouring Men* (London, 1964), pp. 22–33.

Hobsbawm, E.J., *Primitive Rebels* (London, 1974).

Hobsbawm, Eric and Ranger, Terence, *The Invention of Tradition* (London, 1983).

Hudson, Darril, *The Ecumenical Movement in World Affairs* (London, 1969).

Hughes, Michael, *Diplomacy Before the Russian Revolution* (London, 2000).

Hughes, Michael, 'British Methodists and the First World War', *Methodist History*, 41, 1 (2002), pp. 316–28.

Hughes, Michael, 'The Development of Methodist Pacifism, 1899–1939', ✓ *Proceedings of the Wesley Historical Society*, 53, 6 (2002), pp. 203–15.

Hughes, Michael, 'The Foreign Secretary Goes to Court: Sir John Simon and his Critics', *Twentieth-Century British History*, 14, 4 (2003), pp. 339–59.

Hughes, Michael, 'Methodism, Peace and War', *Bulletin of the John Rylands Library of the University of Manchester*, 85, 1 (2003), pp. 147–67.

Hughes, Michael, *Foreign Secretaries in an Uncertain World, 1919–1939* (London, 2006).

Huntington, Samuel, *The Clash of Civilizations and the Remaking of World Order* (London, 1998).

Hurd, Douglas, *The Search for Peace: A Century of Peace Diplomacy* (London, 1997).

Hynes, Samuel, *The Edwardian Turn of Mind* (Princeton, 1968).

*Howard, N. a Hitchcock War . 26 Nov 15 Nov 1970 .*

Ignatieff, Michael, *The Warrior's House* (London, 1998).

Iremonger, F.A., *William Temple: Archbishop of Canterbury* (London, 1948).

Jannaway, F.G., *The Christadelphians during the Great War* (London, 1929).

Jasper, Ronald C.D., *George Bell: Bishop of Chichester* (London, 1967).

Johnson, James Turner, *Can Modern War be Just?* (New Haven, Conn., 1984).

Johnson, James Turner and Weigel, George (eds), *Just War and the Gulf War* (Washington DC, 1991).

Joll, James, *The Origins of the First World War* (London, 1984).

✓ Jordan, E.K.H., *Free Church Unity: A History of the Free Church Council Movement, 1896–1941* (London, 1956).

Judah, Tim, *Kosovo: War and Revenge* (New Haven, Conn., 2002).

Junor, Beth, *Greenham Common Women's Peace Camp* (London, 1995).

Kennedy, Paul, *The Rise of the Anglo-German Antagonism, 1860–1914* (London, 1982).

Kennedy, Thomas C., 'Public Opinion and the Conscientious Objectors, 1915–1919', *Journal of British Studies*, 12, 2 (1973), pp. 105–19.

✓ Kent, John, 'Methodism and Politics in the Nineteenth Century', in John Kent, *The Age of Disunity* (London, 1966), pp. 127–45.

Kirby, Dianne, *Church, State and Propaganda: A Political Study of Cyril Foster Garbett, 1942–1955* (Hull, 1999).

Kirby, Dianne, 'Divinely Sanctioned: The Anglo-American Cold War Alliance and the Defence of Western Civilization and Christianity', *Journal of Contemporary History*, 35, 3 (2000), pp. 385–412.

Kirby, Dianne, 'Harry S. Truman's International Religious Anti-Communist Front, the Archbishop of Canterbury, and the 1948 Inaugural Assembly of the World Council of Churches', *Contemporary British History*, 15, 4 (2001), pp. 35–70.

# Select Bibliography

Kirby, Dianne (ed.), *Religion and Cold War* (Basingstoke, 2003),

Koss, Stephen (ed.), *The Anatomy of un Anti-War Movement: The Pro-Boers* (Chicago, 1973).

Koss, Stephen, *Nonconformity in Modern British Politics* (London, 1975).

Koss, Stephen, 'Wesleyanism and Empire', *Historical Journal*, 18 (1975), pp. 105–18.

Lewis, Bernard, *The Crisis of Islam: Holy War and Unholy Terror* (New York, 2003).

Lockhart, J.G., *Cosmo Gordon Lang* (London, 1949).

Long, Stephen, *Living the Discipline: United Methodist Theological Reflections on War, Civilization and Holiness* (Grand Rapids, Mich., 1992).

Lowe, Peter, *The Vietnam War* (Basingstoke, 1998).

Lukowitz, David C., 'British Pacifists and Appeasement: The Peace Pledge Union', *Journal of Contemporary History*, 9, 1 (1974), pp. 115–27.

Mackinnon, D.M. (ed.), *Christian Faith and Communist Faith* (London, 1953).

Macmillan, Margaret, *Peacemakers: The Paris Conference of 1919 and its Attempt to End War* (London, 2001).

Malik, Shiv, 'The Making of a Terrorist', *Prospect* (June 2007).

Marsh Clive *et al.* (eds), *Unmasking Methodist Theology* (Trowbridge, 2004).

Martin, David, *Pacifism: An Historical and Sociological Study* (London, 1965).

Martin, David, *A General Theory of Secularization* (Oxford, 1978).

Martin, David, *Does Christianity Cause War?* (Oxford, 1997).

Marwick, Arthur, *The Sixties* (Oxford, 1998).

Massie, Robert, *Dreadnought: Britain, Germany and the Coming of the Great War* (London, 1992).

Matthew, H.C.G., *The Liberal Imperialists* (Oxford, 1973).

Mattox, John Mark, *Saint Augustine and the Theory of the Just War* (London, 2006).

McAuley, Martin, *Gorbachev and Perestroika* (Basingstoke, 1990).

McIntire, C.T., *Herbert Butterfield: Historian as Dissenter* (New Haven, Conn., 2004).

Monger, George W., *The End of Isolation: British Foreign Policy, 1900–1907* (London, 1963).

Moore, Robert, *Pitmen, Preachers and Politics* (London, 1974).

Morrill, Dan L., 'Nicholas II and the Call for the First Hague Conference', *Journal of Modern History*, 46, 2 (1974), pp. 296–313.

Morris, A.J.A., *The Scaremongers: The Advocacy of War and Reamarment, 1896–1914* (London, 1984).

Murray, John A., 'Foreign Policy Debated: Sir Edward Grey and his Critics', in Wallace, Lillian Parker and Askew, William C. (eds), *Power, Public Opinion and Diplomacy* (Durham, NC, 1959).

Neilson, Keith, *Britain and the Last Tsar: British Policy and Russia, 1894–1917* (Oxford, 1995).

Newton, Lord, *Lord Lansdowne* (London, 1929).

Nuttall, G.F., *Christian Pacifism in History* (Berkeley, 1971).


Oldstone-Moore, Christopher, *Hugh Price Hughes: Founder of a New Methodism, Conscience of a New Nonconformity* (Cardiff, 1999).

Oliver, Kendrick, *The My Lai Massacre in American History and Memory* (Manchester, 2006).

O'Neill, William G., *Kosovo: An Unfinished Peace* (London, 2002).


Pakenham, Thomas, *The Boer War* (London, 1979).

Parker, R.A.C., *Chamberlain and Appeasement: British Policy and the Coming of the Second World War* (Basingstoke, 1993).

Parker, R.A.C., *Churchill and Appeasement* (Basingstoke, 2000).

Parkin, Frank, *Middle Class Radicalism: The Social Bases of the Campaign for Nuclear Disarmament* (Manchester, 1968).

Pinder, R., 'Religious Change in the Process of Secularisation', *Sociological Review*, 19, 3 (1971), pp. 343–66.

Popovski, Vesselin, 'The Concept of Humanitarian Intervention', in Siani-Davis, Peter (ed.), *International Intervention in the Balkans since 1995* (London, 2003).

Pugh, Michael, 'Pacifism and Politics in Britain, 1931–1935', *Historical Journal*, 23, 3 (1980), pp. 641–56.


Raath, A.W.G. (ed.), *The British Concentration Camps of the Anglo-Boer War* (Bloemfontaine, 1999).

Rack, Henry D., *Reasonable Enthusiast: John Wesley and the Rise of Methodism* (London, 1989).

Rae, John, *Conscience and Politics* (London, 1970).

Ramet, Sabrina Petra, *Balkan Babel: The Disintegration of Yugoslavia from the Death of Tito to Ethnic War* (Boulder, Colo., 1996).

Ramsbottom, Oliver and Woodhouse, Tom, *Humanitarian Intervention in Contemporary Conflict* (Cambridge, 1996).

Ramsey, Paul, *War and the Christian Conscience* (Durham, NC, 1961).

Ramsey, Paul, *The Just War: Force and Political Responsibility* (New York, 1968).

Ramsey, Paul, *Speak Up for Just War or Pacifism* (University Park, Penn., 1988).

Reed, Charles, *Just War?* (London, 2004).

Rempl, Richard A., 'The Dilemmas of British Pacifists during World War II', *Journal of Modern History*, 50, 4 (1979), 1213–29.

Rhodes, Anthony, *The Vatican in the Age of the Cold War, 1945–80* (Norwich, 1992).

# Select Bibliography

Richter, Philip and Francis, Leslie, *Gone but not Forgotten: Church Leaving and Returning* (London, 1998).

Robbins, Keith, *John Bright* (London, 1979).

Robertson, E.H., *George: A Biography of Viscount Tonypandy* (London, 1992).

Rouse, Ruth and Neill, Stephen Charles (eds), *A History of the Ecumenical Movement, 1517–1948* (London, 1967).

Russell, Frederick H., *The Just War in the Middle Ages* (Cambridge, 1975).


Sacks, Jonathan, *The Dignity of Difference* (London, 2002).

Sadhammed, Abdel Salam, *Islamic Fundamentalism* (Boulder, Colo., 1996).

Sakwa, Richard, *Gorbachev and his Reforms* (London, 1990).

Sangster, Paul, *Doctor Sangster* (London, 1982).

Schneer, Jonathan, *George Lansbury* (Manchester, 1990).

Scott-Smith, Giles, *The Politics of Apolitical Culture: The Congress for Cultural Freedom, the CIA and the Post-War American Hegemony* (New York, 2000).

Searle, G.R., *The Quest for National Efficiency* (London, 1971).

Shawcross, William, *Deliver us from Evil: Warlords and Peacekeepers in a World of Endless Conflict* (London, 2000).

Shepherd, John, *George Lansbury: At the Head of Old Labour* (Oxford, 2002).

Siegel, Jennifer, *Endgame: Britain, Russia and the Final Struggle for Central Asia* (London, 2002).

Silber, Laura, *The Death of Yugoslavia* (London, 1996).

Simms, Brendan, *Unfinest Hour: Britain and the Destruction of Bosnia* (London, 2002).

Singer, Peter, *Applied Ethics* (Oxford, 1986).

Slocombe, Ivor, 'Recruitment into the Armed Forces during the First World War: The Work of the Military Tribunals in Wiltshire, 1915–1918', *Local Historian*, 30, 2 (2000), pp. 105–23.

Smith, Martin A., 'Kosovo, Nato and the United Nations', in Badsey, Stephen and Latawski, Paul (eds), *Britain, Nato and the Lessons of the Balkans Conflicts* (London, 2004), pp. 153–77.

Smyth, Sir John, *In This Sign Conquer* (London, 1968).

Spinks, Philip, 'The War Courts: The Stratford-upon-Avon Borough Tribunal, 1916–1918', *Local Historian*, 32, 4 (2002), pp. 210–17.

Stevenson, David, *1914–1918: The History of the First World War* (London, 2005).

Stevenson, William R., *Christian Love and Just War* (Manchester, 1987).

Stonor-Saunders, Frances, *The Cultural Cold War: The CIA and the World of Arts and Letters* (New York, 2000).

Strachan, Hew, *The Outbreak of the First World War* (Oxford, 2004).

Symvoulidis, Charalampos, 'British and Greek Press Reactions to the Disintegration of Yugoslavia, 1991–1999' (University of Liverpol PhD Thesis, 2005).

Taylor, A.J.P., *The Troublemakers: Dissent over Foreign Policy, 1792–1939* (London, 1993).

Taylor, Richard, *Against the Bomb: The British Peace Movement, 1958–1965* (Oxford, 1988).

Teichman, Jenny, *Pacifism and the Just War: A Study in Applied Philosophy* (Oxford, 1986).

Todorov, Tzvetan, *Facing the Extreme: Moral Life in the Concentration Camps* (London, 1999).

Trebilock, Clive, 'Legends of the British Armaments Industry, 1890–1914: A Revision', *Journal of Contemporary History*, 5, 4 (1970), pp. 3–19.

Turberfield, Alan, *John Scott Lidgett: Archbishop of British Methodism* (London, 2003).

Turley, Briane K., 'John Wesley and War', *Methodist History*, 29, 2 (1991), pp. 96–111.

Turner, Barry, *Suez, 1956* (London, 2006).

Turner, J.M., 'Methodism in England, 1900–1932, in Davies, Rupert *et al.* (eds), *A History of the Methodist Church in Great Britain*, 4 vols (London, 1965–88), vol. 3, pp. 309–61.

Turner, John Munsey, *John Wesley: The Evangelical Revival and the Birth of Methodism in England* (London, 2002).

Verrier, Anthony, *The Road to Zimbabwe, 1890–1980* (London, 1986).

Wakefield, Gordon S., *Robert Newton Flew, 1886–1962* (London, 1971).

Walker, R.B., 'The Growth of Wesleyan Methodism in Victorian England and Wales', *Journal of Ecclesiastical History*, 24, 3 (1973), pp. 267–84.

Wallis, Jill, *Valiant for Peace: A History of the Fellowship of Reconciliation, 1914–1989* (London, 1991).

Wearmouth, Robert, *Methodism and the Struggle of the Working Classes, 1850–1900* (Leicester, 1954).

Wearmouth, Robert, *The Social and Political Influence of Methodism in the Twentieth century* (London, 1957).

Weatherhead, Kingsley, *Leslie Weatherhead: A Personal Portrait* (London, 1976).

Webb, Pauline, *A Long Struggle: The Involvement of the World Council of Churches in South Africa* (Geneva, 1994).

White, Mark J., *The Cuban Missile Crisis* (Basingstoke, 1996).

Wilkinson, Alan, *The Church of England and the First World War* (London, 1978).

Wilkinson, Alan, *Dissent or Conform? War, Peace and the English Churches* (London, 1986).

Williams, Rowan, *Writing in the Dust* (London, 2002).

Wilson, H. Harris (ed.), *Christianity and Communism* (Oxford, 1937).

Wilson, Robert L., *Biases and Blindspots: Methodism and Foreign Policy since World War II* (Wilmore, Ky., 1988).

# Select Bibliography

Wittner, Laurence S., *Resisting the Bomb: A History of the World Nuclear Disarmament Movement, 1954–70* (Stanford, 1997).

Wittner, Laurence S., *Towards Nuclear Abolition: A History of the World Nuclear Disarmament Movement, 1971 to the Present* (Stanford, 2003).

Young, Kenneth, *Rhodesia and Independence: A Study in British Colonial Policy* (London, 1969).

# Index

# Index